What Postcolonial Theory Doesn't Say

Routledge Research in Postcolonial Literatures

Edited in collaboration with the Centre for Colonial and Postcolonial Studies, University of Kent at Canterbury, this series presents a wide range of research into postcolonial literatures by specialists in the field. Volumes will concentrate on writers and writing originating in previously (or presently) colonized areas, and will include material from non-anglophone as well as anglophone colonies and literatures. Series editors: Donna Landry and Caroline Rooney.

What Postcolonial
Theory Doesn't Say

Edited by Anna Bernard,
Ziad Elmarsafy, and Stuart Murray

Routledge
Taylor & Francis Group

NEW YORK AND LONDON

First published 2016
by Routledge
711 Third Avenue, New York, NY 10017

and by Routledge
2 Park Square, Milton Park, Abingdon, Oxon OX14 4RN

Routledge is an imprint of the Taylor & Francis Group, an informa business

Library of Congress Cataloging in Publication Data

What postcolonial theory doesn't say / edited by Anna Bernard, Ziad Elmarsafy, and Stuart Murray.
    pages cm. — (Routledge research in postcolonial literatures ; 54)
Includes bibliographical references and index.
    1. Postcolonialism in literature. 2. Postcolonialism and the arts. 3. Postcolonialism.
    I. Bernard, Anna, 1979- editor. II. Elmarsafy, Ziad, editor. III. Murray, Stuart, 1967- editor.
PN56.P555W47 2015
809'.93358—dc23   2015010100

ISBN: 978-0-415-85797-0 (hbk)
ISBN: 978-0-203-79674-0 (ebk)

Typeset in Sabon
by codeMantra

Contents

PART III
Horizons: Environment, Materialism, World

List of Figures

Acknowledgments

As the introduction to this volume makes clear, the debates and ideas began as papers and exchanges presented at a conference at the University of York, UK, in 2010. This event would not have been possible without the financial support of the Department of English and Related Literature, the Centre for Modern Studies, the Leavis Fund and the Roberts Fund, all at the University of York. For the vast amount of work and co-ordination that went into planning the conference we thank the original group of thinkers and planners, including David Attwell and Eleanor Byrne, as well as our colleagues and students, whose dedication proved essential to the success of the event. Furthermore, we would like to thank the conference speakers and attendees whose work, contributions and conversations drove the production of this volume. Donna Landry and Caroline Rooney were, as always, a bedrock of support and sometimes badly needed encouragement. Finally, we would like to thank the Leavis Fund for its support in helping us to cover indexing costs and the Routledge editorial team, especially Nancy Chen, Francesca Monaco, and Ellora Sengupta.

Introduction

What Postcolonial Theory Doesn't Say

Anna Bernard, Ziad Elmarsafy, and Stuart Murray

I

The chapters that make up the contents of this book first came together as papers presented at a 2010 conference with the same title at the University of York. As organizers, we were careful in the ways in which we shaped the panels, which featured an eclectic range of topics, from screening the conflict in Afghanistan and the contemporary Nigerian novel to questions of world ecologies and human-rights ethics, as well as the usual investigations of the "epistemological crisis" surrounding the subject area that always populate large gatherings debating any aspect of the nature of postcolonial studies. Our initial aim was to examine the points of interaction between these different specific critical inquiries and to ask what might be theoretical in the ideas that underpin them. Developing this line of questioning, we wanted to assess the theoretical articulations of these interdisciplinary projects, to see how they say what they say and whether it is what scholars in the field would like to hear said. How, we asked, might the field's cultural and institutional capital best be put to use in an investigation of its theoretical foundations?

The conference's final session was an open discussion, chaired by the three of us with the various participants. We began by outlining the conversations we had shared that had prompted the event and the reasons we believed the topic to be timely, and then reflected on the ways in which various papers had intervened – provoking, troubling, extending, confirming – in the debates we had collectively generated. Finally, we turned the discussion outwards. After all we had shared, what, we asked those assembled in the room, might we might be able to say about the range and resources, the successes and failures, of postcolonial theory seen in the snapshot of that moment? The initial silence that followed may well have been because the question was a difficult one to answer in terms of gathering ideas together in that kind of forum, but reflecting on it afterwards we felt the caution and difficulty articulated something tangible about the discipline itself. Graham Huggan has noted that, as a field, postcolonialism enacts "a *performative* mode of critical revisionism, consistently directed at the colonial past and assessing its legacies for the present, but also intermittently focusing on those forms of colonialism that have surfaced more recently in the context of an increasingly globalized but incompletely decolonized world" (Huggan 2013, 10, emphasis added). The value of the "performative", as well as the multiple opportunities for "consistent directions", is that they have always, of course, offered postcolonial studies numerous variations through which to operate its revisionism – there is never a lack of subjects when it comes to postcolonial critique – but possibly our question caught a moment when the details of these subjects and variations struggled to find expression through a category – theory – that should, but might not, frame and shape them in productive ways.

Postcolonial theory is not spoken of today with the kind of reverence it received in the 1990s in particular. This is, of course, not purely a point about the postcolonial; all manner of critical cultural fields or projects arguably appear less theoretical than they did a generation ago, and work that self-consciously seeks to advance the field of postcolonial criticism is more likely to choose postcolonial studies as the vehicle of choice than the specifically theoretically understood version of the subject. Just what was theoretical about postcolonial theory in its first formative decade also makes for an interesting question. Postcolonialism's poststructuralist formations are often seen as the predominant manifestation of theory in the discipline, rather than the equally theoretical critical Marxism that has been its main challenger. Theory, it now seems, has come to be understood as one avenue among many through which to explore the "revisionism" of which Huggan writes, and not the originating and foundational category it may have seemed in the past.

In seeking to understand how this notion of theory manifests itself, we might note that possibly because of the field's desire to keep an openness in its working method, much critical analysis undertaken in the name of the postcolonial performs a self-reflexivity that takes that openness to be constitutive of its theoretical formations. Robert Young has argued that this kind of relational aspect is in fact central to an understanding of the subject, noting that postcolonial theory is "about relations between ideas and practices: relations of harmony, relations of conflict, generative relations between different peoples and their cultures" (Young 2003, 7). "Relations" is obviously a central term here, which can also be read as a privileging of diversity and difference within both subject matter and method. Young later makes this point more explicitly, arguing that the deployment of the "apparently antithetical positions" of antifoundationalism and empiricism is what characterizes the field (Young 2012, 24). This methodological heterogeneity can be seen as incoherence, as Vivek Chibber, among others, has argued: "It is not that postcolonial studies is an assemblage of theories while Marxism is not. [...] The difference is that Marxism always sought internal coherence and systematicity, while postcolonial studies resists any compulsion to bring together and assess its various strands" (Chibber 2012, 3). Yet we might equally take Young's notion of relation as a way of describing an ongoing position-taking among the field's primary oppositions – materialists versus poststructuralists, activism versus literature, revisionism versus revolution (Huggan 2013, 4), the detail *in* representation versus the method *of* representation – that has facilitated many valuable conversations.

At the same time, for all that we understand the value of the performative, the generative and the relational, we still felt that the initial difficult silence that started our discussion session at the conference spoke of something else, and in fact was rather an example of a critical "not saying". Here was a moment where we could have held that the theoretical aspect to the various papers we had shared lay in articulating the matrix on which they were mapped, stressing the common genesis and relational spaces between them. In fact, we found the space to be problematic rather than generative, indicative of an absence of theory more than an opportunity for performance, and it is our desire to find a language for that absence that shapes the project of this book. In this sense, then, this is not a volume that seeks to map a state of the field, nor to function as a handbook in the ways in which the various chapters can be placed into dialogue with one another. Equally we do not want to repeat well-rehearsed debates about the discipline's supposed various failings. Rather, through the multiple subject matters of our contributors, we are interested in making a claim as to how postcolonial theory has left key questions about both postcolonial praxis and method unsaid. The collection thus picks up from where many of the best-known assessments of the field, most of them published more than a decade ago, left off, to ask with renewed urgency: What do we want postcolonial theory to say, and how might we make it possible to say it?

Postcolonial theory's sins of omission have, of course, been discussed by others, and in many ways. Often, these discussions revolve around the problem of the relationship between theory and practice, especially around a concept such as resistance. Elleke Boehmer has written of the "still underacknowledged antecedents-in-resistance of postcolonial theory" (Boehmer 2013, 307), while Neil Lazarus has, across a number of projects, asserted a more total critique of theory's failure to address the subject's materialist concerns. In *The Postcolonial Unconscious*, for example, Lazarus asserts that postcolonial critical discourse has often "been premised on a distinctive and conjuncturally determined set of assumptions, concepts, theories and methods that have not only *not* been adequate to their putative object – the 'postcolonial world' – but have served fairly systematically to mystify it" (Lazarus 2011a, 16–17). For Lazarus and other critics who share his viewpoint – such as Benita Parry – the mystification of the material realities and capitalist relations of the postcolonial world has been the most conspicuous failure of postcolonial theory's intellectual agenda.

We are interested less in revisiting these debates than in noting that, for the younger scholars who make up many of our contributors here, this critique is often taken for granted, in the wake of what Tim Brennan has described as a new materialist turn within the field, from questions of "discourse, identity, migrancy, and subjectivity [...] to an engaged, activist language of political movements and positions" (Brennan 2013, 68). So our sense of what postcolonial theory leaves unsaid here is not an observation about how, as Boehmer asserts, it "draws attention away from, or pays insufficient heed to, the contexts of political struggle against empire" (Boehmer 2013, 309), but rather a feeling that the materialist/poststructuralist opposition no longer dominates the field. As the essays collected here show, while the battles of the 1990s (and beyond) as to the proper nature of postcolonial studies raged on, a whole range of other topics, events, locations, methods and worldviews went ignored. Whether on Palestine and Eastern Europe or questions of economics, aesthetics and disaster (to name just some of the subjects considered in this volume), much was left unsaid.

In addition, part of our claim here is that contemporary practice in inter- and multidisciplinary scholarship demonstrates that a new assessment of postcolonial theory need not see it as a relational tool that works to juxtapose different fields of inquiry. We argue that there is a specific value to a literary/cultural critical methodology, necessarily now proficient in the languages of subjects such as sociology and politics, which informs our understanding of the postcolonial in ways that open up earlier approaches, whether these stem from humanism, Marxism or post-structuralism. We find this multidisciplinary methodology working across our contributors' essays, detailing a huge range of postcolonial moments, from dance to diaspora and international relations to land seizure. Scholars of the postcolonial now bring the literary into discussion with the material or talk of affect and politics with a skill that means there is now greater opportunity to do justice to the analogous and multiple manifestations of postcolonial cultures and societies. In making this assertion, we see our position not as one of revisionism but rather as part of a more productive and forward-looking critical politics.

II

There is no clearly definable moment when postcolonial theory came into being. If it seemed that no graduate student essay on any postcolonial topic in the early 1990s was complete without some reference to the so-called holy trinity of Edward Said, Homi Bhabha or Gayatri Spivak, that fact – and its then presentism – masked a longer heritage of theoretical exploration of postcolonial topics. Whether in the 1950s Francophone examples of Frantz Fanon or Albert Memmi or the 1960s language debates that took place across the essays of creative writers such as Chinua Achebe and Ngũgĩ wa Thiong'o (and later, Salman Rushdie and Amit Chaudhuri), critical writing from both Europe and the postcolonial world theorized both histories of contact and the new, emerging sets of relations that came to characterize the period of decolonization. Without the self-consciousness that comes with the label of theory as subject, such writing explored topics as diverse as interpersonal relationships and the effects of pedagogy, to name but two major issues.

The period of "high" postcolonial theory that emerged from the 1980s onwards, as the ideas of Said's *Orientalism* (1978) percolated into an era that saw the marketization of university subjects, was part of the production of the disciplinary idea of postcolonial studies, in which theory frequently played the role of the subject's aggressive leading edge. *The Empire Writes Back* (1989), a foundational text in the field, had "Theory and Practice" in its subtitle, as well as two chapters devoted to the specific work literary theory played in assessing postcolonial writing. Such an indication of the prominence of theoretical investigation also made clear the claim being made for its naturalness as a mode of critical inquiry, and for much of the 1990s the theory that animated such investigation was fundamentally poststructuralist. Even as such a situation appeared to become solidified in the classroom, however, a number of significant critiques of postcolonial theory emerged to question its forms and practices. Ella Shohat's 1992 article "Notes on the Post-Colonial" and Arif Dirlik's "The Postcolonial Aura: Third World Criticism in the Age of Global Capitalism" from 1994 formed part of an attack on the ways in which theories of the postcolonial constructed ideas of the global and the manner in which the origins and locations of such writing betrayed themselves as sites of privilege. As Dirlik put it: "Now that postcoloniality has been released from the fixity of Third World location, the identity of the postcolonial is no longer structural but discursive. Postcolonial in this perspective represents an attempt to regroup intellectuals of uncertain location under the banner of postcolonial discourse", while also noting that "postcolonial criticism has been silent about its own status as a possible ideological effect of a new world situation after colonialism" (Dirlik 1994, 332 and 331). Such characterization of "discourse" as a limited vehicle through which to engage the realities of postcolonial experience, and the concomitant link to a potential complicity in the development of a capitalist world order, reframed theory for some not as a productive analytic tool but rather as potentially a marker of a narrow and ahistorical critical conservatism.

Robert Young's *Postcolonialism: An Historical Introduction* (2001) marks possibly the last attempt to position an idea of theory as being central to a global view of postcolonial histories. For Young, postcolonial studies at the beginning of the twenty-first century had yet to acknowledge the full force of the theoretical implications of the anti-colonial struggles that dominated global politics during the previous sixty years. By way of response, he defined postcolonialism as a field in which critical methods were "theoretically and historically fundamentally hybrid, the product of the clash of cultures that brought it into being" (Young 2001, 10). Hybridity, seen here as a productive and insightful mechanism through which to explore postcolonial experience, had been arguably the dominant term in postcolonial theory during the 1990s, from Homi Bhabha's celebrations of its discursive possibilities to Young's claims for its historical and ontological centrality. In *Postcolonialism: An Historical Introduction*, Young named the "hybrid" as both "form and strategy", a method that could bring together historical trajectories and definitions of agency or a revised situated Marxism and new intellectual internationalism under the banner of "tricontinental critiques of eurocentrism" (Young 2001, 345–351).

But rather like the grand double album that emerges from years in the studio just as musical tastes change, Young's book failed to preface the kind of theoretically informed historical criticism he championed. Rather, postcolonial studies fragmented precisely because of the multiple suspicions that now accompanied its claims to view the world whole. In place of this project, the variety of new modes of postcolonial enquiry – ecocritical, queer, indigenous, to name but some – that have emerged in the last ten years are informed by theoretical models, often interdisciplinary in origin, that discuss commonalities among diverse, formerly colonized locations but deliberately eschew ideas of conceptual totality. As new formations of post-colonial theory, they challenge the idea that the label has an automatic right to assume subject status – a matrix of theoretical positions is a long way from assumptions of a unifying hybridity. Nevertheless, it is our contention, evidenced by the work collected in this volume, that this matrix itself has become a way in which theory speaks – says – the postcolonial. For all that a history of postcolonial studies might suggest that its theory phase is over, it is clear that this is, in fact, not the case. The new imperialisms of the contemporary global world, formations that could not have been envisaged during the debates around the postcolonial that took place in the 1990s, increasingly demand theoretical engagement, and in fact it is precisely the legacies of theorizing the postcolonial that become useful here. Without a renewed engagement with the disavowed and under-articulated theoretical paradigms that underpin the field – including traditions of revolutionary thought, which are often invoked but less often worked through – we will remain unable to produce the "new 'history of the present'" (Gopal and Lazarus 2006, 9) that we so desperately need.

III

As we explained above, although there are numerous critiques of the field of postcolonial studies in this volume, the primary aim of the collection is not critique for its own sake. If anything, we are proponents of the "unabashed enthusiasm" that Terry Eagleton once complained was so sorely lacking in the field (Eagleton 1999, 3). Notwithstanding our provocative title, this volume emerges from our investment in the future of postcolonial studies and our commitment to its basic premise, namely the attempt to conceive of particular cultural and literary articulations in relation to larger structures of colonial and imperial domination. We contend that praxis must be theoretically grounded to ensure its effectiveness and its capacity for self-criticism. The theoretical register enables a more consistently lucid purview, not only of the relations between multiple interventions but also of the conditions – intellectual, political, philosophical and literary-critical – that make them possible.

The history of those conditions can be instructive. One version of the story of the relationship between postcolonial theory and postcolonial studies can be seen through the rise of a critical vanguardism that has become more transparent and less satisfying with time. Early poststructuralist theoretical expressions quickly lost their edge with the growing hegemony of their idiom in the early 1990s. Challenges to postcolonial studies from that point on (especially from area specialists) led to a parting of theoretical ways, with greater input from a returned Marxism, the rise of a clearly expressed cultural-studies dimension and the development of distinct subsections in the field such as ecocriticism or settlement studies. Yet each of these new directions seemed to do more to rework postcolonial studies than the other way around, inadvertently reinforcing the impression that the idea of the postcolonial doesn't have much to offer in itself. Arguably, then, postcolonial theory hasn't said certain things due to its inability to reach a more mature sense of its scope or develop theoretical positions capable of responding to urgent global developments, from the fall of the Soviet Union and the rise of "new Europe" to the US-led invasions of Iraq and Afghanistan to the large area of failed and failing states stretching from Congo to Syria.

Nevertheless, the idea of postcolonial theory clearly has had a conceptual purchase and appeal that has extended well beyond its disciplinary origins. The pull of this idea has enabled postcolonial studies to survive accusations of ahistoricism, anti-nationalism (or conversely, making a fetish of anti-colonial nationalism) and, perhaps worst of all, adopting a partial world view riddled with blind spots. We attribute postcolonial theory's resilience to two major factors: first, its commitment to the study of imperialism as a political, economic and cultural force; and second, the resulting salutary transformations of multiple humanities and social-science disciplines. To a certain extent, postcolonial theory is a victim of its own success. The sense of crisis in the field comes in part from the institutionalization of the insights that it has enabled. Now that they no longer seem new, it is hard to know what the field's work should be beyond these general commitments, or what we should be talking to one another about, apart from continuing to affirm and celebrate past accomplishments.

This feeling of stasis looks to us like a missed opportunity. We see the renewal of popular anti-imperial energies across the globe as a chance to reassert the political and theoretical value of the postcolonial as a comparative, interdisciplinary, and oppositional paradigm. The collection thus makes a claim for what postcolonial theory can say through the work of scholars articulating what it still cannot or will not say. Once sectarian and strange, now established and familiar, postcolonial theory cannot afford complacency. There are too many urgent developments worldwide calling

[handwritten marginalia, left margin:] academia a bit slow on the uptake here – its 2016

[handwritten marginalia, right margin:] imperialism an a good thing?! – surely the very way round?! a discipline back to life?! because it brings postcolonialism as

[handwritten marginalia, bottom:] Key statement of book though

for a revitalized critique and new ways of theorizing the imperial past and present. Our position, moreover, is that the theoretical stems as much from praxis as from the ivory tower: that, as we noted above, theory is not without its antecedents in resistance; and that praxis depends on theory for its coherence, or at least as a safeguard against chronic disarray. The theoretical register enables a more consistently lucid purview not only of the relations between multiple interventions but also of the conditions – intellectual, political, philosophical and literary-critical – that make them possible.

Among the many benefits that we might anticipate from a return to the idea of theory is a grammar of ideas that will help to confront, rather than reiterate, structures such as East versus West (or, worse yet, Islam versus the West), and that will dispense with some of the buzzwords (including "hybridity") that have become catch-all terms lacking conceptual precision. This return to questions of theory and method should also enable a return to the universalizing ideals that made early work in postcolonial studies so exciting, but without the "category errors" that distorted the objectives of such work, not least the relative lack of attention paid to the location of colonialism within the broader context of global capitalism (Lazarus 2011b, 7–8). We might hope for a more sophisticated historical understanding of empire and what Said called the "gravity of history" (1994, 367), transcending (without forgetting) the colonial moment of the nineteenth and early twentieth centuries in favor of a more rigorous appreciation of the historicity of the seemingly endless cycle of occupations, exploitations, wars and all-out planetary destruction that characterize late capitalism. If our work is to be worldly, in Said's sense of the term (1983), and to succeed in criticizing the "actual *affiliations* that exist between the world of ideas and scholarship, on the one hand, and the world of brute politics, corporate and state power, and military force, on the other" (Said 2000, 119), then it must be informed not by the narrow considerations of our (or any) profession but rather by the sorts of big ideas that once made theory both thrilling and subversive: thrilling because subversive of the status quo, always daring to proclaim that the current dispensation is neither inevitable nor invincible.

Over two decades ago, Jacques Derrida – whose name has not always carried positive connotations in postcolonial studies – decried the fact that:

> [N]ever have violence, inequality, exclusion, famine and thus economic oppression affected as many human beings in the history of the earth and humanity. [...] [N]o amount of progress allows one to ignore that never before, in absolute figures, never have so many men, women and children been subjugated, starved or exterminated on the earth.
>
> (Derrida 2006, 106)

The years since these lines were written have only brought further confirmation that there are no limits either to capitalism's creativity when it comes to inventing new forms of exploitation or to humanity's *libido dominandi.* It too often seems as if the world's populations are able to do little more than observe and lament the routine assaults on their hard-won rights and dignities. This situation obtains despite the strenuous efforts of generations of activists, scholars and workers across the globe to contest it, not to mention the growth industry in charities that has accompanied the mass resignation of the world's governments from their responsibilities towards their citizens. The seemingly irresistible march towards the concentration of infinite power in the hands of an infinitesimal fraction of the world's population calls for a renewed commitment to the decolonization of knowledge. It is here and now that we, as postcolonial scholars and theorists, are obliged not only to think and act but also to theorize, the better to work towards an interconnected and systemic view of past and present forms of injustice, oppression and violence as part of the larger effort to bring about their obsolescence. What postcolonial theory doesn't yet say – but what our contributors suggest it could – is the promise of a better world.

REFERENCES

Brennan, Timothy. 2013. "Joining the Party". *Postcolonial Studies* 16.1: 68–78.

Boehmer, Elleke. 2013. "Resisting Resistance: Postcolonial Practice and the Antecedents of Theory". In *The Oxford Handbook of Postcolonial Studies*, edited by Graham Huggan, 307–323. Oxford: Oxford University Press.

Chibber, Vivek. 2014. *Postcolonial Theory and the Specter of Capital*. London: Verso.

Derrida, Jacques. 2006 [1994]. *Specters of Marx: The State of Debt, the Work of Mourning and the New International*. Translated by Peggy Kamuf. New York and London: Routledge.

Dirlik, Arif. 1994. "The Postcolonial Aura: Third World Criticism in the Age of Global Capitalism". *Critical Inquiry* 20.2: 328–356.

Eagleton, Terry. 1999. "In the Gaudy Supermarket". Review of *A Critique of Post-Colonial Reason: Toward a History of the Vanishing Present* by Gayatri Chakravorty Spivak. *London Review of Books*, 13 May, 3–6.

Gopal, Priyamvada and Neil Lazarus. 2006. "Editorial". *New Formations* 59: 7–9.

Huggan, Graham. 2013. General Introduction. In *The Oxford Handbook of Postcolonial Studies*, edited by Graham Huggan, 1–26. Oxford: Oxford University Press.

Lazarus, Neil. 2011a. *The Postcolonial Unconscious*. Cambridge: Cambridge University Press.

Lazarus, Neil. 2011b. "What Postcolonial Theory Doesn't Say". *Race & Class* 53:1: 3–27.

Lazarus, Neil. 2013. "'Third Worldism' and the Political Imaginary of Postcolonial Studies". In *The Oxford Handbook of Postcolonial Studies*, edited by Graham Huggan, 324–339. Oxford: Oxford University Press.

Said, Edward. 1983. *The World, the Text and the Critic*. Cambridge: Harvard University Press.

Said, Edward. 1994. *Culture and Imperialism*. London: Vintage.

Said, Edward. 2000. *Reflections on Exile and Other Essays*. Cambridge: Harvard University Press.

Shohat, Ella. 2002. "Notes on the Post-Colonial". *Social Text* 31/32: 99–113.

Young, Robert J.C. 2001. *Postcolonialism: A Historical Introduction*. Oxford: Blackwell.

Young, Robert J.C. 2003. *Postcolonialism: A Very Short Introduction*. Oxford: Oxford University Press.

Young, Robert J.C. 2012. "Postcolonial Remains". *New Literary History* 43.1: 19–42.

Part I
Disciplinary Constellations
New Forms of Knowledge

INTRODUCTION

This section of our volume deals with postcolonial theory's self-understanding via multiple institutional topographies. The section is prompted in part by the "How did we get here?" question: What are the genealogies and epistemologies that went into the making of the current status quo and how might they be transcended? Far from repeating the standard rhetorical move of anaphoric criticisms as a way of opening the debate, the essays in this section constitute a four-way exchange across the sites and boundaries wherein postcolonial theory is invoked, thereby helping to re-map the institutional places and languages through which postcolonial theory knows and speaks. As such they also constitute points of return as well as departure, since the essays in subsequent sections will respond to the arguments presented here.

This section opens with Claire Westall's incisive argument about the class basis of intellectual activity in general and the academic study of English Literature and postcolonial studies in particular. Given the Anglo-American beginnings of postcolonial theory, Westall's essay zooms in on the blind spots of the field's institutional framework and calls for more honesty (or what she calls "probity") in debates about methodologies as they inform and shape the scholarship, teaching and management of postcolonial theory and literary studies. The late capitalist nexus linking English Literature and postcolonial theory in particular, she argues, requires exposure and exploration.

The next two papers take postcolonial theory beyond its humanities base and towards fields with which it has entertained an occasionally difficult, if not hostile and indifferent, rapport. Simon Obendorf interrogates what might happen if, instead of exchanging uneasy glances, postcolonial theory and International Relations (IR) took seriously their common interest in political understanding and change. By tracing the history of recent attempts at opening up the two fields to one other, Obendorf uncovers not only a history of Eurocentric contempt at the heart of IR, but also the very real difficulties that beset attempts to create a dialogue with a version of postcolonial studies that seems to have forgotten its activist dimension. A closer look at postcolonial theory's aims promises a reinvigorated interdisciplinarity better able to fulfil the ever-elusive task of speaking truth to power.

Mrinalini Greedharry and Pasi Ahonen confront another complex inter-disciplinary problem, namely, the relationship between postcolonial theory, with all of its intricacies, and the field of Management and Organization Studies (MOS), which is itself described as a heady mixture of economics, engineering, ethnography, psychology and sociology. Both fields have under-gone multiple shifts and metamorphoses over the past three decades. Can – or even should – they have anything to say to each other? The answer is very much in the affirmative, not only because of the inscription of management knowledge as an integral part of the colonial system's administration of slaves and plantations, but also because of the reconfigurations needed in both post-colonial theory and MOS if they are to effect, rather than merely observe, ruptures within Western epistemologies. In view of the steady advance of putatively objective ideologies and administrative techniques that claim to draw on management science in the operation of universities across the world today, the urgency of the questions raised here cannot be overstated.

The section closes with an intervention on the most basic, and arguably the most difficult, question in this volume: How should postcolonial theory address literature in the contemporary moment? John C. Hawley tackles this through an examination of postcolonial theory's over-reliance on Western aesthetic norms in dealing with texts usually classified under such rubrics as orature, Indian *bhasha* literature or *testimonio*. The tension between the demand for newness, derived from the synthesis of colonial and indigenous forms, and the commitment to representing historical struggle and eman-cipation, has left postcolonial theory unable to address the demands made by such forms. Hawley asserts that if the vocabulary of postcolonial critical aesthetics is to go beyond the terms set out by Adorno, Lukács, Sartre and Jameson, greater attention will have to be paid to the subtle defigurations of established forms in our reading of postcolonial writers.

1 Capitalizing on English Literature
Disciplinarity, Academic Labor and Postcolonial Studies

Claire Westall

This chapter takes up a challenge I set myself on achieving a permanent academic post, namely, to write about the institutionalization of postcolonial studies in relation to the discipline of English Literature, accelerating efforts in the UK, US and elsewhere to globalize English Literature programs, and, the laboring lives of academic staff, especially the "early career" crowd. This means drawing on Marxist critiques of postcolonial studies and reassessments of English Literature; writing on neoliberalization and academic labor; and the everyday efforts of colleagues and friends wanting to resist systemized exploitation (of themselves and others), "enough to be able to look in the mirror and say, 'I'm trying'", as one of them recently put it. It also means using my own experiences as points of reference whilst appreciating that they are notably limited and come via a particular intellectual training. These influences prompted this incursion into debates about academia's postcolonial predicament, including the argument that, for all of its concerns with difference, inequality, representation and the role of the intellectual, mainstream (or institutionally endorsed) postcolonial studies – especially its theoretical and literary wings – has not got to grips with the disciplinary logic of English Literature that shapes, masks and fuels its defining errors and limitations as an academic field. Nor has it sufficiently grappled with the systemic connections between its intellectual history and priorities, and the workaday aspects of academic labor.

On writing I am mindful of numerous warnings about self and field reflexivity as entrapping us in pre-existing modes of inward-looking paralysis (Dean 2010 and 2013), which inhibit transformative thinking and action, as some critiques of postcolonial theory insist (Stam and Shohat 2012). I am also highly conscious of the dangers of personalization being read only as "complaint", as lacking critical or political substance (Gill 2010, 230), and how "complainants" or "killjoys" are managed and silenced by institutionalized demands for "happy talk" (Ahmed 2012, 10). Nevertheless, this is an attempt to think about disciplinary formation and academic labor in the context of the literary-cultural move from the postcolonial to the global. It is also a sign of solidarity with those peers and mentors whose vision, integrity, warmth and humor survive in the face of exploitation, ill health and exhaustion.

Importantly, this discussion is not intended to dismiss all work within or informing postcolonial studies, much of which has been rigorous and significant. However, taking up convincing Marxist explanations of the field's emergence and "misprisions" (Parry 2012a, 117; Parry 2013, 123), I argue that postcolonial studies has been widely endorsed, primarily within core, prestige-bound institutions because it enables and obscures capitalism's organizing principles and ramifications. And it does so, in large part, by proffering a reconciliatory extension of English Literature's imperial and market-oriented version of cultural capital based on precedence as saleable prestige. This argument relies on established readings of English Literature's imperial dimensions and the discipline's ongoing international dissemination and defense of undefined but class-bound "values" (Baldick 1983; Gardiner 2013). As an imperial discipline, English Literature must be reconnected to the development of the capitalist world system and explained as helping mold postcolonial theory and literary studies into a shape that accepts and aids global market creation. For most English Literature departments and universities caught within the anti-educational impetus of neoliberalization, postcolonial studies is supported as a saleable "good" (i.e. a positively valued and seemingly moral commodity) and as a tool facilitating global or international awareness and opportunity for the most advantaged people, groups and countries. Indeed, the field stands against Marxian efforts to call out and dismantle structural inequalities, and its widespread acceptance has exacerbated its authority to do so (see Chibber 2013). It is only when rethought in terms of capitalist modernity that the kinds of critical imperatives postcolonial studies has attributed to itself can be reoriented towards a resistant worldliness within which the reorganization of labor, education and literary studies may be possible.

ENGLISH LITERATURE AND POSTCOLONIAL STUDIES

"[D]isciplinary explanations" (Lazarus and Varma 2008, 321) of the influence English Literature exerts on postcolonial theory and literary studies are significant in ways not typically recognized in critiques of postcolonial studies. This includes how, as the "home" discipline, English Literature imbued postcolonial theory and literary studies with a mode of "perpetual auto-critique" (Stam and Shohat 2012, 372) that functions to stave off first principle, materialist challenges, challenges that are necessarily axiomatic for a radical, and overdue, reorganization of the world we share.

In the wake of postwar mass decolonization, Third World nationalist campaigns, and the rising force of social protest movements and identity-based claims to equality, postcolonial theory and literary studies emerged within and were then propagated by English departments at the most elite universities in the UK and US, making postcolonial studies a top-down academic creation that gained momentum as it penetrated other subject areas, institutions and locations (Lazarus and Varma 2008, 313). According to Arif Dirlik, postcolonialism really began "[w]hen Third World Intellectuals [...] arrived in [the] First World academe" (1994, 329) and became postcolonialists within 1970s "high theory", standing as part of the post-1968 settlement's anti-systemic outlook. As regularly noted, the imprint of post-structuralism and postmodernism, evidenced in the field-defining works of Said, Bhabha and Spivak, helped establish a theoretical idiom (a vocabulary or jargon) that often makes little sense to those outside the English Literature nexus and even some within it. It also set in motion many of the field's prevailing analytical trends and the responses they provoked. Robert Stam and Ella Shohat identify such critiques as including opposition to the seemingly loose approach to historicization; the rereading of political and economic/class/anti-capitalist struggles as "intra-psychic"; intertextual and inter-discursive tensions and ambiguities; and the corresponding celebration of ambivalence, difference hybridity, diaspora and cosmopolitanism (2012, 371–372). Infamously, the "post" of postcolonial studies was both akin to and distinct from other theoretical "posts" (Appiah 1991; McClintock 1992; Quayson 2000). It indicated but did not pin down an approach to "after" and "against" colonialism. Further, it has been repeatedly questioned for impeding accounts of the variance between peoples, places, languages and historic moments; buckling under the weight of exploitative economic continuities; and being unable to respond to the disintegration of the Soviet bloc or the subsequent dominance of the US. A self-declared anti-binarist, anti-universalist and anti-essentialist postcolonialism arose that could be seen as reneging on or contradicting its own moral and intellectual claims, with some works denouncing while also producing forms of binarism, universalism and essentialism (as explained by Dirlik 1994; During 1998; During 2012; San Juan 1998). According to Dirlik, and in line with Benita Parry's ongoing interrogation of the field (2004 and 2012b), postcolonial studies was quick to mobilize its Marxist inheritance, but the field's early poststructuralist anti-universalism led to a decentering and deconstructing of Marxism that ushered in a new, largely silent totality – that of global difference without a structure of relations. Crucially, this allows "postcolonial critics [to remain] silent on the relationship between the idea of postcolonialism to its context in contemporary capitalism" (Dirlik 1994, 331).

Historically situating the emergence of postcolonial studies within the collapse of the postwar economic boom, the related inability of Third World liberationism to hold out against capitalism and the widespread defeat of anti-capitalist ideologies during the restructuring of capital or neoliberalization, Lazarus and Varma describe the field as "janus faced", "having two aspects [...] as an academic enterprise, one accommodationist, the other subversive" (2008, 312), otherwise labeled the "anti-liberationist" and the "anti-anti-liberationist" (Lazarus 2011, 5). Parry links this distinction to Simon During's earlier warning of the "reconciliatory" dimension of academic postcolonialism (2012b, 342), which During defines as an approach that figures "colonialism as a kind of tragedy with a happy ending" – that of global connectivity – and opposed to a "critical postcolonialism" that attempts to "recover or construct differences and marginalized pasts" (1998, 37). We may also relate During's distinction to Graham Huggan's hopeful view of academic postcolonialism as a resistant mode of critique working against imperialism and its consequences, which he sets against the globalized, saleable version of postcoloniality manifest in the publishing, profiling and circulation of "postcolonial", "international" and "cosmopolitan" authors (2001, 4–6). The gap presented by Huggan can be described, to academia's benefit, as the difference between intellectuals working within scholarly debates set towards political resistance and graduates and other workers capitalizing on their exposure to such debates in order to market and sell their "products". However, postcoloniality is already dominant within academia, which is itself the chief arena for the marketing and selling of postcolonialism. Huggan's more recent explanation of the postcolonial field as "torn [...] between competing revolutionary and revisionist impulses" marks an ongoing tension, but he resists conceding that institutional support for revisionist (and largely continuant) causes has won out when this appears to be the day-to-day reality (2013, 4). For, although postcolonial studies emerged as "of and against its time" (Lazarus 2011, 4), the field's accommodationist and reconciliatory aspects have been the most influential, gaining institutional and (where possible) financial backing, especially via endorsements of English Literature's view of itself as a post-imperial discipline working towards a global appreciation of literary culture. We might say that the internationalization and marketization of higher education, particularly of the arts and humanities, relies upon a vision of reconciliation and connection that a globalizing postcolonial studies enables and offers back to English Literature, specifically to its debt-bound student consumers and others looking to purchase English Literature's heritage and use it to join the international creative class of neoliberal laborers (see Brouillette 2014).

Where During and Huggan defend the potential of postcolonial studies, Lazarus and Varma challenge the grounds of such optimism, implicating both aspects of postcolonial endeavor they identify as bound to a failure to recognize imperialism's place within capitalist modernity. Indeed, even when contemporary defenses of postcolonial theory, or studies, oppose imperialism's twenty-first-century manifestations, they still typically start from and stop at imperialism. Weighing up these defense-of-the-field narratives, and seemingly with no scholarly pun intended, Stam and Shohat point to a "Lazarus-like resurrection of the cadaver of postcolonialism" (2012, 371). However, Lazarus' own efforts towards the "plausible reconstruction" needed for a worlded comparative literary practice have pierced the imperial bubble of postcolonial studies. He reprimands scholars for paying "insufficient attention to the fact that colonialism is part and parcel of a large, enfolding historical dynamic, which is that of capitalism in its global trajectory" and for effecting a "category error" that uses "the West" as an ahistorical "euphemism for capitalism" (2011, 7 and 14). As Lazarus puts it, "the field didn't take a wrong turn, it is a wrong turn" (Lazarus in Gunne 2012, 9). Such thinking explodes postcolonial studies, including its efforts at self-transformation, and calls for a badly needed new model of comparative literary analysis that contends with the capitalist world system. This call is echoed in Vivek Chibber's response to Subaltern Studies in *Postcolonial Theory and the Spectre of Capital* (2013). The same type of reconsideration, though, also needs to be wielded against English Literature, against its familial nurturing of postcolonial studies and the manner in which, together, these domains inhibit the creation of alternative models of literary studies that are materially critical in a systemic fashion.

For Simon Gikandi, the positive dimension of postcolonial theory's emergence was as a "reaction against the institutionalization of the discipline of empire", that is, English Literature, with its "imperial imperative" and narrow set of canonically "great men" – most notably Shakespeare, Wordsworth and Dickens (Agnani *et al.* 2007, 635). The predominant view of postcolonial literary studies follows this line of argument, supporting the idea that, from the 1960s onwards, English Literature and its canon were forcibly opened up and diversified in terms of race, gender and class, with representative postcolonial authors and texts providing an anti-imperial, transnational dimension to these changes. Paul Jay explains that literary studies, functioning under the rubric of English Literature (though sometimes labeled differently), is said to have moved from a united or unitary canon, premised on the playing out of Arnoldian principles in the writing of "great" white males along a line of influence and inheritance (2010, 17), to a pluralized mode of "difference recognition" wherein staff and students are bound to study "different literatures" and "differences in literature" as literature becomes a "multicultural object" fit for the globalized contemporary (20–21). As commentators often point out, this occurs with some movement in the demographic makeup of university staff and students along the lines of gender, race and class, but the dominant white, middle-class staff and student pattern holds, most forcefully at the "best" institutions, with an ideological coherence that is reinforced through the self-congratulation achieved with small degrees of "diversity" as exceptional entry (see, for example, Ahmed 2012). In this prevailing view, postcolonial theory and literary studies aid the mutation and survival of English Literature rather than its dissolution in the face of anti-colonial resistance and Britain's imperial decline.

This narrative of the transformation of English Literature is fundamentally problematic. The Gramscian view that hegemonizing processes require and accommodate oppositional pressures as a strategy for self-continuation quickly comes to mind, as do criticisms of postcolonial literary studies that concentrate on the permanence of Anglocentrism, Eurocentrism or Commonwealth bias and on canon elasticity as canon maintenance (i.e. selective inclusion as a means of maintaining a rationale for elitist exclusivity). We should use these points of critique and go further because such a reading of English Literature's adaptability in the face of postcolonial pressure reinforces the idea that reforming the discipline is acceptable, desirable even, when we should be identifying a first-principle challenge to the cultural-as-economic capital English Literature creates and bestows. This reading of adaptation as continuity also ensures that English Literature is criticized only as a "former" imperial discipline rehabilitated via postcolonial and multicultural recognition rather than as a capitalist-imperialist discipline still playing a sizeable role in the development and management of international markets, particularly education markets, and socio-economic inequality. Consequently, this view of disciplinary continuity enables English Literature to retain its imperial claim to being a creator and arbitrator of "universal" value – in aesthetic, literary, cultural, ethical and economic terms – while adding new or extended judgment domains that hold Anglo or "former" imperial centers as literary-critical capitals. In this way, English Literature helps Britain maintain its claim upon the world through cultural precedence, that is, the "firsts" and "greats" it offered the world, while also supplementing this with limited "new" inclusions.

An anti-capitalist, and thereby anti-imperialist, rereading of English Literature and its relation to postcolonial studies should accept and extend beyond studies of cultural imperialism that track the violence of the civilizing mission in empire, of the abuse and mimicry offered in its name and of the imbalance in the power to represent that is crucial for imperialism. It should heed and move past the Eagletonian version of "The Rise of English" (1983) as a replacement for religion and classics, bringing self-reflection and self-improvement to the working masses to quell class tensions at home and bind the colonized to cultural and administrative systems of domination abroad. It should also take on board the insights offered by Gauri Viswanathan's *Masks of Conquest* (1989), but situate literary studies in colonial India between an earlier union-imperial literary formation pivotal to the spread of modern, industrializing capitalism and a later Leavisite model of "literary-critical" disciplining that maintained imperial elasticity for British self (re)assurance via the institutionalization of English Literature.

As I have written elsewhere, English Literature does not know to what its disciplinary name, its "English", refers – whether as of England, as of the English language, as of English in Britain or the United Kingdom or the former empire (Westall 2013, 218). This uncertainty has been stretched with postcolonial theory and literature and debates about literatures in English, global English or world "Englishes". What the "English" of English Literature actually does is offer a sizeable misdirection, pointing to but simultaneously obliterating national space, namely the national space of England, in order to advance British imperialist interests (i.e. the perpetual advancement of capitalist expansion). As Robert Crawford, Michael Gardiner and others writing on Scotland and British literary history have indicated, English Literature, when traced back to its antecedents in the eighteenth-century *belles lettres* tradition of Glasgow and Edinburgh universities, with contributions from Adam Smith and Hugh Blair looming large, can be thought of as part of the cultural formation binding together the British state's emergent ruling class (see Crawford 1998; Gardiner 2013). According to Mary Poovey's study, *Genres of the Credit Economy* (2008), it was Daniel Defoe who persuaded readers into the currency and credit beliefs needed to make the union and its empire workable by maintaining a fact/fiction continuum of value in his writing. Later, English Literature canonized Defoe's realism by casting fictionality as distinct from the economic belief system it helped create (Poovey 2008, 91–124). The Acts of Union (1707–8) themselves might be said to historically signal the shift from the commercial "accident" of empire described by J.R. Seeley to a state-led, or at least officially endorsed, union-empire that was always beyond the national (as British union) and determined by the need for perpetual expansion (as capitalist-imperial). In other words, capitalist market creation precedes formal empire, is the driving force for the emergence of the British state, and sets the terms by which the seeds of English Literature are sown and then exported.

In addition, "the nation" as a political formation and as the geo-spaces of England and Scotland is subsumed within capitalist collectivization for British imperial-union and the *belles lettres* tradition that grounds English Literature. Conceptually, then, "the nation" is antagonistic to English Literature as potentially unruly and destabilizing (Gardiner 2011 and 2013), because it challenges Britain's very existence and the discipline's very British claim to global relevance. This antagonism towards the potentiality of "the nation" has carried over into mainstream postcolonial studies with its rush to emphasize internationalism as across or above rather than between nations or nation-states (Deckard 2012, 8). This makes sense given the scale of European imperialism and the large victories of late capitalism's globalizing intensity (see Lazarus 2011), but in disciplinary terms, English Literature's built-in fear of "the nation" as potentially anti-capitalist has directly influenced postcolonial theory and literature, which have held onto ideas of the national imaginary so as to mask their jettisoning of the kind of Third World nationalism that Fanon and others deemed essential in the move towards a post- or anti-capitalist future.

At the core of British self-projection was, and is, the power of a mythic and imperial Englishness, disseminated via empire and holding as the defining, and most saleable, feature of English Literature. Ian Baucom opens his study of the displaced and disruptive performances of Britain's mythic Englishness with Salman Rushdie's satanic line: "[T]he trouble with the Engenglish is that their his his history happened overseas" (Rushdie 1988, 343; Baucom 1999, 3). While England had been journeying out from the island it shares for centuries, Rushdie's quip conflates British history with the iconic force of English Literature. It marks Britain's deployment of what Gardiner calls "the class-fixed form of Englishness" (2011, 2), which helped Britain demand compulsory inclusion in its imperial narrative of world order and at the same time specify a protected idyllic home of imagined Englishness. This exclusive zone was constantly challenged by and yet maintained through elastic expansion and flexible adaptation of the relationship between Englishness and Britishness. Postcolonial literary studies has predominantly held onto this class-fixed version of imperial Englishness as one of its foundational sites of attack, but regularly mobilizes its international cachet without unpacking the relationship between Britain and England in terms of the trajectory of capitalism – the very façade upon which English Literature stands.

Importantly, English Literature gained its academic hold as Britain's imperial grip loosened. While the canonical "greats" were circulated within empire across the nineteenth century, English Literature's arrival in the academy in the early twentieth century and subsequent growth is testament to its ability to expand, adapt and thrive in the face of, and by means of, imperial self-questioning. This is a skill postcolonial studies inherited and maintains. English Literature should therefore be (re)conceived as a commonwealth discipline, taking its current shape in the 1920s and '30s thanks to the Leavisite influence at Cambridge. This occurred as Britain "softened" its claims to empire in order to argue for shared history and overlapping linguistic and cultural legacies that would protect its future position. With the loss of colonial ground, Britain relies upon English Literature to develop ever-stronger claims to the humanizing and disciplining powers of literary studies in what Gardiner describes as a mode of informal elasticity that underpins the discipline's resilience (Gardiner 2013). Indeed, Leavis' legacy is of "the literary-critical" that makes English Literature an "essential" and "true discipline", training "intelligence and sensibility together, and cultivating a sensitiveness and precision of response" (Leavis 1979, 24). Sensibility, in this disciplinary sense, is the unknown, invisible, and perpetual category of class advancement and co-option that streamlines cultural capital as economic advantage, in the sense of Bourdieu's "distinction". It is also an acquired skill akin to adaptability and flexibility, allowing the trained to learn (or at least mimic) the responses and empathies necessary for professionalized success. Much might be made of Leavis' insider-outsider position at Cambridge, but it is the Oxbridge weight of disciplinary acceptance that comes to define English Literature's academic ascension – passed out to the world's most successful Anglophone universities – and later confirms postcolonial studies as an outgrowth of English Literature's imperial outlook (see Dale 1997). As the Commonwealth mutates, and literary studies takes up the self-questioning enforced by imperial collapse, the discipline remakes parts of itself as a means of self-perpetuation. The arrival of the quickly unpopular Commonwealth Literature, followed by Literatures in English, is testament to a continuity of approach. That postcolonial theory and literary studies evolve partly out of this commonwealth grounding is indicative of the ways in which English Literature maintains British interests, refusing to give way to alternative models of literary study. Moreover, the mutational logic that allows English Literature to carry on exerting a capitalist-imperial impetus is clearly evident in its international manifestations – mostly obviously in North America and Australasia.

The expansionism of the canon is an example of how English Literature's dominance has been (re)crafted and upheld. The Leavisite canon is always-already predetermined and, simultaneously, adaptive, elastic and accommodating, ensuring that new examples – representative and isolated – are brought into the cultural orbit of undefined yet humanizing "greatness". As Karen Lawrence has written, the canon may be ever-changing but canonicity itself is never eradicated (1992, 2–4). In this way, ever increasing but still relatively few new inclusions are made compulsory by English Literature's need to survive via perpetual expansion. New and seemingly exceptional works are then used to reinforce the pre-existing claims to greatness of the disciplinary "classics" to which they are connected. This has been the primary reason for the widespread acceptance of postcolonialism's early "writing back" thesis, and its overuse and lingering effect on under- and post-graduate encounters with postcolonial, global or world literature. (Would Said's *Culture and Imperialism* have been as influential in English institutions without its canonical referencing, without its Jane Austen? Where would postcolonial literary studies and its claims to multicultural drip-down educational benefits for schools and society be without Shakespeare's *The Tempest*?) In this context, Ngũgĩ wa Thiong'o's call for the "Abolition of the English Department" (1972) can be appreciated as a demand not just for the overturning of the dominance of English, the language and its literature in Africa, but also for dismantling the very ordering and absorptive logic of English Literature. Such an overturning would be valuable for literary studies in England as well as in Kenya, and other locations besides, because it could help move literary studies beyond the class-fixed British Englishness of an ever-expanding but exclusive discipline.

Presently, what remains at the center of English Literature are two saleable strands of canon preservation and adaptation – sold all the more fiercely thanks to the necessity narrative of austerity. On one hand, the disciplinary "classics", which are maintained and sold as originators and exemplars of cultural and aesthetic value (still proclaimed as universally relevant), and, on the other hand, small numbers of newly "found" authors and texts, often from "other" places, are included to allow the *frisson* of difference to stand, especially for students coming to comparative literature for the first time. The amalgamation of these two zones constitutes mainstream literary publishing as well as the expressly political rendering of English Literature in the popular British-international imaginary. Few examples better capture Britain's popularizing of the cultural-as-economic value of English Literature's imperializing canon and its reconciliatory glocal, postcolonial multiculturalism than the 2012 Olympic Opening ceremony, with its Brunel/Caliban, its idyllic enclosures of imperial Englishness, its "mix" of cosmopolitan dancing bodies and the encapsulation of the whole world within the London's union flag. As I write, Shakespeare is being hailed by the BBC as Britain's "greatest cultural export", giving away the economic necessity of canonized greatness for Britain's economic futurity while reinforcing the literary-Olympic-economic unity with the forecast that 2016, the 400th anniversary of the death of the "bard", will become Britain's "next Olympic moment" (BBC News Online, 23 April 2014). This is the political and economic purposefulness of English Literature's continuity, a purposefulness being bolstered during the current "crisis of the arts" within universities and set to hold in the face of contraction because the selling of "exclusive" cultural capital is Britain's international calling card.

The very disciplinary logic that uses small degrees of adaptive inclusion to maintain cultural-as-economic advantage is also evident in English Literature's advance of multiplicity, often seen as multiculturalism. This should be expected of an imperial discipline, given that, as Robert Young states, "empire's structure of government was necessarily organized around the accommodation of diversity" (2012, 31). English Literature maintains this self-interested and imperial "accommodation" of difference and advocates for the prioritization of identity politics, cultural difference and multicultural inclusion. Postcolonial literary studies is especially culpable for supporting and taking on this multicultural imaginary so beloved by English Literature. The intellectual fashion across the arts and humanities for multidirectionality, as with multicultural memory, is a recent update within this frame of multiplicity acceptance. Multiple points of recognition – of voices, memories and positions – are permitted and can coexist without resolution. Nevertheless, as with the multicultural impetus more broadly, there should be no applause granted for recognition of polyvocality or pluri-perspectives from within or across groups, places, countries and classes when the relational unevenness, the socio-economic as well as political differentials that determine and define these positions and their connections, are erased. With this multiplicity lens, neither postcolonial studies nor English Literature can account for the compression of capital's contradictions, as within First World/Third World capitals such as London, Los Angeles or Shanghai, and both intellectual fields lack the methodological probity needed to investigate the relationship between capitalism and the complicated literary-cultural expressions that examine or testify to its workings. In fact, multiplicity within English Literature and postcolonial studies does very little to attend to the varying scales of relational inequality that need to be examined for multiplicity to become analytically meaningful. This is why the labels "Global North" and "Global South" as they are typically used are insufficient and can be trapped within a North/South, East/West reductivity that does not get to grips with capitalism's ability to act universally and inculcate difference and complexity across and within specific sites and groups of people (see Lazarus 2002; Chibber 2013).

Where Stam and Shohat are unclear why leftist postcolonialists question or oppose identity politics (2012, 382–383), Lazarus and Varma pinpoint the problem. They write that postcolonial studies' "strategic allegiance with new social movements", especially on university campuses and when combined with the literary and cultural theory's fetishization of difference, led to the "privileging [of] a rhetoric of recognition over one of redistribution", meaning that the "intersection of postcolonial studies and multicultural politics provided a domain within which radicalism could be espoused within the constraints of the seemingly undefeatable global order" (2008, 311–312). This claim is pivotal. Recognition without redistribution is a key procapitalist strategy that English Literature and postcolonial studies continue to deploy. Their calls for change, predominantly as minor adaptations, are offered in ethical or moral terms – enabled by difference recognition – but are typically set towards self-perpetuation and remain within an acceptance of the current global order.

In a 1990 interview, Spivak told of a conversation with Said in which she reminded him of the "scandal of their production" as "postcolonialists", and of the class and power lines that had enabled them to conduct a "wild anthropological experiment" in "the West". Ali Behdad sees this reflexive gesture as usefully underscoring "the ironic accidents of place and privilege that have produced the new kind of cosmopolitan intellectual" (Behdad 1993, 40). Yet "place and privilege" are not accidents, not in the works of Marx, Bourdieu, Foucault (as well as numerous others), and certainly not for Spivak or other postcolonial/cosmopolitan intellectuals and their students. In her related writing on whiteness, Sara Ahmed unpacks how institutions are set to self-question and adapt in low-level ways, as with the inclusion of postcolonial and multi-racial scholars, so as to hold to their dominant ideological outlook and prejudices. She explains that the bind between multicultural recognition and privilege allows racism to be case as "ignorance" and "intolerance". Meanwhile the educated mode of difference acceptance reinforces white middle-class normative values in which "learning to see" and "tolerate" arises within an accepted language of hierarchical relations that fails to oppose the foundations of inequality and are set only to advance the educated "seers" (Ahmed 2004). Additionally, in her work "On Being Included", Ahmed discusses how, as a representative and embodiment of diversity, her institutional role is often to testify to her university's recognition and inclusion of difference, to offset its bourgeois heteronormative whiteness or point up its ability to for self-critique (as it aids self-maintenance). In this way, she repeatedly marks out how a flawed identitarian multiculturalism premised only on recognition – so significant in the development of English Literature and postcolonial studies – is ordinarily reinforced via collegiate and classroom-based encounters in higher education.

FROM POSTCOLONIAL TO GLOBAL AND THE "EARLY CAREER" PROBLEM

By now it should be clear that the role of postcolonial theory and literary studies in my education and employment means that I too have capitalized on English Literature and postcolonial studies and remain caught in the quicksand of (academic) hypocrisy. As a white, female, junior but open-contract (or tenured) lecturer in a successful and somewhat prestigious English Literature department in England, I am complicit with a class, education system and discipline that an eighteen-year-old version of myself today could not possibly hope to join. My experience resonates with Mark Fisher's strikingly familiar portrayal of his inability to fit with the class-set patterns of educational obtainment and acculturation into a professionalized compliance that dominates him while excluding those like him (Fisher 2014). Having entered university as the UK introduced means-tested tuition fees, my debt-free rise from student to salariat meant that my permanency was clinched just as the 2010 Browne Report came into effect in England. And despite, or perhaps because of, the personal success of a (relatively) secure job – increasing described as the "luck" of the few but better understood as the brutal un(der)employment and precarity of the many – this moment brought an acute sense of anger and an activity-based inertia. As the global financial crisis unfolded, and the humanities sought to defend themselves by concentrating on discourses of "value" as they dealt in finance-related topics and tactics, I (like others) felt squeezed by a welcome upsurge of interest in Marxism and debates about capitalism, often related to anti-austerity campaigns and public-sector industrial action, on one hand, and, on the other, ongoing compliance with the vast machinery and debilitating excesses of academic labor as practiced within a growing international "edu-business" rationale (see Gill 2009). For me, this period also underscored how renewed defenses of postcolonial studies, including those with political bite, were enabling the field to hold onto the systemic erasure of structural thinking about material inequalities, and how this weakness was being carried over into the new labels used for comparative literary and cultural studies, especially as "sold" to students. Postcolonial studies and its associated comparative modes were being used by "first" placed institutions (i.e. Oxbridge and the Russell Group in the UK and Ivy League institutions in the US) to legitimize research mantras, curriculum twists and broader branding messages with international or global hooks (e.g. globalization theory, global literature, global career opportunities) precisely in order to continue capitalizing upon the unevenness of the world. In addition, the field's underpinning erasure of capitalist modernity was helping to detract from the overt connections between the field's questioning of inequality and the inequalities played out within our daily work lives. Debates about workloads, staffing levels, income streams and student numbers mostly took place within the language of a downturn, within an acceptance of or a push against hard times, and not within a critique of capitalism's overarching demands that recognized English Literature's investment in its logic of continuity as expansionism.

Like others concerned with postcolonial studies, I am hampered by the field's failure to tackle its own *raison d'être* and (hidden) object of study, namely, capitalist modernity (Lazarus 2011, 7 and *passim*). Yet this hampering is not caused by any blind allegiance to a postcolonial mode of address so much as by a widely held set of assumptions about the form of postcolonial and comparative practice that will remain dominant and be passed down and out to future generations. Perhaps as a direct consequence of my exposure to academic assaults on the pitfalls of the field, the economic strains felt by English Literature departments, my own included, appear to me to fuel an expectation, conveyed in disciplinary and institutional terms, that in the battle for "survival", I, and others like me, should deliver a sanitized, multicultural and reconciliatory postcolonialism or post-postcolonialism: a version that is global, inclusive and forever positive in its outlook, functioning without a probing sense of methodological integrity and firmly in line with neoliberal-ization and internationalization imperatives set to supposedly protect us, our students, the department and subject, institutional and national interests, and much more besides. The managerial idiom of "survival", "best practice" and "international excellence" insists that research, teaching and administrative auditing should be attuned to smooth and exciting versions of global connec-tivity, cross-cultural interaction and transnational trends. Yet it also demands a tapping into resources and markets that offer us the strongest chance of self furtherance – with China and India, Africa and Asia, Rights, Ecology, Medicine and Big Data all ripening as "hot" or "highlight" domains for the arts and humanities, regardless of the rigor or lack thereof being mobilized at any given time. It seems "better" if our comparativism is about "shared values" rather than uneven consequences, and our concern with "other" places, peo-ples, literatures and cultures should help us stand as flag bearers for (prof-itable) international collaborations. We must welcome financialization and narrow our intellectual wares in accordance with the pre-set agendas of fund-ing bodies, always promising more for less (at the expense of others – locally, nationally and internationally), and in line with the preferences of potential student-customers and their parents (again locally, nationally and very much internationally) in order to hold onto or increase our market share without opposing market principles in any active fashion. We also need to accept that we exist within normalized financial lotteries that reinforce the unending and unpredictable nature of our laboring lives – from unclear student debt profiles through long-shot scholarship applications to unlikely-to-be-successful fund-ing bids. Our approach must be financially realist and credit-dependent, as it has been since Defoe, and, simultaneously, we should not look to assess how financialization has been built in to the literary-cultural discipline we claim is critical. We can write and teach about race, gender, poverty, labor, land, differ-ence and subalternity, with power and imperialism in mind, so long as we do not link these issues to the everyday acculturation of staff and students into an education industry that helps advance recognition without redistribution, promotes the silencing of questions about internal labor inequalities and enjoys real-estate acquisition. This is also an industry that practices hierarchical and predetermined decision-making; demands struggling bodies, brains and bank overdrafts; and benefits from the nervous networks and fixed-contract home-lessness of its early-career entrants.

It may be fair to say that this directly affects all academics and apprentice-academics, and this is largely the case, but those with an obvious postcolonial or comparative profile are especially susceptible to being read by recruiters and/or colleagues as potential revenue-raising internationalists, with new topics, projects and global access points. Early-career researchers are also particularly vulnerable to the co-optive pressure built into the erasure of structural thinking in the field, its own compromised history and its individualistic (and therefore moot) mode of gestural opposition. For San Juan, postcolonial studies accepts a paltry allegiance to resistance only as a "refurbishing of the liberal individualist ethos geared to the 'free play' of the market", which is insulting when cast against the actions of "colonized subalterns" (1998, 3 and 10). As he says, such individual resistance is "the valorization of reified immediacies [seemingly] unconnected with institutions and instrumentalities that subtend them" (8). Further, when Parry takes Young to task for his "chutzpah" in aggrandizing the achievements of postcolonial studies, she does so because of his failure to "provide a coherent study on why and to what ends the world is in urgent need of transformation [as he claims], as well as the strategies for insurrection" (Parry 2012b, 341–342). Such failures are common within postcolonial studies, leading Parry and other Marxists writing on postcolonalism to challenge the way postcolonial studies addresses imperialism and power differentials without theorizing why and how such differentials came into being, are maintained and can be opposed, even overturned (see Dirlik 1994; San Juan 1998; Lazarus 2011; Parry 2004 and 2012). These failures, it seems to me, are most consequential for those junior postcolonialists or comparativists trained with and through an absence of systemic and insurrectionary intent presented to them and others as global political engagement. Plus, they are typically drowning in their own exploitation – as the anxious, beleaguered and encumbered bodies of doctoral, postdoctoral and fixed-contract researchers evince. When Terry Eagleton acerbically joked, in the opening issue of *Interventions*, that postcolonialists were stronger on "identity than the International Monetary Fund", he also quipped that there was "a secret handbook for aspiring postcolonial theorists" requiring them to begin essays by calling the field into question, proceed as if this were inconsequential and follow the oft repeated instruction to be "sceptical of totalities" because the postcolonial condition is "nothing as drearily centred, well-founded [...] and undeconstructed as a *system*" (1998, 24–26, emphasis in original). Here Eagleton's reductive humor hones in on the misdirections of the field and their replication in the work of young scholars trained to ignore, and so accept, the history and unfolding of capitalist modernity despite its hidden/haunting role in their work and its (crippling) effects on their laboring positions. Recent interventions, including debates about what lies beyond postcolonialism and world Englishes, too often claim a move forward while relying almost wholesale on postcolonial methods and terminology, maintaining its critical omissions and supporting its complicity with English Literature's erasure of capitalist-imperialist (expand

and adapt) imperatives. Additionally, such work, and more besides, proceeds without a methodological frame that would enable the content to stand in relation to the working practices that produce it.

As English Literature continues to maintain its reach by extending itself into "new" global manifestations of inclusion, there is a fundamental danger of comparative literary interests or expertise being presented to students (of varying types and at different stages) as a pick and mix non-approach that makes, or presents, the world as always-already and everywhere equally different, interesting, consumable and available to those belonging to the right (rightly ranked) institutions, countries and classes. To offer students, especially undergraduate students, questions about difference, inequality, representation and global resource management without a systemic and systemized methodological approach that has a rationale for how and why they need to encounter such texts and debates is to perpetuate the error at the disciplinary heart of English Literature that was carried over into postcolonial theory and literary studies.

On moving into my academic post, it became obvious that the debates about postcolonialism and globalization, fraught since at least the mid-1990s, would color my everyday working life, especially my teaching, and that efforts at methodological transformation to create new forms of literary-cultural investigation (including a mode of anti-disciplinarity) were essential. Relinquishing debates about what should be included in Global Literature in favor of an agreed methodological approach that grapples with the literary-cultural content of capitalist modernity appears to be the only strategic move forward that literary studies can make if it is to develop (or enhance) any political ambition for itself and its students beyond survivalism and compliance. Moving past (or better still, against) postcolonial theory and literary studies would require also moving against the straitjacket of English Literature and the discipline's aptitude for creating class-fixed subjects heavy with cultural capital and mistakenly at ease with capitalism.

REFERENCES

Ahmed, Sara. 2004. "Declarations of Whiteness: The Non-Performativity of Anti-Racism". *Borderlands* ejournal 3.2: http://www.borderlands.net.au/vol3no2_2004/ahmed_declarations.htm.

Ahmed, Sara. 2012. *On Being Included: Racism and Diversity in Institutional Life.* Durham, NC and London: Duke University Press.

Agnani *et al.* 2007. "Editor's Column: The End of Postcolonial Theory? A Roundtable with Sunil Agnani, Fernando Coronil, Gaurav Desai, Mamadou Diouf, Simon Gikandi, Susie Tharu and Jennifer Wenzel". *PMLA* 122.3: 633–651.

Appiah, Kwame Anthony. 1991. "Is the Post- in Postmodernism the Post- in Postcolonial?" *Critical Inquiry* 17.2: 336–357.

Baldick, Chris. 1983. *The Social Mission of English Literature, 1848–1932.* Oxford: Clarendon.

Baucom, Ian. 1999. *Out of Place: Englishness, Empire, and the Locations of Identity*. Princeton: Princeton University Press.

BBC News Online. 2014. "Shakespeare's A Cultural Icon Abroad". 23 April. http://www.bbc.com/news/entertainment-arts-27110234.

Behdad, Ali. 1993. "Travelling to Teach: Postcolonial Critics in the American Academy". In *Race, Identity, and Representation in Education*, edited by Cameron McCarthy *et al.*, 280–288. New York: Routledge.

Brouillette, Sarah. 2014. *Literature and the Creative Economy*. Stanford: Stanford University Press.

Chibber, Vivek. 2013. *Postcolonial Theory and the Specter of Capital*. London: Verso.

Crawford, Robert, ed. 1998. *The Scottish Invention of English Literature*. Oxford: Oxford University Press.

Dale, Leigh. 1997. *The English Men: Professing Literature in Australian Universities*. Canberra: Association for the Study of Australian Literature.

Dean, Jodi. 2010. *Blog Theory: Feedback and Capture in the Circuits of Drive*. Cambridge, MA: Polity.

Dean, Jodi. 2013. "The Neoliberal Trap". *Open Democracy*, 17 July. http://www.opendemocracy.net/jodi-dean/neoliberal-trap.

Deckard, Sharae. 2012. "Editorial". *Green Letters: Studies in Ecocriticism* 16.1: 5–14.

Dirlik, Arif. 1994. "The Postcolonial Aura: Third World Criticism in the Age of Global Capitalism". *Critical Inquiry* 20.2: 328–356.

During, Simon. 1998. "Postcolonialism and Globalisation: A Dialectical Relation after All?" *Postcolonial Studies* 1.1: 31–47.

During, Simon. 2012. "Empire's Present". *New Literary History* 43.2: 331–340.

Eagleton, Terry. 1998. "Postcolonialism and 'postcolonialism'". *Interventions: International Journal of Postcolonial Studies* 1.1: 24–26.

Fisher, Mark. 2014. "Good for Nothing". *The Occupied Times,* 19 March. http://theoccupiedtimes.org/?p=1284.

Gardiner, Michael. 2011. "Introduction". In *Scottish Literature and Postcolonial Literature: Comparative Texts and Critical Perspectives*, edited by Michael Gardiner, Graeme MacDonald and Niall O'Gallagher, 1–14. Edinburgh: Edinburgh University Press.

Gardiner, Michael. 2013. "English Literature as Ideology". In *Literature of an Independent England: Revisions of England, Englishness and English Literature*, edited by Claire Westall and Michael Gardiner, 203–217. Basingstoke, UK: Palgrave Macmillan.

Gill, Rosalind. 2009. "Breaking the Silence: The Hidden Injuries of Neo-liberal Academia". In *Secrecy and Silence in the Research Process: Feminist Reflections*, edited by Róisín Ryan-Flood and Rosalind Gill, 228–244. London: Routledge.

Gunne, Sorcha. 2012. "Mind the Gap: An Interview with Neil Lazarus". *Postcolonial Text* 7.3: 1–15.

Hall, Catherine. 2002. *Civilizing Subject: Metropole and Colony in the English Imagination 1830–1867*. Chicago: University of Chicago Press.

Huggan, Graham. 2001. *The Postcolonial Exotic: Marketing the Margin*. Abingdon and New York: Routledge.

Huggan, Graham. 2013. "General Introduction". In *The Oxford Handbook of Postcolonial Studies*, 1–26. Oxford: Oxford University Press.

Jay, Paul. 2010. *Global Matters: The Transnational Turn in Literary Studies*. Ithaca: Cornell University Press.

Lawrence, Karen. 1992. "Introduction: The Cultural Politics of Canons". In *Decolonizing Tradition: New Views of Twentieth-Century "British" Literary Canons*, edited by Karen Lawrence, 1–19. Urbana and Chicago: University of Illinois Press.

Lazarus, Neil 2002. "The Fetish of 'the West' in Postcolonial Theory". In *Marxism, Modernity and Postcolonial Studies*, edited by Crystal Bartolovich and Neil Lazarus, 43–64. New York: Cambridge University Press.

Lazarus, Neil. 2011. "What Postcolonial Theory Doesn't Say". *Race & Class* 53.1: 3–27.

Lazarus, Neil and Rashmi Varma. 2008. "Marxism and Postcolonial Studies". In *Critical Companion to Contemporary Marxism*, edited by Jaques Bidet and Stathis Kouvélakis, 309–331. Leiden; Boston: Brill.

Leavis, F. R. 1979 [1943]. *Education and the University: A Sketch for an English School*. Cambridge: Cambridge University Press.

McClintock, Anne. 1992. "The Angel of Progress: Pitfalls of the Term Post-Colonialism". *Social Text* 31–32: 85–98.

Ngũgĩ wa Thiong'o. 1972. "On the Abolition of the English Department". In *Homecoming: Essays on African and Caribbean Literature, Culture and Politics*, 149–150. London: Heinemann.

Parry, Benita. 2004. *Postcolonial Studies: A Materialist Critique*. London: Routledge.

Parry, Benita. 2012a. "What is Left in Postcolonial Studies". Edward Said Memorial Lecture 29 May. University of Warwick.

Parry, Benita. 2012b. "What is Left in Postcolonial Studies?" *New Literary History* 43.2: 341–358.

Parry, Benita. 2013. "Edward Said and Third-World Marxism". *College Literature* 40.4: 105–126.

Poovey, Mary. 2008. *Genres of the Credit Economy: Mediating Value in Eighteenth- and Nineteenth-Century Britain*. Chicago: Chicago University Press.

Quayson, Ato. 2000. "Postcolonialism and Postmodernism". In *A Companion to Postcolonial Studies*, edited by Henry Schwarz and Sangeeta Ray, 87–111. Malden, MA: Blackwell.

Rushdie, Salman. 1988. *The Satanic Verses*. London: Vintage.

San Juan, E. 1998. *Beyond Postcolonial Theory*. New York: St Martin's Press.

Stam, Robert and Ella Shohat. 2012. "Whence and Whither Postcolonial Theory?" *New Literary History* 43.2: 371–390.

Viswanathan, Gauri. 1989. *Masks of Conquest: Literary Study and British Rule in India*. New York: Columbia University Press.

Westall, Claire. 2013. "The Rise and Fall of English Literature". In *Literature of an Independent England: Revisions of England, Englishness and English Literature*, edited by Claire Westall and Michael Gardiner, 218–233. Basingstoke, UK: Palgrave Macmillan.

Young, Robert JC. 2012. "Postcolonial Remains". *New Literary History* 43.1: 19–42.

2 Dangerous Relations?

Lessons from the Interface of Postcolonialism and International Relations

Simon Obendorf

INTRODUCTION

The scene is a University of Melbourne seminar room in the mid-1990s. Together with around fifteen other students, I wait for a postgraduate teaching assistant to open discussions in a tutorial accompanying an international relations module. The tutor begins by explaining that he has recently returned to Australia following postgraduate study of the subject in the United Kingdom. He name-drops the institution at which he was enrolled and the eminent British scholars of the discipline he has encountered. With his bona fides thus established, he surveys our group and asks, "So who here has studied international relations before? And I don't mean any of that postcolonial bullshit".

True story. But beyond the academic archetypes – postgraduate bluster, an un-wowed group of undergraduates, the cultural cringe evident in much of the relationship between Australia and the United Kingdom – something significant was taking place. The tutor's dismissal of postcolonialism as irrelevant to a discussion of international relations was, first and foremost, a piece of disciplinary boundary-riding, an attempt to delineate what was, and most importantly what was not, relevant to international relations scholarship. The delivery was nonchalant (subtext: "surely everyone here is intelligent enough to agree with my prejudicial assessment of postcolonialism's relevance"). But the attempt to make postcolonialism an object of mirth, and to buttress students' disciplinary allegiances to a version of international relations that explicitly rejected engagement with postcolonialism, betrayed unease over what was already an emergent postcolonial critique.

At the time, a literature exploring the relationship between postcolonialism and international relations was becoming evident. In 1999, Albert Paolini was to call for a "redrawing of the international relations canvas" (39), denouncing the discipline's Eurocentrism, its orientation towards Western universalism, obsession with Great Power politics and disregard for non-Western cultures and concerns (33–40). Reaffirming Stanley Hoffman's classic (1977) appraisal of the discipline, Steve Smith would declare that at the end of the twentieth century, international relations was "still an American social science" (2000, 374). Others would argue that international relations was so thoroughly contaminated by Eurocentrism and by an obsession with structures and politics universalized by European colonial expansion that entirely new ways of understanding international processes were required (Bleiker 1997; Krishna 2001). What was clear was that a postcolonial challenge was being mounted. My undergraduate seminar was to become an arena where the purity of mainstream disciplinary approaches to international relations was to be defended and where no "postcolonial bullshit" would be allowed to stick.

This chapter uses the complex relationship between disciplinary International Relations (IR) and postcolonialism to explore what we might learn from the dialogues and disjunctures between postcolonialism and the social sciences. Scholars working at the intersection of IR and postcolonialism have been forced to grapple with a range of issues that often lie beyond the experience of those pursuing postcolonial studies in the humanities. Most obviously, there is the challenge of working against the grain of settled orthodoxies and in ways often unrewarded (even penalized) by the discipline. Yet the picture is not all bleak. In carving out intellectual and institutional spaces from which to explore these ideas, those working to bring postcolonialism into dialogue with the politics and processes of international affairs have been pursuing scholarship in ways that should prove of broader interest. Certainly, not all scholarship reflecting on IR and its allied disciplines (globalization studies, development, international political economy, international law) from postcolonial perspectives is marked by a consistent approach. Many of the most productive lessons become visible when scholars disagree or take opposing positions. Nor is it the case that the postcolonial critique of IR has proved an unalloyed success. Yet within the body of scholarly work attempting this task we can identify several key themes worthy of further examination: a sophisticated awareness of the problems of intellectual institutionalization and disciplinary incorporation; a dedicated attention to issues of politics, economics, materiality and the processes of everyday life; and a commitment to interdisciplinary collaboration and outcomes of practical benefit.

This chapter does not rehearse the arguments over the need for a postcolonial intervention into international relations. The point has already been well made by a range of scholars (Shilliam 2011; Krishna 2009; Gruffydd Jones 2006; Darby 2004). Rather, my argument is that examining the ways in which scholarship on postcolonial issues has been undertaken from disciplinary vantage points other than those provided by the conventional institutional and intellectual locations of postcolonial inquiry can serve to signal potential future directions for postcolonial studies and help overcome a looming pessimism over the field's future on the part of its scholars and practitioners. Throughout, the intention is to highlight where the experience of those working at the interface of IR and postcolonialism might prove of broader interest to those concerned with the future development of postcolonial discourses, and how it might assist in addressing some of the more persistent criticisms made regarding the field. The chapter thus contributes to the broader aims of the volume, exploring how postcolonial studies has been deployed and received in locations and debates well beyond its scholarly comfort zones. The chapter concludes by drawing together the lessons of such a process in order to argue for the reinvigoration of a commitment to the normative politics of postcolonial scholarship and to interdisciplinary dialogue.

POSTCOLONIALISM, INCORPORATED?

It is practical to begin with questions of institutional location and disciplinary reception. Postcolonialism has been taken up most enthusiastically in English and cultural studies departments, where it has been lionized as part of the leading edge of the discipline. Indeed, it was the emergence of postcolonial studies that gave impetus to the entrenchment of cultural studies in the contemporary university (Rao 2006; Radhakrishnan 1993). While I shall have more to say about the consequences of postcolonial studies' institutional affiliation with culturalist modes of enquiry in the pages that follow, it is important not to lose sight of the fact that the celebratory welcome accorded postcolonialism in the humanities has not been replicated elsewhere.

For those pursuing postcolonial critiques and analyses of international relations, for instance, matters are in stark contrast. The mainstream of IR still largely resists or remains ignorant of postcolonial criticisms. In pursuing dialogue and engagement, postcolonial studies scholars have had to negotiate with a confident, well-established and powerful academic formation whose reflex instincts are to dismiss any potential postcolonial contribution. Siba Grovogui, in a searing critique of IR's reluctance to pursue meaningful exchange with postcolonial perspectives, has written of how:

> IR scholars are securely guided by disciplinary gatekeepers, road maps of tenure rules and professional journals … [to] dispense with alternative Western and non-Western imaginaries of communities and politics and their modes of inquiry, assumptions, hypotheses and questions.
> (Grovogui 2009, 138)

Echoing this point, Kim Nossal, in a survey of introductory international relations texts, has argued that these are usually "noteworthy for what they do *not* tell their student-readers about international politics, those things deemed to be too unimportant to bother knowing about" (2001, 177). Among these, he argues, are an accurate understanding of politics and concerns other than those of the global hegemons, of the history and consequences of European colonial expansion and of the ethnocentric basis of much international relations theorizing.

The need for postcolonial perspectives seems obvious. Indeed, many scholars have applied insights derived from postcolonial studies in ways that serve to highlight IR's elisions, asserting the signal importance of European colonialism in universalizing the Westphalian state form (Spruyt 2000; Clapham 1999); identifying the imbrication of the doctrine of sovereignty with European imperialism (Anghie 2005); pointing to the derivative nature of discourses of postcolonial nationalism (Chatterjee 1985); identifying the connections between colonialism, imperialism and contemporary patterns of global economic inequality (Hoogvelt 2001); or highlighting the neo-imperialist motivations and colonialist assumptions that feed into contemporary discourses of terrorism, border protection, peace-keeping or national security (Barkawi and Laffey 2006; Darby 2006b; Hage 2003). Yet despite such efforts, their impact on the discipline of IR has been minimal. Analyses of international politics and processes informed by postcolonial theoretical perspectives have proceeded largely outside disciplinary frameworks. Even where engagement has been attempted, it has met with little recognition. Agathangelou and Ling evoke the nature of postcolonialism's relationship to the mainstream of international relations with the image of postcolonialism hovering "outside the House of IR" (2004, 32): illicit, largely disavowed by mainstream realist and liberal theoretical traditions, and raising critiques of the discipline while isolated from it.

The benefits of having a seat at the table of disciplinary IR appear both self-apparent and beguiling. From recognition would flow access to resources, career opportunities, enhanced possibilities for collaboration and, above all, the promise of influence. The connections between international relations scholarship and the practical affairs of diplomacy, foreign policy, military doctrine and inter-state relations make the job of asserting postcolonial politics and perspectives seem all the more urgent. The question thus poses itself: How and to what extent should postcolonial studies seek validation from, and a role within, disciplinary international relations? While a settled consensus on this issue is unlikely to emerge, three main approaches can be identified. The first is that pursued by those scholars who believe that postcolonialism can and should establish a role for itself within the theoretical corpus of IR, even to the extent of establishing a school of postcolonial international relations. Opposing such tactics are those who believe that IR is so irretrievably Eurocentric that scholars should instead direct their attention to supplanting it with alternative accounts of transnational and transcultural politics and exchange. Finally there are those who adopt a more cautious and nuanced approach, preferring to remain at some distance from the discipline and to mount their critiques from the outside.

The first of these three modes of engaging international relations has been pursued by those seeking an accommodation between postcolonialism and those parts of existing IR theory and scholarship perceived as most receptive to postcolonial critique. For instance, reflectivist approaches to the study of international relations have been presented as more able to address IR's disciplinary parochialism due to their greater commitment to normative, historically informed and interdisciplinary thinking in comparison with the descriptive, positivist and model-based methodologies that characterize the predominant (especially American) approaches to IR scholarship (Crawford 2001; Smith 2000). Along these lines, L.H.M. Ling has drawn upon reflectivist IR theories such as constructivism that explore how phenomena in the international domain are constructed socially and historically and how they can be explained by reference to state interests and identities (Wendt 1992). She asserts that blending constructivism with postcolonial theory will overcome much of IR's current cultural chauvinism and lead to the creation of a "postcolonial international relations" (Ling 2002). Elsewhere, others have pointed to theories of international political economy (Chase-Dunn 1991; Wallerstein 1974) and attempts by IR theorists to bring critical theoretical perspectives to bear on understandings of imperialism, class and the state system (Linklater 1990) as providing potential avenues of entry for postcolonial thought (Paolini 1997, 33). A different approach has been pursued within comparative political studies, with scholars seeking to identify how materials from non-Western cultures might contribute to, or even restructure, mainstream IR thinking (Acharya and Buzan 2010; Bilgin 2008; Behera 2007).

What such accounts share is a conviction that postcolonial approaches will be able to carve out a space and a role for themselves within IR theorizing. They present postcolonialism as able to contribute in practical and politically progressive ways to theories of the international, even if this means engaging with its intellectual and disciplinary others, such as development studies, international relations and global neoliberal economics (Chowdhry and Nair 2002b; Sylvester 1999a, 1999b). Yet enthusiasm over a potential rapprochement between postcolonialism and IR is by no means universal and it is not just mainstream scholars of IR who are antagonistic towards postcolonialism assuming a place within the disciplinary canon.

Here the opposing strand of thinking regarding the relationship between postcolonialism and IR becomes apparent. Many of those committed to postcolonial scholarship have expressed grave reservations about the appropriateness of postcolonialism being incorporated into the mainstream of disciplinary IR. In an incisive study, Sankaran Krishna argues that the disciplinary abstractions upon which international relations theorizing relies – a focus on sovereign state actors, strict delineations of international and domestic politics – work to excise from the discipline's consideration entire narratives of violence, dispossession, victimhood and resistance that do not fall into the neat categories of inter-state relations or *realpolitik*. Thus, far from being a desirable platform from which to work towards redressing the inequality and Eurocentrism that shape contemporary global politics, IR instead is exposed as one of the root causes of the problem. Accordingly, Krishna sees little possibility for any meaningful dialogue between postcolonialism and international relations. He unambiguously asserts: "[P]ostcolonial IR is an oxymoron – a contradiction in terms" (2001, 407).

This reluctance to be drawn into IR's theoretical discourses or to present postcolonially informed interventions in the language and terms of in-house debate runs the risk of accusations that postcolonialism constructs IR as a paper tiger, overstating its resistance to outside influence. Yet there is certainly reason to proceed with caution. Speaking on feminism's fate within international relations, Cynthia Weber has written that IR has actively worked to evacuate the discourse of its political content, recasting "what feminism supposedly is and what feminism supposedly does in order to insulate itself from feminism's transformatory potential" (Weber 1999, 444). Specifically addressing the implications of this critique for postcolonial studies, a group of scholars (including the present author) from the Institute of Postcolonial Studies in Melbourne has put it thus:

> The greatest risk [...] is that an entanglement with international relations will blunt the discourse's radical edge. [...] Some distance must therefore be maintained from the encaptive capacities of the discipline. Once inside the house of international relations, it is difficult to escape confinement [...] and the enabling possibilities are drained away.
> (Darby *et al.* 2003, 5)

The consequences of such intellectual confinement are apparent. Many attempts to establish postcolonialism within IR are characterized by a suppliant tone, seeking to establish such projects' value to the discipline and to demonstrate specialist knowledge of its intellectual contours. Less apparent is the reciprocal value such interventions might hold for postcolonial studies, or a sense that in-depth knowledge of postcolonialism might be expected from disciplinary IR. Addressing himself to those scholars who would work towards recasting the language, subject matter and politics of international relations, Roland Bleiker has offered stark guidance: "[F]orget IR theory" (Bleiker 1997).

It is here that the third approach to a postcolonial engagement with IR comes into view. Not all scholarship in this area either seeks inclusion in IR's theoretical fold or entirely rejects the value of critiquing disciplinary international relations from a postcolonial stance. Even from a distance sufficient to avoid the temptations and dangers of incorporation, much of worth can be said and important critiques can be raised. When it comes to interdisciplinary engagement, marginality – long valorized within postcolonial studies – has its merits. Scholars who have chosen to work "at the edge of international relations" (the phrase is taken from the title of Phillip Darby's 1997 edited collection on the relationship between IR and postcolonial studies) have done much to highlight the erasures and violence that underwrite IR as an academic discipline, a source of knowledge and a field of practical politics (Shilliam 2011; Gruffydd Jones 2006; Darby 2006a, 2003).

Together, such authors share a commitment to a project of decolonizing the theoretical discipline of IR; to expanding understandings of processes of transnational and transcultural exchange; and to broadening out the category of the international with reference to non-Western sources and materials and notions of global justice. The project is one of both critiquing the lacunae of contemporary IR and offering up critical insights into how it might be variously transformed and transcended. In many ways this is a process of attempting to speak truth to power. There is a sense that IR is too important – most obviously due to the sway it holds over the definition of the world and to the conduct of transnational affairs – to allow its current practitioners and theorists to escape external scrutiny. As Grovogui argues, IR as a discipline needs to be challenged both for the lack of attention it has paid to non-Western thought and to its attempt to exclude histories of colonial dispossession and violence from its remit. "This exclusion", he writes, "has ethical implications, whether in the actual world of international relations or the discipline that purports to study them" (2009, 138).

THE POLITICS OF POSTCOLONIALISM

This brings us squarely to the question of politics and change. One of the most persistent critiques of postcolonial studies has been regarding the lack of interest it shows towards projects of political praxis. A common line of thinking attributes this outcome at least in part to postcolonialism's success in establishing its disciplinary home within the humanities. Benita Parry characterizes postcolonial studies as "institutionalized" within departments of English and cultural studies, arguing that a predisposition towards poststructuralist theory and a preference for distanced interpretation of texts, images and discourses have led to the field having "an insufficient engagement with the conditions and practices of actually existing imperialism" (2004a, 74). Kwame Anthony Appiah's famous description of postcolonialism as being the concern of a "comprador intelligentsia" (1991, 348), interested only in cultural products, has been echoed in concerns over the field's perceived avoidance of substantial engagement with postcolonial histories, politics or economics (Ahmad 1995; Dirlik 1994). One critic has pungently described such processes as representing a "sacrifice of postcoloniality as potential politics or activism at the altar of postcoloniality as metropolitan epistemology" (Radhakrishnan 1993, 751).

There appears to be a pressing need, therefore, to excavate a politics of postcolonial studies. Despite the institutional legitimacy it has achieved, the discipline has proved reluctant to move beyond a limited range of largely culturalist concerns to challenge the Eurocentrism evident in the canons of Western scholarship (Seshadri-Crooks 1995). For those working at the nexus of postcolonial studies and IR, overcoming this problem is a crucial undertaking. H.D. Harootunian (1999) has argued that a preference for literary criticism has worked to limit postcolonial studies' ability to either intervene in the politics of intellectual theorizing about international processes as they impact upon the non-West or to understand those real-world issues (such as underdevelopment) that confront the postcolony worldwide. Overcoming

arguably which this volume is in fact correcting

but what about its materialist incarnation?

that this is the way postcolonialism needs to go

such limitations holds out the potential not just of reforming IR as a body of theory but of influencing the North-South relations that such theory informs and animates. Vinay Lal highlights the urgency of this task:

> The three decades that postcolonial studies has flourished in the American academy are precisely those where the US has engaged in rapacious conduct around the world, from its illegal mining of Nicaragua's harbours to the Gulf War of 1991 and, more recently, to the wars in Iraq and Afghanistan. One can be certain that postcolonial studies, even if some of its practitioners occasionally deluded themselves into believing that their interventions and interpretations were calculated to make a difference in the 'real' world [...] made no difference to the outcome of US foreign policy.
>
> (Lal 2010, 5)

ideally we all concur

sure, but these are not new positions — basically

Whether or not postcolonial studies can rise to meet such challenges is still open to debate. Certainly, Lal is not alone in his skepticism. Julian Saurin (2006) has argued that postcolonialism does not offer a sufficiently trenchant critique of Eurocentrism, and that more forceful anti-imperialist politics and strategies must be brought to the fore in order to decolonize IR. Yet this does not appear to be the majority viewpoint. The ways in which scholars have sought to bring a postcolonial normative politics to bear on disciplinary IR provide some intriguing pointers towards a more politically effective and materially engaged postcolonial studies. Uniting many of these accounts is a conviction that postcolonial studies do possess a normative quality that can be profitably brought to bear on the knowledge politics of IR and in practical areas such as development, international political economy and activism of benefit to marginalized, minority and subaltern communities.

Such investment in the potential of a postcolonial politics holds out great promise, not just for reformist intervention into the theories and practices of contemporary world affairs, but for a reinvigoration of the normative tradition in postcolonial studies more broadly. To both of these ends, several productive ways to proceed suggest themselves: a serious engagement with postcolonialism's Marxian heritage; an attention to the pasts, politics and everyday life-worlds of non-European societies; and a renewed commitment to activist intervention into the processes of resistance and domination that characterize the North-South divide in the contemporary world.

The call for postcolonialism to re-engage with Marxian approaches and material conditions is by now a common refrain. Ahmad's early criticism of the apolitical nature of postcolonial enquiry due to its "apocalyptic anti-Marxism" (1995, 10) was picked up and expanded by Lazarus and Bartolovich (2002) and Parry (2004b), who identified materialist critique as a powerful and practical source of postcolonial politics. Unsurprisingly, such analyses have fed into the literature on postcolonialism and IR. The thinking is that postcolonialism's Marxist foundations can serve to underpin a politically muscular postcolonialism able to inform a critique of disciplinary IR by identifying practices and politics of anti-colonial resistance, revealing systemic factors working to entrench global economic inequality and underscoring the importance of solidarity (Darby *et al.* 2003). Rumina Sethi, in a recent volume examining global patterns of resistance to domination and imperialism, has provided a spirited justification of the necessity of Marxist perspectives to contemporary postcolonial scholarship. She presents the incorporation of these perspectives as vital to the very survival of postcolonialism as an intellectual endeavor:

> An affiliation between third-world cultures and their social and political histories has to be established so that postcolonial studies might profitably survive. If certain key aspects of postcolonial studies – nationalism, globalization, the subaltern – are issues that Marxists have been involved in from the beginning, why should postcolonialist practitioners be reluctant to embrace Marxist parameters?
>
> (Sethi 2011, 123)

Significantly, Sethi exhibits a reluctance to read materialist and culturalist explanations as necessarily oppositional. In their introduction to *Power, Postcolonialism and International Relations,* Chowdhry and Nair (2002a) similarly argue that the materialist/culturalist split has been overstated. They point to the early influence of Marx and Gramsci on postcolonial scholarship and the ways in which work within the field – most notably that of the subaltern studies collective – sought to remedy Marx's Eurocentrism. Having established the importance of such non-Eurocentric materialist approaches to crafting a postcolonial intervention into contemporary global power relations, they go on to assert that "the imbrication of the discursive and the material [...] illuminates the necessity for a postcolonial re-reading of international relations and political economy" (Chowdhry and Nair 2002a, 24).

The point is well made. If postcolonial interventions in IR help establish the importance of materialist thinking and draw the discipline's attention to axes of economic inequality, class and exploitation, they also highlight the need for IR to be confronted by the politics of difference. Postcolonial readings of IR have been shaped by the attempt to gain insights into the operation of transnational circuits of power from sources other than the usual narratives of great power maneuverings and orthodox theoretical understandings of sovereignty and state self-interest. At the core of such attempts lies the assertion that IR as a discipline has developed largely in ignorance of material conditions, politics and cultures outside Europe and America and of the colonial basis of the expansion of the international system (Seth 2011; Thomas and Wilkin 2004).

Postcolonial critics have sought to show how IR's preference for systemic and generalist theory-building downplays or dismisses local and specific accounts that proceed from the realms of culture and everyday life. The "world has been written from London or Washington without the impediment of having to know much about other places or histories or peoples" (Darby *et al.* 2003, 10). Postcolonial studies – long attuned to the question of difference and better able to provide insights into non-Western cultures and specific life-worlds – has been seen as able to motivate and inform projects of theory-building that draw upon non-Western sources and the grassroots of societies. As Darby explains, the politics that scholars of international theory look to here is one that:

> must in the first instance be drawn from within non-European societies, tapping sources that give us glimpses of other life worlds. These glimpses will tell us something of how people come to terms with external influence and intervention, but they will also tell us much about other concerns, quite unrelated to imperialism and its aftermath. (2004, 31)

Postcolonialism is thus marshaled to help overcome IR's ignorance of non-Western voices, histories and situations and to highlight the partiality of its theories. This is no easy task. There has yet to be a thoroughgoing engagement between much of IR and the sorts of politics that have been anticipated. The contours of any future adaptation or reform remain unpredictable. But, significantly for this chapter's purposes, there is a sense in the literature that postcolonialism is able, at least in part, to provide the methodological apparatus and normative politics necessary for the job. Seth asserts that postcolonial theory works to illustrate the ways in which knowledge formations act "as a potent force for shaping what is 'out there'" and that it is "especially sensitive to the many circumstances in which knowledges born in Europe are inadequate to their non-European object" (2011, 182). There is an investment here in both anticolonial theory and praxis, a belief that postcolonial scholarship can and should move beyond the domain of description and analysis to assert preferable political outcomes and to operate as an agent of change. Vijay Devadas and Chris Prentice capture something of the nature of this potential when they write: "Postcolonial critique remains productive to the extent that it brings its commitment to the analysis of all violent sovereignties that have followed colonialism's modern moment" (2007, 8).

THE CHALLENGE OF INTERDISCIPLINARITY

This principled turn away from Western materials and interests, and the assertion of a politics of difference, draws attention to the issue of working across disciplinary boundaries. The attempts to bridge postcolonialism and international relations are prime examples of interdisciplinarity in action. Postcolonial studies have been used to identify salient issues and inform the political content of critique and intervention. More significantly, they have helped provide access to materials to inform and guide new narratives and theories of international processes. This experience of interdisciplinary working is worth exploring for what it might reveal about the contributions postcolonial studies can make beyond its current intellectual boundaries and the importance of forging working relationships with those working to allied purposes in other disciplines.

It is important to acknowledge that calls for interdisciplinary engagement have not always met with the approval of scholars associated with what might be regarded as postcolonialism's mainstream. Fears have been expressed regarding the potential for a diffusion of intellectual focus and the likelihood of misrepresentation. Peter Childs and Patrick Williams argue that:

> [v]enturing across ... [disciplinary] boundaries has its dangers. [...] [C]ritical assessments of post-colonialism from the 'outside' as it were, may be – indeed usually are – very impressive in the area of the author's specialism (history, international relations, politics, etc.) but may be rather less convincing as analyses of post-colonialism. (1997, 22)

The reluctance to engage is, on one level, understandable. The ways in which the social sciences in particular have approached the study of non-Western artifacts and knowledges – characterizing them in ways that stand at odds with the meanings they derive from their specific cultural, historical, spiritual or social *milieux* – are well documented (Dutton 2002). For postcolonial studies, a field that takes difference as its touchstone and texts derived in specific cultural contexts as its core area of inquiry, there is a reasonable desire to avoid association with universalizing, rationalist and social-scientific methodologies. Such concerns are likely to come to the fore in different scenarios and registers as postcolonialism is increasingly brought into engagement with other disciplines. They should not be too easily dismissed. Dominant discourses hold the potential to envelop and define postcolonialism in ways that might diminish or defeat its purposes.

Yet as we have seen, much of the scholarship bridging postcolonialism and IR has been marked by the extreme care it has taken to preserve postcolonial studies' ability to critique, and to prevent the field being subsumed by dominant disciplinary structures. Those working within postcolonial studies should be more self-confident about working across disciplinary boundaries and more trusting of their ability to maintain the field's intellectual integrity and particularity. Indeed, one of the strongest defenses of postcolonialism's explanatory utility and political contribution have come from those critical of IR, who seek in postcolonialism a set of political and methodological tools that can be put to the task of accomplishing reform (Dutton, Gandhi and Seth 1999).

The experience of how postcolonialism has helped structure a critique of IR is instructive here. Much of the scholarship in this area has required access to the experiences, politics and viewpoints of those in the postcolony. The task has been to explore the extent to which the politics of the international can be read off the realms of the social, the everyday and the personal. In this, postcolonial studies has taken the lead, not just in fleshing out the necessity and politics of such a re-narrativization but in providing guidance as to how it might best be attempted. Scholars working in postcolonial cultural studies have extensive experience in using literary materials to illustrate the ways in which external and internal exercises of power and hegemony act to shape experiences and subjectivities within postcolonial polities.

One example of this has been the turn to postcolonial fiction as a sourcebook from which the politics of everyday life, understandings of external influence, and connections between the discursive and the material might be read. In his exploration of the relevance of fictional accounts to processes of decolonizing international relations, Darby has argued that "literature's concentration on the personal can be a corrective to international relations' preoccupation with aggregates, its mechanistic presumptions about international processes and its positivist approach to outcomes" (1998, 42). Of course, fictional accounts are not the only source at play here. The attempt to gain a more complete understanding of processes of everyday life in the postcolony and to give voice to the concerns of the postcolonial world has prompted those working on international processes to use postcolonialism's modes of enquiry and attentiveness to a variety of textual sources in order to explore real events and everyday life. A sense of the possibilities inherent in such an approach is provided by the work of Gyanendra Pandey. Pandey presents it as a matter of ethical responsibility for scholars to cast as wide a net as possible when garnering source materials about issues such as violence, war and suffering in the postcolony. For Pandey, fragmentary sources such as pamphlets, poems, oral narratives (and their silences) and folk songs provide a necessary counterbalance to the official accounts of generals, police forces and government reports with which scholars and theorists from the social sciences are more comfortable dealing (Pandey 1992). They hold the potential to provide us with key insights into the experience of external influence, of conflict and of how the patterning of everyday life are imbricated with transnational flows and spaces.

While such assertions about the value of engagement with creative literature and a broad range of textual sources materials may seem familiar and relatively unproblematic to those used to working within postcolonial cultural or literary studies, for scholars of disciplinary IR they are more likely to appear novel and unsettling. They signal the possibility that self-consciously political – and locally or personally grounded – narratives might help to overcome the grand-theoretical, Eurocentric and hegemonic tendencies that pervade much of IR scholarship. The influences of a postcolonial politics are certainly discernable in this project. But perhaps more significant is the fact that these politics have been used to frame a range of interdisciplinary engagements that extend well beyond postcolonial studies' usual interest in cultural and literary production. The project of seeking to demonstrate the connections between material conditions, everyday life and international affairs has seen a broader, multifaceted, interdisciplinary project begin to coalesce. Increasingly, there has been an awareness of the need for insights into society, culture and everyday life that can be provided by social science disciplines such as ethnography, anthropology, geography or sociology.

This preparedness to work across multiple disciplinary boundaries has proved fruitful for scholars seeking to demonstrate the connections between what is occurring at the level of lived experience and the politics of trans-national processes. Yet for the purposes of the present argument, what is remarkable about many of these studies is the preparedness they have shown to express their interventions with reference to postcolonial politics and concerns. Thus postcolonially informed critique of international theory has variously been made with reference to non-Western materials derived from (among others) urban geography (Bishop, Phillips and Yeo 2003), sexuality studies (Obendorf 2012, 2006), development (Ng 2006), environmental analysis (Magnusson and Shaw 2003) and ethnography (Comaroff and Comaroff 2003; Das *et al.* 2001). If nothing else, the range of disciplines that now look to postcolonial studies to inform their critical analysis of the theory and practice of contemporary international affairs demonstrates the extent to which postcolonialism is seen as able to contribute to projects of theoretical reform and practical change. It also demonstrates the value of forging interdisciplinary alliances in bringing about particular theoretical or practical acts of reform.

CONCLUSION

Postcolonial studies have a seemingly unique capacity for self-doubt and critical introspection. There is a long-standing tradition of internal debate over parameters, methodologies and politics that stretches back to the earliest phases of postcolonialism's emergence as a field of study. In 1995, Kalpana Seshadri-Crooks opined that postcolonialism had arrived at "that phase in its development in which, like every other revisionary discourse, it is melancholic about its new-found authority and incorporation into institutions of higher learning" (47). Ten years later, Vijay Mishra and Bob Hodge felt able to deploy the past tense when speaking of the field, asking: "What *was* postcolonialism?" (2005). More recently, a symposium in Berlin expressed doubts over postcolonialism's ability to explain its contemporary relevance, with many participants giving the impression that field had largely run its course (Amine *et al.* 2010). Summarizing what he sees as a growing sense of "postcolonial fatigue", Lal has argued that:

> [e]ven among the adherents of postcolonial studies [...] there is a growing recognition that exhaustion has set in, the questions put on

[handwritten marginalia, left margin: "cultural and literary production — results in lack of confidence but enables the ongoing formation of new positions"]

[handwritten marginalia: "agreed — both its weakness + its strength solidarity but"]

offer are predictable, and that one is only likely to encounter regurgitation of familiar arguments.

(Lal 2010, 2)

The reasons for this supposed fatigue are familiar. Lal points both to the repetition and reach of postcolonialism's established successes (its institutional recognition within the contemporary university, its contribution to bringing marginal voices and issues to the attention of the center and its criticisms of the master narratives of the Enlightenment) as well as its reluctance to address many of its failings (its inability to effect real world change, its avoidance of issues of material culture and political economy, and its institutionalization in and for the humanities). Yet he is careful not to characterize postcolonialism as a spent force. Instead he sees attention to particular projects of critique – he identifies the critique of history, of the nation-state and of non-violence – and the development of an ability to contribute in practical as well as epistemological terms to politics of dissent and resistance as critical to postcolonialism retaining future relevance. In each of these areas, he argues, much remains to be done. "[B]efore we convince ourselves of a postcolonial fatigue, perhaps we should seriously ask if postcolonial studies traveled as far as is sometimes alleged" (Lal 2010, 5).

This chapter has sought to trace the consequences of one particular instance of postcolonial studies' travel. The argument has been that the strategies and implications of bringing a postcolonial critique to bear on international theory can illuminate a route towards overcoming the sorts of intellectual lethargy and pessimism that Lal and others have identified. I share with Lal – and with many of those seeking to deploy postcolonial politics, perspectives and methodologies within international relations scholarship – a sense that postcolonial studies are able to structure a range of intellectually rigorous and politically effective interventions and critiques. This has the potential to unlock benefits not merely for the discipline of IR but more broadly.

Bleiker has cautioned scholars "not to ignore the IR practices that have framed our realities" (2001, 39). IR, under such a reading, acts not merely to describe the international realm but works actively to constitute it. Postcolonial critique therefore holds the potential not merely to disturb and challenge dominant discursive models of the international but to actively participate in the theorization and bringing into being of more sensitive, informed, anticolonial and pluralistically conceived translocal processes, spaces and politics.

Yet while the benefits for international studies seem clear, it is important to note that the experience of working at the interface of international relations and postcolonial studies holds great potential for reinvigorating the field of postcolonialism itself. This chapter has explored three areas where such a contribution might be detected: an awareness of the risks and rewards of engaging with other disciplines, the (re)assertion of a politics of postcolonialism and the processes of interdisciplinarity. My intent has been to demonstrate that postcolonial studies, as seen from outside its institutional location in the humanities, does not appear to be suffering from fatigue or irrelevance. In many ways it appears revolutionary, even threatening.

This is not to say that working across disciplinary boundaries will always be easy, of immediate impact or necessarily work to the benefit of post-colonial studies. One of the key insights the experience of working with IR holds is that scholars committed to postcolonial critique need to stand ready to protect and assert the particular politics and methodologies of the field in their interdisciplinary work. A seat at the table will prove of little value if the languages and rules of debate are already set, the agenda not open to amendment and dissenting voices kept at bay. Here, too, we must remain cognizant of the knowledge politics of the contemporary university. The problems flowing from postcolonialism's institutionalization in cultural studies could all too easily be duplicated should postcolonialism wind up similarly institutionalized within one or other of the social sciences. Similarly, the exhortation to work collaboratively with those in the developing world, to access non-Western voices and materials, and to seek allies in disciplines outside our own does not always sit comfortably with the discipline-specific career paths, research audit cultures, pedagogic concerns, student expectations and disciplinary divisions of today's higher education institutions (Darby *et al.* 2003, 10).

Yet the potential benefits that can flow from engagement should counsel against any tendency to conceive of postcolonialism as a closed shop. The risks inherent in engagement with other disciplines should not be used as a justification for insularity or lassitude. The search for alternative futures for both scholarship and society is too important a task to neglect. A desire to contribute to the search for practical solutions informs much of the interest in postcolonial studies exhibited by those seeking reform in disciplines such as international relations. Here, there is a sense that postcolonial studies can and should provide more than description or critique. The instances explored in this chapter demonstrate how a politically engaged and self-confident postcolonialism can make powerful contributions to interdisciplinary problem-solving and the identification of new intellectual concerns.

An oft-quoted maxim within critical IR scholarship is provided by Robert Cox: "[T]heory is always for someone and for some purpose" (Cox 1981, 128). The experience of postcolonialism as it has been brought into dialogue with the discipline of IR is valuable to the extent that it asks us once more to re-engage with the normative traditions of postcolonial scholarship. As we survey the future of postcolonial studies, it impels us to ask just who postcolonialism is for, and what purposes we want it to serve.

REFERENCES

Acharya, Amitav and Barry Buzan, eds. 2010. *Non-Western International Relations Theory: Perspectives On and Beyond Asia*. London: Routledge.

Agathangelou, Anna M. and L. H. M. Ling. 2004. "The House of IR: From Family Power Politics to the *Poisies* of Worldism". *International Studies Review* 6: 21–49.

Ahmad, Aijaz. 1995. "The Politics of Literary Postcoloniality". *Race & Class* no. 36.3: 1–20.

Amine, Khalid, Srinivas Aravamudan, Nicolas Bancel, Dan Diner, Joachim Küpper, Vinay Lal and David Murphy. Panel Discussion – Postcolonialism: What Next? Dahelm Humanities Center, Freie Universität, Berlin, 23 November 2010. Available from http://www.fu-berlin.de/en/sites/dhc/programme/Panels/Panel_Postcolonialism1.html.

Anghie, Antony. 2005. *Imperialism, Sovereignty, and the Making of International Law*. Cambridge: Cambridge Umiversity Press.

Appiah, Kwame Anthony. 1991. "Is the Post- in Postmodernism the Post- in Postcolonial?" *Critical Inquiry* 17: 336–356.

Barkawi, Tarak and Mark Laffey. 2006. "The Postcolonial Moment in Security Studies". *Review of International Studies* 32.2: 329–352.

Bartolovich, Crystal and Neil Lazarus. 2002. *Marxism, Modernity and Postcolonial Studies*. Cambridge: Cambridge University Press.

Behera, Navnita Chadha. 2007. "Re-imagining IR in India". *International Relations of the Asia-Pacific* 7.3: 341–368.

Bilgin, Pinar. 2008. "Thinking Past 'Western' IR?" *Third World Quarterly* 29.1: 5–23.

Bishop, Ryan, John Phillips and Wei Wei Yeo, eds. 2003. *Postcolonial Urbanism: Southeast Asian Cities and Global Processes*. New York and London: Routledge.

Bleiker, Roland. 1997. "Forget IR Theory". *Alternatives* 22.2: 57–85.

Bleiker, Roland. 2001. "Forget IR Theory". In *The Zen of International Relations: IR Theory from East to West*, eds. Stephen Chan and Roland Bleiker, 37–66. Houndmills and New York: Palgrave.

Chase-Dunn, Christopher. 1991. *Global Formation: Structures of World-Economy*. Oxford: Blackwell.

Chatterjee, Partha. 1985. *Nationalist Thought and the Colonial World: A Derivative Discourse?* New Delhi: Zed Books.

Childs, Peter and R. J. Patrick Williams. 1997. *An Introduction to Post-Colonial Theory*. London: Prentice Hall, Harvester Wheatsheaf.

Chowdhry, Geeta and Sheila Nair, eds. 2002a. "Introduction – Power in a Postcolonial World: Race, Gender, and Class in International Relations". In *Power, Postcolonialism and International Relations: Reading Race, Gender and Politics*, 1–32. London: Routledge.

Chowdhry, Geeta and Sheila Nair, eds. 2002b. *Power, Postcolonialism and International Relations: Reading Race, Gender and Class*. London: Routledge.

Clapham, Christopher. 1999. "Sovereignty and the Third World State". *Political Studies* 47.3: 522–537.

Comaroff, Jean and John L. Comaroff. 2003. "Ethnography on an Awkward Scale: Postcolonial Anthropology and the Violence of Abstraction". *Ethnography* 4.2: 147–179.

Cox, Robert W. 1981. "Social Forces, States and World Orders: Beyond International Relations Theory". *Millennium – Journal of International Studies* 10.2: 126–155.

Crawford, Robert M.A. 2001. "Where Have All the Theorists Gone – Gone to Britain, Every One? A Story of Two Parochialisms in International Relations". In *International Relations – Still an American Social Science? Toward Diversity in International Thought*, edited by Robert M.A. Crawford and Darryl S.L. Jarvis, 221–242. Albany: State University of New York Press.

Darby, Phillip, ed. 1997. *At the Edge of International Relations: Postcolonialism, Gender and Dependency*. London: Pinter.

Darby, Phillip. 1998. *The Fiction of Imperialism: Reading between International Relations and Postcolonialism*. London: Cassell.

Darby, Phillip. 2003. "Reconfiguring 'the International': Knowledge Machines, Boundaries and Exclusions". *Alternatives* 28: 141–166.

Darby, Phillip. 2004. "Pursuing the Political: A Postcolonial Rethinking of Relations International". *Millennium: Journal of International Studies* 33.1: 1–32.

Darby, Phillip, ed. 2006a. *Postcolonizing the International: Working to Change the Way We Are*. Honolulu: University of Hawai'i Press.

Darby, Phillip. 2006b. "Security, Spatiality, and Social Suffering". *Alternatives* 31.4: 453–473.

Darby, Phillip, Devika Goonewardene, Edgar Ng and Simon Obendorf. 2003. *A Postcolonial International Relations?*, edited by Devika Goonewardene, Edgar Ng and Simon Obendorf. Vol. 3, *Occasional Papers*. Melbourne: Institute of Postcolonial Studies.

Das, Veena, Arthur Kleinman, Mamphela Ramphele and Patricia Reynolds, eds. 2001. *Violence and Subjectivity*. New Delhi: Oxford University Press.

Devadas, Vijay and Chris Prentice. 2007. Postcolonial Politics. *Borderlands* 6.2, http://www.borderlands.net.au/vol6no2_2007/device_editorial.htm.

Dirlik, Arif. 1994. "The Postcolonial Aura: Third World Criticism in the Age of Global Capitalism". *Critical Inquiry* 20: 328–356.

Dutton, Michael. 2002. "Lead Us Not into Translation: Notes Toward a Theoretical Foundation for Asian Studies". *Nepantla: Views from South* 3.3: 495–537.

Dutton, Michael, Leela Gandhi and Sanjay Seth. 1999. "The Toolbox of Postcolonialism". *Postcolonial Studies: Culture, Politics, Economy* 2.2: 121–124.

Grovogui, Siba N. 2009. "No Bridges to Swamps: A Postcolonial Perspective on Disciplinary Dialogue". *International Relations* 23.1: 135–140.

Gruffydd Jones, Branwen, ed. 2006. *Decolonizing International Relations*. Lanham, MD: Rowman and Littlefield.

Guha, Ranajit, ed. 1997. *A Subaltern Studies Reader 1986–1995*. Minneapolis: University of Minnesota Press.

Hage, Ghassan. 2003. *Against Paranoid Nationalism: Searching for Hope in a Shrinking Society*. Annandale, NSW: Pluto Press Australia.

Harootunian, H. D. 1999. "Postcoloniality's Unconscious/Area Studies' Desire". *Postcolonial Studies: Culture, Politics, Economy* 2.2: 127–147.

Hoffman, Stanley. 1977. "An American Social Science: International Relations". *Daedelus* 106.3: 41–60.

Hoogvelt, Ankie M. M. 2001. *Globalization and the Postcolonial World: The New Political Economy of Development*. 2nd ed. Basingstoke, UK: Palgrave.

Krishna, Sankaran. 2001. "Race, Amnesia and the Education of International Relations". *Alternatives* 26.4: 401–424.

Krishna, Sankaran. 2009. *Globalization and Postcolonialism: Hegemony and Resistance in the Twenty-First Century*. Plymouth, UK: Rowman and Littlefield.

Lal, Vinay. 2010. "The Politics of Culture and Knowledge after Postcolonialism: Nine Theses (and a Prologue)". *Lal Salaam: A Blog by Vinay Lal – Reflections on the Culture of Politics & the Politics of Culture* (28 November 2010), http://vinaylal.wordpress.com/2010/11/28/the-politics-of-culture-and-knowledge-after-postcolonialism-nine-theses-and-a-prologue/.

Ling, L. H. M. 2002. *Postcolonial International Relations: Conquest and Desire between Asia and the West.* London: Palgrave Macmillan.

Linklater, Andrew. 1990. *Beyond Realism and Marxism: Critical Theory and International Relations.* Basingstoke, UK: Macmillan.

Magnusson, Warren and Karena Shaw, eds. 2003. *A Political Space: Reading the Global through Clayoquot Sound.* Minneapolis: University of Minnesota Press.

Mishra, Vijay and Bob Hodge. 2005. "What was Postcolonialism?" *New Literary History* 36.3: 375–402.

Ng, Edgar. 2006. "Doing Development Differently". In *Postcolonizing the International: Working to Change the Way We Are,* edited by Phillip Darby, 125–143. Honolulu: University of Hawai'i Press.

Nossal, Kim Richard. 2001. "Tales that Textbooks Tell: Ethnocentricity and Diversity in American Introductions to International Relations". In *International Relations – Still an American Social Science? Toward Diversity in International Thought,* edited by Robert M.A. Crawford and Darryl S.L. Jarvis, 167–186. Albany: State University of New York Press.

Obendorf, Simon. 2006. "Sodomy as Metaphor". In *Postcolonizing the International: Working to Change the Way We Are,* edited by Phillip Darby, 177–206. Honolulu: University of Hawai'i Press.

Obendorf, Simon. 2012. "Both Contagion and Cure: Queer Politics in the Global City-State". In *Queer Singapore: Illiberal Citizenship and Mediated Cultures,* edited by Audrey Yue and Jun Zubillaga-Pow, 97–114. Hong Kong: Hong Kong University Press.

Pandey, Gyanendra. 1992. "In Defense of the Fragment: Writing about Hindu-Muslim Riots in India Today". *Representations* 37: 27–55.

Paolini, Albert J. 1997. "Globalization". In *At the Edge of International Relations: Postcolonialism, Gender and Dependency,* edited by Phillip Darby, 33–60. London: Pinter.

Paolini, Albert J. 1999. *Navigating Modernity: Postcolonialism, Identity and Inter-national Relations.* Boulder, CO and London: Lynne Rienner Publishers.

Parry, Benita. 2004a. "The Institutionalization of Postcolonial Studies". In *The Cambridge Companion to Postcolonial Literary Studies,* edited by Neil Lazarus, 66–80. Cambridge: Cambridge University Press.

Parry, Benita. 2004b. *Postcolonial Studies: A Materialist Critique.* London: Routledge.

Radhakrishnan, R. 1993. "Postcoloniality and the Borders of Identity". *Callaloo* 16.4: 750–771.

Rao, Nagesh. 2006. "New Imperialisms, New Imperatives:Taking Stock of Postcolonial Studies". *Postcolonial Text* 2.1, http://postcolonial.org/index.php/pct/article/view/386/816.

Saurin, Julian. 2006. "International Relations as the Imperial Illusion; or, the Need to Decolonize IR". In *Decolonizing International Relations,* edited by Branwen Gruffyd Jones, 23–42. Lanham, MD: Rowman and Littlefield.

Seshadri-Crooks, Kalpana. 1995. "At the Margins of Postcolonial Studies". *ARIEL: A Review of International English Literature* 26.3: 47–71.

Seth, Sanjay. 2011. "Postcolonial Theory and the Critique of International Relations". *Millennium – Journal of International Studies* 40.1: 167–183.

Sethi, Rumina. 2011. *The Politics of Postcolonialism.* London: Pluto Press.

Shilliam, Robbie, ed. 2011. *International Relations and Non-Western Thought: Impe-rialism, Colonialism and Investigations of Global Modernity.* London: Routledge.

Smith, Steve. 2000. "The Discipline of International Relations: Still an American Social Science?" *British Journal of Politics and International Relations* 2.3: 374–402.

Spruyt, Hendrik. 2000. "The End of Empire and the Extension of the Westphalian System: The Normative Basis of the Modern State Order". *International Studies Review* 2.2: 65–92.

Sylvester, Christine. 1999a. "Development Studies and Postcolonial Studies: Disparate Tales of the 'Third World'". *Third World Quarterly* 20.2: 703–721.

Sylvester, Christine. 1999b. "In-Between and in Evasion of So Much: Third World Literatures, International Relations and Postcolonial Analysis". *Postcolonial Studies: Culture, Politics, Economy* 2.2: 249–261.

Thomas, Caroline and Peter Wilkin. 2004. "Still Waiting After All These Years: 'The Third World' on the Periphery of International Relations". *The British Journal of Politics & International Relations* 6.2: 241–258.

Wallerstein, Immanuel M. 1974. *The Modern World-System: Capitalist Agriculture and the Origins of the European World-Economy in the Sixteenth Century*. New York: Academic Press.

Weber, Cynthia. 1999. "IR: The Resurrection or New Frontiers of Incorporation". *European Journal of International Relations* 5.4: 435–450.

Wendt, Alexander. 1992. "Anarchy is What States Make of It: The Social Construction of Power Politics". *International Organization* 46.2: 391–425.

3 Managing Postcolonialism

Mrinalini Greedharry and Pasi Ahonen

"Imperialism was *organized* and it was *managed*".

—Bill Cooke

How can we manage postcolonialism now? The question resonates in various ways depending on your view of the postcolonial project. If you are one of the people still committed, as Robert Young writes, "to reconstruct Western knowledge formations, reorient ethical norms, turn the power structures of the world upside down, refashion the world from below" (20), how do you manage to keep it going? If you are one of those who think that the intellectual fuel of postcolonialism has been spent, there is nothing left to manage – it is time to shut the operation down. Young's trajectory suggests that there remains political work that could, and should, still animate postcolonial studies, including the ongoing lack of connection with struggles around indigeneity across the world and the persistence of "unreadable Islam" (Young 2012, 27–31). Nevertheless, the task of managing postcolonialism conveys the affect of tired and disheartened people still struggling to keep a project going, alive, some recognizing that there is so much still left undone, others having moved on into new areas of scholarly life that promise more liveliness.

There is a less affectively charged way to read the word "manage" – not so much how can we go on as what will we do to ensure that the actions we want to carry out can be accomplished by groups of people working together? In other words, quite literally, how do we manage postcolonialism? What do we have to do now, with whom, in what institutional, practical and ethical forms to ensure that the postcolonial project can continue?

KEEPING DISCIPLINARY HOUSE IN THE END TIMES

The sense of a postcolonial ending may be specific to the Anglo-American humanities scholar. As Young observes:

> The postcolonial perspective has spread across almost all the disciplines in the humanities and social sciences, from classics to development

theory to law to medieval studies to theology – even sociology …
along with the creation of related subdisciplines such as diaspora and
transnational studies, that this remarkable dispersal of intellectual and
political influence now makes it difficult to locate any kind of center
of postcolonial theory. (2012, 22)

The implied past disciplinary center is English Literature. Young consistently situates the beginnings of postcolonial critique outside the academy in the work and activism of anticolonial leaders and thinkers such as
M.K. Gandhi, Kwame Nkrumah and Frantz Fanon, so we do not mean
to suggest that Young is making a disciplinary claim. He is careful to say
"spread across" not "spread from" English to other disciplines. Rather, we
suggest that it is the humanities – especially literature – scholar who needs to
be reminded that the postcolonial is not primarily driven by the disciplinary
concerns and methods of literary studies any more, and that this does not
mean the postcolonial project itself is therefore over.

In *Orientalism*, Said locates his critique at the moment when humanities
scholarship is ceding its power to, or being overtaken by, the social sciences.
If the great philologists and classicists were the scholars who produced
knowledge about the Orient in the nineteenth century, by the mid-twentieth
century the same knowledge was the influential sphere of the social science
and "area studies" specialist. However, the disciplinary boundaries between
philology and political science, or literary studies and psychology, matter
less in Said's analysis than the fact that the research object, the "Oriental",
could be readily and eerily reproduced across the disciplinary boundary.
Orientalism introduced us to the idea that in speaking about the Oriental,
the disciplinary boundary was partly an illusion of Western epistemology,
since the same sort of thing was said about him (or her) whatever form of
knowledge was speaking.

Recent laments and discussions about the future of postcolonialism in the
humanities specifically may be just another way of perpetuating the colonial
illusions of Western epistemology. We worry about interdisciplinarity and
transdisciplinarity at a moment when the postcolonial project might have
its greatest impact *because* of its spread across disciplinary lines. However,
like many other tasks in postcolonial scholarship, it is a case of using disciplinarity against the grain, which is always going to be a fraught task for the
disciplinarian in practice. Trained in one discipline, and naturally concerned
about its future (and the future of one's career within the discipline), how do
we put aside such concerns in order to work the postcolonial edge?

The disciplinary question is important here because one possible solution
to the apparent wane of postcolonialism in literary studies is to allow the
project to become decentered. Frederick Cooper makes the claim, with due
acknowledgement to postcolonial theory's original impetus in literary studies, that "it is now the interdisciplinary domains of colonial and postcolonial
studies that could use a new sense of direction, particularly a more rigorous

historical practice" (2005, 13; our emphasis). He argues scrupulously that this is not a bid for the disciplinary dominance of history over literature. Indeed, as a historical anthropologist, he could just as easily make a claim for anthropology over literature. Anthropology is as important as literature in bringing postcolonial concerns into the academy. Thus, although Said remains an important marker and figurehead for postcolonial studies generally and literature specifically, one should equally take note of the importance of work such as the 1973 collection edited by Talal Asad, *Anthropology and the Colonial Encounter*, which provoked a profound and sustained internal critique of anthropology as a colonial practice and form of knowledge. Cooper seems to be suggesting that the natural limit of the literary postcolonial might be the historical postcolonial. For him, if we have exhausted the possibilities of thinking about the textual culture and reproduction of colonialism then it might be time to turn to problems and questions that other disciplines, such as history, are better equipped to illuminate. In some sense, he names a move that has been organically developing in postcolonial theory, connected partly with the publication of and response to Dipesh Chakrabarty's *Provincializing Europe*, published in 2000, and partly with a wider readership of the kind of historical anthropology of colonialism that scholars like Cooper, Ann Stoler and Bernard Cohn have been doing for the last thirty years.

Nevertheless, Cooper's comments also point to a certain ambiguity about where and when the interdisciplinarity of postcolonial studies takes place. Scholars from outside literature seem to agree that in its sense as an academic field, postcolonial studies begins with the work of literary scholars – Said, Bhabha and Spivak – but that it also, almost immediately, begins to turn interdisciplinary. Cooper figures this interdisciplinarity as a problem that requires "not [more] disciplinarity, but discipline: *a more thorough and critical engagement with other fields*, a more rigorous and wider reading of social theory" (2005, 6; our emphasis). We would agree that it is here, in a more attentive, rigorous engagement with the postcolonial theory outside literary studies, where the answer to the persistent sense of ending and exhaustion from postcolonial literature scholars lies. If English Literature is unsure about the future of the postcolonial project, it might examine what the postcolonial is doing in other disciplines in order to become rejuvenated and reinspired.

In this chapter we want to examine the particularly lively incarnation of postcolonialism in Management and Organization Studies (MOS) as one such resource. MOS is itself a thoroughly interdisciplinary field, one without any easy recourse to the pedigree of single disciplinary tradition, while it makes use of several well-recognized social science methodologies and epistemologies. The uneasy amalgamation of psychological, economic, engineering, sociological and ethnographic approaches applied to investigate issues related to managing and organizing that is MOS has been further complicated during the last three decades by the various turns in humanities and social sciences. The turns to language, discourse, theory, culture and practice have all had significant effects on the field and changed the ways in which managing, management and managers, as well as organizing, organization and organizations, are understood, conceptualized and studied. If there is one turn that, to date, the field is struggling to make, it is the turn to history. Even this turn has at least started, as the establishment of the journal *Management and Organizational History* in 2006 attests, although we are still some way away from historicizing management knowledge. This does not mean that historical approaches and methods have not been used within the field. What has remained largely unexplored is what happens to MOS when history is taken seriously both in terms of epistemology and ontology. Apart from some notable exceptions (Cooke 2003a, 2003b, 2003c), scholars in the field have been content with applying history to MOS problematics rather than interrogating the effects of historicity on management knowledge. Though postcolonial MOS is a relative newcomer to the postcolonial project, acquiring a critical mass only in the early 2000s, in that short time it has passed through many of the same issues with which literary postcolonial studies has been grappling and has come to different conclusions about what can be done to "turn the power structures of the world upside down" (Young 2012, 20).

CRITICAL MANAGEMENT STUDIES AND THE POSTCOLONIAL

Management and Organization studies is largely structured by positivist, economicist and managerialist objectives, methods and epistemologies deriving from the "leading" business schools and journals located in the United States that have little in common with the humanities. However, this framework has been challenged from inside the field by Critical Management Studies (CMS), a group of scholars active since the 1980s in the UK, joining similar groups in Canada, Australia, New Zealand, the Nordic Countries and Brazil to form what is an increasingly expansive, though still peripheral, scholarly movement (Adler, Forbes and Willmott 2007, 123). The objective of CMS, broadly understood, has been to bring about "a cultural shift in the image of management, from saviour to problem" (Parker 2002, 9). Over time, the label of CMS has come to define a rather wide and theoretically heterogeneous sub-field, including those who share the objective of the Marxian core of CMS but draw on a range of theoretical traditions including Frankfurt School Critical Theory, postmodernism, poststructuralism (particularly Foucault's work on power, discipline and subjectivity) and feminism (Adler, Forbes and Willmott 2007). More broadly, CMS scholars work from the premise that "management" and "organization" are themselves concepts and categories that should be analyzed rather than assumed to be inevitable or naturally occurring phenomena, historically constituted social constructions with particular dynamics and underlying ideological assumptions (Harding 2003). In contrast with mainstream management studies, CMS research assumes that what management is and what managers do cannot be answered well in the abstract (Adler 2002, 153). Rather, critical management scholars focus on a feeling for organizational context, the nature of managerial work (psychologically, politically and linguistically) and a careful investigation of how social or organizational processes reproduce suboptimal performance or unethical practices and social or organizational harm. At the same time, they are also interested in how managerial action is embedded in wider, politico-economic institutional arrangements that operate to steer and constrain, as well as enable, managerial action. A critical management studies framework emphasizes the practices and discourses that constitute organizations are never politically neutral, and challenges the centrality and the necessity of a dominant elite defining social reality (Alvesson, Bridgman and Willmott 2009). Importantly, one consequence is that managers are studied as human beings who interact with other human beings in particular social settings, with specific discursive resources at their disposal at any given time (Ashcraft, Kuhn and Cooren 2009).

Although CMS in its broad sense is now at least quarter of a century old and well established as an institution and approach within MOS, it is worth noting some features of its emergence. First, it has emerged predominantly in European academia. Though it is important to note that CMS has been a regular feature of the US Academy of Management, it retains most of its scholarly power and value in European research networks and journals. Mainstream MOS is overwhelmingly driven by the research agenda and objectives of the more positivist and managerialist Anglo-American academy. There is an interesting tension here, in a British context, between the UK as a European critical voice and at the same time a beneficiary of and participant in the dominant Anglo-American management studies paradigm. It is in the UK where CMS has the strongest institutional presence in terms of research groups, dedicated courses and UK-based journals. It is not possible, nor perhaps desirable, to try to smooth out this tension, but it does point to the ways in which critical perspectives can only emerge in complex relationship to existing sites of power. The British academy, as a former imperial center, has a capacity to produce critical epistemological spaces, like CMS, that it does not necessarily have the will to fully inhabit. CMS began in the UK with the participation of scholars in other places, but is able to grow and persist because of the value given to British scholarship in the global academy. Like many other critical movements in the humanities and social sciences, CMS has had occasion to ask of itself, "critical in the name of whom and what" (Adler 2002, 388–389). In Adler's account, the objective is at the same time very focused and strangely vague. It is focused on the paleo-Marxist objective of putting an end to capitalist exploitation of workers. However, it is vaguely inclusive, since CMS welcomes anti-racist, postcolonial, feminist, ecological and other perspectives into the paleo-Marxist struggle. Feminist theory and perspectives have similarly been quite successful in CMS, without necessarily creating much space for or pushing postcolonial or transnational feminist scholarship into the field (Calás and Smircich 1996, 2006).

The truth of this is well illustrated by the fact that despite a notable interest in poststructuralist philosophies and a complex engagement with feminist theory, postcolonial theory and perspectives remained strangely absent or at least occluded from the field of critical management studies until 2001, when Anshuman and Pushkala Prasad, two of the earliest advocates and prime movers of a postcolonial perspective in management studies and both based in the American academy, organized a postcolonial stream at the well-established biennial CMS conference. *Postcolonial Theory and Organizational Analysis*, the first book to be published on postcolonial approaches in Management and Organization Studies, was published in 2003.

The twenty-year delay in the emergence of the postcolonial in the management and organization context is curious. It is also worth noting that anti-racist perspectives, as distinct from postcolonial, have not been any more successful in entering the center of CMS scholarship. The discussion of race has rather been subsumed and largely depoliticized under the rubric of "diversity" and discussion of racism under the rubric of "harassment". The Prasads have speculated that:

> conceivably the close association of imperialism with cruelty, plunder, rape, violence and genocide ... turns it into something unsavoury that is jarring to the liberal sensibility. It could be this perception of the unsavoury quality of the object of postcolonial inquiry that may partly explain why, consciously or otherwise, management scholars have largely stayed away from postcolonial theory. (2003, 287)

It seems more likely, given the sub-disciplinary locations where postcolonial analysis first took hold in MOS, that most scholars, mainstream or critical, simply did not see the relevance of postcolonial critique or approaches to their work unless they worked on management across national and cultural contexts. In other words, unless the research object was the management of "Others", the postcolonial did not seem relevant. Implicitly or explicitly, postcolonialism was understood as just (read "essentially the same as") poststructuralism about Others.

The push to postcolonial management and organization studies did not emerge organically from the critical research and activism inaugurated by CMS itself, as one might have expected, but from those working in areas such as human relations management and diversity, corporate social responsibility, and international and cross-cultural management. It is not accidental that the Prasads were able to find a place for a postcolonial stream at a CMS conference because CMS opens an important critical space, as we have indicated, for interrogating the very idea of management. Nevertheless, we would emphasize that the movement is not from CMS to postcolonialism but rather a contingent meeting between those working on issues to do with Others, often working in the settler colonial settings of North America and Australasia, who sought to force a methodological and subsequently episte-mological crisis onto Management and Organization Studies as a whole, via the available space of CMS.

Prasad and Prasad were the first to offer some general rationale for the relevance of postcolonial analysis in research on management and organi-zations. They argued that a postcolonial approach would have the effect of defamiliarizing the workplace from a new perspective; increase the importance of understanding colonialism as constitutive of Western moder-nity (of which, in their turn, theories and practices of management form a central part); provide a means of understanding non-Western management practice without the Western practice as normative referent; and provide a means of understanding the new transformation effected by processes of glo-balization, considering that globalization is redistributing economic power away from the West towards Japan, China and India (Prasad 2004, 29–33). The earliest instances of postcolonial management analyses have been invaluable in revealing the limits of thinking about management problems in terms of abstract universalism, as somehow above particular historical, geographical and cultural contexts. This body of work includes Subhabrata Bobby Banerjee's critique of colonizing narratives of environmentalism in Australia; Michael Frenkel's Bhabhian reading of knowledge transfer in mul-tinational corporations as hybridity; Raza Mir and Ali Mir's reimagination of organizations as sites of postcolonial renewal rather than colonial control; and Dean Neu's account of the ways that accounting techniques reproduce colonialist social relations in their taken-for-granted mundaneness.

Nevertheless, in the 2012 edited collection *Against the Grain: Advances in Postcolonial Organization Studies*, edited by Anshuman Prasad, he more or less reaffirms the value of postcolonial theory primarily as a means of challenging the "metropolitan Anglophone researchers" who continue to rely on "old-fashioned and, frequently Eurocentric, scholarly concerns and/or approaches to social scien-tific inquiry", thereby providing ways of "doing management research differently, and adding new and unique layers to the current understanding of management and organizations" (Prasad 2012, 14). Although Prasad certainly acknowledges that postcolonial critique is not just an attack on Eurocentrism, the rationale for postcolonial theory as retrieving Others from the misunderstanding of the old-fashioned, metropolitan Anglophone researcher does not enable it do much else. Having entered the field of Management and Organization Studies through criticism of the ways in which difference was conceptualized in international cross-cultural management studies, especially in human relations management and related organizational issues, it still does remain largely confined to areas of management and organization where encounters with Others, whether domestic or foreign, is a significant issue, such as International Management, International Business (Westwood 2006; Westwood and Jack 2007) and Human Resource Management (Ahonen *et al.* 2014).

Though postcolonial interventions remain overwhelmingly the concern of scholars interested in the problem of difference, there has been an important development for postcolonial analysis at the center of Management and Organization Studies. Bill Cooke, who is a key scholar in CMS, has demonstrated through careful historical research that management as a distinct form of knowledge was born of the colonialist need to manage slaves and plantations, rather than as a response to the technological innovations and industrialization of the Western world (2003a, 2003b, 2004). In other words, at its core, management knowledge is part of the colonial order of things. Management has not typically located its historical origins so far in the past because slave labor has not been considered a complex enough labor process to require either sophisticated management or managers as distinct subjects. Cooke has shown not only that plantations were complex organizations run on principles recognizable to us as "scientific management" but that there was certainly an evolving managerial identity inextricably connected with White supremacism and racism.[1] The broader point of this historical exercise, as Cooke argues, is that

> [i]nsofar as CMS depicts management as a consequence of capitalism alone, it is not all that far from managerialist orthodoxy. ... Empire, in other words, is absent from CMS; yet imperialism was *organized* and it was *managed*. (2003c, 90)

His historical analysis reveals management as a form of knowledge that emerged to manage the differences that other forms of knowledge, such as literature, history and anthropology, were producing. Here, the difference is less important in itself than the epistemic forms, which have been used to produce, reproduce, organize and manage it.

Cooke's work might seem to echo Cooper's suggestion that we should all return to more rigorous historical practice. However, he asserts that his purpose in writing a different history of management is not so much an exercise in history as a strongly felt ethical impulse to put back into the epistemic frame what has, consistently, implausibly and willfully, been denied. He suggests that "whatever existent or emergent theorization we use to frame the past, the link between management and slavery is always waiting to be obviously made" (2003a, 1916) and it is the fact of making the link that matters to Cooke. The postcolonial might be one means, he argues, but there are any number of others, for example Marxian or Foucauldian, that could accomplish the same task if they took the link between management and slavery, or management and colonialism, seriously. In other words, the historical phenomenon of colonialism and the conditions of possibility it legitimates today should matter to us as scholars *tout court*, rather than as historians, anthropologists or critical management scholars. It is, in fact, in his words, "a legitimate, indeed moral, academic imperative" (2003a, 1916).

We have no argument with Cooke's imperative, but his argument that any method might be able to do the work if we acknowledge that management knowledge is inextricably connected to colonialism and imperialism requires more thought. The most recent wave of critical management studies indicates that even the persistent use of a variety of critical methodologies and approaches has not lead to a significant change in (Western) management theory's self-identification as universal theory. In an editor's introduction to a special issue on critical management studies for the *Academy of Management Review* in 2008, Gavin Jack, Marta Calás, Stella Nkomo and Tuomo Peltonen note that, so far, the range of critical epistemologies from Marxist, feminist and post-positivist philosophies have not made the inroads into management that one might have expected. As they observe:

> [I]t is notable that, over the years, theoretical concerns in this field have been consistently displaced by methodological concerns, as if methodological solutions were capable of solving the theoretical limitations lying at the heart of most of the discipline's assumed problems. (2008, 875)

In particular, Jack and others observe that postcolonial theory has been introduced as a new tool in management studies where it is deemed relevant and supposedly adds a necessary, extra "lens" to the work that improves its accuracy. That is to say, in some cases postcolonial theory may be useful because it offers another perspective on something that Western methods, by themselves, cannot address. This is a familiar move. It is a concession to cultural and social factors in the case of some research objects as a variation on positivism, where some objects need extra or different lenses fitted to the microscope so that we may study them more accurately. Use of the microscope, and the epistemological practices that enable and validate it, is still mandatory, but there is an acknowledgement that the usual lens that is fitted to the instrument will not be sufficient by itself for this special case. It is perhaps because of the necessity of writing and researching in relation to the mainstream positivist assumptions, and in "leading" journals, that a plurality of methodologies has been deployed in CMS as a kind of improvement on positivism, much like what has happened with, or to, the historical turn in the field we discussed above. The Prasads' early rationales about postcolonial theory can be read in exactly these terms. However, as Jack and others point out, this continually sidesteps the epistemological challenge from postcolonial theory that Western management knowledge can no longer be authorized as management knowledge in itself. Cooke's point that any method might carry the analytic load of revealing the connections between management and racism, slavery and colonialism, is true, but as Jack and others argue, there must also be an epistemological shift if management knowledge is to do the work of provincializing itself as knowledge. They argue that even in the work of those who are deeply committed to plurality and equality, there is a subtle and persistent disavowal of the need for any deeper epistemic self-reflexivity so that Western management studies can continue to function as management knowledge in the abstract.

We would argue that the greatest advance in postcolonial Management and Organization Studies, in terms of provincializing (Western) management knowledge, is by Jack and Westwood. They have taken up the challenge to engage in the epistemic self-reflexivity prompted by postcolonial theory in their 2009 book *International and Cross-Cultural Management Studies: A Postcolonial Reading*. Their project is a genuinely ambitious one, encompassing a rationale for postcolonial critique; histories of international cross-cultural management's origins in colonial British anthropology and modern Western science; colonial discourse analysis of several key texts in the modern international cross-cultural management canon; a detailed critique of academic publishing; and an examination of institutional higher-education practice as an apparatus for reproducing the colonial order of things. It is the critique of academic practices, together with lists of actions that can be taken now, that best indicates how far Jack and Westwood think it is possible to take the imperative to put colonialism back into the epistemic frame of Management and Organization Studies. In providing researchers, instructors, journal editors, publishers and professional association members with concrete actions they can take to "legitimize and valorize non-Western forms of knowledge" (2009, 301), Jack and Westwood set the bar high for what postcolonialism should do next in Management and Organization Studies. They acknowledge the sheer weight of institutional and scholarly practice that stands in the way of realizing these goals, but they conclude, "We do not subscribe to responses of inactivity and passivity in the face of these challenges" (2009, 314).

PRACTICING POSTCOLONIALISM

A turn towards thinking about epistemology could lead in quite the opposite direction from Jack and Westwood's study: further and further away from Cooke's moral imperative and towards more abstract and disembodied considerations of what knowledge is or what constitutes an act of knowing. In Management and Organization Studies, however, scholars are invariably turned back to questions of how knowledge is organized and managed in the world, since that is their articulated research object. While being increasingly interested in how people understand their work and represent it, they are also persistently concerned about how it changes or fails to change what they do, what organizations do or what is done in organizations. Jack and Westwood's lists of proposed actions all concern the ways in which academic organizations – universities, publishers, professional associations – might organize themselves and manage their work process differently in order to bring about a change in the kind of knowledge that is produced in Management and Organization Studies. It is this turn to reflections on epistemology in questions of management and organization that we are par-ticularly interested in connecting with the humanities postcolonial project. It is here that we imagine that the melancholy postcolonial critics in English or History might be spurred on to continue with the postcolonial project.

It is not a simple matter to persuade scholars, whether in literature or management studies, that a move from various useful critical methods to a new epistemology is warranted. As we have already noted, even within the field of CMS, itself a sub-field in Management and Organization Studies, postcolonial methodologies have not been adopted readily because they are not seen as relevant to most metropolitan research. In literary postcolonial studies, the case is different because so much scholarship has focused on the ways in which metropole is constituted by colony, as much as the colony is constituted by metropole. Said's exposition of the Orient at the heart of West-ern literary discourse, or Spivak's exhortation that "it should not be possible, in principle, to read nineteenth-century British literature without remem-bering that imperialism ... was a crucial part of the cultural representation of England to the English" (1979, 113) make this clear. The postcolonial method has come to seem potentially relevant for reading Western litera-ture as much as it has for the study of non-Western literature. Nevertheless, literature does seem to evade the epistemological challenges that confront history or anthropology or MOS. In acknowledging the relevance of the postcolonial method, it has been able to avoid dealing more fully with ques-tions of how literature as a discipline continues to reproduce colonialism through the ways in which it is organized, managed and practiced.

We have tried to situate the development of postcolonial MOS care-fully in its context as connected with post-positivist and poststructural scholarship, but it bears emphasizing again, before we discuss this further, that a turn to management and organization perspectives is not a turn to managerialism or a backhanded way of slipping the objectives of neo-liberal management of higher education into humanities research. We emphasize this because our experience presenting these arguments to various audiences in the humanities suggests that humanities scholars persistently understand any discussion of management and organization as inevitably aligned with the neo-liberal discourse that informs the structural changes many of us experience on a daily basis in our institutional work lives. Instead, we want to draw attention to the fact that producing an epistemological shift *is* partly a management problem, and that an epistemological shift, such as the kind postcolonialism aims to achieve, cannot be achieved by a change or reorientation in disciplinary methods alone. To talk about how knowledge produces its effects is to talk about how people use it, organize it, manage it and reproduce it literally. To turn to Management and Organization Studies, then, is to turn to a field of study that has experience in and conceptual instruments for thinking about these questions.

We have already discussed the epistemological challenge that CMS poses to management research, but critical management scholars have also sought to examine the organizational structures and practices that bring management knowledge into being. For example, they have unmasked the paradoxical circularity that produces the "quality" in "quality journals" (Macdonald and Kam 2007), the counter-productiveness of journal rankings, and analyzed the management processes and organizational structures in academic journal publishing that seem to keep management knowledge primarily in Anglo-American hands (Meriläinen *et al.* 2008; Tienari and Thomas 2006), how management knowledge is disseminated and diffused through business schools (Grey 2002) and what possibilities there are to be "critical" in this organizational setting (Currie and Knights 2003).

There are a number of different ways in which we can think about taking up management and organization issues, but to further emphasize that there is no fundamental incompatibility with humanities scholarship, we want to draw here on work that has already been done by literature scholars, in particular how we organize the study of literature, how we manage the study of literature, what effects literary knowledge produces and how research capacity is trained and developed.

The question of how a literature department should be organized in order to achieve postcolonial aims emerges as early as 1968 in Ngũgĩ's well-known "On the Abolition of the English Department". That text situates the organizational problem in terms of the cultural context of Kenya, where oral traditions and a lived-experience of colonialism change the conditions in which we should understand the organizational principle of "the English department". As recently as 2004, Chelva Kanaganayakam asked the same kind of organizational question about literature departments and postcolonial studies in the Western academy. Should postcolonial studies be relocated to its own center and thereby be given a certain epistemological autonomy and status – as, analogously, Departments of Women's Studies or Gender Studies appear to have? Despite the fact that postcolonialism has travelled into various other disciplines since its emergence, in the UK and many of its former colonies the work of postcolonial scholars continues, by and large, to be housed in literature departments, whether English or comparative literature, where

> Comfortably ensconced within the confines of English departments, we function in ways that are not fundamentally different from any other branch of English literary studies. In fact, we may be at times guilty of reinscribing the very practices that we struggled to overturn. By enclosing postcolonial studies within certain institutional parameters, we sometimes reintroduce paradigms that we eliminated after considerable effort. (2004, 727)

The equally complicated, but different question of Comparative Literature as both a disciplinary handle and organizational unit has been the subject of analysis by Spivak. As Kanaganayakam goes on to comment later in the article, it is noteworthy that in job descriptions, the postcolonialist is just another specialist like the Victorianist or the Early Modernist. The implication is that the organizational setting has all but wiped out the postcolonial difference. The postcolonial is just another child in the literature family. The thoroughgoing discussions of canons and curriculum indicate that there has been some serious rethinking of what and who to teach. However, the problem is that how we organize and manage the work of postcolonial scholarship – the postcolonial practice of literature-the-discipline – has not been adequately examined.

Whereas Ngũgĩ's argument for the abolition of the English department seemed to be specific to the situation in which he was writing – where a particular language and cultural identity were at stake – Kanaganayakam's discussion shows that the consequence has not been to trigger discussion of organization more broadly in the Anglo-American university, however pressing and complex such organizational questions remain in those contexts. For example, Kanaganayakam teaches in Canada, where "Canadian literature" is itself subsumed into Departments of English and where, in any case, "Canadian literature" seldom includes indigenous storytelling practices, orature or the study of Francophone Canadian literature. Abolishing a Department of English in this context would be a crude solution to a complex colonial context, and Kanaganayakam is not proposing such an abolition. However, sadly, his article abandons the possibility of reorganizing postcolonial studies, preferring instead, as a literature scholar, to defend the study of literature as grounded in texts and textuality. In his words, "The text may well reflect several aspects of contemporary or historical reality, but its primary function is to work within its own status as an artifact" (2004, 736). He returns to disciplinarity, as many postcolonial scholars undoubtedly would in a moment when the humanities in general are under threat as a field of study. The problems that organizational questions reveal are by no means simple to answer or even, as in this case, to contemplate with professional equanimity. Nevertheless, the question Kanaganayakam poses persists. In saying that we have specific and specifiable practices that characterize English, we also imply that we have locations, spaces and material structures by which we carry out those practices and these must surely be open to reorganization.

Much of the analysis of these kinds of questions in the humanities has focused on practices, rather than organization or management, but the two are closely linked. Postcolonial humanities scholars have, for example, been deeply interested in questions of pedagogy as a form of institutional practice. Understandably, however, the majority of this work has taken the form of discussions about canon formation, curriculum and values, thereby maintaining focus, as Kanaganayakam puts it, on the literary text as artefact.[2]

There are, nevertheless some useful starting points for further investigation of management questions in the work of scholars such as Gauri Viswanathan. Her historical work on literary study as a form for colonial government in

Masks of Conquest, much like Cooke's work on management's origins in slave labor, reveals the inextricable relationship between humanities education and the management of a colony and its subjects. Viswanathan's work refers to "government" rather than management, but insofar as she draws on a Foucaultian understanding of government, one that has been of great interest to CMS scholars, we feel it is appropriate to describe her work as revealing a management problem for contemporary literary pedagogy. The implications of these colonial origins for contemporary literary pedagogical practice have not been explored or developed much further, often leaving individual scholars to reflect on their teaching practices without being able to connect those reflections to a wider discussion with their peers on the organizational effects of their practices.

Indeed, when examined more closely, postcolonial teaching actually appears to be at odds with the disciplinary traditions of English literary pedagogy, but how can the individual postcolonial teacher proceed? Reflecting on her experience of teaching "culturally different" texts, Arun Mukherjee writes:

> The most painful revelation came when I recognized the source of my students' vocabulary. Their analysis, I realized, was in the time-honoured tradition of that variety of criticism which presents literary works as "universal". The test of a great work of literature, according to this tradition, is that *despite its particularity*, it speaks to all times and all people. (1995, 450; our emphasis)

Here the postcolonial teacher is actually in conflict with the students, who are training in the universalism that is proper to their discipline's epistemology. Can she simply teach and assess differently than her colleagues in the department? Perhaps, but at the very least this problem may illustrate how postcolonial method has become acceptable at the heart of Western literature without fundamentally disturbing its epistemology. Mukherjee defines successful practice in the postcolonial classroom – one that must still operate under certain organizational constraints – in the following way: "If I succeed in making my students aware of the universalizing tendencies of western literary theory, I consider my teaching to have attained its desired goal" (1998, 168). Mukherjee's work suggests that more research on how the study of literature is reorganized and practiced will allow the postcolonial pedagogy to be advanced more strategically and collectively, rather than being left to the ingenuity of individual teacher-critics.

Finally, however, we want to turn to postcolonial analysis of research practice, a topic that certainly has not received very much attention in literary studies, perhaps connected to the fact that postcolonial studies continues to be hesitant about examining racism. We deliberately use the word "racism" here because postcolonial literary scholarship has been interested in questions of race and racialization – how race has come to be established as a socially and politically meaningful term – but not in the ongoing and oppressive effects of living under the sign of race. Jack and Westwood devote a significant portion of their book on decolonizing the field of cross-cultural management to questions about who determines, produces and evaluates research practice. Discussions of these kinds of questions in literary studies have frequently unfolded in painfully and unproductively inter-personal terms, such as the battles over the identity of "the postcolonial critic" in the mid-1990s. It is time to give more analysis to the ways in which literature as a form of colonial knowledge has been organized and managed, rather than partisan attacks on particular careers and individuals. Said raised these questions of organization and academic practice in *Orientalism*, noting that "no Arab or Islamic scholar can afford to ignore what goes on in scholarly journals, institutes and universities in the United States and Europe; the converse is not true" (1979, 323). The imbalance in the power of culturally different academics to produce knowledge about themselves in non-Western academic institutions and journals is a problem that we continue to ignore because what Said notes in 1978, Jack and Westwood confirm in 2009. Indeed, peripheries also occur within the West (Meriläinen *et al.* 2008).

Postcolonial management and organization research really comes into its own as a disciplinary resource here. For example, drawing substantially on Linda Tuhiwai Smith's work on decolonizing research methodologies, Jack and Westwood consider how "building indigenous research capacity" (2009, 290) might be addressed by changing organizational practice. Some of these propositions are relatively easy to understand and are already in place in many universities, since they fit well with established practices on widening access to universities, such as "the training of indigenous people as researchers" (2009, 290) or "the employment of indigenous people as researchers" (2009, 290), but others involve more uncomfortable and unfamiliar effort on the part of First World scholars such as "the generating of research questions by communities" (2009, 290) or fostering research networks among indigenous researchers rather than fostering individual indigenous research group's dialogue with one non-indigenous central group. Of course, the division between indigenous and non-indigenous, or West and non-West, is not always so clear. In the UK and Canada, for example, postcolonial scholarship has not produced more of a racial and ethnic balance of academics employed in the humanities and social sciences. Since we continue to imagine the humanities as the discipline that helps people to understand the common human experience, it really ought to be a serious concern why professional organizations and humanities departments are not more representative of the 'Others' we seek to retrieve from Western regimes of representation.

Work of this kind might call upon postcolonial scholars who work in Western universities to devote more of their decolonizing efforts to changing the ways they participate in research networks, publishing, editing and managing researchers than focusing on their own individual research. Jack and Westwood, in their exhortation to their Western peers, are conscious that this is a sensitive question – one of people's individual careers, ambitions and identities as scholars. Here again, however, an organizational rather than autobiographical understanding gives us a less guilty and melancholy approach to what can and should be done.

> Our book is an invitation to a collective conversation involving individuals and institutions to find strategies through which we might transform our discipline. ... A key part of such institutional transformation is the need for political organizing *amongst us*.
>
> (Jack and Westwood 2009, 310; our emphasis)

THE END OF AN ILLUSION

Questions of organizational management and practice return us to the disciplinary questions with which we began. The process of thinking more about how we practice literature as a form of knowledge might also, then, be a means to engage in more dialogue with other disciplinary postcolonial projects, and here we have sought to outline the possibilities offered by postcolonialism in Management and Organization Studies, thus realizing its potential as a rupture in Western epistemologies, rather than simply a way of reading culture and culturally different texts. At the very least, we hope to have demonstrated that postcolonialism is alive and well as an epistemological project, if not in literature then in other disciplines. But we hope to have also made the case that the illusion of "other" disciplines, when speaking of the non-Western world, is one of colonial epistemology's most persuasive illusions.

NOTES

1. Cooke identifies an archive of this managerial identity in periodical publications of the time with titles such as "On the Management of Slaves", "The Management of Negroes", "Judicious Management of the Plantation Force", "Moral Management of Negroes" and "Management of Slaves" (2003a, 1910).
2. Spivak's "How to Read a Culturally Different Book" and Kanaganayakam's response to this are two such examples of pedagogical reflection that seem to become hooked on the question of the particular text, R K Narayan's *The Guide*, under discussion, though they both address the need to change teaching practice.

REFERENCES

Academy of Management. "Critical Management Studies". Briarcliff Manor, NY, 2013. Academy of Management. 13 August 2013. http://aom.org/Divisions-and-Interest-Groups/Critical-Management-Studies/Critical-Management-Studies.aspx.

Adler, Paul. 2002. "Critical in the Name of Whom and What?" *Organization* 9.3: 387–395.

Adler, Paul S., Linda C. Forbes and Hugh Willmott. 2007. "Chapter 3: Critical Management Studies". *Academy of Management Annals* 1.1: 119–179.

Ahonen, Pasi, Janne Tienari, Susan Meriläinen and Alison Pullen. 2014. "Hidden Contexts and Invisible Power Relations: A Foucauldian Reading of Diversity Management". *Human Relations* 67.3: 263–286.

Alcadipani, Rafael, Farzad Rafi Khan, Ernesto Gantman and Stella Nkomo. 2012. "Southern Voices in Management and Organization Knowledge". *Organization* 19.2: 131–143.

Alvesson, Mats, Todd Bridgman and Hugh Willmott, eds. 2009. *The Oxford Handbook of Critical Management Studies*. Oxford and New York: Oxford University Press.

Alvesson, Mats and Hugh Willmott, eds. 2003. *Studying Management Critically*. London and Thousand Oaks, CA: Sage.

Ashcraft, Karen Lee, Timothy R. Kuhn and François Cooren. 2009. "Constitutional Amendments: 'Materializing' Organizational Communication". *The Academy of Management Annals* 3.1: 1–64.

Calás, Marta B. and Linda Smircich. 1996. "From 'the Woman's Point of View': Feminist Approaches to Organization Studies". In *Handbook of Organization Studies*, edited by Stewart Clegg, Cynthia Hardy and Walter R. Nord, 218–258. London: Sage.

Calás, Marta B. and Linda Smircich. 2006. "From the 'Woman's Point of View' Ten Years Later: Towards a Feminist Organization Studies". In *Handbook of Organization Studies*, edited by Stewart Clegg, Cynthia Hardy and Walter R. Nord, 285–346. 2nd ed. London: Sage.

Chakrabarty, Dipesh. 2000. *Provincializing Europe: Postcolonial Thought and Historical Difference*. Princeton: Princeton University Press.

Cooke, Bill. 2003a. "The Denial of Slavery in Management Studies". *Journal of Management Studies* 40.8: 1895–1918.

Cooke, Bill. 2003b. "A New Continuity with Colonial Administration: Participation in Development Management". *Third World Quarterly* 24.1: 47–61.

Cooke, Bill. 2003c. "Managing Organizational Culture and Imperialism". In *Postcolonial Theory and Organizational Analysis: A Critical Engagement*, edited by Anshuman Prasad, 75–94. New York and Houndmills, UK: Palgrave Macmillan.

Cooke, Bill. 2004. "The Managing of the (Third) World". *Organization* 11.5: 603–629.

Cooper, Frederick. 2005. *Colonialism in Question: Theory, Knowledge, History*. Berkeley: University of California Press.

Currie, Graeme and David Knights. 2003. "Reflecting on a Critical Pedagogy in MBA Education". *Management Learning* 34.1: 27–49.

Grey, Christopher. 2002. "What Are Business Schools For? On Silence and Voice in Management Education". *Journal of Management Education* 26.5: 496–511.

Harding, Nancy. 2003. *Social Construction of Management: Texts and Identities*. London and New York: Routledge.

Jack, Gavin, Marta B. Calás, Stella M. Nkomo and Tuomo Peltonen. 2008. "Critique and International Management: An Uneasy Relationship?" *Academy of Management Review* 33.4: 870–884.

Jack, Gavin and Robert Westwood. 2009. *International and Cross-Cultural Management Studies: A Postcolonial Reading*. Basingstoke: Palgrave Macmillan.

Kanaganayakam, Chelva. 2004. "Pedagogy and Postcolonial Literature; or, Do We Need a Centre for Postcolonial Studies?" *University of Toronto Quarterly* 73.2: 725–738.

Macdonald, Stuart and Jacqueline Kam. 2007. "Ring a Ring O' Roses: Quality Journals and Gamesmanship in Management Studies". *Journal of Management Studies* 44.4: 640–655.

Meriläinen, Susan, Janne Tienari, Robyn Thomas and Annette Davies. 2008. "Hegemonic Academic Practices: Experiences of Publishing from the Periphery". *Organization* 15.4: 584–597.

Mukherjee, Arun P. 1998. *Postcolonialism: My Living*. Toronto: TSAR.

Mukherjee, Arun P. 1995. "Ideology in the Classroom: A Case Study in the Teaching of English Literature in Canadian Universities". *The Post-colonial Studies Reader*, edited by Bill Ashcroft, Gareth Griffiths and Helen Tiffin, 447–451. London: Routledge.

Ngũgĩ wa Thiong'o. 1995. "On the Abolition of the Department of English". In *The Post-colonial Studies Reader*, edited by Bill Ashcroft, Gareth Griffiths and Helen Tiffin, 438–442. London: Routledge.

Parker, Martin. 2002. *Against Management*. Oxford: Polity.

Prasad, Anshuman and Pushkala Prasad. 2002. "Otherness at Large: Identity and Difference in the New Globalized Organizational Landscape". In *Gender, Identity and the Culture of Organizations,* edited by Iiris Aaltion and Albert J Mills, 57–71. London and New York: Routledge.

Prasad, Anshuman, ed. 2003. *Postcolonial Theory and Organizational Analysis: A Critical Engagement*. Basingstoke, UK: Palgrave Macmillan.

Prasad, Anshuman, and Pushkala Prasad. 2003. "The Postcolonial Imagination". In *Postcolonial Theory and Organizational Analysis: A Critical Engagement*, edited by Anshuman Prasad, 283–295. New York and Houndmills, UK: Palgrave Macmillan.

Prasad, Anshuman, ed. 2012. *Against the Grain: Advances in Postcolonial Organization Studies*. Copenhagen: Copenhagen Business School Press.

Said, Edward. 1979. *Orientalism*. New York: Vintage.

Spivak, Gayatri Chakravorty. 1994. "How to Read a Culturally Different Book". In *Colonial Discourse/Postcolonial Theory,* edited by Peter Hulme, Margaret Iversen and Francis Barker, 126–150. Manchester: Manchester University Press.

Spivak, Gayatri Chakravorty. 1999. *A Critique of Postcolonial Reason: Toward a History of the Vanishing Present*. London: Harvard University Press.

Tienari, Janne, and Robyn Thomas. 2006. "Penetrating the Academic Publishing Machine: A Rough Guide". *LTA/The Finnish Journal of Business Economics* 3: 369–380.

Westwood, Robert I. 2006. "International Business and Management Studies as an Orientalist Discourse". *Critical Perspectives on International Business* 2.2: 91–113.

Westwood, Robert I. and Gavin Jack. 2007. "Manifesto for a Post-Colonial International Business and Management Studies". *Critical Perspectives on International Business* 3.3: 246–265.

Willmott, Hugh C. and John Mingers. 2013. "Taylorizing Business School Research: On the 'One Best Way' Performative Effects of Journal Ranking Lists". *Human Relations* 66.8: 1051–1073.

Viswanathan, Gauri. 1989. *Masks of Conquest: Literary Study and British Rule in India*. Columbia University Press.

Young, Robert J C. 2012. "Postcolonial Remains". *New Literary History* 43.1: 19–42.

4 Postcolonial Modernism
Shame and National Form

John C. Hawley

Since a foundational conference at the University of Leeds in 1964, postcolonial studies has established itself as an interdisciplinary field of inquiry that frequently blurs boundaries between the humanities and social sciences to analyze the legacies of colonization. Postcolonial criticism applies a range of theories to cultural artifacts and social processes in former colonies or produced by diasporic world citizens from this postcolonial world. The object of these studies is as protean as the disciplines in which they are carried out, but after these five decades there remains disagreement over the definition of postcolonial literature proper to this analysis. Does it include all texts produced either in former colonies or by those living abroad who stake a claim to represent the nation in question? Does it entail only those texts dealing with particular topics or addressed from a particular point of view (such as resistance), and does it valorize a particular genre for one reason or another as more suitably postcolonial (more realistic, for example)? This chapter hopes to consider a few of these questions, though it cannot hope to resolve them.

A defining characteristic of postcolonial theory has been its self-reflexive response to an ascendant position in the academy. This expressed itself at the turn of the last century with criticism from cultural materialists (Dirlik 1994; Brennan 1997; Lazarus 2002; Parry 2004) who argued that postcolonial theory had mitigated any forceful claim to illuminating social inequities and prompting political change. With its institutionalization it had given in to the replication of poststructuralist language dissection and to a selective focus on literature coming from former colonies that duplicated Western valorization of "formal disruption, meta-fictive strategies and labyrinths of narrative structures" (Sorensen 2010, 10). As a consequence, postcolonial theories were celebrated in the West but "treated with hostility or benign neglect in the postcolonial world" (Gikandi 2011, 163). As we advance further into the twenty-first century, such concerns are joined by calls for what some see as a long-overdue focus on the literary as a neglected component of the postcolonial world (Fraser 2000; Bahri 2003; Harrison 2003; Spivak 2003; Attridge 2004; Brown 2005; Crowley and Hiddleston 2011). The political question – an examination of what is being represented in postcolonial texts and by whom – is increasingly bolstered by forays into aesthetic questions, the *how*, which calls for greater examination of the methods and implications of mimesis and of the genres that are favored by postcolonial writers, created by them or newly invigorated in their work. Before considering some of the implications of these aesthetic issues, the prior question of the canonization of particular writers designated "postcolonial" by prominent critics needs to be rehearsed, since it leads quite quickly into the allied questions of form and genre, and whether any forms or genres may be more suitable, as it were, as a postcolonial process of expression.

DEFINING POSTCOLONIAL LITERATURE

In addressing this question there is a great deal that is helpful in *The Postcolonial Unconscious* (2011), written by Neil Lazarus as a colloquy with Fredric Jameson and Edward Said (Jameson 1981; Said 1994). Rather than completely replacing the analyses that have been conducted by postcolonial critics, Lazarus would wish to approach not only their canonized works but also the many others that he lists as completely overlooked by the current system to an additional rubric that investigated the mode of production and class relations as well as questions of land and environment, of state and nation, and of what he calls, after Raymond Williams, "structures of feeling" (35).

His implication is that by expanding the angle of vision, we will likely shatter the rigid uniformity that valorizes only a certain set of texts. In its place we will find not a single alternative tradition of what makes up postcolonial literature and instead will develop multiple such traditions. It would seem this position militates against the demand for *a* postcolonial form or genre. He compares what he is trying to bring about to what Raymond Williams tried to do in criticizing (in *The Politics of Modernism*) the required characteristics (exile, metropolitanism, etc.) demanded by those in his day who categorized some writing as modern (that is, as uniquely responsive to modernity) and other writing as retrograde (27). Lazarus, in proposing multiple alternative traditions in postcolonial literature, criticizes postcolonial theories and critics for their overly selective canon of "truly" postcolonial literature, arguing against the theories' abstraction and "the tenuousness of its grasp of the central realities of life in the 'postcolonial' world" (36). Bucking the trend among the many postcolonial theorists who dismissed Jameson's notion of postcolonial fiction generally being a national allegory, Lazarus asserts that a more inclusive listing of works written in former colonies would, in fact, demonstrate "the sheer prodigiousness of the texts that put themselves forward explicitly and self-consciously as vehicles of national consciousness" (70; cf. 75–76). The condition of the nation when the work is written affects the form in which it is written, and regardless of the form that is utilized, if it is a viable presentation of the current national consciousness it should be read as postcolonial (cf. Siddiqi 2008). Lazarus turns to Edward Said, who argues that in a comparatively stable country (as Egypt had been when Naguib Mahfouz was writing), the realism evident in the fiction was similarly stable. In Palestine, on the other hand, the writing of Ghassan Kanafani, Emil Habiby and Elias Khoury shows that, like the nation in question and the citizens, "form is an adventure, narrative both uncertain and meandering, character less a stable collection of traits than a linguistic device, as self-conscious as it is provisional and ironic" (Said 1989, xv). "Absurd, excessive, carnivalesque, vertiginous, and careering in its formal and narrative aspects", Lazarus (echoing Said) suggests that these "might be taken for postmodern thematics except that Said insists that their manifestation in Khoury's work be grasped as objective correlatives of the social disintegration specifically contingent upon the Lebanese civil war" (Lazarus 2011, 73).

So for Lazarus, it would appear that postcolonial fiction can be either more traditional or more experimental in technique but will reflect the society's "read" of itself at the time of the writing. The regrettable tendency of some postcolonial theorists, he suggests, is that they abstract the "specific inflections (formal and substantive) of received traditions and idioms of poetry, drama, or prose writing ... from their particular contexts" and then read them as "variants of a (putatively) globally dispersed aesthetic mode, such as 'magical realism' or 'the gothic' or 'postmodernism'" (73–74). For Lazarus, there is "a fatal disposition to situate the aesthetic mode of the 'postcolonial' work as derivative of that of a categorically prior 'Western' instance" (74).

The formal response in the writing can be as various as the contexts of that relationship with capitalism, but it is as a response to (imposed) capitalism that all postcolonial literature must be read.

EXCURSUS ONE: BEYOND THE LITERARY ARTS

Critics of postcolonial literature often enrich their analysis with comparative analyses of the music scene or the other arts, and such a move is relevant here as analogous to what Lazarus is suggesting and as a further step towards the questions circling around postcolonial realism/modernism. Chika Okeke-Agulu has recently written about the Nigerian Art Society of 1958 and the "natural synthesis" (Okeke-Agulu 2010, 510; Uche Okeke 1982, 2) attempted by Uche Okeke, Simon Okeke and Demas Nwoko between, on the one hand, the formal artistic demands of the colonial tradition (including European modernism) and, on the other hand, an authentic, imaginary and indigenous culture; members of this school identified its aims with those of *négritude* (Okeke-Agulu 2010, 509). Of particular interest to Okeke-Agulu is Uche Okeke's involvement with the Mbari Artists and Writers Club, founded in 1961 by Wole Soyinka, Chinua Achebe and the German writer Ulli Beier to facilitate a conversation between Anglophone and Francophone African writers, and resulting in an articulation of discursive intersections between those interested in *négritude*, African personality and pan-Africanism and pan-Arabism that concerned "self-affirmation and critical agency" (Okeke-Agulu 2010, 521). Such common thematic interests did not, apparently, invite formal experimentation, though this seemed implied in the general desire for greater autonomy.

Seeking a hybrid form, however, stretched generic norms and silhouetted the viewer's expectations of the work before him/her and, so the argument goes, continues to do so in ways unique to postcolonial situations. Such artists, in Okeke-Agulu's words, share with European modernists "the belief in the significance of the artists' role in fashioning a new art and culture for the new nation", as well as a need "to articulate their relationship with 'tradition'" and a "focus on the invention of formal styles unlike any before" (Okeke-Agulu 2010, 507). This approach entails "the conscious, critical deployment of the technical expertise learned in art classes and the rigorous experimentation with indigenous art forms" (Okeke-Agulu 2010, 510) – so, it seems, a straddling of genres and power centers similar to those Alpana Sharma finds in Toru Dutt's poetry, as we will see below.

Uche Okeke *et al.* sought to "subject the conservative models of colonial art practice to a radical epistemological shift" that would take the formal aspects from European art and find for them a new conceptual hybridized language to "valorize and reinsert the aesthetic resources of pan-Nigerian traditions within the contemporary conditions of postcolonial subjectivity" (Okeke-Agulu 2010, 506). The drive towards political freedom and cultural autonomy motivating the Nigerian Art Society's hybridized goal defines, for many, the grounding conditions for postcolonial theory. Chika Okeke-Agulu joins Kobena Mercer in pointing to a need to study the "broad historical period of modernism between the 1890s and 1980s" (Okeke-Agulu 2010, 506) rather than skipping over all that to get to the "now-fashionable preoccupation with postcolonial visual cultures and non-Western contemporary artists who mine the colonial cultural archive". Noting that modernity and modernism are not "universally singular in terms of their history, meaning and characteristics" (Okeke-Agulu 2010, 507), Okeke-Agulu suggests the broadening terms "vernacular modernities" (Bruce Knauft), "alternative modernities" (Dilip Parameshwar Gaonkar), "cosmopolitan modernisms" (Mercer) or his own preferred "postcolonial modernism". The creation of new formal styles is a tall order, and perhaps a marriage of styles is as authentically postcolonial. Aside from stand-outs like Salman Rushdie and Kamau Brathwaite and various others (mostly poets, perhaps because of this form's intense concentration on the arrangement of words and the effects of sounds crucial to the work's impact), one might note a comparative lack of narrative experimentation in many postcolonial novels that regularly appear on academic syllabi, and characterize them as thematically vibrant but stylistically conservative, closer to the nineteenth-century realist tradition than to twentieth- or twenty-first-century postmodern literary techniques. But the same might be said for some of the art that Okeke-Agulu celebrates, like Simon Okeke's, the originality of whose pictures "does not depend on any radical formal invention but instead derives from their darkly intriguing subject matter" (Okeke-Agulu 2010, 518). Whereas Uche Okeke and Nwoko invented "a new formal style based on exploration of the formal qualities found in the archive of indigenous Nigerian art", for Simon Okeke and Yusuf Grillo "the ideological basis of natural synthesis did not warrant or necessarily imply the extraction of new forms from specific indigenous artistic traditions" (Okeke-Agulu 2010, 518–519). Chika Okeke-Agulu's implication clearly avoids valorizing any of the artists as a purer embodiment of the "synthesis" and "variegated aesthetic" (Okeke-Agulu 2010, 523) he describes as postcolonial Nigerian modernism.

Following Michael Taussig's lead, Okeke-Agulu argues that part of the recuperation of pre-colonial culture centered on a prior "principle of complementarity" (Okeke-Agulu 2010, 524) that saw Western Manichean binarisms as foreign impositions, and thus allowed the postcolonial modernists in Nigeria and in much of Africa to embrace and adapt elements of European styles without a sense of cultural effacement or individual erasure, much as is done in other postcolonial artistic environs in the ambivalent mimicry that Bhabha (1994), Jeyifo (2001, 117) and others have described.

POSTCOLONIAL STYLE

In the view of Simon Gikandi, the works in question are produced in an ongoing time of melancholy that produces its own "postcolonial mimesis" seeking, on the one hand, to "recover the experiences of the colonized from the objective and totalized regimen of the imperium" but, on the other hand, also "call[ing] attention to the limits of any attempt to contain this world in literary form" (Gikandi 2011, 176). As records of states in formation after a time of trauma, postcolonial texts take the master's languages and literary traditions as but a portion of the *donnée* from which they advance a national literary heritage. Ngũgĩ wa Thiong'o, for example, notes that, because "an important history of orature is the migration of its main genres across languages, cultures, and territories", there needs to be more focus on its "constituent elements and worldview, along with their migratory patterns into new regions and cultures and into different aesthetic genres" (Ngũgĩ 2012, 85). The resulting question of the proper role of literary form or genre in a postcolonial state is of interest principally because it situates literature coming from former European colonies in a larger global discussion of the evolution of form in literary studies and the proper place for aesthetics in nation-building.

Postcolonial criticism's dilemma in considering a political history through its literary response forces its theorists belatedly to resist co-optation by literature departments, to fight relegation to the dustbin of history by globalization and to assert its significance against the social sciences – let alone against the hard sciences (cf. Hawley 2010; Hitchcock 2003, 306). Against this backdrop, questions related to its subject matter can be threatening, but questions of postcolonial form emerge as similarly challenging. In their collection on "innovative uses of genre and form in this particularly fraught and irresolute historical moment", Patrick Crowley and Jane Hiddleston's contributors "endeavor to do no less than to ask *how* literature itself thinks, and what it can do, when it is created in these most fractious and unsettled historical circumstances" (Crowley and Hiddleston 2011, 8; emphasis added). Peter Hitchcock elsewhere considers the possibility of postcoloniality itself being a genre, one that must undo every manifestation of classification against which it is precipitate, yet expire at its own rendezvous of victory (Hitchcock 2003, 299). Hitchcock ultimately posits that there "is no genre of postcoloniality", but he offers many forms that the object of its study has historically taken for those who enter its cloudy environs: colonial discourse analysis (the trinity: Said, Spivak, Bhabha); the countering pragmatic and political analysis of Marxist inspiration (Achebe, el Saadawi, *et al.*); "commonwealth criticism", demonstrable in William New's *Critical Writings on Commonwealth Literatures: A Selective Bibliography to 1970, with a List of Theses and Dissertations* (1975); anti-postcolonial postcolonialism (some of the work of Anne McClintock, Aijaz Ahmad, Arif Dirlik, Sara Suleri), which objects to the inadvertent taming of a postcolonial impulse that results from canonizing it in college syllabi and in many of the neatly packaged anthologies for the classroom; the originary founding fathers (Césaire, Fanon, *et al.*); the "metonymic", meaning the move to multiculturalism or globalization as the prior overarching angle of analysis, practiced by social scientists. But Hitchcock notes that these approaches are not genres as such, though they may be "subgenres" of the essay, the tract, the manifesto, etc. (Hitchcock 2003, 302).[1] Postcoloniality, he suggests, "is so tied to the fortunes of genre that make up its object that it proceeds by a logic of utterance that is its agon" (Hitchcock 2003, 300).

For those in literature departments, whether in the West or in former colonies, questioning the object of study has been *de rigueur*, but now, viewed through the lens of aesthetics, this question more frequently addresses the form in which "the object of study" is presented. Intuitively we imagine we know the genres that postcolonialism takes as its object of study, but Hitchcock asks a prior question that introduces some uncertainty to our presumed knowledge. "What if", he writes,

> postcoloniality were read as a more thoroughgoing critique of the genres of such expressivity? What if its particular impetuosity about genre itself represented generic distinctiveness, a sort of supergenre that challenged the logic of classification in genre and beyond ...?
>
> (Hitchcock 2003, 302)

Thus the object of postcolonial theory is not, for example, the sonnet but is instead "the logic of classification" itself. And even though he tentatively posits that "we know almost instinctively" that one real genre of postcoloniality is the novel, he admits the shifting sands of such assertions. On the one hand, the "autocritique" of the "classificatory register" of various genres is a healthy disturbance of the stasis of, for example, the novel, and, on the other hand, no one can step outside of his or her historical moment to fully "measure the crisis to which their critique responds" (Hitchcock 2003, 302). Hitchcock concludes that "the more one examines variations in the genre the more one has to concede that postcolonial writers have wrested the novel from itself" and that, in fact, "the postcolonial novel exists because it is in the nature of the genre to provide form for content that challenges what constitutes the genre" (Hitchcock 2003, 303). Perhaps what Hitchcock has in mind is a modern-day example of what, some decades ago, was described as a self-consuming generic artifact (Fish 1972). But Hitchcock too boldly asserts that "decolonization implies a broad range of delinking from oppression that includes a break from genre's own history" (Hitchcock 2003, 308). Variation in genre, yes; hybridized genres, yes. Re-creation *ab ovo*, unlikely.[2] Instead, let us posit a carnivalesque exuberance that gives a nod towards generic norms handed down from the colonial master, but that then plays games not only with the master language but also with the master's literary primer – making gestures toward the sonnet, for example, but subverting the logic of the Shakespearean couplet or the Petrarchan conversation between the octet and the sestet. Echoing queer theory, Hitchcock contends that the "generic distinction [of postcoloniality] is to question genre ... as a means to dissolve the very classifications and divisions that have produced it" (Hitchcock 2003, 327).

He is, of course, not the first to draw this conclusion. Though it has been a good many years since Fredric Jameson published *The Political Unconscious: Narrative as a Socially Symbolic Act* (1981), in which formal literary expectations were recognized as historical evidence of a particular society and the implied relations among its classes, Patrick Crowley observes as recently as 2012 that "some theorists [still] hope to avoid the marchlands of generic indeterminacy" (Crowley 2012, 80), but probably shouldn't.[3] Jameson had suggested that genres were products of their age. They evolve, and other forms that arguably deviate from their structural norms are as descriptive of the age as are the canonical genres they violate. As Bart Moore-Gilbert summarizes Jameson's argument, form "constitutes 'the political unconscious' of the text and it is the politically responsible critic's role to read symptomatically for indices of its relation to social reality and the political forces which configure that reality" (Moore-Gilbert 2012, 91). The critic has this task because, as Hitchcock puts it, "All genres [...] cannot themselves measure the crisis to which their critique responds" (Hitchcock 2003, 302). It is an ongoing argument as to whether postcolonial critics can see the crises, but as Gikandi suggests, the procrustean limitations of the colonizers' literary genres might be a good focal point to examine the tensions in question.

In her elaboration of Homi Bhabha's complicated analysis of "the temporally conceived pauses or time-lags that fall between modernity as an epochal event/symbol and modernity as a reiterative, circulating sign/meaning in the everyday" (Sharma 2003, 98), Alpana Sharma concludes with him that "the colonized subject as witness of the 'time-lag' of modernity is privileged to speak supplementarily, *beside* the 'Great Event' that then gets estranged and reinscribed differently" (Sharma 2003, 99) – that is, the colonized subject is overlooked, unheard and uninscribed in the history of modernity even as it transpires around him/her. Among the interesting questions raised by this emphasis on the discursive (in what is arguably a primarily political event) is: If one can temporarily bypass that rather large elephant (the political nature of the Great Event, as well as of many lesser ones), then what is the form that this "different" reinscription might take or historically has taken? Is there a postcolonial form in which those without voice can inscribe their account of that Event? Sharma's own interests lead her in a somewhat different direction, applying Bhabha's schema to a nineteenth-century female author and concluding that the "interstitial" position of Toru Dutt (an Indian poet who wrote in English, 1856–77) in Indian society enabled her (forced her?) to "seriously play with the patriarchal norms of her time" and, in a queer reading of that enablement, shaped her "refusal to settle neatly into only one side of any number of binary relations: female/male, colonized/colonizer, Indian/Western, original/imitative, young/old, sheltered/'free' and so on" (Sharma 2003, 108). Provocative enough, but prompting again questions about the form(s) that this straddling of discourses (or power relations) enabled if, in fact, not only the content but also the reinscription was somehow different. Those formal points where Dutt's account and others like it diverge from the generic expressions of the British need more examination, with an eye to the resistant reading of modernity that these changes may sometimes open up.

EXCURSUS TWO: THE *TESTIMONIO*, MAGICAL REALISM AND THE NEOBAROQUE

If many, including recently Pascale Casanova, appear to agree that the dominant contemporary form in supposedly postcolonial nations "does not depend on any radical formal invention", does this imply the inevitability of realism? A recent collection of essays coming out of India claims that "[t]he fiction writers in the post-colonial period are obsessed with new kinds of realism" (Khan 2007, 7). However "new" these realisms may or may not be (social realism, psychological realism, historical realism, mythic realism and magic realism), and whatever impact they may have on their authors' styles and their choice or manipulation of genre, the "obsess[ion]" purportedly "determines the subjects of their fiction" (7). One assumes they are not genres in and of themselves, but if they in fact determine one's subject, perhaps they also necessitate a particular set of formal choices, i.e. this is the way to do magic realism and so forth.

In the special issue on the form of postcolonial African fiction that she edited for the journal *Novel*, Susan Andrade writes that "literary criticism of African novels ... has moved towards a celebration of anti-mimeticist writing" (2008, 196), and summarizes Casanova's argument as follows:

> Realism or neorealism is a sign of political and cultural impoverishment. Nationalism makes for realist works of art; realism itself is a non-autonomous and simple art form. Only when a regional or cultural entity has developed beyond realism to arrive at "literary autonomy" does a culture or state arrive at good art. (189)

Andrade notes the "tendency to privilege realism" (190) among the African critics Chinweizu, Jemie and Madubuike (1983), who demanded that literature be realist (and accessible), politically engaged and written in African languages, and who, in the postcolonial literature they valorized, sought specifically to counter European modernist experimentation. But, respond-ing to the 1983 *Bolekaja* school, Kwame Anthony Appiah warned against its enmeshment in "literary cultural nationalism" (Andrade 2008, 190) and valorized more typically European modernist experimentation whenever it appeared in African novels. Kumkum Sangari tried to find "a marriage of formalism and cultural nationalism that result[ed] in a laudatory reading of marvelous or magical realism" (Andrade 2008, 191), suggesting a need to defend something like magical realism from charges that it is a European imposition and (therefore) non-revolutionary. Nonetheless, countering the valorization of arguably postmodern techniques, Andrade concludes that "literary realism is a neglected mode in postcolonial literature" (2008, 197) for critics who do not have the patience to recognize that "realism makes visible individual histories in the flow of collective histories" (2008, 198) and these histories enact what Georg Lukács in his later writings recom-mended: novels that elucidate "the relation between interiority and action" (2008, 195).

How useful these days are ongoing competitions between modernism and realism in evaluating postcolonial literature – a confusing binary that Nicholas Brown describes as "an antinomy in desperate need of rethink-ing if not of jettisoning altogether" (Brown 2008, 1)? If Brown hits the mark, perhaps the now-familiar dismissal of African novels (among others from former European colonies) as just too realistic is missing the point. Recent students of modernism, for example, argue that the experimental works of modernism in the twentieth century "radically re-conceive the realist project rather than aborting it altogether" (Leslie 2007, 125). Bart Moore-Gilbert pooh-poohs the tendency evinced by some "to assume that aesthetic experimentalism is per se more politically engaged than work which conforms to received rules and conventions", and regrets that some critics feel a "compulsion to choose between Lukács's and Adorno's competing calibrations of the 'progressiveness' of Realism and Modernism respectively" (2012, 104).

Timothy Bewes frames the problematic of postcolonial studies as "a field defined not positively, by the presence of certain cultural motifs, identity formations, historical struggles, or emancipatory goals, but negatively, by an incommensurability that is materialized whenever such presences are produced or named as the object or the subject of a work" (Bewes 2011, 7). Whether or not this problematic can be read as a spur to creation, there is little doubt that it is a source of alienation (most visibly, one supposes, from those likely to purchase the product and, invisibly, from the writer's sense of an authentic self). Choosing an audience that includes both the colonized and the colonizer, and using the master's tools to transgress the master's various cultural hegemonies, comes at a price (cf. Lazarus 2011, 54). In the chronic anxiety towards artistic production that results, forms such as the *testimonio* and other oral-written hybrids work as revisionist histories of a people, or as personal confessions, or as magical realism that defies analysis as truth claims.[4] Has postcolonial criticism relied too easily on Western generic codes in its evaluation of genres as diverse as Rigoberta Menchú's autobiography, Indian *bhasha* literatures in English, various types of orature and novels responding to the Truth and Reconciliation Commission? One suspects that the aporia separating accounts of modernity written by the colonizer from those written by the colonized and expressed in subtle transgressions of an accepted form offer a productive area for future research in postcolonial studies.

For example, Moore-Gilbert singles out autobiography to consider whether its generic demands are "peculiar to Western man". He notes three defining laws undergirding the genre of autobiography in the West: the "unity and sovereignty of the autobiographical subject", the "coherent ... unfolding of the process by which that subject becomes constituted" and "the establishment of clearly defined borders around the autobiographical text" (2012, 93). But the Latina Feminist Group would seem to be testing these sorts of margins for this genre in the collected essays on Latina feminist *testimonios* in their book eloquently entitled *Telling to Live*. The volume "tells" a great deal in the subdivisions in its table of contents: "Genealogies of empowerment", "Alchemies of erasure", "The body re/members", "Passion, desires, and celebrations". Taken together, this is a collection of very individual accounts, idiosyncratic (if sharing significant commonalities of experience), clearly embodied in particular people with bodily memories who seek a voice and cathartic in bringing formerly silent suffering up from personal oblivion and into welcoming community. Does the *testimonio*, far more efficiently than the novel, forcefully cut to the chase and explore what postcolonial fiction is "really" all about: the exposition of personal suffering and the trajectory of individuals into the light, into self-conscious agency? This is certainly one of the questions at the heart of the ongoing controversy over representation and "truth" in this non-Western genre (Barnet 1969; González Echevarría 1985; Beverley and Zimmerman 1990; Yúdice 1991; Gugelberger 1996).

And yet, clearly building on the controversy over Rigoberta Menchú's account and the role of her transcriber, the editors of *Telling to Live* note, first, that "scholars often see testimonies as dependent products" (2001, 13) and, second, that Latin American women's accounts "are seen as disclosures not of personal lives but rather of the political violence inflicted on whole communities" (2001, 13) so, they are in fact more like national allegories than one might initially have expected. Yet "the *testimoniantes* (subjects of the texts) admit that they withhold secrets about the culture or details of their personal lives that, for political reasons, are not revealed in the stories narrated" (2001, 13). The self-editing, the trickster-like manipulation of the "facts" of the narrative, even if filtered through a transcriber with his/her own agenda, allows for our speculation over the fictive nature of these testimonies. A story is being told, and the narrative that is being shaped is not completely dependent upon the haphazard nature of the facts of the narrator's life.

This arguably unreliable testimony to facts, as some have described Menchú's work, is valorized by Jessica Berman in postcolonial novels written by women, as well. In her view,

> critics have long missed the narrative complexity of ... female-authored texts, and at times have denigrated them for their departures from a more seamless realism. [But] these texts show some of the formal hallmarks we have long associated with European modernism: textual merging of fact and fiction; play with external and internal realities; disruptions of time and order of emplotment; attempts at new narrative perspectives ... and focus on the everyday life of ordinary figures. (2011, 143)

Cognizant of this personalized structure, the Latina Feminist Group set out to write a series of *testimonios* addressing a common set of issues, and first among them were the questions: "Why did we pursue higher education? What did we think we were doing? What was the enticement? What did we get out of it?" (2001, 13). This led to more probing questions: "How did collectivity and isolation figure in our lives? What was the process of resistance and recovery?" (2001, 14). These more painful questions arose because "for racialized ethnic women of subjugated peoples, achievement is always a double-edged sword". In constructing an academic persona, many of these women found that "professionalism", "objectivity" and "respectability" negated their humanity (2001, 14). In defense of such writing (cf. Beverley 2004), Moore-Gilbert decries "narrow, if not plainly ethnocentric, conceptions of what the autobiographical self consists of and how it should be written" (2012, 106).

On the other hand, readers of *testimonios* presume a stronger alignment with things that actually happened than they do when reading magical realist texts even if, like magical realism's realism, *testimonios'* testimony may be partly fabulous. Some time ago Stephen Slemon noted, first, that magic realism is an oxymoron, with the two words pointing towards two representational codes. But, originating in "cultures situated at the fringes of mainstream literary traditions" and removed from "established systems of generic classification" (Slemon 1988, 10), this may be a genre tailor-made for postcolonial work. The world of magic and the world of realism are "locked in a continuous dialectic with the 'other'", and this creates "disjunction within each of the separate discursive systems, rending them with gaps, absences, and silences" (Slemon 1988, 11) – echoing, I would suggest, the unspoken secrets and the group-persona that speaks in *testimonios*. Sounding very much like Slemon's analysis of magical realism, Santiago Colás writes that "it is not the testimonio's uncontaminated positing of some pure, truthful, native history that makes it so powerful, but rather its subversion of such a project" (Colás 1996, 170). Little wonder that recent work in Latin American literature resurrects the history of the infiltration of the European baroque in the New World by the iconographies and cultural signposts of the indigenous populations with whom the Jesuits and others worked in the *reducciones* (Chiampi 2001; Zamora 2010). One man's mimicry is another's resistance.

ON BEING READ BY POSTCOLONIAL LITERATURE

If, following the urging of Lazarus and others, the canon of texts acknowledged to be postcolonial is opened up, this would seem more or less to decide the question: no, there is not one postcolonial form, but there are many, some more suitable for this or that purpose for such writing, some more expressive of these human experiences in such situations, some more challenging to the reader or to social structures, etc., but all responsive to and reflective of the national consciousness at the time they were written. Walter Goebel and Saskia Schabio have edited a collection of essays that ask "how postcolonial texts have determined the evolution or emergence of specific formal innovations in narrative genres" (2013, 1). They begin by conceding that "in the field of postcolonial studies questions of subversion, parody, and mimesis have predominated over other aspects of aesthetic form" (1), and then go on to argue that "on the so-called margins [...] questions of self-definition and of the provincializing of the dominant discourses of Others will trigger off more clearly articulated aesthetic trajectories" (2). This will include returns to precolonial literary forms, and will require "a susceptibility for earlier forms of orature, myth, tale, and forms of communal storytelling [...] which were at a later stage individualized" (2). But, as Kevin Barry concludes in his study of the application of postcolonial theories to Irish literature, "it is timely to put a foot in that door and to question the sometimes baseless but always relentless critical systems which identify a specific aesthetic with a specific politics" (Barry 1996, 11). With regard to the dangers of a nativist return to earlier forms, for example, one notes Paolo Magagnoli's caution that "it is only by attending to the specificities of each work that it is possible to evaluate whether nostalgia is progressive or reactionary, critical or ideological, generative or sterile" (2011, 97).

Lazarus summarizes Jameson's suggestions that social disjunctions resultant from capitalist imperialism find a comfortable literary partner in the "generic discontinuities" (Jameson 1986, 83) of styles like magical realism, and he is very good at tackling head on the devalorization of realism in a lot of the postcolonial literature that heretofore has been broadly dismissed as unworthy of inclusion among the more experimental (and, some might argue, more postmodern)[5] literature exemplified by Salman Rushdie – as, in effect, a continuation of the nineteenth-century novel, which had already been replaced by a certain set of books that met the standards of so-called modernism.

Here we might ask the question with which Santiago Colás begins his essay in Georg Gugelberger's collection: "What's Wrong with Representation?" (2010). Lazarus points to someone like Mahasweta Devi, for example, and her effective use of "the resources of literary realism", including direct, indirect and free indirect speech and between "'internal' and 'external' narrativisation" (2011, 42), moving as well between "diegesis and sociological analysis" (2011, 43). He notes the techniques are used not so much for aesthetic purposes as instead for securing the reader's "commitment to the text" (2011, 47). Such a commitment arguably requires a prior commitment from the author to represent and give voice to socially dominated people.

Indeed, Jessica Berman has argued that much postcolonial fiction "destabilize[s] the division between partisanship and aesthetics … using narrative experimentation as a force of social activity, and grounding their formal resistance to consensus-based realism in their oppositional political engagement" (Berman 2011, 8–9). But while most postcolonial theorists would applaud a literature of commitment[6] that tries to do much more than entertain an elite educated audience, such representation of lower classes has become notoriously suspect for postcolonial theorists. Lazarus sees such navel-gazing and self-flagellation from postcolonial critics as premature because it identifies "the other" as solely the subaltern: "popular consciousness devolves to and is understood under the rubric of subalternity", he objects, "which is understood in turn as being constitutively beyond or outside of representation" (2011, 144).[7] For him, the task of a postcolonial novelist, on the other hand, is not the portrayal of only the so-called subaltern but more generally the portrayal of popular consciousness, which is not so completely other that its representation cannot be handled through realism. Just ask Elizabeth Gaskell or Honoré de Balzac or, Lazarus would likely argue, ask the majority of postcolonial (without the scare quotes) novelists. "The writer's success or failure", he writes, "… is not solely a function of 'authenticity' at the level of content, but also of imagination, dexterity, and telling judgement in the selection and manipulation of the formal resources of fiction" (2011, 142). Nicholas Harrison concludes his study of the need for a more careful study of the literary components of postcolonial writing by urging critics to give "due weight to the historical complexities of reception" and to remain "alert to that indeterminacy that marks literature as such" (Harrison 2003, 150). These seem like very traditional critical norms, which render them daring in the context of postcolonial theory preoccupied by poststructuralist norms of valuation. Berman takes Mulk Raj Anand as a counter-example to such postmodern critical norms, analyzing the protagonist in *Untouchable* and noting that Anand's novels "not only challenge the bildungsroman tradition" but also "build a narrative politics out of ... a political mentality cognizant of the perspectives and voices of others and derived from within the web of stories in which we are situated" (2011, 93). Berman is very much in line with Moore-Gilbert, who references Jameson's historicizing of genre to argue that "postcolonial re-articulations of Western generic conventions project 'value-systems' which are materially consequential to the extent that they seek to galvanize readers to reimagine the world as a preliminary to changing it" (Moore-Gilbert 2012, 92). Postcolonial critics and other readers of postcolonial literature, one surmises, can pass through such a comparatively thin membrane of alterity and imagine another place that they might not only help bring about but also inhabit.

NOTES

1. A helpful and concise summary of the debates between the "discursive" theorists and the "materialists" is offered by Vijay Devadas and Chris Prentice in the *Borderlands* special issue on postcolonial politics.
2. *Pace* Hitchcock, who observes that "the English department has been a bastion of genre, and what questions genre also questions its raison d'être" (Hitchcock 2003, 309). In his favor, I would note, is the expanding inclination to move to English Studies and away from historical "coverage" models for departmental curricula.
3. Discussing Francophone texts that are "not autobiographies but nor are they novels in the classical realist tradition", Crowley argues "pragmatic notions [of genre] are necessarily situated within a tradition of Western genre theory that has perhaps less dominion over texts written beyond metropolitan France" (Crowley 2004, 91).
4. Cultural rhetorical strategies unfamiliar to Anglophone critics may offer a window on varying expectations within other discourse communities. See, for example, Tricia Serviss's recent work on the *coadyuvante* (Serviss 2013).
5. Cf. Hawley, 1995. Lazarus directs our attention to Laura Moss's study of this devalorization of realism (Moss 2000, 158) as well as Dominc Head's (Head 2002, 172; Lazarus 2011, 82).
6. Cf. Sartre, 1988.

7. Lazarus favorably compares Said's views to the "austere" ones of Spivak (144). Brent Hayes Edwards perhaps balances this criticism, observing "Spivak has been one of the few theorists to articulate a methodological vision for postcolonial studies that would include the literary without sacrificing an attention to the social sciences and, in particular, to the complexities of a critique of capitalist globalization" (Edwards 2004, 3).

REFERENCES

Andrade, Susan. 2008. "Introduction: Special Issue on The Form of Postcolonial African Fiction". *Novel: A Forum on Fiction* 41.2–3: 189–199.

Attridge, Derek. 2004. *The Singularity of Literature*. London: Routledge.

Bahri, Deepika. 2003. *Native Intelligence: Aesthetics, Politics and Postcolonial Literature*. Minneapolis: University of Minnesota Press.

Barnet, Miguel. 1969. "*La novella-testimonio: socio-literatura*". *Unión* 4 (October): 99–122.

Barry, Kevin. 1996. "Critical Notes on Post-colonial Aesthetics". *Irish Studies Review* 14: 2–11.

Bartolovich, Chrystal and Neil Lazarus, eds. 2002. *Marxism, Modernity, and Postcolonial Studies*. Cambridge: Cambridge University Press.

Berman, Jessica. 2011. *Modernist Commitments: Ethics, Politics, and Transnational Modernisms*. New York: Columbia University Press.

Beverley, John. 2004. *Testimonio: On the Politics of Truth*. Minneapolis and London: University of Minnesota Press.

Beverley, John and Marc Zimmerman. 1990. *Literature and Politics in the Central American Revolutions*. Austin: University of Texas Press.

Bewes, Timothy. 2011. *The Event of Postcolonial Shame*. Princeton: Princeton University Press.

Bhabha, Homi. 1994. "Of Mimicry and Man: The Ambivalence of Colonial Discourse". In *The Location of Culture*, 85–92. New York: Routledge.

Black, Shameem. 2009. "Microloans and Micronarratives: Sentiment for a Small World". *Public Culture* 21.2: 269–292.

Brennan, Timothy. 1997. *At Home in the World: Cosmopolitanism Now*. Cambridge: Harvard University Press.

Brown, Nicholas. 2005. *Utopian Generations: The Political Horizons of Twentieth-Century Literature*. Princeton: Princeton University Press.

Brown, Nicholas. 2008. "African Literature, Modernism, and the Problem of Political Subjectivity". *NOVEL: A Forum on Fiction*. 41. 2–3: 264–278. http://kellogg. nd.edu/projects/FLAD/pdfs/Brown,%20Nicholas.pdf.

Chiampi, Irlemar. 2001. *Barroco y modernidad*. Mexico City: Fondo de Cultura Económica.

Colás, Santiago. 1996. "What's Wrong with Representation?" In *The Real Thing: Testimonial Discourse and Latin America*, edited by Georg Gugelberger, 161–171. Durham and London: Duke University Press.

Crowley, Patrick. 2004. "The Etat Civil: Post/colonial Identities and Genre". *French Forum* 29.3: 79–94.

Crowley, Patrick and Jane Hiddleston, eds. 2012. *Postcolonial Poetics: Genre and Form*. Liverpool: Liverpool University Press.

Devadas, Vijay and Chris Prentice. 2007. "Postcolonial Politics". *Borderlands* ejournal 6.2. http://www.borderlands.net.au/vol6no2_2007/device_editorial.htm. 29 May 2013.

Dirlik, Arif. 1994. "The Postcolonial Aura: Third World Criticism in the Age of Global Capitalism". *Critical Inquiry* 20. 329–356.

During, Simon. 1998. "Postcolonialism and Globalisation: A Dialectical Relation after All?" *Postcolonial Studies* 1.1: 31–47.

Edwards, Brent Hayes. 2004. "Introduction: The Genres of Postcolonialism". *Social Text* 78: 1–15.

Fish, Stanley E. 1972. *Self-Consuming Artifacts*. Berkeley: University of California Press.

Fraser, Robert. 2000. *Lifting the Sentence: A Poetics of Postcolonial Fiction*. Manchester: Manchester University Press.

Gikandi, Simon. 2011. "Theory After Postcolonial Theory: Rethinking the Work of Mimesis". In *Theory After 'Theory'*, edited by Jane Elliott and Derek Attridge, 163–178. London and New York: Routledge.

Goebel, Walter and Saskia Schabio, eds. 2013. *Locating Postcolonial Narrative Genres*. London: Routledge.

González Echevarría, Roberto. 1985. *The Voice of the Masters: Writing and Autobiography in Modern Latin American Literature*. Austin: University of Texas Press.

Gugelberger, Georg M., ed. 1996. *The Real Thing: Testimonial Discourse and Latin America*. Durham and London: Duke University Press.

Harrison, Nicholas. 2003. *Postcolonial Criticism: History, Theory and the Work of Fiction*. Cambridge: Polity.

Hawley, John C. 2010. 1995. "Ben Okri's Sprit-Child: *Abiku* Migration and Postmodernity". *Research in African Literatures* 26.1: 30–39.

Hawley, John C. "The Colonizing Impulse of Postcolonial Theory". *Modern Fiction Studies* 56.4: 769–787.

Head, Dominic. 2002. *The Cambridge Introduction to Modern British Fiction 1950–2000*. Cambridge: Cambridge University Press.

Hitchcock, Peter. 2003. "The Genre of Postcoloniality". *New Literary History* 34.2: 299–330.

Jameson, Fredric. 1981. *The Political Unconscious: Narrative as a Socially Symbolic Act*. Ithaca, NY: Cornell University Press.

Jameson, Fredric. 1986. "Third-World Literature in the Era of Multinational Capitalism". *Social Text* 15: 65–88.

Jeyifo, Biodun. 2001. "Realm of Value in Literature Art: Interview with Wole Soyinka, 1985". In *Conversations with Wole Soyinka: Freedom and Complexity*. Jackson: University Press of Mississippi.

Khan, M. Q. and Bijay Kumar Das, eds. 2007. *Studies in Postcolonial Literature*. New Delhi: Atlantic.

Latina Feminist Group, The (Luz del Alba Acevedo *et al*). 2001. *Telling to Live: Latina Feminist Testimonios*. Durham and London: Duke University Press.

Lazarus, Neil. 2011. *The Postcolonial Unconscious*. Cambridge: Cambridge University Press.

Leslie, Esther. 2007. "Interrupted Dialogues of Realism and Modernism: 'The fact of new forms of life, already born and active'". In *Adventures in Realism*, edited by Matthew Beaumont, 125–141. Malden, MA: Blackwell.

Magagnoli, Paolo. 2011. "Critical Nostalgia in the Art of Joachim Koester". *Oxford Art Journal* 34.1: 97–121.

Moore-Gilbert, Bart. 2012. "A Concern Peculiar to Western Man? Postcolonial Reconsiderations of Autobiography as Genre". In *Postcolonial Poetics: Genre and Form*, edited by Patrick Crowley and Jane Hiddleston, 91–108. Liverpool: Liverpool University Press.

Moss, Laura. 2000. "Can Rohinton Mistry's Realism Rescue the Novel?" In *Postcolonizing the Commonwealth: Studies in Literature and Culture*, edited by R. Smith, 157–166. Waterloo, IA: Wilfred Laurier University Press.

Ngũgĩ wa Thiong'o. 2012. *Globalectics: Theory and the Politics of Knowing*. New York: Columbia University Press.

Okeke, Uche. 1982. "Natural Synthesis". In *Art in Development: A Nigerian Perspective*. Nimo, Nigeria: Documentation Center, Asele Institute.

Okeke-Agulu, Chika. 2010. "The Art Society and the Making of Postcolonial Modernism in Nigeria". *South Atlantic Quarterly* 109.3: 505–527.

Parry, Benita. 2004. *Postcolonial Studies: A Materialist Critique*. London: Routledge.

Said, Edward. 1994. *Representations of the Intellectual*. London: Vintage.

Said, Edward. 1989. Foreword to E. Khoury, *Little Mountain*, trans. M. Tabet, ix–xxi. Minneapolis: University of Minnesota Press.

Sartre, Jean-Paul. 1988. *What Is Literature? and Other Essays*. Cambridge: Harvard University Press.

Serviss, Tricia. 2013. "Femicide and Rhetorics of *Coadyuvante* in Ciudad Juárez: Valuing Rhetorical Traditions in the Americas". *College English* 75.6: 582–607.

Sharma, Alpana. 2003. "In-Between Modernity: Toru Dutt (1856–1877) from a Postcolonial Perspective". In *Women's "Experience" of Modernity, 1875–1945*, edited by Ann Ardis and Leslie Lewis, 97–110. Baltimore: Johns Hopkins University Press.

Siddiqi, Yumna. 2008. *Anxieties of Empire and the Fiction of Intrigue*. New York: Columbia University Press.

Slemon, Stephen. 1988. "Magic Realism as Post-Colonial Discourse". *Canadian Literature* 116 (Spring): 9–24. http://cinema2.arts.ubc.ca/units/canlit/pdfs/articles/canlit116-Magic(Slemon).pdf. 26 January 2014.

Sorensen, Eli Park. 2010. *Postcolonial Studies and the Literary: Theory, Interpretation and the Novel*. New York: Palgrave Macmillan.

Spivak, Gayatri. 2003. *Death of a Discipline*. New York: Columbia University Press.

Yúdice, George. 1991. "*Testimonio* and Postmodernism". *Latin American Perspectives* 18, No. 3 (summer): 15–31.

Zamora, Lois Parkinson and Monika Kaup, eds. 2010. *Baroque New Worlds: Representation, Transculturation, Counterconquest*. Durham, NC: Duke University Press.

Part II

Case Studies
Geocultures, Topographies, Occlusions

[handwritten margin note: really inhibiting]

[handwritten note above INTRODUCTION: that these have been spaces of oversight – perhaps because they fell mostly outside of the British imperium?]

INTRODUCTION

Having framed the question of what postcolonial theory doesn't say in terms of institutions, disciplines and aesthetics in Section I, the middle section of our volume investigates those sites where postcolonial theory falls silent. Accordingly, topographies and toponyms – Cuba, Germany, Palestine, Eastern Europe, Zimbabwe – are foregrounded not only as markers of a distressing failure of communication, but also as the loci of possible theoretical formulations and transformations to come.

The section opens with a searing indictment by Patrick Williams on postcolonial theory's ongoing inability to say "Palestine", despite the central place it occupies in the life and work of Edward Said, one of the founding figures of postcolonial studies. Like Said, Williams reminds us that such silences are not coincidental; they depend on the active collaboration of writers and institutions, governments and armies. The conundrum that Williams raises is not so much the absence as the misreading of Palestine in relation to postcolonial studies, either through the frameworks used to advance theoretical arguments or through the deliberate mis-characterization (one is tempted to say *méconnaissance*) of Palestine. The way forward, Williams asserts, consists of reversing the process of archive destruction and erasure, on the one hand, and – in line with John C. Hawley's arguments in Section I – acknowledging the uses of form in the arts of resistance on the other.

Ashleigh Harris treats the recent history of violent land reclamation in Zimbabwe and its mediatic representation as the last horizon of white accountability for the colonial past. Comparisons of Mugabe to Hitler and white farmers to Hitler's victims recreate colonial modes of behavior that distort, rather than help us understand, contemporary Zimbabwe by trapping its observers in a rut composed of outdated beliefs and values. Worse yet, for Harris, postcolonial theory is structurally complicit with the ideas and actions that such values engender, perpetuating a dangerous form of imperialist nostalgia.

Alison Fraunhar's analysis of the performative dimension of *mulataje* – a term she uses in contradistinction to the widely used *mestizaje* – foregrounds the interdependence between categories of race and ideology in Cuba.

Ranging across a number of cultural events and a series of performative occasions, Fraunhar presents the reader with a history of Cuba as seen through *mulataje* in a way that disturbs both national ideologies and disciplinary frameworks, adding a grounded complexity to our understanding of cultural production.

For Eva Bischoff, the political mythologies that grew out of the presence of African soldiers in Europe following World War I furnish the occasion for a deconstruction of the hoary opposition between "civilized" white men and African "cannibals". In her essay, Weimar Germany emerges as the locus both of a postwar and post-imperial race hysteria, aided and abetted by routine claims of sexual violence and cannibalism perpetrated by African soldiers on hapless white German victims. By juxtaposing the language of such claims with the growing field of sexual pathology and its application to the populations of Europe, Bischoff demonstrates the mutually constitutive nature of such discourses and those that redefine masculinity in interwar Germany.

The section closes with Cristina Şandru's meditation on the place of postcolonial theory in the postcommunist universe. The disjunctions and fractures that characterize post-communist culture, caught as it is between a history of totalitarian failures and the brutal contemporary imposition of late capitalism, suggest comparisons and continuities with the locations that have hitherto been the object of postcolonial analysis. And yet, Şandru suggests, East-Central Europe has been routinely overlooked by postcolonial theory. Greater scrutiny of the region, its history and culture would open up useful vistas of thought and argument, ending the now outdated division of the world into First, Second and Third, or an over-simplistic North/South binary. In doing so, Şandru responds to the theoretical positions presented by Claire Westall and Simon Obendorf in the first section of this volume.

5 Gaps, Silences and Absences
Palestine and Postcolonial Studies

Patrick Williams

[handwritten: Such a welcome and necessary article]

[handwritten vertical note: ABSOLUTELY and again a materialist reading]

It is, at the very least, anomalous. Worse than that, it is embarrassing. Indeed, there is a strong case for regarding it as nothing less than shameful. "It" is the gap, silence or absence that Palestine has constituted within postcolonial studies. It is anomalous, firstly, in relation to Edward Said. Palestine was centrally important in the life and work of Said. Said has been centrally important in the development of postcolonial studies. How does it happen, then, that Palestine is not, and has not been, centrally important in postcolonial studies? That absence (more than any other, perhaps) is, or should be, deeply embarrassing for a discipline that likes to think of itself as critically insightful, politically savvy and the like, but which is incomprehensibly ignoring the most striking contemporary example of brutally-enforced colonialism. To the extent that the situation in Palestine represents arguably the greatest ethical scandal of the last half century, then the near-total silence of postcolonial studies on the subject is indeed shameful.[1] The discipline is, of course, far from alone in that silence, and this paper will attempt to address some of the modalities and the causes of that silencing and its accompanying absences. This is not the first time that I have voiced such misgivings but, as Said pointed out on many occasions, one of the sad facts about engaging with the Question of Palestine is that basic positions need to be repeated – and repeated.

For a (slightly) earlier generation of theorists, gaps, silences and absences were typically seen as the markers of ideology at work, especially in texts. In *A Theory of Literary Production*, Pierre Macherey famously offers a Marxist analysis of the relationship between ideology and the work of literature, the latter being unthinkable without the former. For Macherey, ideology becomes detectable at those points where discursive faultlines – gaps, silences and absences – indicate the difficulty, perhaps the impossibility, of disguising any longer the ideological stratum. In addition, it is important to be aware of ideology as built into material processes and social and historical circumstances, and the way in which these relate to the text.

> In fact, a true analysis does not remain within its object, paraphrasing what has already been said; analysis confronts the silences, the denials and the resistance in the object – not that compliant implied discourse which offers itself to discovery, but that condition which makes the

> work possible, which precedes the work so absolutely that it cannot
> be found in the work.
>
> (Macherey 1978, 150)

The question of what is said, and not said, is central to Macherey's analysis, and in his discussion of Balzac's novel *Les Paysans*, he offers the following thought: "If one is going to speak against the people, effectively, one must speak *of* the people: they must be seen, given form, *allowed to speak*" (Macherey 1978, 265, emphasis in the original). This is interesting, because it appears to run so strongly counter to the way in which Zionist ideology operates. For the latter, the primary correlates are something like "There are no people; they cannot speak", and, related to that, "The land is empty; the land is ours". To the extent that Palestinians must, willy-nilly, be seen or heard, then it should be as little and as badly as possible, in order to approximate as far as possible to the silent/absent premise. There is an interesting tension between, on the one hand, the remarkably blatant nature of Zionist ideology and, on the other, the remarkable amount of effort put into pretending that it is not there, still less actively and aggressively put into practice in the dispossession of the Palestinian people. How these relate to, and work themselves out in, the context of Palestine is, however, a question much larger than the ability of this paper to address, though we will see a number of examples of interaction of ideological formations and material practices in their impact on Palestinians.

The making silent and absent of the Palestinians is, of course, part of a long and unsavory history, only a little of which can be alluded to here. From the time of the papal edict that created the idea of the *terra nullius*, or empty land, unproblematically available for settlement and annexation, colonialists – potential or actual – have demonstrated a remarkable ability to convince themselves that the land they covet is happily empty of inconvenient inhabitants. While that might seem comprehensible in the context of the prevalent mindsets of the sixteenth or seventeenth century, for example in the case of North America, its use in the middle of the twentieth century in relation to Palestine is more shocking, though it does provide a striking example of the ability of ideology to survive across the centuries, regardless of the facts that stand in its way. The Orientalist discourse of nineteenth-century travelers to Palestine,[2] scarcely able to recognize the presence of a Palestinian population or to grant them decently human status, prepares the ground for Zionism and its range of tactics – discursive/ideological and material/military – for making the Palestinians "disappear", and this is supported by British colonial attitudes. As Said comments in *The Question of Palestine*, "[B]oth the British imperialist and the Zionist vision are united in playing down and even cancelling out the Arabs in Palestine as somehow secondary and negligible. Both raise the moral importance of the visions very far above the mere presence of natives on a piece of immensely significant territory" (Said 1992, 18). The best-known of the Zionist ideological claims in this regard is no doubt Israel Zangwill's formulation, "a land without a people, for a people without a land", where the debatable nature of the latter assertion pales into complete insignificance in the face of the complete mendacity of the former. Another of the most resilient claims is that the Israelis were "making the desert bloom", in the apparent absence either of a settled indigenous population or of any productive use of the land by them. Both aspects, it scarcely needs to be said, were not true.[3] Both, nevertheless, continue to be repeated, even inflated, not least by the most influential voices in the land, such as the former Israeli President Shimon Peres, speaking very recently: "I remember how it all began. The whole state of Israel is a millimetre of the whole Middle East. A statistical error, barren and disappointing land, swamps in the North, desert in the South, two lakes, one dead, and an overrated river. No natural resources apart from malaria. There was nothing here. And now we have the best agriculture in the world? This is a miracle: a land built by people" (*Maariv*, 14 April 2013).

The most masterly combination of the ideological and the material occurs in 1948, when, as the Israeli tanks roll into Palestinian towns and villages, they are found to be – remarkably, almost miraculously – empty. Israeli (ideological) explanations for this include: the inhabitants simply vanished; they ran away; they were told to leave by radio broadcasts from the Arab armies approaching to fight the Israelis. Israeli material practices aimed at producing the desired emptiness ranged from leafleting and loudspeaker campaigns telling the Palestinians to leave, to massacring the inhabitants of villages who did not leave quickly enough (and using reports of the massacres – especially of Deir Yassin – to terrify others into leaving). The land was then made more "empty" by the systematic destruction of the depopulated villages, which had the additional advantage of perpetuating the absence of the former inhabitants.[4]

In 1950, Israel introduced the Law of Absentee Property, whereby any Palestinians who were not present (having previously miraculously vanished in the face of the Israeli military advance) when the Israelis assessed the population and landholdings, were entered into the Kafkaesque category of the "Present Absentee" and forfeited their land, which eventually came to constitute something like seventy percent of the totality of Israel. Many of the present absentees, including the family of Mahmoud Darwish, lingered as liminal figures on the border of the newly established state, repeatedly attempting to cross it to return to what they still considered as home, and as a result risking being shot as "infiltrators". It is tempting to see Palestine as an Absent Presence, haunting the borders of postcolonial studies from which it has been incomprehensibly and unjustly excluded, and which it makes sporadic attempts to infiltrate.[5]

In an interview, Darwish talks about the situation in Palestine/Israel as "a struggle between two memories". Here, arguably, we have something like the struggle between two silences. Firstly, there is the silence of the Palestinians: the silence of the absent, the traumatized, the dead; the silence of the emptied land, the unheard, the speechless; the silence of the proscribed, the gagged, the archiveless. Secondly, there is the silence of the Others, including the silence of denial, of ignorance, of coercion; the silence of partiality, of laziness, of cowardice. All of these silences have their own histories; all require analysis.

The archiveless status of the Palestinians has been carefully constructed and maintained by the Israelis at least since 1948, when tens of thousands of books from major Palestinian libraries and collections were seized. Since then, all forms of archive have been subject to seizure and or destruction. These include the administrative, the cultural and the historical/archaeological. At the administrative level, the Israelis have, for example, repeatedly removed or destroyed paper and computer hard-drive records from the Palestinian Authority. They have also removed the records from human-rights groups such as Addameer, most recently in December 2012 (*Electronic Intifada*, 11 Dec 2012). A range of cultural archives have suffered. In addition to the books just mentioned, the Palestinian film archive that the PLO had been assembling disappeared after the siege of Beirut in 1982; cinemas in the West Bank and Gaza were closed down in the 1980s; the offices of perhaps the most prestigious Palestinian journal, *Al-Karmel*, edited at the time by Darwish, were raided and their records destroyed. Notionally the most visible archive destruction has occurred in the area of history and archaeology, though that visibility does not necessarily occasion much political or media comment. From 1948 onwards, physical remains deemed not to be Jewish, or related to Jewish history, have been destroyed – sometimes so wantonly and excessively that even Israeli officials were driven to protest. Priceless sculptures from the city of Caesarea were destroyed by the army, in spite of promises to spare them. Famous "archaeologists" such as Moshe Dayan ordered the dynamiting of 1,000-year old mosques, including the one where the head of the Prophet Muhammad's grandson, Ali, was said to be buried. Remarkably – or perhaps not – the practices of destruction and obliteration still continue, as in the move, despite petitions to the UN and UNESCO, to destroy a Muslim cemetery in Jerusalem, said to contain the graves of companions of the Prophet, in order to build a Jewish "Museum of Tolerance" (*Electronic Intifada*, 25 July 2011).

Even the much-vaunted discipline of Israeli archaeology can be as barbarically destructive as the military, with Dayan embodying both sides of the dichotomy. An article in *Ha'aretz*, commenting on a recent publication (Kletter 2005), says:

> Nevertheless, the story of archaeology comes across in his book to no small degree as one of destruction: the utter destruction of towns and villages, the destruction of an entire culture – its present but also its past, from 3,000-year-old Hittite reliefs to synagogues razed in Arab quarters, from a rare Roman mausoleum (which was damaged but spared from destruction at the last minute) to fortresses at that were blown up one after the other.
>
> (Rapoport 2007)

Needless to say, the obliteration of Palestinian voices from the past has an enormous impact on the ability of Palestinians in the present to make themselves heard appropriately. On numerous occasions, Edward Said lamented the lack of Palestinian voices in the media, the absence/invisibility of the Palestinian narrative generally and the fact that there was still no good, Palestinian-authored account of Palestinian history (Said 2004). The destruction of archives obviously has a major role to play in those absences, especially the latter. Indeed, the absence of archives is doubly silencing for the Palestinians, since what remains as the possible basis for the construction of a historical narrative – the use of oral history, witness testimony and the like – may not count as acceptable evidence for "proper" historians. This is the case with Benny Morris, one of the Israeli "new historians" whose book on the events of 1948, *The Birth of the Palestinian Refugee Problem,* was the first to use Israeli official records to undermine standard Israeli accounts of what happened (Morris 1987). For Morris, however, there are simply no useful archival accounts to be had from the Palestinian side and as a result, "Whatever anybody calls the writing that emerges without historical records, it's not real history" (Massad 2006, 161).

In *Minima Moralia,* Adorno comments: "Consummate negativity, once squarely faced, delineates the mirror image of its opposite" (Adorno 1987, 247). Something along the same lines could be seen as operating here, where the consummately negative mechanisms of silencing and the discourses of denial offer an insight into what we might call appropriate speech. Specific questions to be addressed would include: How might we speak appropriately about Palestine? More particularly, how might we speak appropriately about Palestine in the postcolonial context? What is currently said? What could be said? "Speaking appropriately" is, of course, something the Israelis have always said that the Palestinians can't do – for example, the repeated Israeli assertions that there was no point in thinking about peace talks because there were no appropriate interlocutors on the Palestinian side. At the same time, "appropriate speech" as a discourse of honesty or truthfulness would have to exclude much that emerges from the Israeli side on the grounds of its demonstrable dishonesty or inaccuracy. Said is particularly scornful of such examples of Israeli lies, as also is Joseph Massad.

One aspect of speaking appropriately would be to name things correctly, and in *The Question of Palestine,* for example, Said introduces the concept of "politicide" as a process for making the Palestinians disappear. The idea later became the focus of the book of the same name by the distinguished Israeli sociologist Baruch Kimmerling:

> Politicide is a process that covers a wide range of social, political, and military activities whose goal is to destroy the political and national existence of a whole community of people and thus deny it the possibility of self-determination. Murders, localised massacres, the elimination of leadership and elite groups, the physical destruction of

public institutions and infrastructure, land colonisation, starvation, social and political isolation, re-education, and partial ethnic cleansing are the major tools used to achieve this goal.

(Kimmerling 2003, 4)

Politicide is, however, only one of a range of Israeli strategies for making the Palestinians silent or absent that have recently been identified. Others include verbicide (Barghouti 2003), memoricide (Pappé 2006), toponymicide and spaciocide (Hanafi 2005). In his article "Verbicide" (2003), the Palestinian poet Mourid Barghouti reflects on the brutalization of language, and language that brutalizes – the attempt to kill a certain kind of language, partly through a language that can kill. In opposition to the dehumanizing, racist discourse of Israeli politicians and generals, Barghouti, in a manner that echoes his fellow-poet Darwish, as we will see later, offers the possibility of a different use of language as a path to the inhabiting of a different, better world. For the Israeli historian Ilan Pappé, ironically driven into exile like the Palestinians precisely for the crime of speaking up for the Palestinians, a key element in Israeli policy since the 1940s has been the obliteration of Palestinian memories and memories about Palestine.

We end this book as we began: with the bewilderment that this crime [of ethnic cleansing] was so utterly forgotten and erased from our minds and memories. But now we know the price: the ideology that enabled the depopulation of half of Palestine's native people in 1948 is still alive and continues to drive the inexorable, sometimes indiscernible, cleansing of those Palestinians who live there today.

(Pappé 2006, 259)

Against this background of silence, denial and erasure, how might we begin to account for the absence of Palestine as an appropriate object of study for postcolonial studies? Part of the reason is no doubt to do with the fact that from the beginning, postcolonial scholars were simply looking elsewhere. The major centers of academic interest typically were – and remain so for many – Africa, the Indian subcontinent, the Caribbean, Australasia. This was not least because so much of the burgeoning postcolonial literature, as well as the existing or emerging body of theory, was in English, or if not, at least in some European language reasonably accessible to Anglophone academics. Also important in terms of keeping Palestine off the postcolonial agenda has been the remarkable success with which Israeli policies and practices have been represented as not in fact colonial. Indeed, arguments such as the one that says Israelis could not possibly be colonizers because they are simply reclaiming their own country continue to find support in certain quarters. Alternatively, the Israeli claim that they fought a war of national liberation – in the best anti-colonial tradition – is used as a way of denying that their behavior is colonialist.

Another part of the reason for the absence of Palestine may be to do with the question of timing. Certainly, the emergence of postcolonial studies in the 1980s occurred at a bad time for the Palestinians. In the wake of the catastrophic Israeli siege of Beirut in 1982, the expulsion of the PLO from Lebanon, and the massacres in Sabra and Shatila, the Palestinian cause was at a low ebb. In the US in particular, there were significant and ongoing efforts to silence, delegitimate and demonize: the PLO was labeled a terrorist organization, its offices at the UN were closed down, US government officials refused to negotiate with the PLO and the US ambassador to the UN was forced to resign for speaking to a PLO representative. At the same time, the dominant representations of the PLO and Palestinians, especially, but not only, in the media, were frequently simplistic and negative, creating the image of a people who were potentially less interesting to study – indeed, perhaps even less worthy of being studied. Even among those who could or should have engaged with Palestinian issues, there was a general silence. Said points to the failure of the American Left to take notice of Palestine, even as they demonstrated their theoretical and political astuteness in other areas: "I've talked with many people on the American Left. Somehow they cannot bring themselves to focus on this [Palestine]. ... This is the one place, it seems to me – along with the Nicaraguan case – where American intellectuals have a very direct role to play. And yet there's nothing there. I find it astonishing" (Said 2004, 326). To the extent that the field of postcolonial studies could be construed as being led by ideas or agendas emanating from the US, then acceptance and inclusion of Palestine was, and is likely to remain, problematic.[6]

Surprisingly, something of the same problem (it only seems to make sense as a US-centric model) also relates to Neil Lazarus' more recent and better-argued criticism of postcolonial scholarship, *The Postcolonial Unconscious*. Another global view of the field, and one put forward by a more able critic than Appiah or Dirlik, its stringent critiques carry more weight because of the intelligence of Lazarus' approach. Nevertheless, it, too, uses blanket dismissal as an important weapon in its armory.

> Among these assumptions and investments [predominant in the field of postcolonial studies] I would list in particular the following: a constitutive anti-Marxism; an undifferentiating disavowal of all forms of nationalism and a corresponding exaltation of migrancy, liminality, hybridity, and multi-culturality; an hostility towards 'holistic forms of social explanation' (towards totality and systemic analysis); an aversion to dialectics; and a refusal of an antagonistic or struggle-based model of politics.
>
> (Lazarus 2011, 21)

This is strong stuff, and if Lazarus is in any way correct in his assessment, then it should come as no surprise that a postcolonial studies fundamentally opposed to national self-determination and anti-colonial struggle would have little time for engaging with the issues presented by Palestine. However, in the absence of any greater precision about who is responsible for all these limited, politically and theoretically unacceptable perspectives, I would, reluctantly, have to disagree with Lazarus. It seems to me that the desire to create a model of postcolonial studies deemed to be in need of rescue and reconfiguration by materialist theory unfortunately produces an account of the field that ignores the different, frequently divergent tendencies within it. For example, Lazarus says, "[W]e can register immediately the supplementarity of postcolonial studies to post-structuralist theory" (Lazarus 2011, 1). Can we? Obviously, postcolonial theory draws on post-structuralist theory in various ways. At the same time, and just as obviously, it draws on the radical anti-colonial theorizing of Amílcar Cabral, Frantz Fanon, Aimé Césaire and many more in a way that makes it impossible for it to constitute a mere supplement to post-structuralist theory. Postcolonial studies in the US may well be as dominated by post-structuralism as Lazarus claims the field in general is, but it is much harder to see that as the case elsewhere. Clearly, there is a discussion to be had. Equally clearly, this is not the place for it.

Despite what has just been said, the aim of *The Postcolonial Unconscious* is not to offer a negative critique of the field – as Lazarus points out, he has already done that elsewhere – but to suggest what postcolonial studies could do differently, do better or indeed do for the first time. That would appear to be the perfect opportunity to bring in Palestine, but once again – and all the more remarkably in a work such as this – it does not figure. The final chapter is devoted to Said, but concerns itself with "the battle over Edward Said", particularly in relation to theory. Meanwhile, Palestine continues on its seemingly inexorable postcolonial trajectory as gap, absence, silence. If Palestine does not figure as part of *The Postcolonial Unconscious* for Lazarus, there is, nevertheless, a case to be made for it as something like "the postcolonial repressed": Palestine the unspoken; Palestine the unspeakable. High time, no doubt, for a return of the repressed.

Another possible reason for the absence of Palestine in postcolonial studies is related to the numerous misunderstandings of what postcolonial studies is or does, and hence whether it has anything useful or relevant to say about Palestine. The dismissal of postcolonial studies or a postcolonial perspective is particularly persuasive when articulated by someone who might generally be regarded as possessing a good understanding of the Palestinian situation, such as Joseph Massad. In his chapter "The 'Post-Colonial' Colony: time, space, and bodies in Palestine/Israel", Massad offers a range of criticisms of postcolonialism. These are, however, based on what might be considered a rather limited understanding of the concept and the discipline; for example, "Consequently, colonialism's end, it is said, brings about post-colonialism" (Massad 2006, 13). Well, yes, up to a point – but there is obviously a lot more involved than simple temporal succession. Similarly, there are probably few if any working in postcolonial studies who would consider the following an adequate summary of the field: "Aside from ignoring the material relations of colonial and post-colonial rule and rendering these terms limited to the discursive realm ..." (Massad, ibid.). For Massad, however, the particular problem of the postcolonial occurs in relation to settler colonialism.

> The United States, Rhodesia, South Africa, and Israel, for example, instituted themselves as post-colonial states, territories and spaces, and instituted their political status as "independent" in order to render their present a post-colonial era. Yet the conquered peoples of these territories continue (including the people of Zimbabwe following "independence" and South Africa following the "end" of apartheid) to inhabit these spaces as colonial spaces and to live in eras that are thoroughly colonial. Given such a situation, how can one determine the coloniality and/or post-coloniality of these spaces or times? (Ibid.)

Apart from the fact that none of the states mentioned specifically declared themselves postcolonial as such – though they certainly proclaimed their "independence" – Massad here, strangely, almost naïvely it would seem, takes the notional self-representation of the settler-colonial states for some kind of truth about the status of the postcolonial. They declare themselves to be (by implication) postcolonial, and this, for him, is sufficient to make postcolonialism a rather less than useful concept. "[H]ow can one determine the coloniality and/or post-coloniality of these spaces or times?" he asks. "Quite easily", we can reply, since even in its earliest, arguably least theoretically sophisticated, most "discursive" incarnation as Colonial Discourse Analysis, postcolonial studies was premised on not taking colonial self-representation at face value, particularly not its large-scale, self-serving, ideologically loaded claims. Indeed, Massad himself appears to experience little difficulty in identifying the continuing colonial nature of such states, regardless of what they may say about themselves. Such an apparently uncritical acceptance of settler colonialism's self-presentation does appear strange, however, given that a considerable part of the same chapter is devoted precisely to a critique of "the signifying penis" in the context of Jewish/Zionist representations of bodies and masculinity.

In the end, there is obviously no guarantee that scholars will find postcolonial studies relevant or useful in the Palestinian context, but it is hard not to feel that dismissal ought to be grounded in a fuller and better understanding of what is being dismissed. That is particularly true at the opposite end of the political /ideological spectrum from Massad, in the case of the spectacularly awful *Postcolonial Theory and the Arab-Israel Conflict*, edited by Philip Carl Salzman and Donna Robinson Divine, where the lack of understanding of, or meaningful engagement with, postcolonial theory renders the book intellectually ridiculous.[7] The fact that it is a Jewish/pro-Israeli collaboration whose main aim appears to be to attack and discredit Edward Said does not in any way absolve it of its failure to address one of the two key terms in its title. Fascinatingly, in the context of what has been said so far, for Salzman and Divine and their contributors, Palestine does not constitute any sort of absence. On the contrary, for them, Palestine is the central, indeed almost the only, concern of postcolonial theory and postcolonial studies, to the detriment of both. That contention alone perhaps says everything that needs to be said about the volume's ability to contribute to informed debate in this area.

It is not simply the case, however, that postcolonial studies has continued to remain silent on the subject of Palestine. In 2007, delivering a conference paper on "Re-routing postcolonialism", it seemed to me that ignoring Palestine was indeed the norm for the field. That appeared largely unchanged in 2010, at the conference that formed the basis for the present collection. Now, however, there are welcome, and increasingly substantial, steps being taken to address Palestine within a postcolonial framework, such as a special issue of the postcolonial journal *Interventions* devoted to Mahmoud Darwish; special issues of the *Journal of Postcolonial Writing* on "Palestine and the Postcolonial", as well as one on "Global Checkpoints", which inevitably tackles the Israeli checkpoints regime; and perhaps more importantly, Anna Ball's 2012 *Palestinian Literature and Film in Postcolonial Feminist Perspective* and Anna Bernard's 2013 *Rhetorics of Belonging: Nation, Narration, and Israel/Palestine*. It nevertheless remains the case that there is a great deal more that postcolonial studies could be saying.

Among the terms that postcolonial studies needs to be articulating appropriately in relation to Palestine are some of the most basic in the postcolonial lexicon, such as resistance and representation. ("You're not *still* talking about resistance and representation?!" asks my wife in tones of absolute incredulity. "After all these years?") By way of justification, one could offer the simple fact that these terms have continued to be relevant, indeed essential, to the people at the heart of the struggle, the Palestinians themselves, and returning to them constitutes an important opportunity for postcolonial re-evaluation. An important aspect of the return and repetition is the recognition that, as previously pointed out, there is an ongoing need to maintain certain positions, go over the same ground, fight the same battles, simply because the overall determining context has not changed. On the subject of this kind of conceptual return, the Marxist philosopher Ernst Bloch says we shouldn't be anxious or embarrassed about going back to old concepts. Indeed, it could prove positive, because the concepts may have learned something in the meantime (Bloch 1986). Certainly, we have to hope that postcolonialists have learned something in the meantime.

As far as resistance is concerned, there is a clear need for more nuanced analysis that understands its multiple forms, moments and strategies – from full-scale armed conflict to popular "passive" struggle; from the mutually life-denying tactic of suicide bombing to life-affirming poetry – and within any of those, the very different shapes that resistance can take on. With that in mind, I want to make a brief, unavoidably schematic, excursus through the work of the poet Mahmoud Darwish as an example of some of those various modes and methods. Before his assassination by the Israelis in 1972, the writer and activist Ghassan Kanafani coined the phrase "resistance literature" to describe the more politically engaged forms of Palestinian cultural production, and the figure who came to epitomize Palestinian resistance literature was Darwish. The idea of resistance operates in some markedly different ways in Darwish's work at different points in his literary career. Although he became known as "the poet of Palestinian resistance", and although his early poems in particular are haunted by Israeli violence, Palestinian death and suffering – including the kind of massacres that characterized the *Nakba* of 1948 – there is always a restraint in the way in which Palestinian resistance is envisaged and articulated by Darwish. A possible exception might be the final words of probably his best-known poem, "Identity Card":

> I do not hate people.
> I steal from no one.
> However
>   if I am hungry
> I will eat the flesh of my usurper.
> Beware beware of my hunger
> and of my anger.
>
> (Darwish 1973, 25)

In general, however, Darwish is opposed to anything that might be considered blatant or strident, even where the defense of his people is concerned, and the kind of calls to arms, descriptions of "heroic" Palestinian martyrs and the like, which figure in the work of his compatriots, are usually absent from Darwish's poetry. As he said in an interview towards the end of his life, "I would not want to appear as a patriot or as a hero or as a symbol. I will appear as a modest poet" (Darwish 2007b). At the same time, although an aversion to stridency could be considered Darwish's default position, it did not prevent him being considered the pre-eminent spokesman for the Palestinian resistance, however much he himself grew impatient with that sort of categorization. There were, however, situations in which restraint was inappropriate or indeed impossible. The most obvious of these was the 1982 Siege of Beirut, which Darwish experienced along with Yasser Arafat and the PLO fighters, where the Palestinian resistance appeared all the more desperately heroic as it became increasingly isolated and betrayed.

> Fallen is the mask!
> You've no brothers, my brother,
> No friends, no forts, my friend.
> You've no water and no cure
> No sky, no blood and no sails.
> No front, and no rear.
> Besiege your siege then. No escape!
>
> (Darwish 1995, 58)[8]

The poems composed during the siege were, unsurprisingly, given the context and the need to represent Palestinian resistance, among the most militant Darwish ever wrote, and it was precisely for that reason that he later repudiated them, as works that were too much governed by immediate political necessity rather than what, for him, remained the overriding concerns of the literary text. "When I got to Europe [i.e. after leaving Beirut] I set to work on a reevaluation of everything that I had written up to that point. I sorted them into those that deserved to survive, or not. I shortened, concentrated, softened. And above all: less militancy" (Darwish 1997, 130).[9]

This did not mean, however, that Darwish had abandoned the idea of resistance, rather that he wanted to render it into poetry in different ways. In the 1980s he began writing what he called "the poetry of Troy" to give a voice to those denied one by history – the indigenous peoples of North America, the defeated Arabs in the Spanish *Reconquista*, the Trojans, the Canaanite inhabitants of Palestine – in opposition to dominant representations, dominant narratives of history, dominant cultures.[10] To that end, Darwish developed a new poetic form – the lyrical epic – to embody his resistant aesthetic. Although poems such as "Eleven Stars in the Last Andalusian Sky" and "The Speech of the Red Indian" (Darwish 2000) are extensively researched works, historically grounded in their period, and Darwish insists on them as such, it is hard to avoid the parallels with contemporary Palestine, particularly as the source of another silenced and (thus far) colonized people.

Another approach to resistance by Darwish involved something like a resistance to resistance – even, according to some, a complete betrayal of the revolution. From his earliest collections, Darwish's work has included love poetry – perhaps most famously, or most transgressively, the poems for his Jewish lover, Rita – though these were typically accorded less importance than others that highlighted national identity, Palestinian resistance and the like. In 1999, Darwish published his first collection consisting entirely of love poems, *A Bed for the Stranger*, and was duly attacked by poets, critics and politicians for having allegedly sold out the struggle. Undeterred, Darwish argued that such criticism simply demonstrated a lack of understanding of the fact that Palestinians were first of all human beings and not a political cause, that the book represented a deepening of human experience and that for him, "Love poetry is the intimate, personal dimension of cultural resistance" (Darwish 2006, 92).

A different "moment" of resistance, and a different poetic response by Darwish, occurred in 2002, with the Israeli onslaught on the towns of the West Bank. Darwish had continued with his (frustrating for some readers) practice of not writing poetry that reacted immediately to events, but this was one that he felt it was impossible to ignore, not least because he himself was in Ramallah, one of the most intensively attacked towns, where the Israelis aimed to humiliate and possibly remove Yasser Arafat. The result was the thirty-page poem *State of Siege*. In some ways, this could be seen as a revisiting of the lyrical epic from the 1980s and 1990s, but in length, style and structure it is typically Darwish – something quite new. A work begun in Ramallah under siege by the Israeli army and air force, its fragmentary, epigrammatic form evokes the snatched moments of respite in a life lived between bombardments, where "Soldiers measure the gap between being and nothingness/Using a tank's gunsights" and "We measure the distance between our bodies and the shells using a sixth sense …" (Darwish 2002). More than just an account of Palestinian suffering, however, this is a work of resistance, resistance that again takes many forms, from the "active" mode of the armed "martyrs" through to the "passive" strategy, encapsulated in the term *ṣumūd*, of resisting by simply staying alive, not giving in, not going away, seen through Darwish's perceptive, ironic vision:

> Standing here. Sitting here. Always here. Eternally here.
> And we have one single united goal: to be.
> After that, we differ on everything. …
>
> (Darwish 2002)

In addition, there is resistance for Darwish in the fact of not being reduced to silence by the siege. The act of poetic creation – and that of course includes love poetry – stands in opposition to the military onslaught. "When I write twenty lines about love/I imagine this siege/has gone back twenty metres!" (Darwish 2002). As Darwish said to his neighbor under siege, the lawyer and writer Raja Shehadeh, *State of Siege* is "a poet's journal that deals with resisting the occupation through searching for beauty in poetics and beauty in nature. It was a way of resisting military violence through poetry. The victory of the permanent, the everlasting, the eternal, over the siege and violence" (Shehadeh 2009). This mode of resistance is seen, for example, in moments such as this:

> Cups of our coffee. The birds, and the green trees
> In blue shadow. The sun leaping from one wall
> To another, like a gazelle.
> The water in the endless shapeless clouds of what remains for us
> Of the sky. And other things, their memories postponed,
> Prove that this morning is strong and glorious,
> And that we are the guests of eternity.
>
> (Darwish 2002)

Despite the oppressive effects of the siege on time (memories having to be postponed) and space (so little of the sky is left available to the besieged), the kind of resistance, even victory, that Darwish envisages is here imaginable. And in case anyone might think that he is so immersed in the poetic as to be likely to forget the broader needs of the campaigns of resistance, Darwish has this to say: "Resistance to the occupation is not just a right, it is also a duty. It can take various forms, including the rejection of any Israeli practice which aims at the annihilation of Palestinians. We have to invent new forms of struggle which can help the greater national good" (Darwish 2006, 68).

This brief overview is nothing like an appropriate postcolonial analysis of the question of resistance in the work of Mahmoud Darwish, but it is at least a preliminary indication of some of the terrain on which such an analysis might operate, aware of the historical and political contexts, cultural specificities and personal agendas that interact in the production of a rich and complex literary oeuvre.

In another instance of an Ernst Bloch-type return to the concepts, postcolonial studies needs to revisit and rethink fundamental aspects of the Palestinian situation. One example to follow would be Ilan Pappé, in his reconceptualising of the nature of the Palestinian *Nakba* as a key moment in a process of colonialist ethnic cleansing lasting more than half a century. Apart from the provocative, but entirely appropriate, use of the term "ethnic cleansing" to describe what has been done and continues to be done to the Palestinians, Pappé's important move is to see the *Nakba* not, as it is typically regarded, as just the events of 1948, traumatic though they were, but as an integral part of the continuing Israeli project for control of the land of Palestine. That has so far been a colonizing project. At the point at which it is fully achieved and successful, it will (arguably) no longer be colonial, since the native population will have been removed. This seventy-year history of ethnic cleansing, both unending and unacknowledged, epitomizes the silence and denial that are so prevalent in this context, while in its oppressive persistence it offers a strong parallel with Walter Benjamin's words from the "Theses on the Philosophy of History": "The tradition of the oppressed teaches us that the 'state of emergency' in which we live is not the exception but the rule. We must attain to a conception of history that is in keeping with this insight" (Benjamin 1973, 259). From what we have seen so far, recognition of the former is difficult enough. The creation of the latter is altogether a more challenging task, but one in which postcolonial studies ought to be centrally engaged.

At the same time, Pappé's rethinking of the *Nakba* has potential effects in other areas. Some recent work in trauma studies, most notably that of Stef Craps, has identified a need to "postcolonialize" the field, to make it more aware of, and responsive to, the kind of issues more typically found in postcolonial studies. Among the range of criticisms leveled at what might be considered the dominant form of trauma studies is its tendency to privilege the experience of Holocaust survivors, particularly certain individuals, to see trauma as located in a one-off incident and to regard the traumatic event as fundamentally non-narratable – or at least in the form of a consecutive, coherent narrative. This combination of privilege, individualization, discontinuity and fragmentation has appeared increasingly unhelpful in efforts to understand and represent trauma appropriately. Pappé highlights the way in which Palestinian trauma is turned into silence and absence. The *Nakba* is neither remembered nor celebrated; the little that remains of the ruins of Palestinian villages is obliterated – materially, by the planting of non-native conifers over the site; discursively, by the creation of explanatory narratives for these parks that contrive not to explain that these were in fact the homes, farms and communities of the displaced indigenous people. Pappé comments:

> In this way, the information provided at these JNF [Jewish National Fund] sites is a pre-eminent model for the all-pervading mechanism of denial Israelis activate in the realm of representation. Deeply rooted in the people's psyche, this mechanism works through exactly this replacement of Palestinian sites of trauma and memory by spaces of leisure and entertainment for Israelis. In other words, what the JNF texts represent as an 'ecological concern' is yet one more official Israeli effort to deny the Nakba and conceal the enormity of the Palestinian tragedy.
>
> (Pappé 2006, 229)

What emerges, in direct opposition to the dominant trauma theory model, is the ethnic cleansing of the Palestinians as an ongoing, eminently narratable, non-Jewish, colonially-induced trauma in urgent need of postcolonial analysis.

Above all, it is the persistent effort of Palestinians to represent themselves – to make themselves present and audible – that requires postcolonial engagement. As a final snapshot, we can return to the problem of the Palestine film archive. As mentioned, the one being created by the PLO vanished in Beirut in 1982. That was not the end of the story, however. In 2006, Azza El Hassan made *Kings and Extras*, documenting her ultimately fruitless efforts to track down the absent archive. The following year, filmmaker Annemarie Jacir managed to trace not only one of the missing films – *They Don't Exist*, made in 1974 by Mustafa Abu Ali, founder of the PLO film unit – but to reunite the filmmaker and his film by smuggling Abu Ali into Jerusalem for a special screening. Jacir is, of course, one of the significant figures in the slow, difficult emergence of postcolonial Palestinian cinema. Her film *Like 20 Impossibles* is one of the best-known of Palestinian shorts; she became the first Palestinian woman to direct a feature-length film, the prize-winning *Salt of this Sea* (2008); her latest film, *When I Saw You*, saw international release in 2012. Both films were Palestinian entries for the Oscars, overcoming yet another form of silencing and removal that had previously blocked Elia Suleiman's *Divine Intervention* on the grounds that Academy Awards submissions have to come from a specified country and there was no country called Palestine. Although the PLO archive may never be recovered, Jacir, Suleiman, Hani Abu Assad, Tawfik Abu Wael, Michel Khleifi and others continue with the task of creating its replacement, denying absence, opposing the silence.

NOTES

1. The silence is widespread, rather than absolute. It is, as noted later in this essay, being challenged by a number of individuals. That it has lasted for so long is, nevertheless, a matter of concern.
2. See, among others, Shehadeh 2008 and Said 1992.
3. See Pappé 2006.
4. See, for example, Pappé 2006 and Masalha 2000.
5. Anna Bernard also argues for the Present Absentee status of Palestine in postcolonial studies in her recent book (Bernard 2013).
6. I personally do not regard the field as being US-dominated, but a number of widely accepted critiques, such as those articulated by Arif Dirlik and Anthony Appiah, seem to me only to make sense if a US-led or US-centric model is accepted. The career-chasing "native informants", the ideologically co-opted critics and the like in Dirlik and Appiah do not match any of my experience of the world of postcolonial studies outside the US.
7. I have written about this collection at greater length in the volume *Postcolonialism and Islam* (Williams 2013b).
8. For a discussion of Darwish's most important work to emerge from the siege, the prose memoir *Memory for Forgetfulness*, see Williams, "'Besiege your siege!': Mahmoud Darwish, Representation, and the Siege of Beirut" (2013c).
9. All translations from collections in French are my own.
10. For a more extensive discussion of this phase in Darwish's work, see Williams, "Writing the Poetry of Troy" (2013a).

REFERENCES

Adorno, Theodor. 1987. *Minima Moralia*. Verso: London.

Ball, Anna. 2012. *Palestinian Literature and Film in Postcolonial Feminist Perspective*. London: Routledge.

Barghouti, Mourid. 2003. "Verbicide", *New Internationalist* 359, August. www.newint.org

Benjamin, Walter. 1973. *Illuminations*. London: Fontana/Collins.

Bernard, Anna. 2013. *Rhetorics of Belonging: Nation, Narration, and Israel/Palestine*. Liverpool: Liverpool University Press.

Bloch, Ernst. 1986. *The Principle of Hope*. Oxford: Blackwell.

Craps, Stef. 2012. *Postcolonial Witnessing: Trauma Out of Bounds*. London: Palgrave Macmillan.

Darwish, Mahmoud. 1976. *Selected Poems*. Cheadle Hulme: Carcanet.

Darwish, Mahmoud. 1995. *Memory for Forgetfulness*. Berkeley: University of California Press.

Darwish, Mahmoud. 1997. *La Palestine comme métaphore*. Arles: Actes Sud.

Darwish, Mahmoud. 2000. *The Adam of Two Edens*. Syracuse, NY: Syracuse University Press.

Darwish, Mahmoud 2002. *State of Siege*. Trans. Amina Elbendary. *Al-Ahram Weekly Online* 580, 4–10 April. http://weekly.ahram.org.eg/2002/580/cu1.htm.

Darwish, Mahmoud 2002a. Interview with Maya Jaggi. *The Guardian*, 8 June. http://www.theguardian.com/books/2002/jun/08/featuresreviews.guardianreview19.

Darwish, Mahmoud 2002b. "Siesta in the Midst of Siege": Interview with Amina Elbendary. *Al-Ahram Weekly Online* 617, 19–25 December. http://weekly.ahram.org.eg/2002/617/cu7.htm.

Darwish, Mahmoud 2003. *Unfortunately, It Was Paradise.* Berkeley: University of California Press.

Darwish, Mahmoud. 2004. *State of Siege.* Trans. Sarah Maguire and Sabry Hafez. *Modern Poetry in Translation,* series 3, No.1 http://www.mptmagazine.com/poem/a-state-of-siege-extract-4/#commentarea.

Darwish, Mahmoud 2006. *Entretiens sur la poésie.* ActesSud.

Darwish, Mahmoud 2007a. *Comme des fleurs d'amandier, ou plus loin.* Arles: Actes Sud.

Darwish, Mahmoud 2007b. "Return of the 'Modest Poet': Interview with Dalia Karpel". *Ha'aretz,* 12 July. http://www.haaretz.com/weekend/magazine/return-of-the-modest-poet-1.225367.

Hanafi, Sari. 2005. "Spacio-cide and Bio-politics: The Israeli Colonial Conflict from 1947 to the Wall". In *Against the Wall: Israel's Barrier to Peace,* edited by Michael Sorkin, 158–173. New York: New Press.

Kletter, Raz. 2005. *Just Past? The Making of Israeli Archaeology.* London and Oakville, CT: Equinox.

Kimmerling, Baruch. 2003. *Politicide: Ariel Sharon's War against the Palestinians.* London: Verso.

Lazarus, Neil. 2011. *The Postcolonial Unconscious.* Cambridge: Cambridge University Press.

Masalha, Nur. 2000. *Imperial Israel and the Palestinians: The Politics of Expansion.* London: Pluto.

Massad, Joseph. 2006. *The Persistence of the Palestinian Question.* London: Routledge.

Morris, Benny. 1987. *The Birth of the Palestinian Refugee Problem, 1947–1949.* Cambridge: Cambridge University Press.

Pappé, Ilan. 2006. *The Ethnic Cleansing of Palestine.* Oxford: Oneworld.

Philo, Greg and Ian Berry. 2004. *Bad News from Israel.* London: Pluto.

Qumsiyeh, Mazin B. 2012. *Popular Resistance in Palestine.* London: Pluto.

Rapoport, Meron. 2007. "History Erased". *Ha'aretz,* 6 July. http://www.haaretz.com/weekend/magazine/history-erased-1.224899.

Said, Edward W. 1992. *The Question of Palestine.* New York: Vintage.

Said, Edward W. 1994a. *Representations of the Intellectual.* London: Vintage.

Said, Edward W.1994b. "On Mahmoud Darwish". *Grand Street* 48: 112–115.

Said, Edward W. 2000. *Reflections on Exile and Other Essays.* London: Granta.

Said, Edward W. 2004. *Power, Politics and Culture.* London: Bloomsbury.

Said, Edward W. 2006. *On Late Style.* London: Bloomsbury.

Salzman, Philip Carl, and Donna Robinson Divine, eds. 2008. *Postcolonial Theory and the Arab-Israel Conflict.* London: Routledge.

Shehadeh, Raja. 2008. *Palestine Walks: Notes on a Vanishing Landscape.* London: Profile Books.

Shehadeh, Raja. 2009. "Mahmoud Darwish – a poet of peace in a time of conflict". *The Guardian.* 7 August. http://www.theguardian.com/books/booksblog/2009/aug/07/mahmoud-darwish-poetry-palestine.

Williams, Patrick. 2009. "Naturally, I reject the term 'diaspora': Said and Palestinian Dispossession". In *Comparing Postcolonial Diasporas,* edited by Michelle Keown, David Murphy and James Procter, 83–103. London: Palgrave Macmillan.

Williams, Patrick. 2010. "Outlines of a Better World". In *Rerouting the Postcolonial*, edited by Janet Wilson *et al*. London: Routledge.

Williams, Patrick. 2013a. "Writing the Poetry of Troy". In *Locating Postcolonial Narrative Genres*, edited by Walter Goebel and Saskia Schabio. London: Routledge.

Williams, Patrick. 2013b. "Postcolonialism and Orientalism". In *Postcolonialism and Islam*, edited by Geoff Nash *et al*. London: Routledge.

Williams, Patrick. 2013c. "'Besiege your siege!': Mahmoud Darwish, Representation, and the Siege of Beirut". In *The Ethics of Representation in Literature, Art, and Journalism: Transnational Responses to the Siege of Beirut*, edited by Caroline Rooney and Rita Sakr, 56–70. London: Routledge.

6 Facing/Defacing Robert Mugabe

Land Reclamation, Race and the End of Colonial Accountability

Ashleigh Harris

In 2012, a spate of Internet petitions, blogs and websites emerged seeking the support of an international public to stop what they called the genocide of whites in southern Africa. More recently, Steve Hofmeyr, the South African popular Afrikaans musician, made headline news (and mobilized significant public support) with the statement that the white "tribe is dying", a claim that he made alongside his call to expose "the lie of white on black genocide during apartheid" (Brodie 2013). Paul Gilroy warns us that such "revisionist accounts of imperial and colonial life" (2005, 2) are on the rise. Writing about Britain, Gilroy sees this revisionism as a sign of the condition of postcolonial melancholia, which "promote[s] imperialist nostalgia" and "endorse[s] the novel forms of colonial rule currently being enforced by economic and military means at the disposal of a unipolar global order" (3). Postcolonial melancholia is not only a wish to return, nostalgically, to the time of imperialism and a disavowal of responsibility for the aftermaths of apartheid and colonial history but it also endorses a colonial approach to the present moment.

As Wendy Willems (2005) has argued, Gilroy's notion of postcolonial melancholia gives us critical purchase on the broader significance of the major and sustained British press coverage of Zimbabwe's fast-track land redistribution program of the 2000s, in which white farmers were often violently dispossessed of their land. Building on Willems' reading of the British media's portrayal of Zimbabwe's land reclamation, I argue that this redistribution campaign contributed to a broader revision and reversal of colonial accountability in Africa. Indeed, this revisionism might be seen to feed back into a larger justification of the large-scale land acquisitions by multinational corporations, nation states and even wealthy institutions as diverse as Harvard University and the World Bank that have occurred across sub-Saharan Africa since the economic and food shortage crisis of 2008;[1] a land grab that has received relatively little attention in the Western media compared to the disproportionately large coverage of Zimbabwe's land reclamations.

It is my contention that postcolonial scholarship and theory are in a structural state of complicity with the colonial structures and patterns of meaning that drive this global condition of postcolonial melancholia. In my field of African studies, this is most evident in the fact that postcolonial theory remains a body of scholarship that by and large circumvents knowledge production on the continent of Africa itself (see Harris 2012; Hawley 2010; Mbembe and Nuttall 2004; Mignolo 2011; Nnaemeka 2003). Indeed, one might argue that postcolonial theory is in danger of actively refusing to engage knowledge production from Africa for the purpose of sustaining its own project of advocacy. The point recalls to us Spivak's famous warning of the epistemic violence wrought by Western scholarship ([1989] 1994, 74) and the problem of Habermas's universal intellectual who, in "[intervening] on behalf of rights that have been violated and truths that have been suppressed" (Habermas 1989, 73; cited in Sanders 2002, 5), is in danger of actively positing such advocacy as a silencing strategy.[2] This is what Walter Mignolo attempts to address in his critique of cosmopolitan models of inclusion. He writes:

> [I]nclusion doesn't seem to be the solution to cosmopolitanism any longer, insofar as it presupposes that the agency that establishes the inclusion is itself beyond inclusion: "he" being already within the frame from which it is possible to think "inclusion". Today, silenced and marginalized voices are bringing themselves into the conversation of cosmopolitan projects, rather than waiting to be included. Inclusion is always a reformative project. Bringing themselves into the conversation is a transformative project that takes the form of border thinking or border epistemology – that is, the alternative to separatism is border thinking, the recognition and transformation of the hegemonic imaginary from the perspectives of people in subaltern positions. Border thinking then becomes a "tool" of the project of critical cosmopolitanism.
>
> (Mignolo 2000, 736–737)

Yet to what extent does postcolonial theory harness such transformative potential, given that it remains dominated by scholars in the developed global North? And how do we harness such transformative critical cosmopolitanism in an era of global finance capital, where our scholarly enterprise itself relies on a global distribution of resources that ensures the continued circumvention of precisely those vernacular cosmopolitanisms?

These global economic conditions are fundamental to my analysis below. Is border thinking a possibility in a scholarly context where some of the most established and wealthy US universities are buying large tracts of African land via hedge funds, speculating against future global resource crises in order to secure their financial futures and scholarly dominance in the world (see Vidal and Provost 2011)? The materiality of this economic imbalance demonstrates the politics of knowledge production that troubles postcolonial scholarship. In presenting a case study of how representations of Zimbabwean president Robert Mugabe sustain a project of postcolonial melancholia, this chapter seeks to get critical purchase on the larger problem that such discursive entanglements pose for the future of postcolonial studies.

LAND AND THE RHETORICAL USES OF RACE

Robert Mugabe is no stranger to the international press. Images of the ageing statesman pervade the global media, inevitably accompanied with an account of the fall of the Zimbabwean nation. Mugabe is, indeed, the *bête noire* (and I use the term advisedly) of the global North. His image has come to signify the Zimbabwean crisis but is also often tethered to a broader critique of the postcolonial African nation state. Nowhere was this more apparent than in the British media's coverage of the Zimbabwean crisis in the daily papers during the 2000s, a time when Britain confronted increasing civil tensions about immigration and national belonging following the instigation of the global rhetorical and actual "war on terror". The 2000s, too, saw Mugabe's government, ZANU(PF), launch its land reclamation program in Zimbabwe. A chaotic, violent and un-programmatic series of reclamations of white-owned land ensued and the Zimbabwean situation was thrown into global view. Not only did the British media provide extensive coverage of the (often-personalized) story of black peasant reclamations of white-owned farms in Zimbabwe in that decade but a profusion of memoirs, autobiographies and reportage accounts of land reclamation were also published then, almost all of them from the perspective of, or in sympathy with, white farm owners. As Jocelyn Alexander notes, in this "spate of biographies" and reportage accounts of the country's decline, "Mugabe was placed centre stage, and portrayed as a singularly violent tyrant" (180). That centrality is made clear by a brief browse through the covers of these books, which more often than not include an image of Mugabe on them.[3]

To understand why the scene of land reclamation in Zimbabwe became the site of British postcolonial melancholy *par excellence*, we need first to outline some of the important historical and discursive factors at play in the representation of this scene. The first step towards a more equitable distribution of land at the end of white rule in Zimbabwe was made with the Lancaster House Agreement of 1979. This was a transitional contract, drawn up in advance of the handover of power from Rhodesia's premier Ian Smith to the incoming president of the newly democratic Zimbabwe, Robert Mugabe. The agreement, which denied Mugabe the power to seize and redistribute white-owned land within the first ten years of independence, was a compromise, brokered in the interests of political and economic stability during the country's transition. The Lancaster House Agreement outlined that all transfers of land had to be governed under a "willing-seller, willing-buyer" agreement at full market prices.

Both Smith and Mugabe had good reasons for agreeing to this compromise: Smith was invested in protecting the economic interests and securing the social position and safety of the minority white community whilst Mugabe was being handed a strong and stable economy and a nation that was known as the "breadbasket of Africa". Yet in reality, what Mugabe inherited was a country with deeply inequitable land distribution. At that time "about 70 percent of Zimbabwe's landmass, including communal areas, was owned by the [Rhodesian] state and 24 percent owned by large-scale commercial farmers" (Juana 2006, 296). The racial implications of this were massive. About forty percent of the country's arable land was owned by approximately six thousand white farmers, whilst around four million black Zimbabweans lived in state-owned "communal areas".

It is no surprise, then, that at the time of his rise to political prominence in the 1970s, land was Mugabe's greatest priority, as well as his most powerful political tool. Before signing the Lancaster House Agreement at the end of the successful war for liberation, Mugabe had promised his people land as compensation for their support during the war. Importantly, the promise of land was the chief incentive for young men to join Mugabe's forces. Yet, while the Lancaster constitution subdued Mugabe's initial ambitions (and promises) of large-scale land redistribution, he failed even to achieve his more modest goals, tempered by the agreement: "By the end of 1996, a total of 71,000 farm families were re-settled on 3.6 million hectares of land", a far cry from the initial goal of resettling 162,000 families on 8.3 million hectares by 1990 (Juana 2006, 298). Indeed, in the middle to late 1990s, around seventy percent of the country's most arable land remained in the hands of white farmers.

Mugabe's failure to make good on the promises of land redistribution coincided, in the second half of the 1990s, with a number of other failures of the ruling party: gross mismanagement and corruption on every level of government; a lack of basic health care at a time in which Zimbabwe had the highest HIV/AIDS infection rate in the world; unprecedented levels of unemployment; and the complete breakdown of the basic conditions of democracy, including intensified censorship, political intimidation and punitive withholding of basic resources on the basis of political allegiance. All of this amounted to a rising civil dissatisfaction with ZANU(PF) that became tangible with the official formation of the Movement for Democratic Change (MDC) in 1999, the most powerful political opposition the ruling party had encountered since the dissolution of the Zimbabwe Africa People's Union (ZAPU) in 1987.

In an anxious attempt to rein in this discontent, Mugabe proposed to replace the Lancaster House constitution with a new one that would significantly extend presidential power, giving him the power to seize white-owned farms without compensation, which, he argued, would be the responsibility of the previous colonial power, Britain. Mugabe knew that Britain had no intention of accepting this responsibility, given that as early as 1997, then International Development Secretary Clare Short had written a letter to the Zimbabwean government, clearly stating Britain's stance on its responsibilities in Zimbabwe. She wrote, of the Labour government of the time, "We are a new government from diverse backgrounds without links to former colonial interests" and thus "[w]e do not accept that Britain has a special responsibility to meet the cost of land purchase in Zimbabwe" (Short 1997). Nevertheless, convinced that the land question would win him back the support of his people, Mugabe put the adoption of this new constitution to referendum vote in February 2000. It was duly rejected. This constituted the first political defeat ZANU(PF) had ever suffered in its twenty years of rule. With Mugabe facing a parliamentary election in June 2000, the rejection of his proposed constitution made him particularly vulnerable.

At this time, the War Veterans Association, a loose but powerful association of veterans of the war for liberation from Rhodesian rule, were mobilizing intensely for the seizure of white-owned farms. Highlighting Mugabe's early promise of compensating the soldiers of his liberation war with land, the War Veterans' campaign redoubled the President's vulnerability. With the association growing in support (to the point of including members far too young to have fought in the liberation war) and threatening large-scale dissent, Mugabe was eager to win their support. He did so by effectively ignoring the results of the referendum vote and giving the "war vets" the green light to seize white-owned farms.

Mugabe immediately embarked on a rhetorical campaign to justify the unlawful seizures, dubbing them the third *chimurenga*. The *chimurengas* (a Shona word meaning "revolutionary struggle") are key points in Zimbabwe's history towards liberation from colonial power. The first *chimurenga* refers to the 1890 uprisings of the Matabele and Mashona against colonial settlement. The second *chimurenga* describes the liberation war against the Rhodesian government. Mugabe rhetorically posited his third *chimurenga*, the eviction of white farmers from the land, as "our last struggle for the complete decolonization of our country and continent as a whole" (Mugabe 2001, 55). Mugabe used the discursive pre-histories of *chimurenga*, then, as a way to embed his land redistribution campaign in this broader historical sweep towards a final, and total, decolonization.

In 2000, twenty years after independence, Mugabe was waging a rhetorical war against colonization, but for the purposes, it would seem, of his own more immediate political crisis, an expedience that historian Terence Ranger sees as "a cheapening [of] liberation history" (Ranger 2002, 161). Yet Mugabe's rhetoric carried political weight precisely because of the long-lived effects of Zimbabwe's colonial history, observable in the country's continued economic racial inequalities at the time. It is unsurprising, then, that Mugabe's rhetoric turned upon racially essentialist statements such as "Africa is for Africans. [Our] Land is ours by birth, ours by right" and "We call on all blacks to stand together to isolate these whites" (Shaw 2000).[4]

Such racialized rhetoric was, indeed, effective. In 2000, the violent seizure of white-owned farms began in earnest, with the war veterans acting with impunity (Solidarity Peace Trust 2003, 11). By the end of 2003, approximately forty-three hundred farms had been seized, amounting to around 8.6 million hectares of land. This was a little over the original ten-year goal (8.3 million hectares), set at the time of the Lancaster House Agreement and supported by £44-million of British compensation. Thus the fast-track land reform program achieved its goals through a disorganized, violent, opportunistic campaign in the course of only three years. The consequences are well known. The international community responded strongly with sanctions, eliciting even stronger anti-white and anti-British rhetoric from Mugabe and accelerating the county's economic crisis. Debates have been ongoing as to the longer-term economic consequences of the division of large-scale commercial farms, which were distributed to numerous small-scale (sometimes subsistence) farmers.[5]

These events, of course, received massive coverage in the British press during the 2000s. Yet instead of interrogating the extent to which colonial racial meaning continued to pervade the Zimbabwean situation in ways that were, indeed, detrimental to white farmers, this coverage became – as Wendy Willems illustrates – complicit in reiterating those very colonial repertoires of race, which in turn fuelled Mugabe's own anti-white sentiment. Willems argues that the British media response to land reclamation "sought to frame and represent [those] events in Zimbabwe in terms of a racial conflict between black and white" (2005, 103) and that the "Zimbabwean government [...] successfully managed to exploit these discourses on what they termed as 'Britain's kith and kin'" (2005, 104).

Such crude, autochthonous versions of race are equally present in the considerable outpouring of white memoir and autobiography that emerged at this historical juncture. Both Ranka Primorac (2010) and Rory Pilossof (2009), quite rightly, see a neo-colonial presentation of race in this genre, which dominates writing from the area in its sheer output. The ways in which this version of Zimbabwe, reiterating as it does a crude ethnicization of the contemporary moment in that country, emerged in a larger international arena has received the attention of scholars trying to get beyond the dichotomizing discourses that pervade the public sphere.[6] Willems takes this point further in grappling with the British media's investment in the narratives of white dispossession in Zimbabwe as a form of British postcolonial melancholia. Below I analyze the popular documentary *Mugabe and the White African* within the context that Willems describes.

THE *BÊTE NOIRE* AND THE GLOBAL RACIAL IMAGINARY

I have argued elsewhere that the fast-track land reform program enabled "white Zimbabwean land owners to shed the identity of 'settler'" (Harris 2004, 106) and with it all sense of accountability to the colonial past. Moreover, the fact that land reclamation was often violent enabled white Zimbabweans to mobilize a language of victimhood, often describing themselves as exiles and refugees in the lands to which they subsequently migrated. The rhetorical uses of this notion of victimhood have ranged from nostalgic figurations of Rhodesia to reactionary idealizing of Ian Smith and his regime, which gives substance to Mugabe's otherwise seemingly hysterical claim that white Zimbabweans "continue to nurture and pledge membership to the Rhodesian lobby across the world" (2001, 41). The more extreme the ideological position, the greater the investment in configuring a narrative of white victimhood, to the point of drawing lines of comparison between Nazi Germany and contemporary Zimbabwe. White Zimbabwean identification with Jews in Hitler's Germany became unsettlingly common in the aftermath of the land grabs, both prompted by and prompting Robert Mugabe's infamous statement of 21 March 2003: "This Hitler has only one objective: justice for his people, sovereignty for his people, recognition of the independence of his people and their rights over their resources. If that is Hitler [...] then let me be a Hitler tenfold" ("US slams Mugabe's 'black Hitler' speech", 2003). It is important to note, as does Blessing-Miles Tendi ("Whitewashing Zimbabwe's History", 2010), that the statement is often quoted out of context. In this speech Mugabe was attempting to utilize the rhetoric aimed against him by white Zimbabweans by inverting it, rather than simply identifying himself with Hitler. That point notwithstanding, the statement consolidated Mugabe's nativist prose – and gave white Zimbabweans the rhetorical stage for their claim to victimhood, which in turn became an expedient site for the erasure of colonial history.[7] On this discursive stage, enacted on the very real scene of land reclamation, the white African is no longer the stranger-turned-usurper attached to settler identity but has become the victim of an unconquerable dictator, "the black Hitler" as Mugabe has come to be called.

Chloe Traicos, director and writer of the film *A Stranger in my Homeland* (2005), gives voice to this position. She states:

> Hitler used the Jews, a wealthy minority group, as a scapegoat in the same way Mugabe has used the whites. Hitler told the starving Germans that it was the Jews' fault they were all starving. In exactly the same way, Mugabe has blamed the starvation of the blacks on the whites.
>
> (Brown 2003)[8]

The sentiment is also reiterated in one of the most successful commentaries on the Zimbabwean situation, Peter Godwin's book *When a Crocodile Eats the Sun*, where he writes: "A white in Africa is like a Jew everywhere – on sufferance, watching warily, waiting for the next great tidal wave of hostility" (2005, 266). Even more pertinent to this study, I argue that such statements operate performatively so as to evoke a very specific form of British empathy. As Paul Gilroy points out in *Postcolonial Melancholia*, "[T]here is something neurotic about Britain's continued citation of the anti-Nazi war", and the "memory of the country at war against foes who are simply, tidily, and uncomplicatedly evil has recently acquired the status of an ethnic myth" (Gilroy 2005, 89). The rhetorical evocation of Hitler as "uncomplicated evil" against which Britishness is defined gives greater substance to my claim here that the figure of Mugabe operates to consolidate a certain version of Britishness, too.

Gilroy elaborates this postcolonial melancholy thus: "Neither the appeal of homogeneity nor the antipathy towards immigrants and strangers who represent the involution of national culture can be separated from that underlying hunger for [national] reorientation" (2005, 89). Similarly, we might argue that turning Robert Mugabe into the "uncomplicated evil" antagonist of the British nation serves a much larger rhetorical purpose, one that has more to do with the dynamics of immigration politics, the war on terror and resource crises than it does with the rights of white land ownership in postcolonial Africa.

The violent scene of black peasants reclaiming ex-colonial territory from white owners (rhetorically identifying themselves expediently, yet effectively, with a British audience) was, then, compulsively reiterated in Britain as a symptom of the nation's contemporary struggle to come to terms with its post-imperial national identity. It is for this reason that it is worth paying close attention to the film *Mugabe and the White African* (2010), which received multiple accolades in Britain and the United States[9] and was, for the most part, highly acclaimed in reviews in the British press.[10] What is surprising about this high acclaim is that so few commentators saw beyond the personalized tale of a family of farmers who suffer a terrible attack on their farm, Mount Carmel, in the district of Chegetu, Zimbabwe.[11] Pervading that narrative of personal trauma, I argue, is a distinctive and unremitting colonial semiotics of race, reiterating a nostalgia for a racial taxonomy of the human and of civilization. In this colonial semiotic, as Achille Mbembe writes, "African human experience" is understood only through a "negative interpretation" (2001, 1) in which it

> is assumed that, although the African possesses a self-referring structure that makes him or her close to "being human", he or she belongs, up to a point, to a world we cannot penetrate. At bottom, he/she is familiar to us. We can give an account of him/her in the same way we can understand the psychic life of the *beast*. We can even, through a process of domestication and training, bring the African to where he or she can enjoy a fully human life.
>
> (Mbembe 2001, 2)

Approaching the racial limits of the human in another context, Judith Butler in *Precarious Life* discusses Emmanuel Levinas's ethical notion of the face, "which operates as a catechresis, displacing meaning along a series of invisible connections so that the representation of the face becomes a figuration of an unspoken meaning" (Butler 2004, 133–134). For Levinas, this meaning is, in the first instance, humanity and the human. We see the face of the other and it speaks their (and our) shared humanity. Butler's project to interrogate "the domain of representation where humanization and dehumanization occur ceaselessly" (2004, 14) and to provide an "account of the relationship between violence and ethics" (2004, 140) leads her to reflect on the ways violence occurs "precisely *through* the production of the face, the face of

Osama bin Laden, the face of Yasser Arafat, the face of Saddam Hussein" (2004, 141), which is to say, faces constructed in the Western presses as the faces of "evil". She writes:

> Although it is tempting to think that the images themselves establish the visual norm for the human, one that ought to be emulated or embodied, this would be a mistake, since in the case of bin Laden or Saddam Hussein the paradigmatically human is understood to reside outside the frame; this is the human face in its deformity and extremity, not the one with which you are asked to identify.
>
> (Butler 2004, 143)

Butler is contemplating the catachrestic production of these faces (as evil) in the context of the Gulf wars and the "war on terror", of course. The circulation of the image of Robert Mugabe's face at this time is, then, just as charged, providing as it does a catechresis of the right to reclaim an imperial imaginary. In this context, it is no surprise that much has been made of Mugabe's "Hitler-like moustache", which has become (alongside his iconic glasses) a de-realized symbol of his personage. Both of these de-realized symbols of the man are blatantly manipulated on the DVD cover and advertising poster for *Mugabe and the White African*. (See Figure 6.1.)

Figure 6.1 DVD cover, *Mugabe and the White African*, directed by Andrew Thompson and Lucy Bailey, 2009, Arturi Films.

Here, the face of Mugabe has been reduced to caricature, recognizable through the glasses and the moustache that the film's title replaces. It is, one might say, a defacing of the face as human, so that Mugabe comes to represent inhumanity itself. This reading of the visual image is supported by the words "If good men do nothing, evil will prevail", a tagline that instantly positions Mugabe as the incarnation of evil against the "good men", binaristically encoded in the poster as "the White Africans" of the title. If, in Butler's analysis, "the hyperbolic absorption of evil into the face itself, the eyes" (2004, 143) in representations of bin Laden and Hussein enables the viewer's disidentification, the disidentification of the viewer with Mugabe's face is here doubled. The caricature defaces at the same time as we confront an eyeless representation of evil, one that draws on a broader repertoire of the face of evil in reinforcing the rhetorical link between Hitler and Mugabe. The eyeless image presents the face as the absolute, impenetrable other.

This visual palimpsest is strongly reiterated by the opening scenes of the film. Immediately after the title screen appears, a series of covertly filmed footage follows: the hand-held camera moves violently across an otherwise peaceful scene of a road in Zimbabwe, spliced with images of a mob attack. These images are followed by longer shots of a burnt-down farm (04:30 – 05:10), over which the following text is superimposed: "In the last ten years Zimbabwe has descended into chaos. Mugabe's land reform has evicted 4000 white farmers. Thousands are starving under Mugabe's regime". This is immediately followed by the sound clip, also overlaying the images of Zimbabwe's decay, of Mugabe's oft-cited Hitler quote, mentioned above. The quote begins here, slightly inaudibly, with the line "I am still a Hitler of the times" and then continues with excerpts from the quotation cited above, with textual re-enforcement of the words "Justice for his people", "sovereignty for his people" and "let me be a Hitler tenfold". This final phrase remains on screen for some time, over the image of a burnt wheat field, before dissolving into a blank screen.[12]

Of course, the rhetorical function of framing Mugabe as a Hitler figure is the counterpoint this portrayal produces of presenting white Zimbabweans as victims. The real victims of this film are not the "thousands, starving under Mugabe's regime". Indeed, the continued and intense violence, poverty and political oppression suffered by black Zimbabweans are at the very margins of this film. While the film does detail a beating of an unnamed chief guard of Mount Carmel farm (19:00 – 19:58), as well as the vicious beating of Gift Kanyana, a candidate for ZANU(PF)'s opposition, the Movement for Democratic Change (51:20), for the most part poor black farm workers are presented as a nameless mass, in need of white protection and employment to sustain their lives and the lives of their children. Instead, the film focuses on the court case between farmer Mike Campbell and Robert Mugabe, a case heard in the SADC international court between 2007 and 2009. Both Campbell's Chief Counsel, Jeremy Gauntlett, and the instructing attorney for the case, Elize Angula, speak of the racism behind the

Zimbabwean government's land seizure without any further reflection on the discursive history of race in this context. Furthermore, Gauntlett takes the charge of racism further in his statement, "[O]ne doesn't want to use the emotive term 'ethnic cleansing', but [the land seizures are] distinctly racially discriminatory" (41:41). The rhetorical staging of the sentence, in which Gauntlett claims not to want to use the emotive term but does so anyway, is an example of how the signs of race operate in the film.[13] This is all the more apparent since Gauntlett's "ethnic cleansing" statement follows shortly after a close-up shot of Mike Campbell reading the independent newspaper *The Zimbabwean*. The paper bears the headline "We are like Jews during the Nazi Era" (37:40).[14] The analogy is further extended by Prof. Jeffrey Jowell, QC who states, "Democracy is not only about popular will. We know that through European experience. The German government in the 1930s was elected popularly and they went on to do terrible things" (50:14).

The analogy between contemporary Zimbabwe and Nazi Germany is iterated and reiterated in the film through the reproduction of Mugabe's face as the face of evil. And this analogy becomes even more discursively complex when we are confronted with the powerfully emotive narrative of the brutal beating of Mike Campbell, his wife and his son-in-law, Ben Freeth, that follows. The extreme violence of these beatings is poignantly and powerfully portrayed through photographs of the beaten faces of these three victims (104:42 – 114:00). This is the key spectacle in the film. The images are reinforced in their repetition. We see them a second time through the eyes of instructing attorney Elize Angula as she looks over the photographs (116:00), and then a third time when they are presented as evidence in court (124:00). As Slavoj Žižek points out in his book *Violence*:

> [T]here is something inherently mystifying in a direct confrontation with [violence]: the overpowering horror of violent acts and empathy with the victims inexorably function as a lure which prevents us from thinking. A *dispassionate* conceptual development of the typology of violence must by definition ignore its traumatic impact. (2008, 3–4)

It is not the actual events or the real beatings of these people that are up for discussion here. It is, rather, in Žižek's dispassionate sense that I would like to discuss the portrayal of, and return to, the face of the victim in this film. I am, once again, guided by Butler, who writes of the 9/11 attacks in New York:

> [T]he extensive reporting of the final moments of the lost lives in the World Trade Center are compelling and important stories. They fascinate, and they produce an intense identification by arousing feelings of fear and sorrow. One cannot help but wonder, however, what humanizing effect these narratives have. By this I do not mean simply that they humanize the lives that were lost along with those that narrowly

escaped, but that they stage the scene and provide the narrative means by which "the human" in its grievability is established.

(Butler 2004, 38)

Similarly, *Mugabe and the White African* produces an intense identification with the faces of the white victims of violence, an identification that is racially framed and produced. While the film does depict black victims of the violent farm attacks, it does so fleetingly, without attention to the individual narratives of these victims and in ways that do not carry the symbolic weight of the images of the white victims (the attack on the white victims is the emotional climax of the film). It is clear, as Butler notes, that

> [s]ome lives are grievable, and others are not; the differential allocation of grievability that decides what kind of subject is and must be grieved, and which kind of subject must not, operates to produce and maintain certain exclusionary conceptions of who is normatively human: what counts as a livable life and a grievable death?
>
> (Butler 2004, xiv–xv)

This formulation of grievable life betrays a deep entanglement in the global media with the racial meanings produced and concretized in the epistemes of empire.

Achille Mbembe has illustrated how the contemporary African *commandement* is deeply entangled in colonial legacies of rule and abuse of power (Mbembe 2001). It is perhaps an obvious addition to Mbembe's lucid claim to state that the entire globe remains entangled in the deep matrices of racial meaning laid down across the long histories of colonization. More than mere nostalgia for the colonial episteme, we see an increasing justification for its reiteration today. It is, then, for precisely this reason that the events of the fast-track land reform are distilled sites of deeply entangled relations of colonial and postcolonial power and history, and are, in my analysis, over-determined knots of political and discursive meaning. Furthermore, in their entanglement, on the one hand with colonial configurations of racial meaning and, on the other, their rhetorical seduction in presenting the face of the victim *par excellence* in Zimbabwe, specifically, but by extension Africa more broadly, as white, these discourses place themselves beyond accountability for colonial history. This is perhaps nowhere better illustrated than in the words of Ben Freeth, whose voice we hear above all others in *Mugabe and the White African*, when he states, "Mugabe has only got two cards: and that is [sic] race and land" (26:04). That race and land, the two single most important issues in the history of colonial rule and its aftermath, become for Freeth ephemeral justifications behind the violence he and his family have suffered – a violence that takes absolute precedence – indicates a profound detachment from the racist histories that precede the attack. Violence against the white body is the final frontier of colonial apologism.

Mugabe himself, in somewhat more emotive registers, makes a similar point to the one this chapter is outlining, stating: "These Anglo-Saxon bigots glibly use the language and vocabulary of democracy to duck their colonial responsibility so they can prolong their evil control and ownership of our land and resources" (2001, 137). As mentioned above, Mugabe often draws on dichotomizing structures in his rhetoric in much the same way as his detractors do. Yet both remain so deeply entangled in the racial epistemes of colonial history that the transformational potential of their critiques are undermined.

This kind of discursive trap may also illustrate a much larger snare for postcolonial theory *per se*. Is there a viable "outside" to the ways that the global academy structures the values of knowledge production today, values that produce epistemic violence? Or, to put it another way, can postcolonial scholarship leverage a critical "outside" to the condition of postcolonial melancholia? Perhaps the best we can do, following Mark Sanders' model (2002), is to acknowledge complicity as a precondition of our intellectual work. But given the institutional and economic realities that govern and shape our work as postcolonial scholars today, Mignolo's border thinking seems a horizon beyond a present moment pervaded by the condition of postcolonial melancholia.

NOTES

1. What some scholars have dubbed the "new scramble for Africa" (see for example Carmody 2011 and Okeke 2008).
2. This problematizes Mark Sanders' deconstruction of complicity, too. For Sanders, even "opposition does not free one from complicity, but depends on it as its condition of possibility", and yet it is within the acknowledgement of this complicity that "responsibility is sharpened" (2002, 10). That subaltern silence might be seen to validate the work of intellectual opposition, though, is a form of epistemic violence that requires more than critical self-awareness on behalf of the scholar to repair.
3. See, for example, Auret, Blair, Chan (2002), Godwin (2010), Hill (2005a&b), Holland and Norman.
4. See Ranger 2004 for a discussion of the historical uses of this racial essentialism and Mugabe's *Inside the Third Chimurenga* for his own justification of such racial categories.
5. Cliffe *et al.* point out that "[d]ebate continues as to what extent the overall economic meltdown was caused by or generated declines in post-land reform production or whether and how these processes interacted" (2011, 907). See also Brian Raftopoulos and Tyrone Savage (eds). 2000, *Zimbabwe: Injustice and Political Reconciliation*. Weaver Press: Harare, and Scoones *et al.* 2010. *Zimbabwe's Land Reform: Myths and Realities*. Harare and London: Weaver Press, Jacana Media and James Currey, both cited in Cliffe *et al.*
6. See specifically Chan and Primorac (2004 & 2007). Phimister and Raftopolous (2004) also interrogate the international dimension of the Zimbawbean crisis,

though from a different perspective to my own study. Their focus is on how Mugabe's anti-imperialist rhetoric garnered support from various solidarity movements and other African nations (discussed and cited by Willems 2005, 102).

7. See, too, Karin Alexander's "Orphans of Empire: An analysis of white identity and ideology construction in Zimbabwe" (2004).

8. For a longer discussion of Traicos's and other white memoirists' discursive use of victimhood and nostalgia, see Harris (2004).

9. The film won a British Independent Film Award for Best Documentary, a Sterling World Grand Jury Prize, Washington DC and a Special Jury Prize, US, and was shortlisted for an Oscar nomination for Best Documentary Feature.

10. In a brief overview of the center-left newspapers' reviews of the film, it is worth noting that only *The Guardian's* Blessing-Miles Tendi offers a thorough critique of the film, stating it "puts a heroic gloss on the colonial attitudes that endure in independent Zimbabwe" (Tendi 2010). Two other reviewers offer more tempered critiques. Tom Sutcliffe's review in *The Independent* 19 May 2010, "Last Night's TV – True Stories", and, despite its seemingly positive title, David Smith's "Mugabe and the White African: the brave film that puts a human face on Zimbabwe's troubles" in *The Guardian* 14 May 2010 both point to the film's failure to place the land-reform process in a longer and more critical historical arch. Philip French's "Mugabe and the White African: Film Review" in *The Observer* 10 January 2010 and Peter Bradshaw's "Film review: Mugabe and the White African" in *The Guardian* 7 January 2010 are both exceedingly adulatory of the film. Indeed, Bradshaw later placed the film in his Best Films of 2010 list (see *The Guardian* 1 December 2010). This, too, was the overwhelming reception of the film in the center-right and conservative presses.

11. It is also worth noting how one-sided this public discussion was, entirely ignoring texts that sympathized with the land-reclamation program, such as Nyaradzo Mtizira's *The Chimurenga Protocol*, Gabarone: Botshelo, 2008.

12. In his trenchant review of the film, Blessing-Miles Tendi also notes the directors' demonizing of Mugabe through "rude juxtaposition with the 'good' white farmer" (Tendi 2010).

13. Willems points to various examples where the term "ethnic cleansing" emerges in British media reports on the Zimbabwean crisis. See Willems 2005, 97.

14. The other discernable text on the newspaper's cover is the list of prices: "UK60p | SA R5.00 | Z\$ 100 Million", which is a strong visual marker of Zimbabwe's economic crash.

REFERENCES

Alexander, Jocelyn. 2006. *The Unsettled Land: State-making and the Politics of Land in Zimbabwe, 1893–2003*. Athens, OH: Ohio University Press.

Alexander, Karin. 2004. "Orphans of the Empire: An Analysis of Elements of White Identity and Ideology Construction in Zimbabwe". In *Zimbabwe: Injustice and Political Reconciliation*, edited by Brian Raftopolous and Tyrone Savage, 193–212. Cape Town: Institute for Justice and Reconciliation.

Auret, Michael. 2009. *From Liberator to Dictator: An Insider's account of Robert Mugab's Descent into Tyranny*. Cape Town: New Africa Books.

Blair, David. 2003. *Degrees in Violence: Robert Mugabe and the Struggle for Power in Zimbabwe*. London: Continuum.

Brodie, Nechama. 2013. "Are whites really being killed 'like flies?'" *Mail & Guardian*, 10 October. http://mg.co.za/article/2013-10-10-are-sa-whites-really-being-killed-like-flies.

Brown, Penny. 2003. "Refugees recall a different Zimbabwe". *The Australian*, January 13.

Butler, Judith. 2004. *Precarious Life: The Powers of Mourning and Violence*. London: Verso.

Carmody, Pádraig. 2011. *The New Scramble for Africa*. Cambridge: Polity Press.

Chan, Stephen. 2002. *Robert Mugabe: A Life of Power and Violence*. London: IB Tauris.

Chan, Stephen and Ranka Primorac. 2004. "The Imagination of Land and the Reality of Seizure: Zimbabwe's Complex Reinventions". *Journal of International Affairs* 57.2: 63–80.

Chan, Stephen and Rank Primorac, eds. 2007. *Zimbabwe in Crisis: The International Response and the Space of Silence*. London: Routledge.

Cliffe, Lionel, Jocelyn Alexander, Ben Cousins and Rudo Gaidzanwa. 2011. "An Overview of Fast Track Land Reform in Zimbabwe: Editorial Introduction". *The Journal of Peasant Studies*, 38.5: 907–938.

Gilroy, Paul. 2004. *Postcolonial Melancholia*. New York: Columbia University Press.

Godwin, Peter. 2010. *The Fear: The Last Days of Robert Mugabe*. London: Picador.

Godwin, Peter. 2005. *When a Crocodile Eats the Sun*. London: Picador.

Habermas, Jürgen. 1989. "Heinrich Heine and the Role of the Intellectual in Germany". In *The New Conservatism: Cultural Criticism and the Historians' Debate*, translated by Shierry Weber-Nicholsen, 71–99. Cambridge: MIT Press.

Hill, Geoff. 2005a. *The Battle for Zimbabwe*. Cape Town: Struik Publishers.

Hill, Geoff. 2005b. *What Happens After Mugabe? Can Zimbabwe Rise from the Ashes?* Cape Town: Zebra Press.

Holland, Heidi. 2010. *Dinner with Mugabe: The Untold Story of a Freedom Fighter Who Became a Tyrant*. Camberwell: Penguin.

Harris, Ashleigh. 2012. "An Awkward Silence: Reflections on Africa and Theory". *Kunapipi: Journal of Postcolonial Writing and Culture*. 34.1: 28–41

Harris, Ashleigh. 2004. "'The home I never knew I had': Inscriptions of Whiteness/ Descriptions of Ownership in White Zimbabwean Autobiography". In *Versions of Zimbabwe: Literature, History and Politics*, edited by Robert Muponde and Ranka Primorac, 103–118. Harare: Weaver Press.

Hawley, John C. 2010. "The Colonizing Impulse of Postcolonial Theory". *Modern Fiction Studies* 56.4: 769–787.

Juana, James S. 2006. "A Quantitative Analysis of Zimbabwe's Land Reform Policy: An Application of Zimbabwe SAM Multipliers". *Agrekon* 45.6: 294–318.

Mbembe, Achille. 2001. *On the Postcolony*. Berkeley: University of California Press.

Mbembe, Achille and Sarah Nutall. 2004. "Writing the World from an African Metropolis". *Public Culture* 16.3: 347–372.

Mignolo, Walter. 2011. *The Darker Side of Western Modernity: Global Futures, Decolonial Options*. Durham: Duke University Press.

Mignolo, Walter. 2000. "The Many Faces of Cosmo-polis: Border Thinking and Critical Cosmopolitanism". *Public Culture* 12.3: 721–748.

Mugabe, Robert. 2001. *Inside the Third Chimurenga: Our Land is Our Prosperity*. Harare: Department of Information and Publicity ZANU(PF).

Nnaemeka, Obioma. 2003. "Nego-Feminism: Theorizing, Practicing, and Pruning Africa's Way". *Signs: Journal of Women in Culture and Society* 29.2: 357–385.

Norman, Andrew. 2004. *Robert Mugabe and the Betrayal of Zimbabwe*. Jefferson, NC: MacFarland & Co.

Okeke, Chris Nuwachukwu. 2008. "The Second Scramble for Africa's Oil and Mineral Resources: Blessing or Curse?" *International Lawyer* 43.1: 193–209.

Phimister, Ian and Brian Raftopolous. 2004. "Mugabe, Mbeki and the Politics of Anti-imperialism" *Review of African Political Economy* 31.101: 385–400.

Pilossof, Rory. 2009. "The Unbearable Whiteness of Being: Land, Race and Belonging in the Memoirs of White Zimbabweans". *South African Historical Journal* 61.3: 621–638.

Primorac, Ranka. 2010. "Rhodesians Never Die: The Zimbabwean Crisis and the Revival of Rhodesian Discourse". In *Zimbabwe's New Diaspora: Displacement and the Cultural Politics of Survival*, edited by JoAnn McGregor and Ranka Primorac, 202–228. Oxford: Berghahn Books.

Ranger, Terence. 2004. "Nationalist Historiography, Patriotic History and the History of the Nation: The Struggle over the Past in Zimbabwe". *Journal of South African Studies* 30.2: 215–234.

Ranger, Terence. 2002. "The Zimbabwe Elections: A Personal Experience". *Transformation* 19.3: 159–169.

Sanders, Mark. 2002. *Complicities: The Intellectual and Apartheid*. Durham, NC: Duke University Press.

Shaw, Angus. 2000. "Zanu-PF backs Mugabe, says Zim state media". *SAPA-AP*, 15 December. http://www.iol.co.za/news/africa/zanu-pf-backs-mugabe-says-zim-state-media-1.56626?ot=inmsa.ArticlePrintPageLayout.ot.

Short, Clare. 1997. "Letter to the Zimbabwean minister of agriculture and land". *The Guardian*, 5 November. http://politics.guardian.co.uk/foi/images/0,9069,1015120,00.html.

Solidarity Peace Trust. 2003. "Report on Youth Militia". http://www.solidarity peacetrust.org/205/national-youth-service-training/.

Spivak, Gayatari Chakravorty. [1985] 1994. "Can the Subaltern Speak?" In *Colonial Discourse and Post-Colonial Theory: A Reader*, edited by Patrick Williams and Laura Chrisman, 66–111. New York: Columbia University Press.

Tendi, Blessing-Miles. 2010. "Whitewashing Zimbabwe's history". *The Guardian*, 5 February. http://www.theguardian.com/commentisfree/2010/feb/05/mugabe-white-african-zimbabwe.

Thompson, Andrew and Lucy Bailey, dirs. 2009. *Mugabe and the White African*. Arturi Films.

2003. "US slams Mugabe's 'black Hitler' speech", *The Mail & Guardian Online*, SAPA-AFP, 25 March. http://www.mg.co.za/Content/l3.asp?ao=12422.

Vidal, John and Claire Provost. 2011. "US universities in Africa land grab". *The Guardian*, 8 June. http://www.theguardian.com/world/2011/jun/08/us-universities-africa-land-grab.

Willems, Wendy. 2005. "Remnants of Empire? British media reporting on Zimbabwe". In *Westminster Papers in Communication and Culture*: 91–108. http://www.west-minster.ac.uk/_data/assets/pdf_file/0017/20177/007zim_art6.pdf.

Žižek, Slavoj. 2008. *Violence*. New York: Picador.

7 Staging the *Mulata*

Performing Cuba

Alison Fraunhar

Figure 7.1 "*Mulata* de Rumbo", Victor Patricio de Landaluze, in *Tipos y costumbres de la isla de Cuba colección de artículos por los mejores autores de este género*. Antonio Bachiller y Morales, ed. (Miguel de Villa, Havana 1881).

The well-known lithograph *Mulata del Rumbo* by Victor Patricio de Landaluze depicts a young woman standing with her body in three-quarter profile, gazing over her right shoulder at an unseen admirer (Fig. 7.1). With frizzy hair, deep skin tone, round nose and full lips slightly parted in a seductive, knowing smile, her face is animated, but her features lack refinement. Carnality is asserted in her arms and neck, which appear strong and robust rather than frail and delicate. She leans to the left, holding a fan in her left hand, while her right hand rests on her hip, elbow cocked in a pose both jaunty and sinuous. Wearing a pretty dress trimmed with lace and a ruffled hem swirling on the ground, she has a fringed shawl draped loosely around her waist in a graceful but insouciant style. The shawl, rather than modestly covering her, reveals more of her neck, décolleté and arms than a white woman would have shown in public. Nor would a white woman ever appear alone in public, while the nameless *mulata* is posed in front of what appears to be an exterior wall and sidewalk. Her manner of dress, body language, location and physical features all combine to flaunt her "not-quite-ness" – not quite white, not quite black (Bhabha 2004).

This sense of in-between-ness that Bhabha articulated is the starting point for a wide range of colonial practices and negotiations embedded in visual and textual representations and performances of *mulataje* – the attributes and qualities associated with being a *mulata*. I italicize the Spanish *mulata* instead of the English mulatta to signal an epistemological difference between the two words that resists translation. By italicizing the word, I want to emphasize the Spanish meaning of the word while simultaneously marking its difference. *Mulataje* signals both the lived experience of the mixed-race children of colonial relations and the symbolic valence of the idea of the *mulata* as an ambivalently privileged colonial subject. The problematics of race and racial mixture were well documented in the Spanish colonial world, and relations of race were a source of great desire and anxiety. While perhaps the casta paintings of New Spain are better known, nowhere was racial nuance better articulated than in *costumbrismo*, a popular nineteenth-century visual and literary movement that sought to painstakingly (if superficially) depict the racial, occupational and regional particularities of metropolitan and peripheral subjects. Landaluze was a master of the *costumbrismo*, as indicated in the title of the volume in which this lithograph first appeared. The lithograph's title, *Mulata del Rumbo*, and the image announce ambivalence, relying on the interplay of visual and textual signs that bear multiple meanings. The first meaning of *rumbo* is course or direction, suggesting that the *mulata del rumbo* is a girl on the move, confident, even brash. *Rumbo* also refers more colloquially to the street, the disreputable public space off limits to proper white ladies, suggesting that it is the proper place for the disreputable *mulata*. *Rumba* is also a Cuban dance form originating in Afro-Cuban culture, and *mulatas* were considered to be particularly adept at dancing it; indeed, the posture and attitude of the *Mulata del Rumbo* suggest dance. Finally, *rumbo/rumba* is slang for party: the smiling *mulata* is a party girl (Lane 2005, 198). The various meanings of *rumbo* all coalesce as defining attributes of the *mulata*. *Mulata del Rumbo* is a performative image, conveying self-awareness through the *mulata*'s pose and her gaze as she embodies the stereotype that had become, by then, congealed: a young woman who is desirable, graceful, sexually available, materialistic, flirtatious, shallow and vain.

While the stereotype of the *mulata* that I have just described in some detail was constructed during the colonial era and contributed to pervasive racial anxiety in the colony, it persists to this day. The racial category *mulata* encompasses a wide range of skin colors and phenotypes, often troubling attempts to determine a mixed-race person's racial identity and contributing greatly to colonial anxiety. Usually erroneously defined as the female child of European and African parents, the *mulata*'s racial composition also includes indigenous people and Asians who contributed to Cuba's makeup, although they are often overlooked in the narrative of Cuban identity. Ambiguity weaves through depictions of *mulatas* and performances of *mulataje* reflecting, contesting and revealing changing ideologies of the nation. Here I take the liberty of insisting on the term *mulataje* to refer specifically to the attributes and qualities associated with the *mulata* rather than the term *mestizaje* more commonly used throughout the hemisphere, usually in reference to the offspring of European and indigenous liaisons both licit and illicit. This tension becomes the core and the central paradox of Cuban identity, what Vera Kutzinski calls "the erotics of Cuban nationalism", a libidinal sense of the nation that is embodied and affective (Kutzinski 1993). As I will show, through racial mixture and affiliation with both sinners and saints, the *mulata* embodies the notion of Cuba, the eroticized nation, in all its paradoxical glory. This essay is meant to be a preliminary consideration of the relation between *mulataje* and ideology in Cuba through its representation in fine and graphic arts, and its performance on stage, screen and, as it is depicted in *Mulata del Rumbo*, on the street.

In colonial Cuba, categories of race and class were permeable rather than rigidly fixed; people migrated up and down racial, social and economic scales (Martinez Alier 1989). Within this mutable system, the *mulata* came to stand for what was uniquely Cuban, albeit endowed with greater symbolic value than agency. The trope of the *mulata* was prescriptive and performative in theater, in music and cabaret, and eventually on film, stretching across to the performance of everyday life, where identity, constituted through race, gender, ethnicity, religion, sexuality and profession, is performed. Judith Butler has argued that gender is "an identity tenuously constituted in time – an identity instituted through *a stylized repetition of acts*" (Butler 1989, 519; my emphasis). Alicia Arrizon and Angela and Onik'a Gilliam also privilege performativity as the primary constituent of *mulataje*, disavowing the phenotypical basis of racial classification (Arrizon 2006; Gilliam and Gilliam 1999). *Mulataje* is constituted from geographical, phenotypical and cultural markers that are recruited as signifiers of identity, albeit unstable ones, and is interpreted through an epistemological framework of colonialism and imperialism. It is constituted through activation, rather than being determined by a specific racial configuration. Angela Gilliam situates *mulataje* as a condition of youth (young women are *mulatas*, old women are black), and Alicia Arrizon calls particular attention to the hybrid and performative *mulata* body within a field of agricultural products also synonymous with Cuba. *Mulataje* draws authority from European, indigenous and African traditions: the European *gitana* (gypsy), the Arawak mother deity, Attabeira, and the Yoruban *orisha* (deity) Ochún, goddess of sweet water, flirtation, dance and romance. Through repetition and reiteration, the disreputable, desirable European gypsy is combined with the *orisha*, who is then conflated with the Virgin of Charity, patron saint of Cuba. The hybrid figure that accommodates all these predecessors is canonized as *la mulata cubana*. Homi Bhabha, Robert J.C. Young and other postcolonial theorists develop the notion of hybridity to describe an epistemology produced at the site of contact between colonizer and colonized: the *mulata*, as a mixed-race body, constitutes its embodiment (Bhabha 1994; Young 1995). Along with the indeterminacy of race, the performance of gender, including, as we shall see, cross-dressing, complicates attempts to fix a stable meaning to *mulataje*.

Tipos y Costumbres de la isla de Cuba (Cuban types and customs), the volume in which in *Mulata del Rumbo* appeared, was comprised of *costumbrista* literary sketches written, as the subtitle informs us, by "the best writers of this genre" and illustrated by Victor Patricio de Landaluze, perhaps the most iconic artist of nineteenth-century Cuba. Landaluze (1830–1889) had immigrated to Cuba around 1850 and was a staunch loyalist. At a time when nationalist sentiment and opposition to Spanish rule were surging in Cuba, he held a Spanish military commission. While Landaluze's ideological leanings certainly contributed to a European rather than Creole world view, he nevertheless sought to document a unique sense of place and identity through the description of types, activities and settings that were specific to Cuba. The sense of national identity in this instance was neither contingent upon nor coeval with national sovereignty in the visualization of *cubanidad*, an essential sense of being Cuban. The nation was imagined and visualized before it came into being. *Mulata del Rumbo* and *Tipos y Costumbres de la isla de Cuba* visualized Cuba through a bourgeois, Eurocentric lens, making bourgeois subjective visuality the zero point of normativity, the invisible center from which different subject positions were viewed and evaluated. As popular graphics, the illustrations in *Tipos y Costumbres* do not fit neatly within the canon of art history but as the work of an academy-trained European artist, neither are they entirely marginalized. Like so many other aspects of coloniality and of Cuba itself, this work hovers in between: in between fine art and "mere" illustration, in between civilization and the rest. For a nation such as Cuba in which relations of power and race implanted during the colonial era have persisted well beyond independence, Latin American postcolonial theory can help to explain the operation of such relations. The issues and debates about specificities and commonalities embedded in Latin American colonial, postcolonial, national and regional discourses are well represented in a recent volume, *Coloniality at Large*, edited by Mabel Morana, Enrique Dussel and Carlos A. Jauregui (2008). This volume theorizes Latin America with a continental focus and largely overlooks the Caribbean. Once more, the Caribbean constitutes the margin of the margin. United neither by common language nor common colonial history, the region itself resists unifying theories, as was so eloquently noted by Antonio Benitez Rojo in *The Repeating Island* (1992).

Visualizing the nation in the nineteenth century was effected not through the so-called fine arts but through new, popularizing technologies of mechanical reproduction: lithography and chromolithography, along with popular theater and the proliferation of periodicals. These visual technologies worked between the narrative and the spectacular. Vision and visuality are deeply implicated in colonial and postcolonial relations of power, a charge that continues to reverberate to this day (Landau and Kaspin 2002; Ryan 1997). The visual turn towards self-representation was an international phenomenon that began in the late eighteenth century, and volumes of subjects *pintados por si mismos* appeared throughout Europe and Latin America. These volumes include the English *Heads of the People* (1840–41), the French *Les Français peints par eux-mêmes* (1841), the Spanish *Los españoles pintados por si mismos* (1844) and Mexican *Los mexicanos pintados por si mismos* (1854). *Costumbrismo* was concerned with "typical" characters, details of dress, activity or vernacular speech, occupations and geo-historical features in light, humorous essays, poems and sketches. Proclaiming by their titles an agenda of self-representation, *costumbrista* volumes highlighted and codified characteristic types and tastes found in the respective nations, both representing and constructing a vision of national identity. *Costumbrista* volumes included images that contain a high degree of authenticating detail, presenting views that reinforced bourgeois values by delivering a set of fantasy relations of class, race and gender to a literate bourgeois constituency for its pleasure and elucidation: nineteenth-century "info-tainment". *Costumbrismo* typologized modern life by reducing social life to a set of stock characters and set situations, including pretentious social climbers, naïve innocents, labor and laborers, peasants, street scenes and the racialized others of Empire. *Costumbrismo* fits between two styles that likewise contributed greatly to colonial imaginaries. *Casta* painting in eighteenth-century Nueva España (Mexico) preceded *costumbrismo*, and Orientalism, the late nineteenth-century realist mode of describing the British and French colonial territories of the Middle East and North Africa, followed it (Carrera 2003; Katzew 2004).

In visual culture, Orientalism focused less on the mechanics of colonial raciality (since racial mixing was a less visibly prominent feature of Middle Eastern and North African colonialism than was the case in Spanish American colonies) than did *costumbrismo*, and more on scenes of native life painted in the academic style, with laser-sharp detail and highly selective compositions. Like Orientalism, Cuban *costumbrismo* was an offshoot of romanticism, and served to parse the nuances of subject formation and as travelogue of the exotic for European consumers, but it also helped to consolidate self-recognition and self-construction for subjects and soon-to-be citizens of the island/nation. Engaging with contemporary scientific, evolutionary and anthropological discourses of race and culture, *costumbrismo* flourished through the burgeoning print-culture industry in which newspapers and journals proliferated (see Thomas 2012, 104). In addition to *costumbrista* volumes dedicated to scenes of Cuban life, nineteenth-century Cuban writers used the many periodical publications, *Album de lo bueno y bello* (1860), *Almanaque de Juan Palomo* (1870–73) and *Don Junipero* (1862–1869), as discursive sites in which to critique the gamut of Cuban life, from social events to current events, political commentary to literature, comic sketches, caricatures and satire. The visual lexicon established by *costumbrismo* remained a touchstone for subsequent cultural production, as types, customs and settings were recycled over and over. By the time *Tipos y costumbres* was published in 1881, *costumbrismo* was on the wane globally, perhaps a victim of changing fashion as photography gained popularity as the medium of choice for visual documentation and graphic arts began to draw upon a more expressionistic style. But the importance of *Tipos y costumbres* in Cuban culture as a source for later artists, as a document of the time and as a template for national identity is unparalleled, and *costumbrismo* has survived in Cuba to the present day.

Under the sign of *costumbrismo*, the unique qualities of *cubanidad* were worked out in popular culture, in theatrical performance, caricature and graphic art, verse, song and in the practice of everyday life. As early as the 1830s, the Spanish-Cuban writer and actor Bartolomé Crespo Borbón gave voice to an invented Afro-Cuban identity, writing and performing in blackface as the "African" Creto Ganga (Rio Prado 2010; Leal 1975; Lane 2005; Cruz 1975; Thomas 2008). Like his contemporary Landaluze, Crespo y Borbón was a Spanish immigrant and loyalist who strategically deployed African characters as figures of ridicule to reinforce the idea of European superiority and hence to justify European domination. Crespo y Borbón is always associated with the holy trinity of Cuban *costumbrismo* that featured so prominently in his *œuvre*: the *negrito* (the comic African), *gallego* (the naive Spanish immigrant) and *mulata*. These figures were invented through the enmeshed processes of colonial appropriation, nascent capitalism and world systems, slavery and the plantation economy, reified and authorized through repetition and performance. As subalterns, they threatened the social order either through irreverence, encroachment or outright rebellion. Fear of this latent if unrealized power was deflected through a particularly Cuban form of satire, *choteo*, in which pretentiousness and social striving were exaggerated and ridiculed. In the plays of Creto Ganga, the *gallego* was portrayed as the naïve and gullible Spanish immigrant, the *negrito* as pompous, mischievous and sly, and the *mulata* as vain, frivolous and materialistic (Mañach 1955; Laguna 2012). As Creto Ganga, Crespo Borbón created a paradoxical space in the Cuban public sphere for the representation of Afro-Cubans (in the dual sense of speaking for and standing in place of). The popularity and ubiquity of Creto Ganga's Afrocuban characters on the Cuban stage foreclosed on more nuanced and authentic self-representation of and by blacks and *mulatos*, and yet, by their very visibility and presence, Creto Ganga's characters normalized blackness on the larger stage of Cuban identity.

The figure of the *mulata* was performed in popular theatrical genres including *zarzuela* and *teatro bufo,* the light theater forms that derived from Spanish *zarzuela* and Italian light opera. These were the dominant popular musical theater forms in Cuba in the nineteenth century, and although imported from Spain, each was adapted and reconfigured to express Cuban cultural, musical and even political themes (Thomas 2008). Although *bufo* did not originate in Cuba, it did play a particularly crucial role in visualizing national identity on the island (Leal 2002; Lane 2005). In Cuban *teatro bufo*, nationalist desire eschewed imported characters and narratives in favor of Cuban scenarios that deployed popularizing and stereotypical characters in scenarios that defamiliarized the operation of Spanish colonial authority. While drama was not highly esteemed as an art form in nineteenth-century Cuba (indeed regarded as the poor stepsister of literature), the freshness, immediacy and relevance of Cuban *bufo* and *zarzuela* made them extremely popular. Like popular graphics, they reached a far greater percentage of the population than loftier forms such as novels, appreciated and read by only a few. The first *bufo* performance took place in May 1868, just months prior to the outbreak of the first Cuban war of independence, the Ten Years War. *Bufo* immediately had a galvanizing effect in Cuba. As Jill Lane notes, "[I]t marks the moment in which audiences recognized themselves on stage, and in that moment of recognition, in that mutual gaze from audience to stage and back, recognized themselves as *Cuban*" (Lane 2005, 60). It did not take long for this empowering sense of identification to make *bufo* dangerous to the authorities. In a well-known incident several months later, the cry of "*Viva la gente que produce la caña!*" ("Long live the people that produce the [sugar] cane!") shouted by an audience member during a *bufo* performance in January 1869 precipitated a brutal crackdown from the colonial government and drove most *bufo* companies into exile until after the end of the war (Rio Prado 2010, 24). This incident demonstrates the paradoxical relation between representation and identity. While *bufo* served as a vehicle to express Cuban identity and desire for independence, it did so through the use of stereotypical characters and texts often written by loyalists like Creto Ganga.

Notwithstanding the popularity of *teatro bufo*, rituals and performances by Africans and Cubans of color pre-date the advent of professional theater in Cuba by centuries. Among the earliest performances in Cuba were those staged by Africans in ceremonies held in honor of Yoruba deities conflated with Catholic saints in a religious practice that later became known as Regla de Ocha or Santería (Castellanos, Jorge and Isabel 1994; Leal 1975; Ortiz 2001). The Cuban carnival tradition, conflating European and Yoruban ritual (hence, in itself, "*mulata*"), first documented in the early nineteenth century and still performed today, had a major impact on and continues to shape and reflect social reality on the island. In *comparsas* (carnival parades) and masking traditions, the beautiful *mulata*, frequently dressed in Ochún/ Caridad's bright yellow dress, is a prominent and celebrated figure.

The characteristics that were admired and burlesqued onstage in the nineteenth century constituted the raw material of tragedy prominent in literature of that time in which the *mulata* was overwhelmingly presented as a tragic figure. While parody and humor were effective strategies for the kind of immediate social critique enacted in popular theater, the longer form of the novel created space for a more in-depth analysis of social problems. During the nineteenth century, debates about the future of slavery and burgeoning national desire destabilized colonial authority in Cuba. The crisis of the colonial patriarchy played out on women's bodies, particularly *mulata* bodies, through attempts to regulate and suppress women's sexuality, participation in the public sphere and economic agency. The most noteworthy literary exploration of the effects (on men and women, blacks and whites) of the protonational crisis is the great Cuban *costumbrista* novel by Cirilio Villaverde, *Cecilia Valdés o la loma del Angel* (1882), the book that established the template for tragic erotic *mulatas* for generations to come. Considered by many the definitive Cuban novel of the nineteenth century, *Cecilia Valdés* was a masterpiece of *costumbrismo*. Villaverde's progressive social views and political activism earned him the wrath of the colonial government, and he spent many years in exile in the US. In brief, *Cecilia Valdés* relates the story of the beautiful *mulata* Cecilia, who is having a passionate affair with Leonardo, the son of a wealthy Spanish merchant, who just happens to be her halfbrother. Unbeknownst to Cecilia, Leonardo is betrothed to a wealthy, white girl and his betrayal drives Cecilia crazy. She descends into madness and meets a tragic end, as did her *mulata* mother before her. Critics have long read *Cecilia Valdés* as an allegory of Cuba. Cecilia's racial in-between-ness, along with the tropes of illegitimacy and incest that were the by-products of slavery and colonialism, come to stand for the tragedy of the nation *avant la lettre* (de la Torriente 1940; Raimundo 1979; Summer 2002). *Cecilia Valdés* has resonated powerfully with generations of Cuban artists and writers, and has inspired myriad interpretations since its publication. In addition to being read as a national allegory, *Cecilia* has inspired myriad interpretations. Noteworthy among these are an opera (Ernesto Lecuona's *Maria La O*, 1930), a postcolonial, queer re-writing (Reinaldo Arenas' *Graveyard of the Angels*, 1987) and a film (Humberto Solas' *Cecilia*, 1981).

In the nineteenth century, *mulata* stage characters were created by white writers and performed by white performers, but early in the twentieth century, *mulata* performers began to gain prominence, particularly in musical and cabaret performance. During the 1910s and 1920s, *mulata* singers, musicians and composers created and performed powerful personas grounded in the compliance with and rejection of tropes. In this photograph, dated July 11, 1916, Maria Teresa Vera (1895–1965) is seated – not in a submissive position but as if enthroned (Fig. 7.2).

Figure 7.2 Maria Teresa Vera and Rafael Zequiera, NY, July 11, 1916.

Her gaze is clear and direct; she wears a masculine hat and plain dress, and sits holding her guitar. The photograph was taken in New York while Vera was recording and performing with her professional partner, Rafael Zequeira, who stands beside her, pointing to her as if to acknowledge her as the central figure of the image and indeed their partnership. Although infrequently photographed, she always appeared in photographs dressed in simple clothes with little jewelry, no makeup, her hair was always conservatively styled. In her strategic refusal to perform feminine beauty and desirability, she subverted conventional expectations of *mulataje*. Perhaps the first Cuban *mulata* to achieve wide renown nationally and abroad, her first public performance was at the age of sixteen. She was the first woman in Cuba to perform in the open-air cafés in Havana. Vera's most remarkable accomplishment was to attain success in the music business in Cuba at a time when this was unprecedented for a woman, and her success was far from inevitable. Vera began her career at a turbulent time in the young republic. With the recent emancipation of slaves (1888) and more recent independence from Spain (1899), discourses of race and citizenship were highly charged. Theoretically entitled to full enfranchisement, Afrocubans were in fact systematically denied opportunities in education, jobs, health care and living conditions, in addition to being subjected to a vicious military backlash in 1912 against Afrocuban war of independence veterans protesting unfair treatment (Helg 1995). At the same time, the first two decades of the republic saw tremendous social upheavals in Cuban society. Cuba sought to shake off its brutal and conservative Spanish colonial legacy and, among other sweeping social changes, women in Cuba flooded into the cities seeking employment and education.

Not only did she lack formal musical training and was obviously not white but she sang in a direct, unembellished voice in the everyday vernacular of the streets. She is credited as one of the founders of the *trova* or folk music movement in the first decade of the twentieth century. Her music was an important bridge between older folk music and the burgeoning urban sound of *son*, comprised of African syncopation and Spanish melody. It superseded the older, more sedate *danzon* and was a slightly disreputable sensation when it was first introduced. Cristobal Diaz Ayala notes that *son*'s success was due in part to economic considerations, as the *danzon* required a larger, more expensive classically trained orchestra than did the smaller, more improvisational *son*.

Although details of her romantic life were never included in any official biographical data, Vera was widely believed to be lesbian. In the 1930s she was rumored to be romantically as well as professionally involved with Guillermina Aramburu, an elite white poet who wrote the lyrics to one of Vera's most famous songs, *Veinte Años*, although Aramburu allegedly denied that there was any romantic involvement between them. In any event, Vera's personal conduct was exceptionally discreet, and she was never publically linked romantically with anyone of either sex. She was, however, initiated into Regla de Ocha (also known as Santería, the Afrocuban religion conflating Yoruban deities or *orishas* with Catholic saints) as daughter of Ochún, the Afrocuban deity depicted as a sensual, graceful *mulata*. Ochún is associated with the Virgin of Charity, the (*mulata*) patron saint of Cuba. Vera was a serious devotee. Ordered by the *babalawo* (Regla de Ocha priest) to retire from her musical career, she stopped performing and recording for almost three years. Although dedicated to Ochún, the supreme deity of femininity, Vera became an icon of Cuban music in spite of her apparent rejection of the conventions of *mulataje* and her lack of formal training, succeeding through the force of her prodigious musicality.

In contrast with the working class, rurally born Vera, Rita Montaner (1900–1958) was born into a middle-class, mixed-race family in Guanabacoa, a suburb of Havana that was a locus for the Afrocuban religious practices of Santería and Abakua. The atmosphere of the town was steeped in the rhythms and chants of "*la religion*", as African religious practice was collectively known. Guanabacoa was also home to the pianist and singer Bola de Nieve and the composer Ernesto Lecuona, two other great figures in Cuban popular music of the republican era. Both of them were frequent collaborators of Montaner. Montaner's white, professional father ensured that she was well educated, fluent in several languages, and was classically trained in voice and piano, grooming her for middle-class status, catering to elite cultural preferences. As early as her teens, Montaner had attracted attention for her prodigality, garnering publicity and prizes for voice and piano. But Montaner was drawn to the African cultural forms of her neighborhood, and became increasingly sensitive to the racial prejudice she experienced in the elite world. Although she achieved critical acclaim and success as a classical musician, she became hugely popular nationally for her interpretation of roles and personae of the black underclass, most famously the *calesero* (the black coachman) in the *sainete* (one-act musical theater piece) *La Niña Rita o La Habana de 1830* (Grenet, Lecuona, 1927) at the Teatro Regina. Even before her appearance in *La Niña Rita*, Montaner had already performed and recorded in important venues in New York, Spain and France, and regularly starred in light operatic productions in Havana. In *La Niña Rita*, she appeared in blackface, dressed as a male coachman or *calesero*.

Figure 7.3 Rita Montaner as El calesero in *La Nina Rita*, Sept. 29, 1927.

Opportunities for Cuban artists and performers were limited, and those who were able to left the island for lucrative contracts and expanded audiences abroad. Montaner, a *mulata,* flaunted her own racial ambivalence through her blackface performance and her cross-dressing that both transgressed normative feminine behavior, albeit in the socially sanctioned context of the theater (Fig. 7.3). Her performance as the *calesero* crossed the divide between the staged and the everyday, as well, as her very appearance onstage with a white company was in itself controversial. This instance of blackface and cross-dressing is an example of the suppressed, "queer" yet highly visible counter discourse to the heroic, white, masculine norm of the nation. Montaner's transgressive, carnivalesque performance complied with at the same time as it put pressure on *costumbrista* stereotypes and relations of race within the liminal space of the theater. Montaner entertained without threatening the largely white audiences, although at a high psychic price. She suffered deeply from a sense of cultural ambivalence and the racism and rejection from high society that she experienced as a *mulata*. Although she proudly claimed her Afrocuban heritage and advocated against racial prejudice and oppression, off stage her volatile personality and sometimes unruly conduct crippled her career. Composer and orchestra leader Gonzalo Roig claimed that Montaner would have achieved greater success than that of the African American diva Josephine Baker were it not for her unpredictability and tendency to act out publicly. While she never attained the international profile of Baker, she has remained an idol in Cuba, known as "*Rita de Cuba*" and "*Rita la unica*". Her widespread adulation testifies to Cubans' willingness to accommodate complexities in identity.

During the post World War II period, Cuba became the privileged "other" to Mexican national identity construction and contestation. Cuban musicians, Cuban actresses and directors were welcomed in Mexico, and the *cabaretera* film genre that began in the late 1940s was a great fit for Cuban femininity, dance and sexuality. Cuban actress/dancers Ninon Sevilla, Maria Antonieta Pons and Rosa Carmina epitomized the *cabaretera*, becoming stars of Mexican cinema, performing Cuban *mulataje* in their stage and film performances. *Cabaretera* films were melodramas set in the demimonde of the nightclub or dance hall, spaces at once modern, liminal and dangerous. This genre bloomed at the tail end of Mexican cinema's *edad de oro* or golden age. This spanned the mid-1930s to the mid-1950s, a period in which the Mexican film industry released films with local and national themes, narratives and characters characterized by high production values. In the eponymous *Mulata* (Martinez 1953), the dancer and actress Ninon Sevilla played a dual role of (black) mother and *mulata* (daughter), in both brown and blackface. *Mulata*, while hardly one of Sevilla's classic films, makes explicit the link between Cuban femininity, sensuality and race. It is a fascinating and disturbing film, incorporating an almost ethnographic scene of a *toque de tambor* (Afrocuban drum and dance session dedicated to the *orishas*) in which Sevilla dances the classic moves of the physically embodied worship of Regla de Ocha within a conventional melodramatic narrative. Sevilla, although extremely fair, was particularly adept at Afrocuban dance because she grew up in the largely Afrocuban neighborhood of Centro Habana, and was familiar with Afrocuban religious and cultural practices.

Figure 7.4 Poster, *Mulata* (Martinez, 1953).

The scene was shot on location on a beach with *cinéma verité* cinematography and live sound, the editing and changing available light and shadow suggesting that the dance and trance session took place over several hours. As the scene progresses, all the dancers except Sevilla fall into ecstatic trances that without exception cause them to rip open their dresses and expose their breasts. The scene and the photograph reproduced in the movie poster (Fig. 7.4) offer a striking example of the projection of Eurocentric desire and fantasy onto African or Afrocuban ritual. Nowhere in the history of Afrocuban religious or secular performance was bodice-ripping normative behavior. This scene strikingly situates what I call tropi-erotics, the unquestioned stereotype of tropical erotics within purported ethnographic observation, producing a reality effect that endorses the fictions of erotic possession and African sexuality. Yet Sevilla's performance complicates our understanding of *mulataje*. Although she was a white woman performing racialized characters, her background and personal affinities authenticate and authorize the performance.

Mulatas and *rumberas cubanas* circulated beyond Mexico to other Latin American countries. The burgeoning popularity of Cuban music and dance, especially the *rumba*-based *mambo*, opened markets for Cuban orchestras and musical combos who began performing to great acclaim around Latin America in the late 1940s. Orchestras like Lecuona Cuban Boys and Casino de la Playa (Miguelito Valdez), Benny More y el Conjunto Matamoros,

Conjunto Casino, Perez Prado, la Orquesta America toured Latin America with dancers and singers, including Sevilla. The extremely sensual rhythm and dance style of the *mambo* provided a liberatory sound track for much of a continent slowly emerging from centuries of cultural domination by conservative Spanish norms. Among the principal exponents of this phenomenon were the *Mulatas De Fuego* (the *Mulatas* of Fire or Fiery *Mulatas*), a troupe of six dancers and three singers and two models, all young *mulatas*, that was assembled by Rodney (Rodrigo Neyra), dancer, choreographer and designer who went to achieve great renown as the artistic director of the famed nightclub the Tropicana. The singers included a very young Celia Cruz and Elena Burke, who became two of the great divas of popular Cuban music of the twentieth century. *Las Mulatas del Fuego* constitute a lesser-known episode in the history of *mulataje*. They and the troupes they inspired were all directed by men but nevertheless, they were all *mulatas* (indeed, Rodney himself was *mulato*) and represent a rather unusual conflation of staged and lived identity.

Rodney assembled the group in 1947 for a film and a stage show, *Zamba Rumba*, presented at the Faust Theater in Havana to tremendous critical and popular success. They inspired numerous other *mulata* revues, none of which attained their level of popularity or fame. *Las Mulatas del Fuego* initiated the rise of the *mulata* showgirl in Cuba, and Rodney took the formula with him to the Tropicana nightclub in Havana, where it became canonic. The Tropicana was a legendary nightclub in the decade before the revolution, although inaccessible to the majority of Cubans. It generated and reinforced codes of exotic tropical music and femininity for the multitudes of tourists who visited Cuba in the 1950s, most of them coming from the US. In numerous revues, *mulata* showgirls, dancers and models performed the exotic, racialized female for a new, international audience of tourists.

During the first two decades of the revolution that abruptly foreclosed on the excesses of late-republican Cuba, the erotics of *mulataje* were radically proscribed if not entirely suppressed, re-emerging only due to the exigencies of the Special Period (Fraunhar 2004). The so-called "Special Period in Time of Peace" refers to the economic crisis in Cuba precipitated by the collapse of the Soviet Union in 1990, which lasted until 1997, although arguably the country has still not entirely recovered from its devastation. Recent changes and continuities in the presentation and representation of *mulataje* are pervasive in the publicity and packaging of the popular Cuban rum, Ron Mulata. Ron Mulata was launched in 1993 but distributed only in Cuba until 2005 (when very limited European distribution began) at a lower price point for a domestic consumer base than Havana Club, the internationally distributed prestige brand. Unlike Havana Club, Ron Mulata and its images are aimed at a national market, not a touristic imaginary, although for some reason, it was advertised in the pages of *Cine Cubano*, the Cuban film-industry magazine that is distributed abroad as well as in Cuba even before it was available internationally. The publicity for Ron Mulata features an image of a racially indeterminate young woman garlanded with a wreath of sunflowers, invoking the visual heritage of nineteenth-century lithographs like *Mulata del Rumbo* (Fig. 7.5).

Figure 7.5 Label, Ron Mulata, n.d.

The protagonist of the image, for she is clearly performing a role, engages the spectator with an expression at once grave, self-reflexive, modest and sultry. The image and the persona being performed in it are based upon a long line of sexy *mulatas*. The *mulata* is here recruited to explicitly represent rum (evoking intoxication, carefree abandon), the sugar from which rum is refined, a product deeply implicated in Cuban history, and the code of *mulataje*.

It may be useful to consider this image alongside the *Mulata del Rumbo*. The contemporary/nineteenth-century *mulata* of Ron Mulata has been whitewashed, sanitized and made appealing for a different constituency. Against this refashioned return of the repressed, we might want to consider the case of the *jinetera*, the street prostitute whose re-emergence on the streets of Havana after decades of virtual absence, was another result of the exigencies of the Special Period, which began with the fall of the Soviet Union. The collapse of government subsidies made access to dollars, and what they could buy on the black market, important for survival. And while prostitutes had been condemned, reviled and demonized since nineteenth-century discourses of public health (and officially rehabilitated and reintegrated in the revolution), at this post-revolutionary moment of crisis they emerged as everyday heroines. The earnings of the *jineteras* gave them power as players in the dollar economy and they were also recognized as providers for their families who were willing to make great sacrifices. In Daniel Diaz Torres' 2012 film *La Pelicula de Ana*, Ana (Laura de la Uz) plays the role of an actress pretending to be a prostitute to earn money from a German documentary production and recites an impassioned monologue about the exigencies of daily life during the Special Period, personalizing Cuban stories about the lengths to which people had to go to meet necessities for survival. As *La Pelicula de Ana* nimbly demonstrates, prostitution is a form of performance, blurring the boundary between everyday life and theatrical or filmed performance. Commodified feminine desirability and availability are enacted through the performance of the repertoire of *mulataje*.

Throughout Cuban history the iconic *mulata* served and continues to serve now as a visible sign of Cuban identity and as a form of social control, one that ostensibly celebrates visibility while at times foreclosing on agency. In Cuba, the trope of the *mulata* is performed daily. For many young *Cubanas* even today, the embodiment (looking like a sexy *mulata*) and performance (flirting, dancing well, etc.) of these characteristics is a template for personal and professional success. In Fernando Perez's classic, lyrical, city-symphony film *Suite Habana* (2003), a brief scene reframes the classic discourse of the desirable *mulata* in contemporary performative lexicon. A beautiful young *mulata* with the almond eye shape suggestive of Asian heritage walks down a crowded city street where she is appreciatively ogled by male construction workers, loiterers and passersby. One man in particular tries to join her, casting ardent looks at her; she cuts her eyes at him, dismissing him with a disdainful expression on her face as she leaves him behind. Thus she performs both her desirability as well as self-awareness of its value in a commodified marketplace of gendered, sexualized relations of power (Fig. 7.6).

While I have provided several examples of the contemporary iteration of *mulataje*, I end with an example that takes the notion of *mulataje* from the phenotypical and biological into the realm of self-invention. This is the adoption of the *mulata* persona in contemporary transvestite culture in Havana. In another key scene in *Suite Habana*, Ivan, a quiet, serious young man who works in a hospital laundry, comes home after work and enacts an elaborate ritual of transformation as he dresses in a long brocade dress, luxurious wig, full makeup, with false eyelashes, long fingernails and platform high heels, becoming a glamorous *mulata*. He then goes out to a nightclub where, as a drag performer, he lip-syncs "*Ya no me hace falta*" ("I don't need you"), a song made popular by the group Bamboleo. (Bamboleo, incidentally, was fronted by two glamorous *mulata* singers, Vannia Borges and Haila Mompie.) Drag performances like this have become popular in both Havana and provincial cities around Cuba as attitudes about sexuality in

Figure 7.6 Still from *Suite Habana* (Fernando Perez, dir., 2003).

the heavily patriarchal and *machista* nation are gradually changing. In this photograph by Mariette Pathy Allen, a performer at Havana's famous Las Vegas Club dressed in Ochun's vibrant yellow and gold dances alongside a giant inflatable bottle of Havana Club rum (Fig. 7.7).

Figure 7.7 Performer at the Las Vegas Club, Havana © Mariette Pathy Allen 2012.

It is in its iteration as drag that the queer potential of *mulataje* comes full circle. In the colonial era, the *mulata*'s simultaneous desirability and transgressive nature were rooted in the racial ambiguity that eventually came to signify Cuba's unique identity. The contemporary drag performance of *mulataje* simultaneously disavows, flaunts, foregrounds and evacuates biological bases for defining identity.

Shifting depictions of *mulatas* and performances of *mulataje* reflect, reveal and correspond to changing ideology. The concerns of nation-building in the nineteenth century required a figurehead who could unite the island's population and distinguish it from metropolitan and other hemispheric polities, and this found expression in the beautiful, young, mixed-race female. The trope was later complicated by its performance and counter-performance in the Republican era, corresponding to a growing consciousness of modern cosmopolitan and national identity taking place in a repressive, although putatively democratic, regime. At the present time, widely seen as an era of ideological paradigm exhaustion, neither the broken promises of revolution nor any visible alternatives seem to offer the kinds of enfranchisement and opportunities that citizens expect. In the colonial episteme, the *mulata* embodied the racial tension that bestowed identity as it perpetuated colonial anxiety. In contemporary Cuba, the queered *mulata* body of desire performs at the limit of the nation: a disruptive, liberatory body that menaces the somnolent mythologies of ideology.

REFERENCES

Arenas, Reinaldo. 1987. *Graveyard of the Angels*. New York: Avon.

Arrizon, Alicia. 2006. *Queering Mestizaje Transculturation and Performance*. Ann Arbor: University of Michigan Press.

Bachiller y Morales, Antonio ed. 1881. *Tipos y costumbres de la isla de Cuba colección de artículos por los mejores autores de este género*. La Habana: Miguel de Villa.

Benitez Rojo, Antonio. 1992. *The Repeating Island: The Caribbean and the Postmodern Perspective*. Durham, NC: Duke University Press.

Bettelheim, Judith. 2001. *Cuban Festivals: A Century of Afro-Cuban Culture*. London: Ian Randle.

Bhabha, Homi. 1994 "The Other Question: Stereotype, Discrimination and the Discourse of Colonialism". In *The Location of Culture*, 94–120. London: Routledge.

Bhabha, Homi. 2004. "Of Mimicry and Man". In *The Performance Studies Reader*, edited by Henry Bial, 279–286. London: Routledge.

Boix, I. ed. 1844. *Los españoles pintados por si mismos*. Madrid: Calle de Carretas.

Butler, Judith. 1989. "Performative Acts and Gender Constitution: An Essay in Phenomenology and Feminist Theory". *Theater Journal* 40.4: 519–531.

Cámara Betancourt, Madeline. 2000. "Between Myth and Stereotype: The Image of the Mulatta in Cuban Culture of the Nineteenth Century as a Truncated Symbol of Nationality". In *Cuba, the Elusive Nation: Interpretations of National Identity*, edited by Damien J. Fernandez and Madeline Cámara Betancourt, 100–115. Gainesville, FL: University Press of Florida.

Carrera, Magali M. 2003. *Imagining Identity in New Spain: Race, Lineage, and the Colonial Body in Portraiture and Casta Paintings.* Austin: University of Texas Press.

Castellanos, Jorge and Isabel Castellanos. 1994. "El Negro en el Teatro Cubano". *Cultura Afrocubana,* Tomo IV, 195–263. Miami: Ediciones Universal.

Cecilia. 1992. Dir. Humberto Solas, Cuba.

Cecilia Valdes. 1930. Zarzuela; music by Gonzalo Roig, libretto by Agustin Rodríguez and José Sánchez-Arcilla.

Céspedes, Benjamín de. 1888. *La prostitución en la ciudad de La Habana.* La Habana: Establicimiento Tipgrafica O'Reilley.

Cruz, Mary. 1975. *Creto Ganga.* Havana: Unión de Escritores y Artistas de Cuba.

Ezponda, Eduardo. 1878. *La mulata. Estudio fisiológico, social y jurídico.* Madrid: Imprenta de Fortanet.

Les Français peints par eux-mêmes: Encyclopédie morale du dix-neuvième siècle. 1841. Paris: L. Curmer.

Fraunhar, Alison. 2008. "*Marquillas cigarerras cubanas*: Nation and Desire in the Nineteenth Century". *Hispanic Research Journal* 9.5: 457–477.

Fraunhar, Alison. 2004. "*Mulata Cubana*: Between narration and nation". In *Latin American Cinema: Modernity, Gender and the Nation* Shaw, edited by Lisa Shaw and Stephanie Dennison, 160–179. Raleigh, NC: McFarland.

Garcia Riera, Enrique. 1992. *Historia documental del cine mexicano.* Guadalajara: Universidad de Guadalajara.

Gilliam, Angela and Onik'a Gilliam. 1999. "Odyssey Negotiating the Subjectivity of *Mulata* Identity in Brazil". *Latin American Perspectives* 26.3: 60–84.

Gottberg, Luis Duno. 2008. *Solventando Las Diferencias: La Ideología Del Mestizaje en Cuba.* Austin: University of Texas Press.

Helg, Aline. 1995. *Our Rightful Share: The Afro-Cuban Struggle for Equality, 1886–1912.* Durham, NC and London: University of North Carolina Press.

Katzew, Ilona. 2004. *Casta Painting: Images of Race in Eighteenth-Century Mexico.* New Haven: Yale University Press.

Kenny Meadows, Joseph. 1840–41. *Heads of the People or Portraits of the English.* London: Willoughby and Co.

Kutzinski, Vera. 2003. *Sugar's Secrets: Race and the Erotics of Nationalism.* Charlottesville and London: University of Virginia Press.

La Pelicula de Ana. 2012. Dir. Daniel Diaz Torres, Cuba.

Laguna, Albert. 2010. "*Aquí está Alvarez Guedes*: Cuban Choteo and the Politics of Play". *Latino Studies* 8.4: 509–531.

Lam, Rafael. 1999. "*La Leyenda de las Mulatas de Fuego*". *Musica Cubana* 3. Havana: Unión de Escritores y Artistas de Cuba.

Landau, Paul S. and Deborah D. Kaspin, eds. 2002. *Images and Empires.* Berkeley and London: University of California Press.

Lane, Jill. 2005. *Blackface Cuba.* Philadelphia: University of Pennsylvania Press.

Lazo, Raimundo. 1979. *Cecilia Valdes o la Loma del Angel, novela de costumbres cubanas, estudio critico.* Mexico: Editorial Porrua.

Lazo, Rodrigo. 2002. "Filibustering Cuba: *Cecilia Valdés* and a Memory of Nation in the Americas". *American Literature* 74.1: 1–30.

Leal, Rine. 1975. *La Selva Oscura.* La Habana: Editorial Arte y Literatura.

Mañach, Jorge. 1955. *Indagación del choteo.* La Habana: Editorial Libro Cubano. http://lilt.ilstu.edu/jjpancr/Spanish_305/indagaci%C3%B3n_del_choteo.htm.

Martinez Alier, Verena. 1989. *Marriage Class and Color in Nineteenth-Century Cuba*. Ann Arbor: University of Michigan Press.

Martínez-Malo, Aldo. 1988. *Rita la Única*. La Habana: Editorial Abril.

Mohanty, Chandra Talpade. 2003. "Under Western Eyes: Feminist Scholarship and Colonial Discourses". In *Feminism without Borders: Multiculturalism, Globalization, and the Politics of Liberation*, 17–42. Durham and London: Duke University Press.

Moraña, Mabel and Enrique Dussel, eds. 2008. *Coloniality at Large*. Durham and London: Duke University Press.

Mulata. 1953. Dir. Gilberto Martinez Solares, Mexico. DVD.

N.A. *ca.* 1854. *Los mexicanos pintados por si mismos*. Mexico: Imprenta de M. Murguía.

Ortiz, Fernando. 2001. *El Baile y el Teatro de los Negros en el Folklore de Cuba*. 2nd ed.: La Habana: Editorial Letras Cubanas.

Renan, Ernest. 1882. "What is a Nation?" http://www.nationalismproject.org/what/renan.htm.

Rio Prado, Enrique. 2010. *La Venus de Bronce : Una historia de la zarzuela cubana*. La Habana: Ediciones Alarcos.

Ryan, James R. 1997. *Picturing Empire: Photography and the Visualization of the British Empire*. Chicago: University of Chicago Press.

Said, Edward. 1979. *Orientalism*. New York and London: Verso.

Suite Habana. 2003. Dir. Fernando Perez, ICAIC.

Summer, Doris. 2002. "Who Can Tell? Filling in the Blanks in Villaverde". In *Mixing Race, Mixing Culture: Inter-American Literary Dialogues*, edited by Monica and Debra J. Rosenthal, 220–230. Austin and London: University of Texas Press.

Thomas, Susan. 2009. *Cuban Zarzuela*. Springfield: University of Illinois Press.

Torriente, Lolo de la. 1946. *La Habana de Cecilia Valdés*. La Habana: Jesus Montero.

Young, Robert J.C. 1995. *Colonial Desire: Hybridity in Theory, Culture and Race*. London: Routledge.

8 Amongst the Cannibals
Articulating Masculinity in Postcolonial Weimar Germany

Eva Bischoff

When the German Empire collapsed under the double stress of a lost war and a revolutionary movement in 1918, it also lost its colonies. The Treaty of Versailles stipulated that all German colonies were to be transformed into mandates of the League of Nations under the jurisdiction and rule of other European colonial powers. Germany became, legally speaking, a "Postcolonial State in a Still-Colonial World" (Klotz 2005). Yet for a long time, the German colonial past was regarded to be of little consequence to German society as a whole. Sebastian Conrad has coined the term "double marginalization" to describe this traditional perception, which, on the one hand, generally denied the notion of modernity as the result of a co-constitutive, shared historical process and on the other, assumed that the brief colonial encounter and its negligible impact distinguished the German national history from that of other European nation states (Conrad 2002, 148). Given this background, it is no surprise that many German scholars ignored postcolonial critique for a long time.

In recent years, this has changed dramatically. An increasing number of studies devote themselves to the reconstruction of Germany's colonial past or its condition as a postcolonial, immigration country in denial (Steyerl and Rodríguez 2003). There are multiple reasons for this dramatic change. Some of them are of a more academic nature: the impact of path-breaking studies by English-speaking scholars, most of all Susanne Zantop's monograph *Colonial Fantasies*, first published in 1997, or the influence of scholarly endeavors such as New Imperial History or Global History. Other reasons for this postcolonial shift are a growing critical awareness of racism and racist discrimination within German civil society, public debates on *Leitkultur* and multi-culturalism, or the centenary of the genodical war against the Herero in German Southwest Africa (1904–07) (Perraudin and Zimmerer 2011).

The following case study is located within this context. Unlike other historical studies, which stress reconstructing continuities between the German colonial project and the genocidal expansion of the Third Reich (Zimmerer 2009; Langbehn and Salama 2011; Baranowski 2011), my focus will be on the interconnectedness of criminological, anthropological and colonial discourses in the articulation of hegemonic masculinity in 1920s Germany. In other words, I am interested in recovering an entangled postcolonial gender history.

Which brings us back to the particular postcolonial moment of the Weimar Republic. During the early 1920s, German masculinity was perceived as being threatened on multiple levels, most of all by the presence of French colonial soldiers. To prevent Germany from taking up arms against their Western neighbors in the near future and to ensure reparations, French, British, Belgian and American forces occupied the Rhine-Ruhr-area between 1919 and 1930 (the US forces, however, withdrew in January 1923 and their territory became part of the French occupation zone). Part of the French troops garrisoned on German soil were colonial troops, more specifically, the *Tirailleurs Sénégalais*. The deployment of colonial troops triggered a racist campaign supported by all political parties (apart from the radical left), which claimed that these African men raped women and children, mutilated their bodies and fed on their flesh (Maß 2006, 76–105; Koller 2001, 201–261). Thus in German public discourse, the nation was seen as cannibalized: metaphorically by the Entente powers and literally by the French colonial troops. Yet these were not the only anthropophagi that provoked public anxieties. Reports of white males (*Lustmörder*) killing women, men or children, consuming their flesh or selling it on the black market unsettled the population. Accordingly, cannibals supposedly not only resided in colonial spaces but quite possibly lived next door.

So far, Anglophone postcolonial scholarship has focused on reconstructing the cannibal as the representation of the colonial other (Arens 1987; Kilgour 1990; Hulme 1992; Obeyesekere 2005). In scrutinizing the relationship between the white (male) self and cannibal other, most of these scholars rely on psychoanalytic categories, namely on Jacques Lacan's concept of the "mirror stage". Maggie Kilgour summarizes this position succinctly. The "modern Cartesian subject depends for its self-definition as an independent entity, clearly differentiated from others, on the image of an 'other' who destroys such boundaries", she states. The cannibal serves "as a mirror to the European subject", while simultaneously threatening to destabilize it by incorporating European men both physically as well as culturally. The latter representing "the danger of 'going native'", i.e. the return "to an original state of barbarism" (Kilgour 1998, 240).

This conceptual framework, as I will demonstrate in this chapter, flattens the complexities of the relationship between the white (male, bourgeois) self and the cannibal other. Drawing on the findings of my research on the complex and multi-layered discourse on cannibalism in postcolonial Weimar Germany, I will argue that postcolonial theory has to rethink its conceptual framework. Instead of accepting binary categories such as self and other, thereby reaffirming the ontological hygiene imposed by colonial discourse, we have to focus on the complex network of practices through which categories such as race or masculinity came into being in the first place.

Starting in the colonial context and then shifting my gaze to the German "motherland", I will first reconstruct the anthropological knowledge of the cannibal. In contrast to Anglophone studies, I will discuss the accounts of nineteenth-century German explorers and travel literature, concentrating on the example of Georg Schweinfurth. Next, I will take a look at the public debate surrounding the *Tirailleurs Sénégalais*. I will show that the stereotypical descriptions of these French-African soldiers relied on notions developed in anthropological discourse and combined the accusations of anthropophagy, homosexuality and sadism in a manner that was similar to the portrayal of white sexual killers (*Lustmörder*) in both medico-psychiatric literature and press reports, which I will focus on in my third and final section. Here, I will look at one particular case, that of Friedrich (Fritz) Haarmann, to exemplify how medical discourse relied on anthropological concepts of the link between savageness and masculinity, thereby establishing the notion of the male "anachronistic body" and the necessity of self-control (Bischoff 2011, 204).

While retracing these entangled discourses, I will take a theoretical step sideways and think about the relationship between "normal" masculinity and the cannibal, not in terms of a binary opposition but in reference to Rosi Braidotti and Édouard Glissant as a multiplicity of relations or an *agencement* (Braidotti 2002, 69, 75; Kaiser 2012, 133). Following their cue, I will trace the network of connections that established white hegemonic masculinity in 1920s Germany. As I will demonstrate, its articulation did not rely on a clear-cut binary differentiation between "normal" men and others, whether criminals or so-called savages but referred to a concept of a continuum of male sexual ab/normality. Every man, according to authoritative medico-psychiatric discourse, was driven by violent sexual impulses. "Normality" was not a matter of binary biological differences but male self-conduct.

THE SAVAGE CANNIBAL

Accusing the members of the indigenous population of a newly "discovered" territory of practicing cannibalism was part and parcel of the European colonial project since its inception in 1492. Descriptions of cannibals, who threaten to devour European explorers, became a central *topos* in European travel literature. Numerous popular adventure novels exploited the topic up until the nineteenth century; "amongst the cannibals" became almost a synonym for colonial adventure. Often these novels circulated across different colonial contexts (see Powell 1883 and 1884). German-speaking authors (male and female) contributed to this discourse throughout the eighteenth and nineteenth centuries. As explorers, missionaries, scientists and anthropologists they were engaged in the European colonial project long before the German Empire developed its colonial aspirations in 1884 (Zantop 1997). One of the most influential of these texts was botanist Georg Schweinfurth's travelogue *Im Herzen von Afrika*, published in 1874. Its English version, entitled *The Heart of Africa*, had appeared the previous year (Schweinfurth 1873). In the following, I will refer to the third and revised German edition of his publication (Schweinfurth 1918). Schweinfurth envisioned himself as part of a larger European tradition, explicitly referring to Jules Pocet as his predecessor and source of inspiration (331).

In the travelogue, Schweinfurth described the adventures and scientific findings of an expedition he conducted between 1869 and 1871 to the upper Nile River basin. During his journeys, he encountered two African societies, the Mangbetu (also Monbuttu) and the Niam-Niam (or Azande), which, according to him, represented the epitome of cannibal communities. He established a close link between indigenous, African masculinity and anthropophagy in his descriptions of these two societies. Female cannibals played a much less prominent role in his account (337–338, 410–411). He was much more concerned about their sexual practices. He especially scorned the self-determination and freedom enjoyed by Mangbetu women (336). The Azande, according to Schweinfurth, were extremely savage, bellicose and superstitious (238, 254, 304–305). He described them as typical representation of humanity's evolutionary past. Initially he even believed them to be the "missing link" between man and animal (287, 293). The Azande wore the hides of colobus monkeys as garments and left the animals' tails to dangle down. This simian resemblance resulted in fierce debate, about which Schweinfurth was well aware, in nineteenth-century anthropology about the Azande's evolutionary status (248, 287, 289). The Azande warrior in particular was, in his view, an embodiment of animal-like savagery and bellicose masculinity, further debased by near negligible morals and ethics (293).

Yet, Schweinfurth noted in his travelogue, juxtaposed with the Mangbetu's practices, the Azande's cannibalism paled in comparison. He argued that because the Mangbetu had evolved to a comparatively higher level of cultural development, their anthropophagy was similarly superior (337). This assessment seems to be a contradiction in terms. However, considering that the contemporary general paradigm of evolutionary progress stipulated that it was synonymous to the development of European bourgeois norms and morals, an evolved African society allegedly practicing cannibalism appeared to be even more horrifying, effectively emphasizing racist assumptions about the cannibalistic "nature" of Africans.

Just as he did in his descriptions of the Azande, in detailing Mangbetu culture Schweinfurth established a close discursive connection between African masculinity and man-eating. Here, he focused on King Munsa, their leader, who functioned in his travelogue as a *pars pro toto* for Mangbetu society as a whole. This "king of cannibals" behaved like a "dusky Cesar" and often lapsed into fits of extreme rage. Moreover, Schweinfurth noted, the king performed "Dervish-like" dances on official occasions that induced an ecstatic state, similar to epilepsy (311, 324,

328–329). In employing the term "Dervish" in pejorative terms, the German explorer semantically equated animalistic African religions and Islamic spiritual practices with a state of mindless unconsciousness. King Munsa, the description continues, had a neronic disposition, his demeanor was characterized by tedium and repletion, his eyes were alight with the "wild fire of animal passion" and the lines around his mouth bespoke his "lust for cruelty", his greed and his brutality (312–313). His favored food was the tender flesh of small children, of which he devoured one on a daily basis (337).

Schweinfurth's report inspired numerous scholars to conduct other expeditions and to explore the interior of the African continent and his ethnological descriptions were referred to by multiple authors and fellow explorers such as Wilhelm Junker (1840–1892) and Eduard (Karl Oskar Theodor) Schnitzer (1840–1892), also known as Emin Pascha (Bischoff 2011, 84–85). Thus the Azande warriors and King Munsa became the role model of savage, African cannibals. In following Schweinfurth's example, his fellow scientists not only accepted the explanatory models he provided for the occurrence of anthropophagy, namely ritual, greed and superstition, but also the connection he had established between masculinity, primal urges and man-eating. This knowledge about the "savage cannibal", as Gananath Obeyesekere has identified it, informed, as we will see, the debates about the French colonial troops occupying the Rhine-Ruhr area (Obeyesekere 2005, 1, 13–14, 223–236). Few African men and women had been to Germany before, mostly as participants of colonial exhibitions or *Völkerschauen* (Bruckner 2003; Dreesbach 2005), or as individual migrants living in the larger cities such as Hamburg or Berlin (Oguntoye 1997; El-Tayeb 2001; Bechhaus-Gerst and Klein-Arendt 2004). Therefore, Germans had limited first-hand experience with people of African origin (Ciarlo 2011). In fact, the *Tirailleurs Sénégalais* were "the first large-scale [African] presence in Germany" (Campt 2004, 35).

CANNIBALISM COMING HOME

As occupied territory, Germany was often depicted as the helpless victim of the allied forces' decisions – sometimes explicitly as being cannibalized. One of many examples is a caricature from the German weekly journal *Kladderadatsch* referring to the London conference in September 1924, which reads: "The conference brothers waiting for the Germans". In the foreground, the representatives of the three key members of the entente are squatting right next to a large cauldron: Uncle Sam, Jacques Bonhomme and John Bull (left to right) with more cannibals/representatives of allied forces lurking in the background, all brandishing large knives (*Kladderadatsch* 1924, 511) [Fig 8.1]:

Die Londoner Konferenzbrüder

in Erwartung der Deutschen

Figure 8.1

German critique of the French employment of colonial troops built on the link between low evolutionary status, the "nature" of Africans, masculinity and the forms of anthropophagy we recognize from the anthropological discourse on the "savage cannibal" outlined above. It also added an extra level to these cannibalistic imaginations: the allegation of sexual violence. Press reports and propaganda material issued by the German Foreign Office during the war described the French-Africans as extremely brutal, filled with blood lust and uncontrollable sexual urges. African men allegedly had raped female prisoners in French internment camps or had forced them into sexual (or white) slavery. They were suspected of same-sex practices and pedophilia. The soldiers were described as animals or apish brutes, as nameless hordes without any sense of manly or military honor (Koller 2001a, 119–124). Their alleged sexual assaults on white women were interpreted as the result of their enhanced sexual urges and underdeveloped self-control (Koller 2001b, 156). They were believed to practice cannibalism, to have eaten (at least parts of) the bodies of the German soldiers (Auswärtiges Amt 1915, 20, 48–49, 53–54). There were also allegations of mutilation of fallen or wounded German soldiers and of homosexual violence (35, 36–37, 44–45, 7, 8, 12, 15, 22, 42, 51–52). German post-war accusations against the *Tirailleurs Sénégalais* continued these themes but emphasized the connection between savagism, masculinity and sexuality. White German men, forced to watch the sexual assaults without weapons to defend the honor of their sisters, wives and mothers, were deeply humiliated. This added to the perceived post-war "crisis of masculinity", triggered by the high number of maimed or cognitively disabled returnees, the post-war demographic gender imbalance and women entering the professions in larger numbers in response to war economy (Maß 2001, 29–30). The alleged sexual and racial danger was summarized as the "black dishonor" (*Schwarze Schmach*) or the "black shame" (*Schwarze Schande*), referring to both the dishonored, violated white women and the shame French political and military leaders had brought upon France in the eyes of the whole civilized world (Koller 2001b, 158). Although they were very present to the public eye, it is important to note that non-Europeans never held the majority among the French soldiers stationed on German territory. Maß estimates a total of 25,000 men, most of them from Morocco and Algeria, approximately 5,000 to 7,500 from West Africa, namely Senegal and Madagascar, and a few hundred from Annam and Tonkin. Keith Nelson, one of the first historians to discuss the topic, assumes that 45,000 soldiers were deployed between 1920 and 1921 (Maß 2006, 79–80; Nelson 1970, 610–611).

Many civil organizations rallied against the colonial soldiers' employment. The *Deutsche Evangelische Kirchenbund*, for instance, passed a resolution during its congress in June 1920 directed at fellow Christians, urging them to speak out against the situation in Germany:

> Depressed by hunger and poverty, restricted in its ability to help herself, our nation must watch with horror as her women and children, girls and boys are being defiled and violated. [...] *Scandalous shame is brought upon our fellow citizens.* The bodies and souls of pure/virtuous [*rein*] women and innocent children are contaminated, the weak are ensnared. *Mouth and quill both refuse to describe the atrocities*, which exceed all horrors of the war (*Deutsche Allgemeine Zeitung* 1920, 2, emphasis in the original).

The reasons for the sexual violence exerted by the French-African soldiers, according to the resolution, were their savage instincts which "no military and manly discipline" could possibly restrain. Even more so, they lacked any form of Christian upbringing and had been uprooted from their ancestral homes (2). The *Kirchenbund* represented a bourgeois middle class. Yet its resolution shared racist assumptions about the nature of male African sexuality with extreme right-wing propaganda directed against the *Tirailleurs Sénégalais*. A typical example of this extreme form of discrimination is Wilhelm Saar's *Der blaue Schrecken (la terreur bleue) und die schwarze Schmach* (The Blue Terror and the Black Shame), first published in 1921. Here, we find an even more explicit reference to colonial cannibal discourse than in the *Kirchenbund*'s resolution. By describing them as blood-sucking, deranged animals that lost all self-control under the influence of alcohol, Saar reduced the soldiers to their instincts. He wrote:

> The black beasts literally run amok, when overwhelmed by alcohol and sexual frenzy, and behave themselves just like wild animals towards their victims. "Unconscious girls, whose veins were completely drained of blood, have been taken to hospitals. The blacks, especially the Moroccans, in their rage bite into the carotid artery of their victims and suck greedily from their blood; they are simply genuine beasts".
>
> (Saar 1921, 48)

A number of historians have discussed this extreme sexualization, analyzing the racist stereotypes that form the basis of the allegations against the French-African soldiers (Koller 2001b, 155–156; Maß 2005, 141). None, however, has commented on the fact that these descriptions bear a close resemblance to descriptions we also find in medico-psychiatric literature on the topic of sexual murder or so-called *Lustmord*.

THE CANNIBAL WITHIN

At the turn of the nineteenth century, parallel to the emergence of the German colonial empire, a scientific debate developed about the "nature" of criminality. A new paradigm was introduced and soon gained wide acceptance among specialists: the notion that criminality was the result of corporeal deviancy. Historians speak of the invention of the "naturalisation of criminality" (Wetzell 2000; Becker 2002, 259). Along with the introduction of this new, biological paradigm, experts also pondered the inherent characteristics of male sexuality. Here, we find two, occasionally intertwined lines of argument: one emphasizing the impact of upbringing and environment (nurture), the other stressing the impact of hereditary and corporeal deficiencies (nature). The latter is the one of primary interest to the topic at hand. Among the criminal acts central to this debate was the sexual murder, or *Lustmord*. It was generally considered to be the consequence of a sexual deviancy derived from sadistic practices. As a term, sadism designated the experience of sexual arousal or pleasure while either observing or actually inflicting pain, shame or other cruelties on other beings, human and animal alike. It was introduced into the debate by Richard von Krafft-Ebing (Krafft-Ebing 1998, 53). His seminal study, *Psychopathia Sexualis*, originally published in 1886 was quickly translated; its first English edition was printed in 1893 (Krafft-Ebing 1893).

According to the Austro–German psychiatrist, sadism was the monstrous excess of a "natural" aggressiveness that was generally part of "normal" male sexuality (9, 56). In pathological cases, Krafft-Ebing pointed out, cannibalistic acts were not uncommon: the killer craved the flesh or blood of his victim and ate parts of its body (62). In other words, sexual crime was connected to cannibalism. Krafft-Ebing's theory on sadism, sexual murder and the connection between anthropophagy and the male sexual drive was not uncontested within both the national and the international scientific community (Eulenburg 1902, 5; Bloch 1907, 616; Ellis 2001, 57). Nevertheless it became the hegemonic model of explanation within forensic medicine, psychiatry and criminology. Erich Wulffen in his highly influential handbook for legal practitioners, police officers, physicians and pedagogues, entitled *Der Sexualverbrecher* (The Sexual Criminal), for instance, assumed that if it were not for the historical process of civilization, humans would be as cruel and violent as animals. Children and so-called natives (*Naturvölker*) were still in this original, pre-civilization state (Wulffen 1928, 306). Similarly, male physiology carried this evolutionary past within it until the author's present day. Wulffen advised his readers: "The mere act of cohabitation with its physiologically inherent violence and lust can induce the sadistic feelings and make him kill his victims" (458). In reference to Anne McClintock's concept of the "anachronistic space", I have suggested thinking about this particular form of male corporeality as an "anachronistic body" (McClintock 1995, 30; Bischoff 2011, 204).

But if, according to authoritative medico-psychiatric discourse, all men were inherently sexually violent and dangerous, why did not all of them act upon these urges in a similar way? Or, to put it more bluntly, was every man a *Lustmörder*? The answer to this question simultaneously brings the connection between colonial and psychiatric discourses on cannibalism into view. It demonstrates how the notion of the savage cannibal other and that of the cannibal within were closely interconnected.

Experts assumed that while "normal" i.e. healthy men were able to restrain their violent urges, individuals of hereditarily "tainted" physiology were not. Their ability to control their sexual drive was allegedly impaired by a degenerative neurological weakness, a form of neurasthenia, which could be both inherited and acquired (by alcoholism and/or masturbation) (Krafft-Ebing 1900, 4–8). This disorder, also called *Entartung*, supposedly resulted in a general enhancement of sexual urges and of sexual deviations such as sadism or homosexuality. As such, sex criminals were seen as having individually devolved to the evolutionary status of so-called savages and were regarded as practicing "atavism" as the living embodiment of humanity's evolutionary and civilizatory past (Lombroso 2004, 345; Galassi 2004, 148–152).

Just after the public outrage about the "black shame" had subsided in 1923, a series of criminal cases involving sexual violence, allegations of anthropophagy and homicide unsettled the newly founded Weimar Republic. One among these was the case of Friedrich (Fritz) Haarmann. He was taken into custody on 23 June 1924 in the city of Hanover and confessed to having murdered several young men who had gone missing since 1918 and who had taken to prostitution to secure their income in times of economic crisis. Haarmann was known to the Hanover police as a part of the city's homosexual community (Hoffschildt 1992, 76). Rumor had it that he had sold the flesh of his victims, a possibility he persistently and vehemently denied. He did, however, admit that he killed his victims in a sexual frenzy, giving details about how he bit their throats and dug his teeth into their flesh (Hann. 155 Göttingen 864a, 701, 710, 712, 722). Haarmann's contemporaries, however, were not convinced by his constant denial of cannibalism. Press reports often described him as a man-eater and drew parallels between his crimes and the cannibalistic practices of so-called savages. The social-democratic newspaper *Vorwärts*, for instance, noted, with reference to his crimes, on 31 December 1924: "It would be [...] a mistake to believe, that man-eating is restricted to the savages. It also exists among the civilized parts of humanity" (*Vorwärts* 1924). Or he was depicted killing his victims, tearing apart their throats with his teeth, for example in the communist newspaper *Die Rote Fahne*, on 13 July 1924 (*Die Rote Fahne* 1924) [Fig 8.2]:

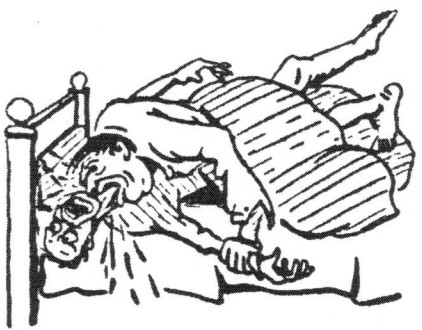

Figure 8.2

His trial in 1924 was not Haarmann's first contact with the juridical system. His crimes included damage to property, fraud, begging, and assault and battery. He had spent twelve years in prison before 1924 (Hann. 173 Acc. 30/87, 80, 110–112). In the context of the numerous trials that were brought against him, he was repeatedly examined by psychiatric and medical experts. They searched in vain for visible corporeal signs of "degeneration" but nevertheless diagnosed numerous mental defects: "epileptic insanity", "hebephrenia" (a form of schizophrenia), "moral and mental inferiority", "feeble mindedness" and "neurasthenia" (Hann. 155 Göttingen 864a, 107–111). The experts in Haarmann's last trial considered him to be "morally insane", mentally unstable because of the adverse influences of his family, his social environment and the psychiatric institutions he had been confined to during his adolescence. Generally, they concluded, he was "a psychopathic personality", a prime example of a neurotic, sex criminal (130).

Haarmann was charged with murder. The prosecution claimed that he had tried "to satisfy his sadistic-perverted desires", implying he had base motives, a juridical characteristic for homicide not manslaughter (Hann. 173 Acc. 30/87, 80, 94). The medical expert appointed by the court, the psychiatrist Ernst Schultze, even went one step further. He argued that Haarmann knew about his neurotic condition and that he therefore had a moral obligation to exercise manly self-restraint. Haarmann, according to Schultze, should have kept himself apart from the homosexual community (Hann. 155 Göttingen 864a, 115–116). His murderous deeds were not the effect of his neurotic disorder but the result of his lack of manliness, of giving in to his lower instincts. The court found Haarmann guilty of having murdered twenty-four men. He was sentenced to death on 19 December 1924 and executed on 16 April 1925 (Hann. 173 Acc. 30/87, 80, 107; Kl. Erwerb. A 401, 12).

AMONGST THE CANNIBALS – CANNIBALS AMONGST US?

"Amongst the cannibals": this phrase captures more than the title of a popular adventure novel or the *topos* of colonial travel literature. In terms of postcolonial Weimar Germany it had several dimensions. Politically speaking, it first referred to the occupation of Germany territory by allied forces. The motherland was imagined as being cannibalized by its former enemies. Second, it represented the defamation of the *Tirailleurs Sénégalais* as anthropophagi and sadistic rapists, ravaging the female German population. Finally, it articulated the plight of brothers, husbands and fathers, emasculated and maimed by military defeat, war injuries and post-war economic crisis, who had to watch helplessly as African men satisfied their primitive sexual desires unchecked by their French masters.

Yet the distinction between African savages and white (German) men was not as clear cut as this picture suggests. As the male body in general was considered an unruly, evolutionary remnant, carrying all the animal urges, instincts and violent desires of the so-called natives, the term "amongst the cannibals" had a third dimension in 1920s Germany. In terms of masculinity, it signified that aggression was considered to be an inherent element of "normal" masculine sexual desire based on male physiology. The only way to keep these desires in check was to exercise self-control. This form of self-discipline was, according to contemporary scientific discourse, the exclusive privilege of white, healthy men. Both psychopathic and non-white men supposedly lacked the necessary strength of mind, as seen in the racist defamations against the *Tirailleurs Sénégalais* and the medico-psychiatric literature. Manly discipline and self-restraint were held in such high regard that criminals such as Fritz Haarmann were nevertheless expected to confirm to these standards. Consequently, "normal" masculinity or, to be more precise, white, healthy and heterosexual masculinity, was not distinguished from "abnormal" masculinity, i.e. African, homosexual or psychopathic masculinity in a binary mode.

Instead, every male individual was located along a continuum of ab/normality. Or to put it bluntly, everybody was amongst cannibal/s.

The conceptual framework Anglophone postcolonial scholarship has relied on to analyze the relationship between the European male self and the cannibal other does not, so far, capture the complexity of the discourses and practices I have reconstructed above. The cannibal was an essential point of reference in this network, but white hegemonic masculinity was not articulated by way of establishing a simple binary opposition to it but in a recursive loop. Every white man shared the pre-civilizatory physiology of the savage whose transcendence by will power and self-restraint was the key element of hegemonic masculinity. To become a man was to become a cannibal and vice versa. Thus by focusing on the postcolonial moment of Weimar Germany as a case study, it becomes apparent that binary categories, such as self and other, do not suffice as categories of postcolonial analysis. Instead we have to reconstruct the complex network of intersecting practices that articulated these categories in the first place.

ILLUSTRATIONS

Courtesy of Staatsbibliothek zu Berlin, Stiftung Preußischer Kulturbesitz.
Erich Wilke. "Die Londoner Konferenzbrüder". *Kladderadatsch*. 77, 32, August 10, 1924, 511.
"Massenmörder und Menschenfleischhändler Haarmann als Vertrauensmann der Polizei". *Die Rote Fahne*. July 13, 1924.

REFERENCES

Unpublished Archival Material

Niedersächsisches Hauptstaatsarchiv Hannover
Kl. Erwerb. A 401.
Sterbeurkunde Friedrich Haarmann.

Hann. 173 Acc. 30/87, 80. Generalakten betreffend Schwurgerichtsberichte (betreffend Haarmann-Prozeß)
Anklageschrift gegen Fritz Haarmann, 4 November 1924, Bll. 3–106.
Urteil im Prozess gegen Fritz Haarmann, 19 December 1924, 107–155.

Hann. 155 Göttingen 864a. Haarmann-Akten
Gutachten Ernst Schultze über Friedrich Haarmann, 1 October 1924. 106–130.
Vernehmungen (Protokolle) Haarmann durch Ernst Schultze in Hannover, 26 July–9 August 1924. 630–734.

Published Primary Sources

Auswärtiges Amt, ed. 1915. *Völkerrechtswidrige Verwendung farbiger Truppen auf dem europäischen Kriegsschauplatz durch England und Frankreich*. Berlin: nd.

Bloch, Iwan. 1907. *Das Sexualleben unserer Zeit in seinen Beziehungen zur modernen Kultur*. Berlin: Louis Marcus Verlagsbuchhandlung.

Ellis, Havelock. 2001. *Love and Pain: Studies in the Psychology of Sex, Vol. 1*. Honolulu: University Press of Hawai'i.

Eulenburg, Albert. 1902. *Sadismus und Masochismus*. Wiesbaden: Bergmann.

Krafft-Ebing, Richard von. 1900. *Nervosität und neurasthenische Zustände*. Vienna: Hölder.

Krafft-Ebing, Richard von. 1893. *Psychopathia Sexualis: With Especial Reference to the Antipathic Sexual Instinct. A Medico-Forensic Study*. London: F.J. Rebman.

Krafft-Ebing, Richard von. [1893] 1998. *Psychopathia Sexualis: With Especial Reference to the Antipathic Sexual Instinct: A Medico-Forensic Study*. Translated from the 12th German edition by Franklin S. Klaf. New York: Arkade Publishing.

Lombroso, Cesare. 2004. "The Criminal". In *The Criminal Anthropological Writings of Cesare Lombroso: Published in the English Language Periodical Literature During the Late Nineteenth and Early Twentieth Centuries*, edited by David M. Horton and Katherine E. Rich, 343–349. Lewiston: Edwin Millen Press.

Powell, Wilfred. 1883. *Wanderings in a Wild Country: Or Three Years Amongst the Cannibals of New Britain*. London: Low Marston Searle & Rivington.

Powell, Wilfred 1884. *Unter den Kannibalen von Neu-Britannien: Drei Wanderjahre durch ein wildes Land*. Translated by M. Schröter. Leipzig: Hirt.

Saar, Wilhelm F. von der. 1921. *Der blaue Schrecken (la terreur bleue) und die schwarze Schmach*. Stuttgart: Winkler.

Schweinfurth, Georg. 1873. *The Heart of Africa. Three Years' Travels and Adventures in the Unexplored Regions of Central Africa, from 1868 to 1871*. London: Gregg.

Schweinfurth, Georg 1918. *Im Herzen von Afrika: Reisen und Entdeckungen im zentralen Äquatorial-Afrika während der Jahre 1868–1871. Ein Beitrag zur Entdeckungsgeschichte von Afrika*. Leipzig: Brockhaus.

Wulffen, Erich. 1928. *Der Sexualverbrecher: Ein Handbuch für Juristen, Polizei- und Verwaltungsbeamte, Mediziner und Pädagogen*. Berlin: Langenscheidt.

Newspapers and Periodicals

Deutsche Allgemeine Zeitung. 1920. "Die Kirche und die schwarze Schmach". June 26, morning edition, 2.

Vorwärts. 1924. "Kannibalen". December 31, morning edition, supplement.

Secondary Sources

Arens, William. 1987. *The Man-Eating Myth: Anthropology and Anthropophagy*. Oxford: Oxford University Press.

Baranowski, Shelley. 2011. *Nazi Empire: German Colonialism and Imperialism from Bismarck to Hitler*. Cambridge: Cambridge University Press.

Barker, Francis, Peter Hulme and Margaret Iversen, eds. 1998. *Cannibalism and the Colonial World*. Cambridge: Cambridge University Press.

Bechhaus-Gerst, Marianne and Reinhard Klein-Arendt, eds. 2004. *AfrikanerInnen in Deutschland und schwarze Deutsche - Geschichte und Gegenwart: Beiträge zur gleichnamigen Konferenz vom 13.-15. Juni 2003 im NS-Dokumentationszentrum (EL-DE-Haus) Köln*. Münster: Lit.

Becker, Peter. 2002. *Verderbnis und Entartung: Eine Geschichte der Kriminologie des 19. Jahrhunderts als Diskurs und Praxis.* Göttingen: Vandenhoeck & Ruprecht.

Bignall, Simone and Paul Patton, eds. 2010. *Deleuze and the Postcolonial.* Edinburgh: Edinburgh University Press.

Bischoff, Eva. 2011. *Kannibale-Werden: Eine postkoloniale Geschichte deutscher Männlichkeit um 1900.* Bielefeld: transcript.

Braidotti, Rosi. 2002. *Metamorphoses: Towards a Materialist Theory of Becoming.* London: Polity.

Bruckner, Sierra A. 2003. "Spectacles of (Human) Nature. Commercial Ethnography Between Leisure, Learning and *Schaulust*". In *Wordly Provincialism: German Anthropology in the Age of Empire,* edited by Matti Bunzl and Glenn Penny, 127–155. Ann Arbor: University of Michigan Press.

Campt, Tina M. 2004. *Other Germans: Black Germans and the Politics of Race, Gender and Memory in the Third Reich.* Ann Arbor: University of Michigan Press.

Ciarlo, David. 2011. *Advertising Empire: Race and Visual Culture in Imperial Germany.* Cambridge: Harvard University Press.

Conrad, Sebastian. 2002. "Doppelte Marginalisierung. Plädoyer für eine transnationale Perspektive auf die deutsche Geschichte". *Geschichte und Gesellschaft* 28: 145–169.

Dreesbach, Anne. 2005. *Gezähmte Wilde: Die Zurschaustellung "exotischer" Menschen in Deutschland 1870–1940.* Frankfurt: Campus.

El-Tayeb, Fatima. 2001. *Schwarze Deutsche: Der Diskurs um 'Rasse' und nationale Identität 1890–1933.* Frankfurt: Campus.

Galassi, Silviana. 2004. *Kriminologie im Deutschen Kaiserreich: Geschichte einer gebrochenen Verwissenschaftlichung.* Stuttgart: Steiner.

Hoffschildt, Rainer. 1992. *Olivia: Die bisher geheime Geschichte des Tabus Homosexualität und der Verfolgung der Homosexuellen in Hannover.* Hanover: Verein zur Erforschung der Geschichte der Homosexuellen in Niedersachsen e.V.

Hulme, Peter. 1992. *Colonial Encounters: Europe and the Native Caribbean, 1492–1797.* New ed. London: Routledge.

Kaiser, Birgit M. 2012. "*Poésie en étendue*: Deleuze, Glissant and a Post-Colonial Aesthetics of the Earth". In *Revisiting Normativity with Deleuze,* edited by Rosi Braidotti and Patricia Pisters, 131–144. London: Bloomsbury.

Kilgour, Maggie. 1990. *From Communion to Cannibalism: An Anatomy of Metaphors of Incorporation.* Princeton: Princeton University Press.

Kilgour, Maggie. 1998. "The Function of Cannibalism at the Present Time". In *Cannibalism and the Colonial World,* edited by Francis Barker, Peter Hulme and Margaret Iversen, 238–259. Cambridge: Cambridge University Press.

Klotz, Marcia. 2005. "The Weimar Republic. A Postcolonial State in a Still-Colonial World". In *Germany's Colonial Pasts,* edited by Eric Ames, Marcia Klotz and Lora Wildenthal, 135–147. Lincoln: University of Nebraska Press.

Koller, Christian. 2001a. *"Von Wilden aller Rassen niedergemetzelt:" Die Diskussion um die Verwendung von Kolonialtruppen in Europa zwischen Rassismus, Kolonial- und Militärpolitik (1914–1930).* Stuttgart: Steiner.

Koller, Christian. 2001b. "Feind-Bilder. Rassen- und Geschlechterstereotype in der Kolonialtruppendiskussion Deutschlands und Frankreichs, 1914–1923". In *Heimat - Front: Militär- und Geschlechterverhältnisse im Zeitalter der Weltkriege,* edited by Karen Hagemann and Stefanie Schüler-Springorum, 150–167. Frankfurt: Campus.

Langbehn, Volker M. and Mohammad Salama, eds. 2011. *German Colonialism: Race, the Holocaust, and Postwar Germany*. New York: Columbia University Press.

Maß, Sandra. 2001. "Das Trauma des weißen Mannes: Afrikanische Kolonialsoldaten in propagandistischen Texten, 1914–1923". *L'Homme. ZFG* 12,1: 11–33.

Maß, Sandra. 2005. "'Wir sind zu allem entschlossen. Zur Vernichtung dieser schwarzen Halbmenschen.' Gewalt, Rassismus und Männlichkeit in der deutschen Kriegspropaganda, 1914–1940". In *Ethnizität und Geschlecht: Postkoloniale Verhandlungen in Geschichte, Kunst und Medien*, edited by Graduiertenkolleg Identität und Differenz, 137–150. Köln: Böhlau.

——— 2006. *Weiße Helden – schwarze Krieger: Zur Geschichte kolonialer Männlichkeit in Deutschland, 1918–1964*. Köln: Böhlau.

McClintock, Anne. 1995. *Imperial Leather: Race, Gender and Sexuality in the Colonial Contest*. London: Routledge.

Nelson, Keith. 1970. "The 'Black Horror on the Rhine:' Race as a Factor in Post-World War I Diplomacy". *Journal of Modern History* 42.4: 606–627.

Obeyesekere, Gananath. 2005. *Cannibal Talk: The Man-Eating Myth and Human Sacrifice in the South Seas*. Berkeley: University of California Press.

Oguntoye, Katharina. 1997. *Eine afro-deutsche Geschichte: Zur Lebenssituation von Afrikanern und Afro-Deutschen in Deutschland von 1884–1950*. Berlin: Hoho-Verlag Hoffmann.

Perraudin, Michael and Jürgen Zimmerer, eds. 2011. *German Colonialism and National Identity*. New York: Routledge.

Steyerl, Hito and Encarnación G. Rodríguez, eds. 2003. *Spricht die Subalterne deutsch? Migration und postkoloniale Kritik*. Münster: Unrast.

Wetzell, Richard F. 2000. *Inventing the Criminal: A History of German Criminology, 1880–1945*. Chapel Hill: University of North Carolina Press.

Zantop, Susanne. 1997. *Colonial Fantasies: Conquest, Family, and Nation in Precolonial Germany, 1770–1870*. Durham: Duke University Press.

Zimmerer, Jürgen. 2009. "Nationalsozialismus postkolonial: Plädoyer zur Globalisierung der deutschen Gewaltgeschichte". *Zeitschrift für Geschichtswissenschaft* 57: 529–548.

9   Postcolonial Postcommunism?

Cristina Şandru

In the past decade or so, a growing number of studies and articles have taken issue with matters that postcolonialism silences or simply chooses not to discuss, and with the new hierarchies and hegemonies it has set up in Western academe. Privileged subjects include a certain type of politically correct discourse; a certain type/genre of literature (say, "hybrid" metropolitan fiction) and perhaps even certain points of origination of this literature, such as India or South Africa; the Anglophone colonial sphere over other types of colonial experience, although this particular gap is being quickly filled by the rise in postcolonial Francophone, Latin American, Middle Eastern and First Peoples studies; and so forth. In a parallel movement, a significant number of new critical approaches have emerged within its fold (environmentalism, new geographies and temporalities, etc.), each trying to address the multiple challenges that globalization poses and to confront contemporary neo-imperial practices. By and large, postcolonial studies has succeeded in adapting its modes of critique to the new, post-Cold War dispositions of power and influence and their resultant inequities. Indeed, so successful has it been that the postcolonial has moved in recent years from being a historical marker to a globally inflected term applicable to a variety of regions, as the collection of essays I co-edited with Janet Wilson and Sarah Lawson Welsh (*Rerouting the Postcolonial*, Routledge, 2009) suggests. Yet in one crucial respect the postcolonial paradigm has fallen short of its critical potential and ethical ambition, namely in its interaction – or lack thereof – with the communist "Second World" and its post-communist aftermath.

Clearly, the two great struggles that shaped the late twentieth and early twenty-first centuries have been decolonization in the Third World and de-Sovietization/de-communization in the Second World. The post-1989 break up of the former Soviet Union and its outlying satellite system has been posing a variety of challenges – ideological as well as economic – ever since. In particular, as far as our discipline is concerned, these events have stressed the need to reformulate neo-Marxist models of postcolonial critique to account for a post-communist set of realities and the resurgence of neo-liberalism in the former Second World. Yet, with notable exceptions, the historical experience of Soviet-controlled territories or satellite states is strangely absent from theorizations of the postcolonial. Indeed, as Alexander Edkind remarks in his study of imperial Russia, the two movements, although "historically [...] intertwined" have been kept "intellectually [...] separate" (2011, 25). Both sides suffer, I believe, from this disjunction between the postcolonial and the post-communist, and if they continue to avoid engaging in a constructive debate they risk falling into what Edkind aptly calls "methodological parochialism" (26). In what follows, I will share some critical reflections on how the two "posts", both marking the nominal fall of empires, can be seen to simultaneously converge and diverge, yielding an interwoven kind of intellectual fabric – a more capacious and flexible version, perhaps, of Said's contrapuntal approach to empire and its legacies. I have treated some of these issues more extensively in my book *Worlds Apart? A Postcolonial Reading of Post-1945 East-Central European Culture* (2012), which reads post-communist cultures through the lens of postcolonial theory, but also against its grain.

Insofar as East-Central Europe has been seen through a postcolonial lens, the main approaches have been variations on the Orientalist model (in key studies by Larry Wolff, Maria Todorova and Vesna Goldsworthy), which highlight the specific character that imperial domination has taken in the region, of which the tendency towards self-colonization in relation to the West is central and goes a long way in explaining the current ideological climate in East-Central Europe. Yet this analytical framework, while of undisputed scholarly significance, does not in itself explain the persistence of certain modes of thinking in the West in relation to the new members of the European family (by "European family" I specifically mean the EU; the East European nations – either ex-Soviet or ex-Yugoslav republics – which have not yet joined this political organization pose an even more challenging problem). Nor is it particularly helpful in situating on a postcolonial axis the volatile mix of geography, ideology and economic and political subservience that characterized East-Central Europe's communist half-century. The most salient difficulty concerns the multiple levels of disjuncture that one must consider concurrently when attempting a comparative analysis of the two major "posts" of the twentieth century: different inflections in terms of historical and geographical co-ordinates; divergent types of imperial occupation; asynchronous advents of modernity; different practices of othering; and, finally, post-Cold War ideological emphases.

Thus if one looks at an abridged version of the century that has recently ended, one can discern an asymmetrical historical timeline between much of the Third World and the East-Central and South-East European regions. Europe's Eastern regions entered their first post-imperial decades immediately after the end of World War I, and experienced thereafter the birth pangs of national projects of development, as well as the excesses of nationalism and the lures of extreme ideologies. Meanwhile, colonialism elsewhere was still very much alive, even though signs of its impending decay were already evident to perspicacious analysts. Then, after the end of World War II, when the colonial world started crumbling, East-Central Europe entered a new imperial age, driven by a different ideology but equally imposed by the military and political might of the Soviet Union. In this respect, as many commentators have argued, the true significance of the Cold War, beyond its political repercussions, emerges from its role as a form of knowledge and representation of the world that has neatly filled the gap left by the rapid dissolution of Western empires after World War II. It laid down, in a different fashion but using old assumptions and binaries, the conceptual geography grounded in the East/West opposition. Not only was East-Central Europe part of this new epistemic paradigm, but so was the "third" (non-aligned) world, itself a creation of the Cold War and subject to its action on both sides of the ideological divide. Indeed, the communist experiment took hold of a sizable part of the liberated Third World as well, before it crumbled under the weight of the new regimes' atrocities or mismanagement. In a parallel but reverse movement, the post-1968 decades in East-Central Europe lost much of their revolutionary Marxist flavor and became bureaucratically frozen in a state capitalism of sorts, the contours of which were best described by Vaclav Havel's term "post-totalitarianism" (Havel 1986). After 1989, the blanket domination of global capitalism has placed the two regions in even closer proximity to each other, though arguably the East/West rhetoric has given way to an earlier North/South divide. East-Central Europe is now going through its own accelerated postcolonial period, replicating in many respects the post-independence moment in much of the Third World half a century earlier, which saw the desired achievement of decolonization drown in excessive nationalism, political authoritarianism and economic failures.

Another level of difficulty concerns the ambivalent positioning of former imperial territories with respect to the perceived or actual metropole. This phenomenon is particularly acute in East-Central Europe, a region distinguished by its liminal location between East and West; by a composite political structure that incorporates both Western and Eastern elements; and by the self-reflexive bent of its culture, in which Orientalism and Occidentalism play off each other in creative – but also deeply problematic – combinations. As many postcolonial theorists have pointed out, one result of extended hegemony and mind-colonization is compensatory behavior on the part of subjected peoples, either in the form of reverse ethnocentrism (the desire for authentic sources, the return to a set of mythic-heroic genealogies etc.) or in the form of mimicry. This dynamic is played out differently in East-Central Europe, where the desire to imitate does not involve the former Soviet center, but the Western hegemon. This attitude is conclusively illustrated by a large number of articles, essays and books written (especially) by Central European intellectuals (Kundera's 1984 "The Tragedy of Central Europe" being amongst the most virulent of its kind), which adamantly reject any type of Eastern-cum-Soviet colonialism, even while their attitude towards what they, too, designate as "Western civilization" (whether it refers to German or French cultural influence, or the newer American hegemony of globalized pop culture), is compounded by an uneasy combination of identification and distance. This "double-centred peripherality" (Băicoianu 2005, 51) accounts for the outright vilification of all post-1945 historical developments (including educational reforms that widened opportunity and created social mobility, better standards of sanitation and health care etc.) as invariably stained by communism, and a converse idealization of Western capitalist achievements. This is both a tendency in general popular culture and a dominant mode of analysis among the intellectual elite and the professional class in many Central and East European countries. Hence the delay or reluctance in East-Central Europe of confronting its communist past, which is associated, on the one hand, with a post-1989 triumph of libertarianism and free-marketeering and, in an opposite (but mirror) reaction, with the resurrection of various stripes of chauvinistic nationalism.

Indeed, the post-Cold War period harks back in this particular respect as well to the immediate post-decolonization period following the end of World War II, during which traditional colonial polarizations were at least partly replaced by a resurgence of ethnic, nationalist and religious fundamentalisms. These at times burst into full-blown conflict followed by partitions (at the borders of India/Pakistan/Bangladesh/Kashmir, in the former Yugoslav space, in the Caucasus). Many such conflicts were caused, on the one hand, by inadequate and ill-thought-out colonial borders (as in much of Africa, but also India/Pakistan), as well as ethnocentric resentments and historical traumas suppressed or distorted for decades under communism (involving in particular the trauma of fascist occupation/collaboration/resistance). On the other hand, the pressures of globalization have produced ever more parochial and localized ideologies in response, as new forms of imperialism have reinforced the "international division of labor and appropriation [...] benefiting First World countries at the expense of Third World" (Ebert in Corniş-Pope 2004, 1) and, I must add, Second World post-communist societies. These, too, have often been a contributing factor to post-decolonization conflicts. Indeed, the suppression or incitement of ethnic and national sentiment and sectarian aspiration are, as various commentators have remarked, an important point of intersection between postcolonial and post-communist scholarship. The end result is a deeply disjunctive post-communist culture, in which resurrected nationalism(s) coexist rather unhappily with accumulated historical frustrations over European integration and where savage market capitalism is superposed on a generalized distrust of mass consumerism. These are all phenomena that postcolonial polities and cultures recognize well, having been a staple of their public discourses for a long time, though the ideological underpinnings differ substantially.

The neo-colonial attitude dominating post-Cold War relations between the countries of East-Central Europe and their Western European counterparts is visible at the level of both economic development and intellectual discourse. The critical space occupied by dissident voices in communist times has by and large been filled in the post-communist decades by unrestrained capitalism, conspicuous consumption and an ever-widening gap of wealth and opportunity between various categories of citizens. As Katharine Verderey and Sharad Chari remark in their seminal article on the conjunctures and disjunctures between postcolonialism and post-socialism, the process of transition in post-Cold War East-Central Europe has brought with it a cocktail of accelerated marketization, commodification and integration in the global circuit of capital. This, coupled with a large supply of cheap labor and the very postcolonial phenomenon of economic migration to the affluent metropolis (from brain drain to the siphoning off of skilled labor), has turned the region into the capitalist West's proximate Third World.

From the perspective of a postcolonial critic, therefore, it seems to me that there are two relevant questions to ask here. The first one should seek to uncover not only the construction of the "West" and its forms of globalized capitalism, but also how numerous postcolonies were affected by socialist ideological pressures and promises. The second question to pose is not *whether* postcolonial modes of analysis are applicable in the wider post-communist context but, rather, *how* they might be applied. In this respect, Verderey and Chari's analytical model, bringing together as it does "European empires of previous centuries, Cold War empires and their Third World client-states, late twentieth-century corporate power, and forms of twenty-first-century capitalism" (2009, 16), makes possible the examination of differing post-totalitarian legacies in a manner similar to postcolonial theory's problematization of the colonial and the postcolonial through and beyond specific localities. In some sense, their post-socialist approach, in which the economic factor plays a crucial role, does hold out the promise of sustained critique of the current orthodoxies supported by "transitology" experts – not only of the socialist past, but also of the "neoliberal verities about transition, markets, and democracy [that] were imposed upon former socialist spaces" (Verderey and Shari 2009, 6). In this, their model can be seen as the necessary analytic complement to materialist forms of postcolonial critique applied to post-Cold War configurations of knowledge and power in the global South (concerning free markets, property rights, political institutions, community relations, forms of consumption, the media and so on). An approach along these lines can throw light on the multiple ways in which postcolonialism and post-communism may be seen to challenge and subvert forms of imperialism while at the same time treating Marxism divergently – as enabling critique of neo-colonial relations for the former and, for the latter, as a complex interplay of failed ideology (relating to the recent past) and newly relevant (if highly contentious) critical toolbox.

The difficult question remains, however, of how one can conceptualize postcolonial futures in the absence of a viable intellectual and socio-political framework to compete with capitalism. At this point, I wish to make a clear distinction between the traditions of critical Marxism – or, rather, the use of ideas, arguments and modes of critique that have their origin in Marxist and neo-Marxist philosophy – and the congealment of Marxism into an ideology and its systemic application as communism. The former, when used in specific political, economic and cultural contexts and in conjunction with critical instruments of different extraction, can continue to provide a discursive alternative to the dominance of neo-colonial capital and its global inequities. The latter must be recognized as the massive political and moral failure that it was. An honest appraisal of the legacies of communism in Europe and throughout the world must start, I believe, from acknowledging the failure of leftist ideologies of Marxist extraction to have produced egalitarian, compassionate and affluent societies anywhere in the world where they have been applied. This is an intellectual position that does not have many supporters among the educated elite in the West, whether homegrown or of postcolonial extraction, a state of affairs that has not changed substantially (despite the lip service occasionally paid to condemnations of communism's excesses) after the fall of the Berlin wall. In this respect, it is worth remembering that the Cold War logic that shaped the world after 1945 had a substantive bearing not only on economic and military policies but also – crucially – on wider cultural trends and attitudes. Indeed, "the intellectual Left's silence about the Second world and the Right's anticommunist preoccupations were interrelated processes, mutually enforcing constraints" (Condee 2009, 236). The awareness of this political reality, however, does not justify the disturbing imbalance between the way in which the Leftist intellectual establishment has conceptualized and discussed the crumbling of empire in the Third World and how it has reckoned with – but most often shied away from – the end of the Cold War and the collapse of communism. Edkind calls this, with direct reference to Edward Said's work, "partial worldliness", which "omits the Second World as a nuisance" (2011, 41), and it is a regrettably widespread phenomenon still. The claim that attacks on communist politics are "today's cultural racism" (Kovacevic 2008, 16), which is made by a sizeable number of left-leaning intellectuals both East and West (a few names immediately come to mind, among whom Slavoj Žižek, Aijaz Ahmad, Alain Badiou) is, in actual fact, a gesture of containment and critical oblivion that denies the very possibility of a non-Marxist critique of the dominant world capitalist system. Such commentators join the ranks of the few believers left in the socialist project in East-Central Europe after 1989, for whom, in Patrick McGuinness's felicitous description in his recent novel *The Last Hundred Days* (2011), "[A]ll the failures of the idea were due to the misapplication of the ideal, [and] all the barbarity of the system was extraneous to that system and accidental to it" (location 3103).

In some important respects, what such commentators object to is the uncontested reign of free-market capitalism, which is now the only game in town in East-Central Europe. To the extent to which this objection has been borne out by recent trends in speculative capitalism, which has spiraled out of control and has left states and individuals alike struggling in the grip of enormous debts while the chief players of the system continue to command the money-making game as dexterously as before, their critique is not only accurate but necessary. In this sense, studies such as Natasha Kovacevic's account of post-communist East-Central Europe as a neo-colonial space, and various analyses of the negative consequences of the post-1989 transitions to liberal capitalism in the region – including the impoverishment of the most vulnerable (the old, the peasantry, the unskilled); the withdrawal of basic state amenities; the growing gap between the ultra-rich and the middle-earning masses; a culture of conspicuous (and often indiscriminate) consumption; a political culture marred by corruption, media frenzy and populist discourses; the resurgence of various brands of nationalism, ethnicism and xenophobic prejudice etc. – offer a corrective vision to the celebratory stances embraced too easily and too uncritically by many of the opinion-makers who control the public sphere. The collapse of socialism has left a large ideological gap in Europe's political imaginary. In East-Central Europe, despite increasing popular frustrations and resentment, intellectual discourses coming from the progressive left are emptied of strength and meaning, while all critique in the name of equality or solidarity is immediately branded as dangerously "communist".

The crux of the matter, in my view, lies in the incapacity of progressive left-of-center politics to offer viable alternatives to the doctrines and practices of capitalism in the rapacious embodiment that has taken over the global economy and many state policies, East and West. This is a situation that social-democratic – but staunchly anti-communist – historians and commentators have deplored with respect to the fading away of the social state and the very idea of welfare that has followed the neo-liberal decade of the 1980s and the transformation of industrial into financial-speculative capitalism (see, for instance, Tony Judt's remarkably lucid pronouncements on the crisis of social democracy in the West in his volume of essays *Ill Fares the Land* (2011)). One explanation for the current ideological gap on the left side of the political spectrum is the fact that Marxist ideology has been enormously successful in appropriating ideals of social egalitarianism that have emerged from earlier reformist movements (the Chartists, the Fabian movement, even quasi-conservative paternalistic movements in the England of the 1840s) and, in the process, has irremediably transformed them. It is clearly not state communism that "created the potential for thinking beyond the politics of private property and class divisions" (Kovacevic 2008, 99), as Kovacevic seems to suggest,[1] but many critics nonetheless choose to neglect other historically progressive ideas of social equity and liberal reform and fall back on old Marxist orthodoxies, in the process evading, or occluding, the question of the ideology's moral responsibility towards its past progeny.

It is this myopia of the Western left – its failure to see that the Marxist-derived communist utopia predicated on absolute rationality, "scientific" social organization, and purity of purpose was anti-humanistic in its very essence, despite its radical emancipatory nature – that I find objectionable. When confronted with the ever-clearer fact that "the Messianic promise of the age-old utopian dream of socialism as a cure for the clearly obvious pathologies of capitalism had merely led to new pathologies in the form of the virulent psychoses of totalitarian dictatorship" (Gottlieb 2001, 6), leftist intelligentsia in the West chose to interpret the flaws inherent in the system as exclusively the product of human error. They therefore failed to acknowledge the implication of Marxist political theory in the development and legitimization of a totalitarian system responsible

> for the slaughter of individuals on the altar of the great historical ideals – justice or progress or the happiness of future generations, or the sacred mission or emancipation of a nation or race or class [...] which demands the sacrifice of individuals for the freedom of society.
> (Berlin 1969, 167)

Steven Lukes' perceptive assessment of why the communist system has generated such an inexplicable "moral blindness" (Lukes 2001) rests on its evacuation of ordinary ethics and individual human rights from Marxist-Leninist discourse and ideology. Since "Marxism offered the emancipating vision of a world in which the principles that protect human beings from one another would no longer be needed" (Lukes 2001, 120) – in other words since it conceived of a future in which the main conditions of ethical behavior and legality, namely want, scarcity, selfishness and diversity of values, would no longer exist – then it was justified to dispense with present morality for the sake of a future world emancipated from the shackles of justice and rights (Lukes 2001, 7–8). For those intellectuals in the West who were all too ready to excuse the crimes perpetrated in the name of noble ideas,[2] Vassily Grossman's painful observations in his epic novel *Life and Fate* (1959) might have served as cautionary food for thought:

> I have [...] seen the unshakeable strength of the idea of social good that was born in my own country. I saw the struggle during the period of general collectivization and again in 1937. I saw people being annihilated in the name of an idea as good and fine and humane as the ideal of Christianity. I saw whole villages dying of hunger; I saw trains bound for Siberia with thousands and thousands of men and women. [...] This idea was something fine and noble – yet it killed some without mercy, crippled the lives of others, and separated wives from husbands and children from fathers. (1959, 405–407)

It is thus that a set of utopian ideals has led to the most barbarous consequences in practice.[3]

As the brief analysis above suggests, "post-colonialism does not translate perfectly its language and strategies into post-communism, and post-communism, with its rejection of Marxism, cannot match perfectly the aims of post-colonialism" (Popescu 2003, 417). But it is important, I believe, to think comparatively and interconnectedly about imperialism and totalitarian communism while fully aware of their specific historical contexts and diverse incarnations in various locations. The communist imposition in

East-Central Europe can fruitfully be seen as a particular historical embodiment of a persistent and widespread imperial drive that has characterized the behavior of stronger states towards territories perceived as providing opportunities for economic, political or ideological expansion. Lack of sovereign power, military occupation, domestic economy subordinated to the Soviet one and cultural hegemony are clear signs of imperial overlordship that the USSR's internal republics and its Eastern European satellites share with formerly colonized nations – and which followed previous histories of imperial subjugation in most of these states.

In addition, it is worth observing that the discourse of ideological othering at the basis of both fascist and communist totalitarianisms is underwritten by a series of assumptions similar to those on which colonial racism operated, particularly in its most extreme forms: slavery on Caribbean plantations and the US South, apartheid and calculated genocide in parts of Africa. Indeed, in regimes informed by scientifically sanctioned state racism (or white supremacism), the treatment of the Other has much in common with the policies and practices of communist regimes towards their class enemies. State-sanctioned racism can function not only on considerations of color, blood and ethnicity, but class, creed and political conviction. It "rel[ies] on institutional and biopolitical mechanisms, which differentiate populations into sub-groups having varied access to means of life and death" (Verderey and Shari 2009, 7). And while the exercise of epistemic, social and punitive power (what Foucault calls "biopolitics") over internal enemies and variously othered populations was a chief characteristic of communist totalitarianism, it has been used with various degrees of systematicity by colonial administrations as well. (The term "enemy" was not frequently found in colonial contexts, as other terminologies of inferiorization were used, chief among which that of the "native savage" in need of civilizing.)

An analytical framework that starts from such concrete particulars would be premised on variant forms of power imposition, in which race and the historical experience of overseas colonialism would not be allowed to obscure other Western (and non-Western) constructions of alterity. The (post)colony can thus become a signifier of cultural and ideological violence – a colonization of the mind as much as a project of geographical expansion and economic exploitation. Such an approach would excavate the epistemological and cultural similarities that underlie the more visible political and economic differences. In particular, it would yield interesting results in the contrapuntal analysis of the Western Enlightenment project of modernity, a project that, in the eyes of many commentators, was embedded in the very ideology of empire and reached its destructive culmination in the two totalitarianisms of the twentieth century. Indeed, if nineteenth-century colonialism can be seen as the logical development of an earlier, mercantile phase of capitalism, then in some important sense communist totalitarianism is its equally logical next step. It follows to a large extent (even if we admit that Soviet communism was not quite the future Marx had in mind) Marx's *fair point!*

picture of the communist future as latent in the womb of the capitalist present. The chief attribute of communist totalitarianism that makes it and its post-period suitable for comparison with (post)-colonialism rests precisely on communism's systemic character, its creation of new modes of production and consumption, new social and political configurations, new cultural models and a systematic determination to change – often annihilate – precommunist modes of life and traditions. In this sense "applied Marxism" (i.e. communism) was, like industrial capitalism, a purveyor of enforced modernization. Many of its policies – rapid industrialization and urbanization, development of infrastructure, fight against religious prejudice, tribalism and "traditional ways" (seen as barbaric by the colonial masters and "bourgeois" by the communists) – are similar to those deployed in newly colonized countries. In this, as well as its relative length and stability, it is more similar to the colonial system than to fascism. The latter thankfully had a shorter shelf life, and – with few exceptions such as Spain or Portugal – has not created a distinct form of governmentality and economy in the countries in which it took hold. Even in countries where fascism lasted longer, its aftermath was followed by relatively smoother transitions in which the break between the pre-fascist past and the post-fascist present was not as traumatic as in the case of either de/post-colonization or post-communism. The advantage of thus thinking the two posts together lies, moreover, in the underlying "refusal of the Three-Worlds ideology that associates postcoloniality with a bounded space called the Third World and postsocialism with the Second World" (Verderey and Shari 2009, 7). Not only are there institutional, political and ideological overlaps between the two but also geographical ones, with areas of the Third World under the direct neo-colonial influence of the Soviet Union, and where quasi-socialist economic and political structures are either still present or in process of being dismantled.

The competition between capitalism and Marxist-based/Soviet-sponsored ideologies in large swathes of the Third World in the post-1945 period is indicative of the uneasy conjuncture between imperialist practices of different stripes in their common pursuit of developmental and modernization policies. To briefly illustrate this point on the level of literary responses, although the vast majority of postcolonial novels take issue with the shape of the postcolonial nation under the combined forces of neo-colonial capitalism and home-bred violence and rapacity, a few dramatize the radical gap between the utopian rhetoric of socialism and the dystopian reality of the postcolonial country that has become in all but name a client state of the Soviet Union. In his article on African fiction and dystopia, M. Keith Booker looks at some of the dystopian environments dramatized in postcolonial fictions from African societies under the influence of Stalinist and post-Stalinist Soviet Union, particularly Somalia under Siyad Barre (in Nuruddin Farah's *Sweet and Sour Milk*, 1979, and *Sardines*, 1981) and Ethiopia under Mengistu (in Hama Tuma's *The Case of the Socialist Witchdoctor*, 1993). In these fictions the parallels between the real historical circumstances and the

this is actually a really colossal oversight – but remember the distinction between theoretical Marxism & communism she made earlier

universe depicted in the book are rather transparent – the allegorical veneer is thin, and the books read more like Orwellian dystopias or satires than elaborately built parables, although the common heritage in Orwell, Huxley and Zamyatin is shared with the dystopic fictions of East-Central Europe (such as Jerzy Andrzejewski's *The Inquisitors*, 1960; A.E. Baconsky's *Black Church*, 1990; I. D. Sîrbu's *Europe, Adieu!* 1992–1993; Ferenc Karinthy's *Metropole*, 1970). In the prologue to *Sweet and Sour Milk*, the reader is openly provided with the key to decoding the meaning of the novel: "Is this Africa or is this Stalin's Russia?" (1979, 10). Indeed, the similarities are striking. Not only is the anonymous General a dictatorial figure modelled directly on Stalin, but all the instruments and practices of the police state are deployed with the same degree of efficiency and brutality: an elaborate arsenal of propaganda and indoctrination supplements an essentially carceral system, in which society is merely an extended version of the smaller prison system used to put away the dissidents. Moreover, there is a crusade of terror waged by a KGB-trained secret police apparatus and Ethiopia's Great Chairman exerts his absolute power through a violent campaign of indoctrination and repression. As Booker remarks, the torture and brutality described in these fictions are clearly reminiscent of those described in anti-Stalinist works such as Arthur Koestler's *Darkness at Noon* or Danilo Kiš' *A Tomb for Boris Davidovich* (Booker 1995, 148). But perhaps the most disturbing element in these African anti-communist dystopias is the remarkable level of continuity with previous – or concurring – authoritarian and repressive ideologies, very similar in nature to the continuity between the fascist and the communist totalitarianisms to which East-Central Europe succumbed for much of the twentieth century. In the context of Somalia, it is a fundamentalist and patriarchal Islamic system that condones and supports Soviet-sponsored socialism, and the similarities between the two are exposed relentlessly in Farah's *Sardines*.

As the brief analysis above suggests, another feature that postcolonial and post-communist cultures share is the experience of trauma and the predominance of the retrospective look, an almost obsessive calling to account of the past in all its forms; their major tonality is the confessional, with undertones of nostalgia or anger. Clearly, where "post-" historical periods are concerned, issues of identity and remembrance, memorializing and using the past, questions of what and why we choose to forget or what stories we choose to tell are not only culturally relevant, but formative on the level of the national narrative as expressed in commemorative public practices or educational policies. Studies such as Tzvetan Todorov's *Hope and Memory* (2003) and Svetlana Boym's *The Future of Nostalgia* (2001) have shown how the excavation of the past is always bent in the direction of either restorative or reflective impulses. The social fabric is torn between nationalist revivals, collective myths and commemorative gestures that "museumify" the past, and the underground, partial, fragmentary collage of personal testimonies, where the emphasis is often on loss, on the irretrievability of the past as well as its irreparability. In addition, I contend, one can also detect a nostalgia for the "might have been". Originating in the desire to retrieve the unfulfilled promises of socialism in East-Central Europe, this nostalgia seeks to revalorize the critical potential of Marxism in the face of the perceived levelling of the nations and cultures of the region into one undifferentiated mass of subservient adjuncts to global capital. There is, thus, a very interesting connection to note between the formation of the (post)colonial and (post)communist subject, a simultaneous acknowledgment and denial of the subject's ambivalent past. Such hypertrophy of history has always been a chief characteristic of borderlands, hybrid identities and post-imperial spaces, as Dennis Walder's admirable comparative study *Postcolonial Nostalgias: Writing, Memory and Representation* (2010) – in which widely different post-imperial writers such as Naipaul, Ballard, W. G. Sebald and the black South African writer Jacob Dlamini rub literary shoulders – makes abundantly clear. Their works are haunted by a prior history that often cannot be adequately verbalized: not only the major histories of empire, oppression and occupation, but also a history of personal responsibility and betrayal, of complicity and accommodation, or simply of a shapeless, haunting guilt for something that is beyond retrieval or repair. The present as revealed by this writing is forever inhabited – indeed, one could almost say possessed – by the shapes, textures and narratives of the past. But these texts do not simply enact a nostalgic rememoration of a lost time, place or home, nor do they pronounce, moralistically, condemnatory sentences. What they suggest, disturbingly, is a certain degree of intimacy between colonized and colonizer, oppressor and oppressed, a blurring of boundaries between perpetrator and victim that renders any implacable moral judgments uneasy, inevitably colored by the difficult negotiations of individual people caught within unaccountable historical situations, often at the mercy of callous decision-makers. As Walder shows in his example of Jacob Dlamini's *Native Nostalgia* (2009), the master narrative of the "struggle" and the suffering under apartheid is always balanced by the remembrance of a happy childhood, despite the lack of basic services. Like communism, the world of apartheid is revealed as "a world of moral ambivalence and ambiguity in which people could be both resisters and collaborators at the same time" (Walder 2010, 17).

While I agree with Neil Lazarus' contention that post-communist literary works cannot be seen to belong within the postcolonial studies arena per se, I maintain that the exercise of comparison, "translation" and transposition can be illuminating. The literatures of post-1945 East-Central Europe[4] share a number of important characteristics with a wide variety of literary texts that are usually labeled postcolonial, partly because they have emerged as responses to a deeply traumatic past and its many divisive legacies in the present. Among these are a preference for oblique modes of narration, grotesque humor, and fantastic or magical realist topoi, a penchant for boundary transgressions and generic hybridity, as well as a relatively large supply of ex-centric and liminal (exilic or diasporic) places of articulation. As in the case of postcolonial fictions, these tendencies arose as a distinct imaginative response to a highly coercive discursive regime. They formed a network of counter-discourses that confronted the officially sanctioned norms of socialist realism. It is this tenor of resistance and subversion that most closely aligns them with postcolonial literatures, which similarly seek to deconstruct the language, rhetoric, mental set-up and symbolic representations underpinning the imperial project. In addition, and again much like postcolonial texts, these narratives unmask the potential of the dominant/repressive discourse for falsification, what Achille Mbembe calls "the stock of falsehoods and the weight of fantasizing functions without which colonialism [and communism, I would add] as a historical power-system could not have worked". To paraphrase Mbembe's conclusion on the role of postcolonial thinking, that "it reveals how what passed for European humanism manifested itself in the colonies as duplicity, double-talk and a travesty of reality" (2008), post-totalitarian texts reveal how the rhetoric of equality, fraternity and justice at the basis of the communist project in actual fact served to obscure the brutality, oppressiveness and stultifying misery of the political regime it engendered. Yet the revelations are almost always at an angle, couched in coded storylines and embedded symbolism, reflecting the ambiguous threshold between accommodation and resistance that is the hallmark of all literary production policed by coercive ideological regimes.

If the characteristic landscape of post-imperial and post-totalitarian fictions is one of moral ambivalence, so is the conflicting public reflection on the narrative of the recent past, which tends to oscillate between two extremes – either the repressive component is downgraded and lines between oppressor and victim blurred to the point of interchangeability, or public discourse is infested by a virulent condemnatory rhetoric that lumps together very different degrees of accommodation, collaboration and resistance. In the context of post-communist East-Central Europe, very often

> [t]he trial of the Communist Party turned into a bureaucratic farce, and no version of the Truth and Reconciliation Committee was ever established. The collective trauma of the past was hardly acknowledged; or if it was, everyone was seen as an innocent victim, or a cog in the system only following orders.
>
> (Boym 2001, 58)

There was no emblematic Nuremberg-type trial, nor a symbolic figure such as Eichmann to give a face and a name to the communist version of the "banality of evil". And, despite highly documented studies of the global effects of communist systems of governance, which have supplemented numerous personal testimonies linking the Nazi and the Stalinist concentration camps and extermination policies, the global memorial valence of communist atrocity has never approached in gravity that accorded to the Nazi genocide.[5]

Hence the resentment that pervades much of public consciousness in Central and Eastern Europe, caused by the perceived detachment of the Western intellectual establishment in its assessment of communist totalitarianism. The contention is that while the memory of fascist crimes has been indelibly imprinted on the consciousness of successive generations of West Europeans, the condemnation of communism is usually equivocal and hedged:

> [W]hile the Holocaust remains the symbol of absolute evil in human history, the horrors of the GULAG and of Stalinist terror, despite being publicly condemned Europe-wide after the collapse of the Soviet empire, have not received comparable institutional recognition (e.g. museums, educational programmes, victim compensation).
>
> (Zhurzhenko 2007)

This asymmetry in European memory can be explained in a variety of ways. One persuasive explanation concerns the different levels of mediatization, as well as the perceived "closeness" of the memory in question. The crimes of communist regimes tended to happen elsewhere in the East, to other peoples, not in the midst of (Western) Europe.[6] These crimes also did not lie so squarely on the shoulders of former Western imperial powers, as much of the violence, exploitation and indignity of colonial behavior did. Surely, any evaluative impulse must be based on fine contextualization and an accumulation of historical evidence, and it usually takes time. Yet the need for more historical contextualization should not obscure the fact that the use of history is seldom disinterested, and that it very much depends on who is doing the interpretation and evaluation, and to what purpose. Suffice to say that the kinds of competition and hierarchization of evil (whether slavery, apartheid, Nazi extermination policies or communist camps) that are still being practiced in certain corners of academic and public discourse are deeply divisive and cannot foster either lucid historical assessment or reconciliation. Compassionate and balanced comparative studies, which do not minimize or dilute the singularity of particular historical experiences, can open up a space of dialogue in which political and ideological uses of memory can be more readily examined and their interested premises exposed.

To conclude, there is an evident postcolonial sensibility in the way East-Central Europe articulates both its recent past and its embattled present: how it places itself at the heart of the European project yet at the same time feels acutely, and seeks to articulate and manifest, its separateness; how it struggles to rememorize, rewrite and reinterpret its history, both more distant and more recent; and how it negotiates its continued semi-peripheral status in the European Union. The advantages of imagining Eastern Europe and the former colonial world within the same intellectual paradigm would thus be reciprocal. What gives the postcolonial its theoretical force and makes it a suitable point of departure in such a comparative analysis is the articulation of how structures of domination work; how models of alterity are formed; and how the imbrication of power and knowledge produces ideologically interpellated subjects, as well as the emphasis on how subjects negotiate and contest these hegemonic ideological structures. On the other hand, post-communism can offer the neo-Marxist versions of postcolonialism a necessary reality check. The crumbling of the systems based on Marxist utopia and the failure of their revolutionary projects need to be interrogated and reassessed, and their implications brought to bear on any contemporary critique of neo-colonial systems.

[handwritten annotation: Key insight, oft-overlooked]

NOTES

1. Whether one agrees it is, in effect, the existence of private property and social classes that creates inequality (a standard Marxist position) or believes, as I do, that it is an excess of inequality beyond and above what one can reasonably expect from a naturally unequal distribution of talents, health and luck among the human population that justifies the current disenchantment with socially irresponsible capitalism.
2. Sartre's own *mauvaise foi* regarding the developments in the Soviet Union is a case in point, but it is far from singular. An interesting study in this respect is Tony Judt's *Past Imperfect: French Intellectuals, 1944–1956.*
3. *The Black Book of Communism* (1997), the most massive study on the phenomenon produced so far, attempts to evaluate the magnitude of its disastrous effects by a systematic and detailed incursion into its historical manifestations, from Lenin's Bolshevik revolution in 1917 Russia, to Pol Pot's Khmer Rouge and the collapse of the regime in East-Central Europe in 1989. According to the raw numeric estimates in the book, communism was in truth "a tragedy of planetary dimensions" (1997, x) that has produced a grand total of approximately 100 million victims. Courtois lists a variety of methods: "firing squads, hanging, drowning, battering, and, in certain cases, gassing, poisoning, or 'car accidents'; destruction of the population by starvation, through man-made famine, the withholding of food, or both; deportation, through which death can occur in transit [...], at one's place of residence, or through forced labour (exhaustion, illness, hunger, cold)" (Courtois 1999, 4).
4. One cannot label literary works written before 1989 as in any salient way "postcommunist", chiefly because the term itself (unlike postcolonialism) has not acquired the same pervasiveness in literary and cultural analysis as it has in social and political studies, where it designates the institutional configurations and economic arrangements superseding the socialist system. This is why I prefer to call these literatures "post-totalitarian" rather than postcommunist, a term that better reflects the multilayered nature of the texts in question and their ambivalent positioning vis-à-vis the ideological field within which they were inevitably inscribed but which they also sought to challenge. For more on this matter, please see Chapter III of my study *Worlds Apart* (2012).
5. *The Black Book of Communism* is only one of these studies, certainly the most massive and systematic, but there are many others, including François Furet's *The Passing of an Illusion*; Anne Applebaum's *Gulag: A History*; Robert Conquest's *Reflections of a Ravaged Century* and *The Great Terror*; and Robert Service's *Communism: A World History.*

6. In fact, as historian Timothy Snyder demonstrates conclusively in the landmark study *Bloodlands: Europe between Hitler and Stalin* (2011), the lands that lie between Stalin's Russia and Hitler's Germany (Poland, Ukraine, Belarus, Lithuania etc.), and which suffered the heaviest toll of atrocity during WWII and after are, geographically at least, at the very heart of Europe.

REFERENCES

Ahmad, Aijaz. 1992. *In Theory: Classes, Nations, Literatures.* London: Verso.

Andzrejewski, Jerzy. 1960. *The Inquisitors.* Translated by Konrad Syrop. London: Weidenfeld & Nicholson.

Applebaum, Anne. 2003. *Gulag: A History.* New York: Doubleday.

Băicoianu, Anca. 2005. "Top Hat and Fur Cap: Postcolonialism, Postcomunism and Their Discontents". *Euresis: Cahiers roumains d'études littéraires et culturelles* 1: 48–53.

Bakonsky, A. E. 1990. *Biserica Neagra [The Black Church].* Bucuresti: Cartea Romaneasca.

Balibar, Etienne A. and Immanuel Wallerstein, eds. 1991. *Race, Class, Nation.* London: Verso.

Berlin, Isaiah. 1969. *Four Essays on Liberty.* London: Oxford University Press.

Booker, Keith M. 1995. "African Literature and the World System: Dystopian Fiction, Collective Experience, and the Postcolonial Condition". *Research in African Literatures* 26.4: 58–75.

Boym, Svetlana. 2001. *The Future of Nostalgia.* New York: Basic Books.

Condee, Nancy. 2009. "Emigration to E-migration: Contemporaneity and the Former Second World". In *Antinomies of Art and Culture. Modernity, Postmodernity, and Contemporaneity,* edited by Okwui Enwezor, Nancy Codee and Terry Smith, 235–249. Durham, NC: Duke University Press.

Conquest, Robert. 1999. *Reflections on a Ravaged Century: Reign of Rogue Ideologies.* London: John Murray.

Conquest, Robert. 2008. *The Great Terror: A Reassessment.* London: Pimlico.

Corniş Pope, Marcel and John Neubauer, eds., 2004–2010. *History of the Literary Cultures of East-Central Europe: Junctures and Disjunctures in the 19th and 20th Centuries.* 4 vols. Amsterdam: John Benjamins.

Courtois, Stéphane, Nicholas Werth, Jean-Louis Panné *et al.* 1999. *The Black Book of Communism: Crimes, Terror, Repression.* Translated by Jonathan Murphy and Mark Kramer. London: Harvard University Press.

Edkind, Alexander. 2011. *Internal Colonization: Russia's Imperial Experience.* Cambridge, Oxford, Boston: Polity Press.

Farah, Nuruddin. 1992. *Sweet and Sour Milk (Variations on the Theme of an African Dictatorship).* Minneapolis: Graywolf Press.

Farah, Nuruddin. 2003. *Sardines (Variations on the Theme of an African Dictatorship).* Minneapolis: Graywolf Press.

Furet, François. 1999. *The Passing of an Illusion: The Idea of Communism in the Twentieth Century.* Chicago: University of Chicago Press.

Goldsworthy, Vesna. 1998. *Inventing Ruritania: the Imperialism of the Imagination.* New Haven: Yale University Press.

Gottlieb, Erika. 2001. *Dystopian Fiction East and West: Universe of Terror and Trial.* Montreal and Kingston: McGill-Queen's University Press.

Grossman, Vassily. 1986. *Life and Fate*. Translated by Robert Chandler. London: Fontana.

Havel, Vaclav. 1986. *Living in Truth*. Edited by Jan Vladislav. London: Faber & Faber.

Judt, Tony. 2011. *Ill Fares The Land: A Treatise On Our Present Discontents*. London: Penguin.

Judt, Tony. 2011. *Past Imperfect: French Intellectuals 1944–1956*. New York: New York University Press.

Karinthy, Ferenc. 2008. *Metropole*. London: Telegram Books.

Kiš, Danilo. 2001. *A Tomb for Boris Davidovich*. Champain, IL, Dublin, London: Dalkey Archive Press.

Koestler, Arthur. 1969. *Darkness at Noon*. London: Penguin.

Kołodziejczyk, Dorota and Cristina Şandru. 2012. "Introduction: On Colonialism, Communism and East-Central Europe: Some Reflections". *Journal of Postcolonial Writing* 48.2: 113–116.

Kovacevic, Natasha. 2008. *Narrating Post/Communism: Colonial Discourse and Europe's Borderline Civilization*. London: Routledge.

Kundera, Milan. 1986. "The Tragedy of Central Europe". *New York Review of Books*, 26 April.

Lukes, Steven. 2001. "On the Moral Blindnes of Communism". *Human Rights Review* 2.2: 113–124.

Mbembe, Achille. 2008. "'What is Postcolonial Thinking?' An Interview with Achille Mbembe".*Eurozine*, 1 Sept. http://www.eurozine.com/articles/2008-01-09-mbembe-en.html.

McGuinness, Patrick. 2011. *The Last Hundred Days*. E-book. London: Seren.

Popescu, Monica. 2003. "Translations: Lenin's Statues, Post-communism, and Post-apartheid". *The Yale Journal of Criticism* 16.2: 406–423.

Said, Edward. 1994. *Culture and Imperialism*. London: Vintage.

Şandru, Cristina. 2012. *Worlds Apart? A Postcolonial Reading of Post-1945 East-Central European Culture*. Newcastle upon Tyne: Cambridge Scholars.

Service, Robert. 2008. *Comrades: Communism: A World History*. London: Pan Macmillan.

Sirbu, I. D. 1992–1993. *Adio, Europa!* [*Goodbye Europe!*]. Bucuresti: Cartea Romaneasca.

Snyder, Timothy. 2011. *Bloodlands: Europe between Hitler and Stalin*. London: Vintage.

Todorov, Tzvetan. 2003. *Hope and Memory*. Translated by David Bellos. London: Atlantic.

Todorova, Maria. 1997. *Imagining the Balkans*. Oxford: Oxford University Press.

Todorova, Maria and Zsuzsa Gille, eds. 2012. *Post-Communist Nostalgia*. New York: Berghahn Books.

Tuma, Hama. 1993. *The Case of the Socialist Witchdoctor and Other Stories*. London: Heinemann.

Verderey, Katherine and Sharad Chari. 2009. "Thinking Between the Posts: Postco-lonialism, Postsocialism, and Ethnography After the Cold War". *Comparative Studies in Societies and History* 51.1: 6–34.

Walder, Dennis. 2010. *Postcolonial Nostalgias: Writing, Memory and Representation*. London: Routledge.

Wilson, Janet, Cristina Șandru and Sarah Lawson-Welsh, eds. 2009. *Re-routing the Postcolonial: New Directions for the New Millenium*. London: Routledge.

Wolff, Larry. 1996. *Inventing Eastern Europe: The Map of Civilisation on the Mind of the Enlightenment*. London: Stanford University Press.

Zhurzhenko, Tatiana. 2007. "The Geopolitics of Memory". *Eurozine*, 5 Oct. http://www.eurozine.com/articles/2007-05-10-zhurzhenko-en.html.

Žižek, Slavoj. 2001. *Did Somebody Say Totalitarianism? Five Interventions in the (Mis)use of a Notion*. London: Verso.

Žižek, Slavoj. "The Two Totalitarianisms". 2005. *London Review of Books*, 17 March. http://www.lrb.co.uk/v27/n06/slavoj-zizek/the-two-totalitarianisms.

Part III

Horizons

Environment, Materialism, World

INTRODUCTION

This final section of our volume seeks to reanimate what postcolonial theory can articulate through outlining projects that further its primary political goals; namely the understanding of imperialism as a structure endemic to the production of environments, subjects and the world. The new modalities of saying and listening that previous sections have explored lead to a set of discursive diagnoses, methodological manifestoes and prescriptions in the pages that follow.

The section begins with an examination of an influential parable: Garrett Hardin's 1968 article "The Tragedy of the Commons". Echoes of a version of Hardin's argument—that there is not enough to go around, and that privatization is the only way to save the world from ruin—have now become standard fare from politicians and policy-makers eager to persuade their constituents about the benefits of austerity for most, while wealth accumulation remains in an ever-shrinking number of hands. By tracing the history of misreadings and misappropriations of Hardin's ideas in the realm of government and policy, Rob Nixon narrates the making of a topsy-turvy political order wherein the greatest threat to the public good is considered to be the very existence and shared character of that good, rather than neoliberalism's rapacious praxes. Such aporias are sadly widespread in the contemporary moment and must, perforce, constitute a new front in postcolonial theory's efforts to unite scholarship with the struggle for justice.

Jennifer Wenzel engages with another aspect of Rob Nixon's research; namely his study *Slow Violence and the Environmentalism of the Poor* (2011), which focuses on violence that is neither spectacular nor explosive, but whose corrosive effects on lives and environments are diffused in space and time. The normal bias towards fast, spectacular forms of violence increases the vulnerability of those populations caught in the shadow of turbo-capitalism. For Wenzel, a proper assumption of the responsibilities implied by Nixon's seminal work would necessarily mean adopting a critical stance towards received, hegemonic ideas about nature and environmentalism. This, in turn, means reading Frantz Fanon with particular attention to the ecocritical dimension of his writing, the better to avoid facile oppositions between nature and society, and to force postcolonial theory to say what ecocriticism cannot.

Originating from a similar postcolonial/ecocritical nexus, Anthony Carrigan makes an eloquent plea for a transformation of the way in which we think about disaster. Postcolonial theory and disaster studies have much to say to each other, not least because of the common genesis of many recent disasters and the ongoing vulnerabilities of the postcolonial condition. Far from being merely an attempt at opening up another channel of communication between disciplines, Carrigan's incisive reading of Kamau Brathwaite's epic magic realist poem *MR* demonstrates what the literary foundation of such an interdisciplinary metamorphosis might look like, and the potential it holds for postcolonial theory, disaster studies and literature.

Crystal Bartolovich's essay unfolds at the intersection between oil as commodity and way of life, nature and postcolonial theory. In a searching analysis of the neoliberal rhetoric of contemporary corporations such as Chevron and Shell, set alongside Patrick Chamoiseau's novel *Texaco*, Bartolovich calls for a re-reading of the contemporary place of oil in the world and in postcolonial theoretical debate. The presumed "foreignness" of oil so prevalent in the commercial and political idioms of the USA and the UK overlooks the reality of oil's commonality within that of the world. It is only by listening to oil's constant challenge to the norms of privatization and nationalism that we can begin to create a more just political and ecological order.

Our volume closes with Sharae Deckard's manifesto for a world-systemic analytical framework. Long caught up in outdated Eurocentric imperialisms and reified binaries, postcolonial theory has yet to fully take on board the implications of a world-systems approach. As a result the implications of the recent scramble for land and resources by non-western states and the formation of new imperial elites outside Europe have yet to be properly theorized. Deckard calls for new innovative methodologies that address the contemporary neoliberal world-system, its literature and concomitant ecology, as a means of demythologizing everyday slogans about new ascendant global economies. In closing on this note, our volume returns to some of the concerns of the opening chapter as a way of presenting a complex whole rather than a heterogeneous collection of essays.

10 Neoliberalism, Genre and "The Tragedy of the Commons"

Rob Nixon

In December 1968, the journal *Science* published "The Tragedy of the Commons", a slender tract by the ecologist and geneticist Garrett Hardin that would become one of the twentieth century's most influential essays. Hardin's thinking resonated in particular with policy-makers at the IMF, the World Bank, conservative think tanks and kindred neoliberal institutions advocating so-called trickle down economics, structural adjustment, austerity measures, government shrinkage and the privatization of resources. Although Hardin's paramount, Malthusian concern was with "overbreeding", it is his general critique of the commons that has had a far more lasting impact. He memorably encapsulated that critique in a parable that represented the commons as unprofitable and unsustainable, inimical to both the collective and the individual good (Ehrlich 1971). According to this brief parable, a herdsman faced with the temptations of a common pasture will instinctively overload it with his livestock. As each greed-driven individual strives to maximize the resource for personal gain, the commons collapses to the detriment of all. Together, Hardin's pithy essay title and succinct parable have helped vindicate a neoliberal rescue narrative whereby privatization through enclosure, dispossession and resource capture is deemed necessary for averting tragedy.

Hardin's account of the commons has been challenged by political scientists, economists, sociologists, demographers, geographers, environmental historians and ecologists. But there is a decisive literary component to his argument that also warrants consideration, namely the way he deploys genre – specifically, tragedy and parable – to fortify the sociobiological case he mounts against the commons. Hardin's crucial move is to pair up genetic and generic forces, creating a muscular tag team pulling for determinism. To change metaphoric registers, in presenting the commons as an innately imminent calamity, he uses genre to strip commonage of its complex cultural histories so that it becomes a blank stage for predictable, biologically driven actions and outcomes.

This process of cultural stripping assumes particular pertinence for our understanding of the neoliberal era's new enclosures, a term first articulated by the Midnight Notes Collective in the early 1990s and elaborated upon by David Harvey and Ashley Dawson, among others. If, in Harvey's phrase, the new enclosures involve "accumulation by dispossession", we need to probe the role that genre plays in what we might in turn call Hardin's disinheritance plot (Harvey 2003, 176). Plot is a usefully layered term here that draws together notions of narrative, property and strategic intent – all crucial to the way the parable of the tragic pastoralist has been appropriated by apologists for the new enclosures.

Early in his essay, Hardin meditates upon William Forster Lloyd's "Two Lectures on the Checks to Population", delivered at Oxford University in 1832 and published the following year. Lloyd, noting that cattle on the commons were "puny and stunted" compared with those on private lands, asked why this was the case (Lloyd 1833, 38). Lloyd's conclusions about human nature, greed and commonage give Hardin a launching pad for his arguments. But what Lloyd, like Hardin after him, doesn't ask are textured historical questions. Crucially, in Lloyd's case, to what extent does the bovine emaciation he observes result from overcrowding on a commons already traumatically shrunken by enclosures – by land transfer from public to private hands, most recently through the Enclosures Acts of 1815–20?

While endorsing Lloyd's conclusions, Hardin makes one decisive intellectual addition, superimposing a generic name, "tragedy", on the incremental ruin that both writers deplore. In his judgment, "the inherent logic of the commons remorselessly generates tragedy" (Hardin 1968, 1244). Hardin doesn't use the term "tragedy" casually. He is at pains to ground his understanding of the genre in a definition he culls from A.N. Whitehead's 1948 volume, *Science and the Modern World*:

> The essence of dramatic tragedy is not unhappiness. It resides in the solemnity of the remorseless working of things. [...] This inevitableness of destiny can only be illustrated in terms of human life by incidents which in fact involve unhappiness. For it is only by them that the futility of escape can be made evident in the drama.
>
> (Quoted in Hardin 1968, 1244)

Through Whitehead, Hardin imports into his arguments a veritable thesaurus entry for determinacy: "ineluctable", "inescapable", "inevitable", "inexorable", "fateful", "remorseless", "preordained", "doomed", "futility of escape" echo through his text. The ensuing portrait of the commons as doom-sealed thus assumes a double force as the deterministic logics of genre and gene converge.

If, for Hardin, biology, like tragedy, is destiny, what strikes a twenty-first-century reader is how narrow a view he takes of the selfish gene's survival strategies (Dawkins 1976). Throughout his writings, Hardin regarded altruism as an insufficient brake on self-interested, survival-driven behavior. Yet by now, most sociobiologists accommodate a broader vision of species self-perpetuation, one that acknowledges how altruism – forms of apparent selflessness – may be genetically beneficial, collectively enhancing the prospects of survival. Hardin's genetic-generic method fails to acknowledge the evolutionary role that the paradox of selfish selflessness may play.

Hardin's restrictive view of the commons as a sociobiological tragic stage ignores circumstances where communities have sought to manage shared resources, so that rather than inducing poverty, the commons may become, however imperfectly, a hedge against future miseries. In striving to forestall or arrest the putatively innate, downward spiral towards a tragically eroded commons, such communities have frequently developed intergenerational resource safeguards, often adapted over centuries. To say as much is not to sentimentalize stewardship or to suggest that such communities have persisted in states of harmonious equity. It is merely to acknowledge that complex motives and mechanisms for stewardship exist, while also acknowledging that such practices may buckle beneath historically specific stressors, as when, for example, adjacent communities are thrust into competition for resources overstretched by the arrival of refugees fleeing war or climate chaos. Or, for that matter, overstretched when an advancing private-property regime whittles down the commons, thereby generating or intensifying competitive desperation.

This is more than an oversight on Hardin's part. It is premised on a category mistake, whereby he conflates common property (*res communis*) with unowned resources (*res nullius*). Access to *res communis* is typically managed through institutionalized practices, whereas access to *res nullius* entails little if any governance (Ciriacy-Wantrup and Bishop 1975). But Hardin makes no such discrimination, tethering both to the genre of tragedy.

He reinforces this category mistake by enlisting a second genre – parable – that scours the commons of its diverse, complicating cultural histories of governance. If sociobiological tragedy is the subject of Hardin's essay, parable becomes its supplementary method. Parable – a genre that Hardin favored throughout his career – is a succinct, overtly instructive form inimical to historical specificity (see Hardin 1974). Be it Jesus' parable of the prodigal son or Hardin's parable of the profligate pastoralist, the genre typically involves a small, didactic story that performs a large, luminous lesson. The narrative ordinarily entails little more than a stark setting, a brief action and an unambiguous outcome.

Hardin summons parable – in the fullest literary sense of the phrase – to help him characterize the commons. For the tragic eco-drama that purportedly follows from the commons as property regime demands characters or actors. Hardin, more in the spirit of Beckett than Shakespeare, provides a minimalist one. The essay's inexorable eco-drama involves a solitary actor, a skeletal pastoralist referred to, in the spirit of parable, as "everyman". What do we know about him? Not much. He is a "rational being", he is greedy and he owns livestock that he grazes on the commons (Hardin 1968, 1244). From those three spare details his tragedy unfolds.

Rather than being steadily disrobed until forced to face his own bare, forked being, Hardin's thespian pastoralist enters the stage of the commons pre-stripped – culturally butt-naked. He is the man from nowhere, shorn of history and values; he feels no culturally constraining pressures and possesses no allegiances except to his solitary, innate greed. This monadic figure is free-floating and self-seeking, exhibiting no social ties and existing, with regard to land usage, outside any evident cultural constraints, taboos, customary decrees or collectively negotiated compromises. His tragic flaw is unanchored in specifics; his hubris, if we can call it that, is the timeless hubris of sociobiological avarice. He departs the stage of the commons in as rarified a condition as he arrived with one critical difference: both he and the commons are now both greed-destroyed. Thus together, parable (a schematic genre denuded of historical content) and tragedy (a genre marked by inexorability) aid the causal transfer from culture to biology that distinguishes Hardin's method.

Why, we may ask, did Hardin choose a pastoralist (and not, say, a gardener) as his solitary actor? The herdsman in question has wandered onto Hardin's tragic stage from the past and the future. He is a ghost and a premonition. He arrives as a holdover from Lloyd's 1832 lectures and from the longer, anti-pastoralist, pro-enclosure tradition that underpins Lloyd's judgments. But Hardin's herdsman has a second, unstated origin. He is also a harbinger against an emerging future – against the decolonization that, in 1968, was spreading internationally in force and influence. This second, implicitly premonitory role of the herdsman is deeply pertinent, on the one hand, to overlapping neocolonial attitudes to Third World land tenure and, on the other, to neoliberal economic policies for resource capture – of the land itself, or of the oil, mineral, timber and water wealth that it sustains. In these terms, the pastoralist is a relic figure, a throwback whose ghostly ancestors frequented pre-enclosures Europe but who still roams the Third World as an embodiment of a profligacy awaiting market rationalization.

The pastoralist in Hardin's tragic parable may be alone but he is many. He is the wretched of the earth whose claims on a finite planet have to be averted. Although Hardin expressed alarm at earth's demographic carrying capacity, he was evidently more horrified by the breeding poor than by the breeding rich, who were wreaking far more devastation on the planet through over-consumption and over-militarization. This double standard, threaded through Hardin's writings, also permeated his private life. Here was an affluent Malthusian professor who had no hesitation in siring four children, thereby exacerbating – in his own terms – an ecological-demographic disaster that he preferred to embody in the figure of a herdsman.

The nomad or herdsman has long served as (to use a pastoralist dead metaphor) a convenient scapegoat to be exorcized in the name of economic rationalization. The commons-dependent, wandering pastoralist can be dismissed as an unanchored, rogue anachronism, someone who, in Lockeian terms, refuses to take root in a private-property regime of purported individual (and thereby collective) self-improvement (Dawson 2010). He is, in the fullest etymological sense, uncultivated. Thus the pastoralist's mobile presence on the land becomes an embodiment of tragic waste – and an impediment to the appropriative ambitions of capitalist and colonialist private-property regimes.

In 1838, just five years after Lloyd's essays advocating enclosure, the *Sydney Herald* vindicated, in related terms, British colonial seizure of territory from nomadic Aboriginals unredeemed by possessive individualism:

> [The Aboriginals] bestowed no labor upon the land and that – and *that only* – it is which gives a right of property to it. [...] Who will assert that this great continent was ever intended by the Creator to remain an un-productive wilderness? [...] The British people found a portion of the globe in a state of waste – they took possession of it; and they had a perfect right to do so, under the Divine authority, by which man was commanded to go forth and people, and till the land.
>
> (Quoted in Muir 2011, 139)

The Aboriginals are non-cultivating and hence can be figured as uncultivated. They are wasteful encroachers whose territories ought to be appropriated by the civilizing forces of possessive enclosure. Although Hardin's anti-hero is not just a nomad but more specifically a pastoralist, he too can be stigmatized as a squanderous presence on the land, someone with no motive for respecting limits rather than as, say, someone motivated to move in adaptive response to seasonal plenitude and scarcity.

In Lloyd's time, landlords who accumulated property through enclosure and forced displacement referred to these practices as "improvements". In allied terms, neoliberalism's developmental logic tends to treat any commons as an unprofitable wasteland awaiting improvement through free market liberation. This assumption gets played out on a transnational scale as, for example, in this advertisement placed by the Philippine government in *Fortune* magazine: "[T]o attract companies like yours, we have felled mountains, razed jungles, filled swamps, moved rivers, relocated towns [...] all to make it easier for you and your business to do business with us" (Korten 2001, 159). Invisible here are the communities displaced by such clearances – communities that the anthropologist Thayer Scudder has called "developmental refugees", those forced into flight by development and barred from once accessible commonage (Scudder 1990; see also Nixon 2011, 150–175). Such common resources may not necessarily be a primary source of food, water and livelihood but are often an indispensable component in a precarious patchwork of survival strategies. What's invisible, then, is the way a deregulated, environmentally hubristic neoliberal order imposes new enclosures and thereby generates new nomads, desperate people ricocheting between rural and urban impossibility.

By the time Hardin's essay appeared in 1968, rich-nation growth was slowing, creating new pressures for global appropriations in a decolonizing world. These circumstances contributed to the appeal of Hardin's anti-pastoral logic and, with neoliberalism's ascent in the 1970s, helped vindicate economic practices that refused to acknowledge global environmental limits. Neoliberals have aligned themselves with the notion of an innately tragic commons in part because it is consistent with their hostility to shared goods, a hostility insepa-rable from the neoliberal drive for resource appropriation and for dismantling regulatory oversight, whether by international, nation-state or local bodies. Neoliberal efforts to institute the "efficiencies" of the "free market" have been coupled, moreover, to efforts to erode the expectation that the state should help safeguard the well-being of citizens at home, not to speak of non-citizens abroad. In the neoliberal narrative, welfare systems, public health care, public amenities, taxation, trade unions, public pensions, public education, public transport, social benefits and the environmental commons are all impediments that need to be privatized, shrunk or eliminated. In Margaret Thatcher's blunt judgment: "There is no such thing as society. There are individual men and women, and there are families" (Thatcher 1987).

Because Hardin's history-stripping tragic parable represents the com-mons as inherently lawless, neoliberals could reference his essay's title to bolster their arguments for the closure of the commons as an absolute good. In these terms, the commons needs to be enclosed – and thereby liberated – for the indissociable double gain of freeing the individual and the market. After all, didn't Hardin speak of "the evils of the commons"? Didn't he insist, in an apparent spirit of neoliberal prescience, that "injustice is prefer-able to total ruin" (Hardin 1968, 1248, 1247)?

However, contra neoliberalism's core tenets, Hardin also argued for an intensified state role in imposing taxes and regulations in order, he insisted, to prevent corporations from polluting recklessly, privatizing profits while socializing health and environmental costs. He saw unchecked privatiza-tion as posing a planetary threat because "our particular concept of private property [...] favors pollution" (Hardin 1968, 1245). Elsewhere, Hardin even contended that the state's regulatory role could be furnished either by socialism or capitalism (Bajema 1991, 199). In lauding Hardin's economic vision, neoliberals suppress the parts of his argument where he rails against unchecked growth on a finite planet. Such growth, he argued, would turn the earth into a "cesspool" (Hardin 1968, 1245).

Hardin slowly became aware that his essay's charismatic title encouraged this kind of misapprehension. He returned, again and again – in essays, books and interviews – to correct what he saw as a pervasive misreading of his argument. In one such essay, "The Tragedy of the Unmanaged Commons", Hardin conceded that "a managed commons, though it may have other defects, is not automatically subject to the tragic fate of the unmanaged commons" (Hardin 1994, 163). He lamented omitting from the title of his original essay some qualifying adjective like "unmanaged" or "unregulated". Had he shown the foresight to include such a qualifier it would surely have tempered his essay's neoliberal appeal, its afterlife – through brisk allusion – as a neoliberal meme.

Hardin was not alone in trying to complicate the crude causal link between the commons and tragedy that his essay title established. Scholars from a dozen disciplines have sought to rein in his runaway phrase. Many have done so by trying to ascribe to the commons a different relationship to genre. We see this in the outpouring of books, essays and chapters with titles like "The Comedy of the Commons", "The Myth of the Tragedy of the Commons", "No Tragedy on the Commons", "The Commons is Not a Tragedy", "The Tragedy of the Tragedy of the Commons", *Commons Without Tragedy*, "The Non-Tragedy of the Commons", "The Tragedy of the Capitalist Commons", "The Tragedy of the Anticommons" and "The Tragedy of the Private".

No one has done more for this concerted effort to decouple tragedy from the commons than Indiana University political scientist Elinor Ostrom. In 2009, Ostrom received the Nobel Prize in Economics for her persistent, detailed research into the immensely variable, and sometimes favorable, outcomes of culturally specific efforts to manage common resources. However, no arguments that the later, somewhat rueful Hardin, or Ostrom, or Hardin's interdisciplinary critics have mounted can fully undo the tenacious public power that "the tragedy of the commons" continues to exert – five small words that draw together into a reductive, conveniently portable phrase a set of formulaic assumptions about generic, genetic, economic and environmental logics.

That said, neoliberalism's Achilles heel is the crisis of futurity, as Mary Louise Pratt has noted (Pratt 2012, 298). If access to resources becomes radically, explosively uneven, if more and more people feel as if they are inhabiting – in both senses of the phrase – futureless states, if they sense that they are being asked to bear more and more communized costs while the few privatize, monopolize and hoard the profits, social movements will arise demanding a different distributive politics of the commons, in all its forms. When people feel reduced (in Rebecca Solnit's phrase) to "non-occupants" of society, such discounted casualties – such resource outcasts – will have every incentive to make common cause against neoliberalism's disinheritance plot (Solnit 2011). In this regard, the 99% or Occupy Movements that have spread across the world's wealthier nations can be seen to be playing catch up with movements in the global South, from the Cochabamba uprisings against the privatization of water to the Maldive protests against the global warming that threatens to submerge that island nation. In such scenarios, the predatory threat arrives not in the form of the greedy, unattached pastoralist but in the form of neoliberalism's unregulated, voracious emissaries who have no respect for limits and no sustainable, inclusive vision of what it means, long term, to belong.

REFERENCES

Anon. 1838. "Crown Lands", *Sydney Herald*, 7 November.
Andelson, Robert V., ed. 1991. *Commons Without Tragedy: Protecting the Environment from Overpopulation – A New Approach*. London: Shepheard-Walwyn.
Angus, Ian. 2008. "The Myth of the Tragedy of the Commons". *Monthly Review*. mrzine.monthlyreview.org/2008/angus250808.html.

Bajema, Carl Jay. 1991. "Garrett James Hardin: Ecologist, Educator, Ethicist and Environmentalist". *Population and Environment* 12: 193–212.

Ciriacy-Wantrup, Siegfried von and Richard Bishop. 1975. "Common Property as a Concept in Natural Resources Policy". *Natural Resources* 15: 713–727.

Cox, Susan Jane Buck. 1985. "No Tragedy on the Commons". *Environmental Ethics* 7: 49–61.

Dawkins, Richard. 1976. *The Selfish Gene*. New York: Oxford University Press.

Dawson, Ashley. 2010. "Introduction: New Enclosures". *New Formations* 69: 8–22.

De Angelis, Massimo. 2009. "The Tragedy of the Capitalist Commons". *Turbulence*. turbulence.org.uk/turbulence-5/capitalist-commons/.

Ehrlich, Paul. 1971. *The Population Bomb*. Cutchogue, N.Y.: Buccaneer.

Hardin, Garrett. 1974. "Commentary: Living on a Lifeboat". *Bioscience* 24: 561–568.

Hardin, Garrett. 1959. *Nature and Man's Fate*. New York: Signet.

Hardin, Garrett. 1968 "The Tragedy of the Commons". *Science* 162: 1243–1248.

Hardin, Garrett. 1994. "The Tragedy of the *Unmanaged* Commons: Population and the Disguises of Providence". *Trends in Ecology and Evolution* 9.5:199.

Harvey, David. 2003. *The New Imperialism*. New York: Oxford University Press.

Heller, Michael. 1998. "The Tragedy of the Anticommons: Property in the Transition from Marx to Markets". *Harvard Law Review* 111.3: 621688.

James, Deborah. 2006. "The Tragedy of the Private: Owners, Communities and the State in South Africa's Land Reform Programme". In *Changing Properties of Property*, edited by Franz von Benda-Beckmann *et al.*, 243–268. Oxford: Berghahn.

Korten, David C. 2001. *When Corporations Rule the World*. San Francisco: Berrett-Koehler.

Lloyd, William Forster. 1833. *Two Lectures on the Checks of Population*. Oxford: Oxford University Press; rept. Garrett Hardin, ed. 1964. *Population, Evolution, and Birth Control*. San Francisco: Freeman.

Midnight Notes Collective. 1992. *Midnight Oil: Work, Energy, War, 1973–1992*. Jamaica Plain, MA: Autonomedia.

Muir, Cameron. 2011. "Broken Country: Science, Agriculture, and the 'Unfulfilled Dreams' of Inland Australia, 1880 To Present". Unpublished Ph.D. dissertation. Australian National University.

Nixon, Rob. 2011. *Slow Violence and the Environmentalism of the Poor*. Cambridge, MA: Harvard University Press.

Ostrom, Elinor. 1990. *Governing the Commons: The Evolution of Institutions for Collective Action*. Cambridge: Cambridge University Press.

Pratt, Mary Louise. 2012. Review of Rob Nixon, *Slow Violence and the Environmentalism of the Poor*. 2011. *Interventions* 14.2: 298–300.

Rose, Carol M. 1986. "The Comedy of the Commons: Commerce, Custom and Inherently Public Property". http://digitalcommons.law.yale.edu/fss_papers/1828.

Scudder, Thayer. 1990. "Victims of Development Revisited: The Political Costs of River Basin Development". *IDA Developmental Anthropology Network* 8.1:1–5.

Solnit, Rebecca. 2011. "This Land is Your Occupied Land". *TomDispatch*. www.tomdispatch.com/archive/175455/.

Tierney, John. 2009. "The Non-Tragedy of the Commons. *New York Times* science blog, October 15. tierneylab.blogs.nytimes.com/2009/10/15/the-non-tragedy-of-the-commons/.

Thatcher, Margaret. 1987. "Interview with *Women's Own*", September 23. www.margaretthatcher.org/document/106689.

Whitehead, A.N. 1948. *Science and the Modern World*. New York: Mentor.

11 Reading Fanon Reading Nature

Jennifer Wenzel

"The time is right to reread Fanon. ..."
—Homi Bhabha, foreword to *The Wretched of the Earth*, x

"For a colonized people the most essential value, because the most concrete, is first and foremost the land: the land which will bring them bread and, above all, dignity".
—Frantz Fanon, *The Wretched of the Earth*, 44

"We are reminded that we by no means rule over nature like a conqueror over a foreign people, like someone standing outside nature – but that we [...] belong to nature, and exist in its midst, and that all our mastery of it consists in the fact that we have the advantage over all other creatures".
—Friedrich Engels, *Dialectics of Nature*, 242

One can hardly claim any more that postcolonial theory doesn't say anything about nature. Several books – Rob Nixon's *Slow Violence and the Environmentalism of the Poor* (2011), Elizabeth DeLoughrey and George Handley's *Postcolonial Ecologies* (2011), Graham Huggan and Helen Tiffin's *Postcolonial Ecocriticism* (2010), Pablo Mukherjee's *Postcolonial Environments* (2010), and Bonnie Roos and Alex Hunt's *Postcolonial Green* (2010) – have put the emergent subfield of postcolonial ecocriticism on the map. These groundbreaking texts all confront questions of belatedness. Why has it taken so long for postcolonialists to think about nature? Or for ecocritics to remember colonialism? Why has it been so difficult to think across the intellectual and activist traditions of environmentalism and postcolonialism? How can contemporary struggles for environmental justice be understood in relation to mid-twentieth-century anti-colonial struggles for national liberation?

Postcolonial ecocriticism's first wave was shaped by Nixon's "Environmentalism and Postcolonialism" (2005), which argued that many anti-imperialist critics and activists have wrongly dismissed environmental concern as the purview of the bourgeois, white and male. Nixon's indispensable account of mutual silences between postcolonialism and mainstream American environmental thought enumerated four oppositions obstructing conversation between them: hybridity vs. purity, displacement vs. place, transnational vs. national frames of analysis and history vs. timeless transcendence. Nixon echoed concerns about "disjunctures" between the fields' respective apprehensions of world and text, which, Susie O'Brien argued in 2001, made their "intersection [...] until recently, virtually unimaginable" (142). For O'Brien, the simultaneous publication of Edward Said's *Orientalism* and William Rueckert's "Literature and Ecology: An Experiment in Ecocriticism" demonstrates how the two fields, founded in the same moment, have run on parallel tracks.

Like all space-clearing gestures, including colonialism, these arguments about the lack of engagement between environmentalism and postcolonialism have elicited some resistance. Other postcolonial ecocritics trace alternative genealogies that recognize the importance of the environment for colonialism and anti-colonial resistance: "the most essential value", Fanon declares, is the land.[1] Mukherjee observes:

> At first sight, it seems very strange that the "greening" of postcolonial studies is of such recent vintage. For if the scholars who shaped the literary and cultural theories of postcolonialism from the mid-1970s were paying any attention at all to the voices of anti-colonial resistance [...] surely they could not have missed the importance placed on the issues of land, water, forests, crops, rivers, the sea – in other words, on the centrality of the environment to the continuing struggle of decolonization. (2010, 46)

And yet, Mukherjee sees postcolonial studies only beginning to apprehend "the idea of colonialisms and imperialisms old and new, as a state of permanent war on the global environment" (2010, 68). The question of whether postcolonial theory says anything about nature is connected to broader debates about its genealogy – what debts it owes to anti-colonial liberation praxis, French poststructuralists or Marx. We might say that postcolonial theory in its late-twentieth-century ascendancy seemed largely to disavow nature, along with nationalism.[2]

Mukherjee reads Aimé Césaire and Amílcar Cabral to excavate their materialist and environmentalist understanding of colonial and anti-colonial culture and politics. This chapter works similarly, reading *The Wretched of the Earth* for what Fanon says about colonialism-and-nature in conjunction, to think anew about questions of belatedness. A decade ago, rereadings of Fanon by David Scott (2004) and Homi Bhabha measured his moment of decolonization against later geopolitical and academic developments: the end of the Cold War, the rise of theory, globalization and 9/11. Unlike Scott, Bhabha insisted upon the contemporary urgency of *The Wretched of the Earth*. Only after the shift from decolonization to globalization and the demise of Cold War Manicheism could we truly understand Fanon's "project of futurity", as if for the first time, he claimed (Bhabha 2004, xiv–xvii).

Now, as ever, the time is right to reread Fanon. I argue that Fanon would be surprised to hear that questions of nature and environment are something new under the postcolonial sun, but also that he cannot have the last word. Yet I am mindful of Nixon's warning that postcolonial ecocritics who undertake retrospective examinations of mid-twentieth-century anticolonialism risk an anachronistic "retrofitting [of] contemporary meanings of environmentalism". Nixon notes that many liberation theorists were "hostile or indifferent to environmentalists" at a time when environmentalism was associated with colonial-era state conservation projects that, by accident or design, further marginalized or dispossessed the colonized (2011, 260–261). I take Nixon's point, but I wonder whether he underestimates the implications of his larger argument that there are versions of environmental concern beyond those of white, middle-class Americans or European colonizers before them. These alternatives do not come from nowhere; they have histories and genealogies, even if fragmented, interrupted or suppressed ones. Nixon's warning risks cutting off the environmentalisms of the poor from their own history. I argue that it is crucial not to cede the ground of environmental concern, in any historical period, to the colonizer or to hegemonic versions of what counts as nature, environment or environmentalism, and to understand where what we now call the environmentalisms of the poor come from. Rereading Fanon is a good place to start.

So listen again, to Fanon's provocative metaphor of colonialism as a species divide. Decolonization is a dialectical reversal, "quite simply the replacing of a certain 'species' [*espèce*] of men by another 'species' of men": the moment the native rejects the "zoological terms" of the colonizer's "bestiary", the "allusion to the animal world in the other's words. For he knows that he is not an animal, and it is precisely at the moment he realizes his humanity that he begins to sharpen the weapons with which he will secure its victory" (Fanon 1968, 35, 42). Fanon's valorization of the native's self-recognition as a non-animal human might smack of a troubling anthropocentrism in need of Animal Studies intervention, but his vivid account of colonization as bestialization offers a prescient reminder of how the species divide has been deployed historically to cast some humans as sub- (rather than non-) human. The tension at stake here – between postcolonialism's attention to histories of dehumanization and environmentalism's critique of anthropocentrism and its conception of humans-as-animals in a more-than-human world – should be added to Nixon's list as a fifth schism between environmentalism and postcolonialism.

As Donna Haraway observes, political and social categories have been conflated with the species divide: "The discursive tie between the colonized, the enslaved, the noncitizen, and the animal – all reduced to type, all Others to rational man, and all essential to his bright constitution – is at the heart of racism and flourishes, lethally, in the entrails of humanism" (2008, 18). Haraway's analysis resonates with Fanon's denunciation of the hypocrisy of European humanism. In the conclusion to *The Wretched of the Earth*, Fanon exhorts, "Come then, comrades. [...] Let us [...] [l]eave this Europe where they are never done talking of Man, yet murder men everywhere they find them. [...] [T]oday we know with what sufferings humanity has paid for every one of their triumphs of the mind" (1968, 311). Yet Fanon also envisions a newly and truly universal humanism when he concludes, "For Europe, for ourselves and for humanity, comrades, we must turn over a new leaf, we must work out new concepts, and try to set afoot a new man" (1968, 315–316). Fanon suggests a way forward for a postcolonial environmental humanities unencumbered by the baggage of an ethnocentric, anthropocentric humanism.

Or listen again to Fanon's account of the "colonial world" as a "world cut in two". He contrasts "the settlers' town [as] a strongly built town, all made of stone and steel" where "the garbage cans swallow all the leavings, unseen, unknown, and hardly thought about", with its native counterpart, "a town wallowing in the mire" with "huts ... built one on top of the other" (1968, 38–39). Fanon understands that (post)colonial environments are urban as well as rural. His distinction between settler and native as that between adequate waste management and "wallowing in the mire" anchors the literary topos of postcolonial trash, where privilege is not having to see, smell or think about waste and shit, whether one's own or that of other people.

These observations may seem small and local, fleeting images that leap off the page while rereading Fanon with an eye to ecology. But nature and natural resources are fundamental to Fanon's analysis of the historical processes that turned decolonization into continuing underdevelopment. He offers an alternative accounting of European colonial domination in relationship to nature:

> This European opulence is literally scandalous, for it has been founded on slavery, it has been nourished with the blood of slaves and it comes directly from the soil and from the subsoil of that underdeveloped world. [...] Colonialism and imperialism have not paid their score when they withdraw their flags and their police forces from our territories. [...] The wealth of the imperial countries is our wealth too. [...] Europe has stuffed herself inordinately with the gold and raw materials of the colonial countries. [...] From all these continents [...] there has flowed out for centuries toward that same Europe diamonds and oil, silk and cotton, wood and exotic products. Europe is literally the creation of the Third World. (1968, 96, 101–102)

Fanon's cartography of underdevelopment reverses the traffic lines of diffusionist progress narratives where Europe is the font from which all blessings flow. Instead, all good things flow towards Europe. The pillage and ruination of the Third World have made the development, wealth and modernity of Europe possible. Drawing a link between captive labor and expropriated natural resources as twinned objects of colonial exploitation, Fanon identifies a structural inequality in what Fernando Coronil called the "international division of nature", a "neglected structuring principle of capitalist development" that Coronil theorized in order to "counter Eurocentric conceptions that identify modernity with Europe and relegate the periphery to a pre-modern primitivity" (Coronil 1997, 29; 2000, 356–357).

Fanon's condemnation of centuries of underdevelopment remains timely in an age of resource wars and climate change. His counter-accounting of European colonialism can be extended into the present and near future, in order to understand that Africa will have paid at least four times for the development of the First World: once in human capital through the slave trade; again in natural capital in the extraction of resources during high imperialism and after; again in financial capital (and the social costs of structural adjustment) through debt-servicing in the era of development and neoliberalism; and finally in the disproportionate effects in Africa of climate change that is largely caused by carbon emissions elsewhere. Extending Fanon's analysis into the climatological predicament of the Anthropocene casts in a different light Homi Bhabha's rereading of *The Wretched of the Earth* as a "weather report on our own day" (2004, xv).

For Fanon, national liberation entails reclaiming control over human and natural resources. Political and economic sovereignty requires resource sovereignty: the right to dispose freely the natural resources within national territories. Decolonization demands not only a new humanity and humanism but also a new materialism and political ecology: a shift in the valuation and disposition of nature. He explains, "Up to the present no serious effort had been made to estimate the riches of the soil or of mineral resources" beyond the narrow colonial imperative of providing raw materials to create European wealth (1968, 100). Echoing his earlier image of decolonization as *tabula rasa*, Fanon writes, "Perhaps it is necessary to begin everything all over again: to change the nature of the country's exports, and not simply their destination, to re-examine the soil and mineral resources, the rivers, and – why not? – the sun's productivity" (1968, 100). He calls for a new inventory of nature and a new kind of economy, based on an alternative valuation of the riches of the soil and perhaps (why not?) even renewable solar energy. Fanon's understanding of the challenge of national liberation is grounded in what we now call political ecology.[3] The post-independence era threatens to repeat the past not merely because the same people remain in charge, or different people play the same roles, but also because postcolonial regimes too often accept the colonizer's spurious argument that the "economic channels created by the colonial regime" and the substances flowing through them towards Europe must remain unchanged "or catastrophe will threaten" (Fanon 1968, 100). *Après moi, le déluge*, the departing colonizer warns, ensuring the continuing flood of riches out of the postcolony.

While we may want to read this passage as part of Fanon's strange, anonymous *agon* between native and settler, it actually indexes a mid-twentieth-century legal debate that the Third World seemed at first to win but then lost all over again. Beginning in the 1950s, newly independent nation-states attempted to establish in international law the principle of Permanent Sovereignty over Natural Resources (PSNR), which held that natural resources of a territory belonged to its inhabitants before, during and after colonialism. Colonial concessions to charter companies or other imperial entities were illegitimate because they lacked "meaningful [popular] consent". These ill-gotten gains should be calculated against any claims for compensation that former colonial powers or corporations made when Third World resources were nationalized (Anghie 2004, 211–213). Fanon's call to inventory soil, rivers and sun, which he framed as part of the need to demand reparations for centuries of colonial theft, is not abstract rhetoric but instead resonant and contemporary with this attempt to establish resource sovereignty as a legal aspect of postcolonial sovereignty.

This effort achieved some success at the United Nations, particularly in General Assembly Resolution 1803 of 1962: "'The rights of peoples and nations to permanent sovereignty over their natural wealth must be exercised in the interest of their national development and the well-being of the people concerned'" (qtd. in Anghie 2004, 216).[4] However, former colonial powers derailed this effort by interpreting these legal instruments through a tendentious understanding of history, where colonized peoples "possess no history or existence which may be asserted in international law until that precise time when they are 'created' by colonialism". At the moment of contact, they enjoyed "just that degree of sovereignty necessary to make the concessions binding" (Anghie 2004, 219–220). In other words – reversing Fanon's reversal of received history – the Third World is literally the creation of Europe. Anghie concludes, "Even while the West asserted that colonialism was a thing of the past, it nevertheless relied precisely on those relationships of power and inequality that had been created by that colonial past to maintain its economic and political superiority which it then attempted to entrench through an ostensibly neutral international law" (2004, 215).

The fate of PSNR reveals the material dimension and economic implications of Fanon's famous statement in "On National Culture" that "Colonialism is not satisfied merely with holding a people in its grip and emptying the native's brain of all form and content. By a kind of perverted logic, it turns to the past of the oppressed people, and distorts, disfigures, and destroys it. This work of devaluing pre-colonial history takes on a dialectical significance today" (1968, 210). Against this "devaluing", arguments for resource sovereignty envisioned a dialectic of decolonization in which a new inventory and counter-accounting of natural resources would effect a radical revaluing of the balance sheets of empire. The eventual weakening of PSNR in international law is an instance of the former colonizers' derailment of decolonization, as Fanon poignantly warned in the middle chapters of *The Wretched of the Earth*.

And yet, in Anghie's account of PSNR, sovereignty – in the political and economic sense – is the core value that underwrites the narrative. Other scholars are more ambivalent about the principle because of its divergent economic and ecological implications. Examining tensions between human-rights law and environmental law, Conor Gearty cites Article 1.2 of the International Covenant on Economic, Social, and Cultural Rights: "All people may, for their own ends, freely dispose of their natural wealth and resources, without any prejudice to any obligations arising out of international economic co-operation, based upon the principle of mutual benefit, and international law". This statement of PSNR, Gearty observes, amounts to "authorized plunder" of natural resources that is no less ecologically harmful for being undertaken by postcolonial citizens rather than colonial buccaneers (2010, 13). PSNR is not only a way to arrest and claim redress for colonial-era exploitation; it's also a license for further plunder. Ngũgĩ wa Thiong'o captures this dynamic in *The Wizard of the Crow*:

> This forest was now threatened by charcoal, paper, and timber merchants who cut down trees hundreds of years old. When it came to forests, indeed to any natural resource, the Aburĩrian State and big American, European, and Japanese companies, in alliance with the local African, Indian, and European rich, were all united by one slogan: *A loot-a continua*. They knew how to take but not how to give back to the soil. (2007, 201)

Ngũgĩ's pun on the 1970s slogan *a luta continua* transposes its affirmation of ongoing struggle for national liberation (and resource sovereignty) into a satiric recognition of the continuous looting of nature in the colonial and postcolonial eras.

Anghie's notion of postcolonial sovereignty differs from the "biotic community" theorized by American conservationist Aldo Leopold not long before advocates of PSNR were working the channels of the UN. For Leopold, "biotic community" was a republic of things underwritten not by political sovereignty but instead a "land ethic" that "simply enlarges the boundaries of the community to include soils, waters, plants, and animals: the land. [...] In short, a land ethic changes the role of *Homo sapiens* from conqueror of the land-community to plain member and citizen of it" (1966, 204). The land ethic decolonizes human dominion over nature, a line of thinking congruent with Engels' equation of colonial conquest with human/nature dualism in my epigraph. I contrast PSNR with Leopold's land ethic to acknowledge that Fanon's political ecology of colonialism is not very ecological, in the sense of a non-anthropocentric understanding of ecosystems that views humans as one species-actor among many forms of nonhuman nature and modes of agency.

The very notion of natural resources, many critics have pointed out, assumes the disposition of non-human nature for humans' economic use. The point of contention in resource sovereignty – no matter how crucial in shaping the way of the world under global capitalism – is limited to which humans claim that authority. Nature becomes a Heideggerian "standing reserve" awaiting instrumentalization for human use, rather than having its own ontology. As Neil Evernden writes, "[O]ne who looks on the world as simply a set of resources to be utilized is not thinking of it as an environment at all. [...] The whole world is simply fodder and feces to the consumer, in sharp contrast to the man who is in an environment in which he belongs and is of necessity a part" (1996, 99). At first glance, this assertion may seem unobjectionable (save for the gendered language) in distinguishing between the unenlightened consumer's "transient" interest in nature as a standing reserve of things he can use and throw away (another sense of dispose) and the "resident" who recognizes himself in a historical interrelationship with nature.

Yet reading Fanon, one recognizes how much unexamined history hangs on that word "simply". (Leopold uses it too.) Or how fraught claims of "residence" or "transience" are in the context of colonialism. Land, bread and dignity, Fanon insists. The native quarter is where garbage cans can't swallow the leavings; he is too decorous to mention the inadequacy of latrines to dispose of the shit. Evernden's easy dismissal of resource thinking – mere "fodder and feces", itself an oddly bestializing locution – is implicitly, simply, dependent on his privilege within a structure of global inequality where questions of resources (or vulnerability to the aftermath of their extraction), food security, and disposal of feces and other waste have been asked and answered such that his daily survival is not on the line. These questions – those raised by the environmentalisms of the poor – suggest that accusations of anthropocentrism sometimes belie the ethnocentrism of an unacknowledged privilege. It is relatively simple to disavow the idea of nature-as-resource as a "conquest" of nature when one inhabits the position of opulent Europe or its "monst[rous]" mimic, the US (Fanon 1968, 313).

This is not to say that environmentalism is a luxury the poor cannot afford, but rather that its meaning, like so many things, is determined Humpty-Dumpty style, by who is to be master: "[W]hat comes to count as the environment is that which matters to the culturally dominant" (Mazel 1996, 142). Fanon was no tree-hugger – and the tree-huggers of Chipko were not really tree-huggers either, in the anti-environmentalist sense of elevating concern for nature over humans[5] – but he did know who will owe whom if nature (including the dehumanized "resource" of slave labor) comes to count in tallying the history of colonialism. His perspective is not ecological in an ecosystem sense, but it is environmental in the weak-anthropocentric sense of understanding human relationships to the natural world in which they are embedded.[6] Fanon's accounting of colonialism's ecological debt makes his geographic concern an environmental concern.

I want to bring this hypothesis of Fanon as weak-anthropocentric environmentalist to a final example from *The Wretched of the Earth* that concerns Cold War debates about continuities between imperialism and post-war modernization and development, to demonstrate how complex the intersections of environmentalism and postcolonialism were in that moment. In the first chapter of *The Wretched of the Earth* appears a remarkable passage:

> All values [...] are irrevocably poisoned and diseased as soon as they are allowed in contact with the colonized race. The customs of the

colonized people, their traditions, their myths – above all, their myths –
are the very sign of that poverty of spirit and their constitutional
depravity. That is why we must put the DDT which destroys parasites,
the bearers of disease, on the same level as the Christian religion which
wages war on the embryonic heresies and instincts, and on evil as yet
unborn. The recession of yellow fever and the advance of evangeliza-
tion form part of the same balance sheet. (1968, 42)

Parsing this passage, one wonders, who is this "we"? One must read care-
fully to catch the moment Fanon shifts from analyzing Manichean colonial
discourse – where "the settler paints the native as a sort of quintessence of
evil" – to ventriloquizing it, picking up the settler's infinitely broad brush.
Fanon reports a *pied-noir* representative's argument in the French National
Assembly "that the Republic must not be prostituted by allowing the Algerian
people to become part of it" (1968, 41–42). From there follows the declaration that all values are diseased upon exposure to the colonized, from which
follows the claim that "we" must understand DDT as the functional equiva-
lent of Christianity in eliminating pestilential heresy and "evil as yet unborn".
The Algerian native's spiritual contagion must be quarantined, this settler
voice proclaims, to keep it from infecting French civilization. The DDT that
kills lice and mosquitoes – vectors of typhus, malaria and yellow fever – is like
colonial Christianity: both insecticide and ethnocide are necessary, Fanon's
ventriloquized settler declares, to neutralize these evils before they hatch.

Fanon shows how colonial discourse posits the native as the "negation of
values" (1968, 41). Readers must attend carefully to grasp the negation of
the negation, whereby Fanon mouths the settler's vilification of the native
and his prescription of chemical and spiritual pesticides in order to expose
and subvert such vile words. From this passage follows Fanon's discussion
of the "logical conclusion" of colonial Manicheism: it "dehumanizes the
native, or to speak plainly, it turns him into an animal" (1968, 42). The
equation between evil natives and pestilent mosquitoes epitomizes the "allusion to the animal world in the other's words" that Fanon registers in his
account of colonialism as a species divide.

One reason this passage is treacherous, its ventriloquism easily missed, is
Fanon's ambivalence about the pre-colonial past – an ambivalence too often
misread as a modernist rejection of tradition. Another reason is that Fanon
repeatedly deploys imagery of Christian apocalypse and millennium to envi-
sion decolonization as a world made new – a strange rhetorical choice in a
polemic the most immediate context of which was Algeria. In this same passage, he appropriates the idiom of Christianity to turn it against muscular,
colonizing versions of itself: "the Church in the colonies [...] does not call
the native to God's ways but to the ways of the white man, of the master, of
the oppressor. And as we know, in this matter many are called but few chosen" (1968, 42). Here and elsewhere, Fanon ventriloquizes Jesus. He uses
the usurping master's tools to reclaim the rightful Lord's house.

But what about DDT? If colonialism instrumentalizes Christianity as a weapon of alienation, does that make yellow fever or malaria an aspect of native culture unjustly assaulted by colonialism or its post-war analogues? Or is Fanon a Third World Rachel Carson, railing against the indiscriminate use of pesticides, the hidden harms of the spray gun? The Fanon-Carson connection is not incidental. As Rob Nixon has also noticed, *Les damnés de la terre* was published in 1961, one year before Carson's lyrical polemic against DDT in *Silent Spring*. To make sense of Fanon's juxtaposition of DDT with Christianity, it is necessary both to note Fanon's ventriloquism and to recognize (as I believe Fanon did) the role of DDT in a broader Cold War project of modernization and development. This is a subject about which postcolonial theory should have much to say.

Between 1955 and 1969, the World Health Organization's Global Malaria Eradication Program sprayed millions of gallons of DDT in more than one hundred countries, with over $500-million in US support (Kinkela 2011, 100, 92). This global initiative – conducted mostly in the Global South – built upon the seeming success of mid-1940s campaigns against typhus in Naples and malaria in Sardinia and Egypt, led by the US military and the Rockefeller Foundation. As David Kinkela writes in *DDT and the American Century*, the spray gun came to symbolize these public health initiatives to prevent human disease by eradicating insect populations. It attained iconic status after *LIFE* featured photographs of the Allied Typhus Commission's Italian delousing campaign in 1944 (Kinkela 2011, 37–40). The spray gun became an unconventional weapon in the Cold War: one could fight communism by killing bugs, thereby eliminating disease and uplifting the undeveloped world. This largely forgotten battle was a different kind of proxy war, where insect vectors of human disease, rather than newly independent nations, stood as proxies for rival superpowers. The geopolitical struggle to align new nation-states with the First World bloc was also fought on a miniaturized scale. American farms, gardens and households became fronts in this war, with insect pests figured as menacing hordes, foreign invaders, even "guerrillas of the underground" (McMillen 1965). This nexus of DDT and anticommunism helps explain the vicious attacks on Carson, as well as Fanon's striking juxtaposition of DDT and colonial Christianity. We should not be surprised to find an echo of Fanon's image in *Silent Spring*, which rejects "'the belief that salvation lies at the end of a spray nozzle'" (Jacob in Carson 1962, 259).

Carson was a fierce opponent of this belief. She challenged mid-twentieth-century faith in the capacity of science to control nature. "Under the philosophy that now seems to guide our destinies", Carson wrote, "nothing must get in the way of the man with the spray gun" (1962, 85). But unlike Fanon, Carson's critique of the arrogance of technoscience and its promises of "salvation" drew upon, rather than rejected, Cold War geopolitical logic. Her condemnation of indiscriminate use of DDT had ideological and geographic limits, which become visible when we peer between the lines of *Silent Spring* and reread Carson with Fanon.

One need not look to the US chemical industry or the Rockefeller Foundation for examples of bugs-figured-as-communists. *Silent Spring* is full of them, and not in a Fanon-ventriloquizing-to-attack kind of way. In a chapter titled "Nature Fights Back", Carson shows how DDT kills insect friends and foes alike, thereby weakening ecosystem defenses against pestilent species. "[E]ach time we breach these defenses a horde of insects pours through. [...] [A]ll these [beneficial species] have been our allies in keeping the balance of nature tilted in our favor. Yet we have turned our artillery against our friends. The terrible danger is that we have grossly underestimated their value in keeping at bay a dark tide of enemies that, without their help, can overrun us" (1962, 246, 251). Carson brings racialized images of the balance of powers and puppet rulers to the suburban backyard.

In addition to arguing for the indispensability of what we might term "comprador beetles", Carson addresses the problem of insect populations developing resistance to pesticides through natural selection. In "The Rumblings of an Avalanche", Carson turns her attention beyond the US to chart the emergence of insect resistance to DDT in the late 1950s. The first report of DDT resistance came in 1947, just after the US campaigns in Italy but before the WHO launched its global program. Amidst debate about what pesticide resistance meant for public health initiatives, the Global Malaria Eradication Program aimed to escalate malaria eradication efforts before pesticide resistance became widespread (Kinkela 2011, 58, 93–95).[7] Although it may seem strange to note the coincidence of 1947 as the year that insect resistance to DDT was first reported, and the Cold War discourse of containment first articulated, the resonances between the insect threat and the anticolonial/communist threat are impossible to ignore in Carson's account.

Charting the emergence of pesticide resistance, Carson writes: "When by 1957 the list of countries in which lice had become resistant to DDT was extended to include Iran, Turkey, Ethiopia, West Africa, South Africa, Peru, Chile, France, Yugoslavia, Afghanistan, Uganda, Mexico, and Tanganyika, the initial triumph in Italy seemed dim indeed". She continues: "In 1956, only 5 species of these mosquitoes displayed resistance; by early 1960 the number had risen from 5 to 28!" (1962, 269). Carson's lists of countries and tallies of species uncannily echo the cartographic contrasts (maps of Africa in 1956 vs. 1960) and numerical tallies that visualize the spread of anticolonial resistance, swept by the "wind of change" across the Third World in the late 1950s, opening new fronts in the Cold War. Carson's map of nature fighting back overlaps with the map of dark subjects of empire striking back. To a remarkable extent, resistant insects and resistant humans shared the same habitat.

If the Global Malaria Eradication Program waged total war against malaria and an arms race against pesticide resistance, Carson advocated what could be described as "soft power". Her observation about the increasing cost of insect control resonates with post-war calculations of the increasing cost and diminishing returns of empire: "The very substantial financial invest-ment involved in backing and launching an insecticide may be swept away as the insects prove once more that the effective approach to nature is not through brute force" (1962, 272). Carson cites Dutch biologist C. J. Briejer's recommendation of a biological (rather than chemical) approach to insect pests that would "'guide natural processes as cautiously as possible in the desired direction rather than to use brute force'" (Briejer in Carson 1962, 275). This advice might apply as much to the putatively softer civilizational/developmentalist impulses (what Gauri Viswanathan has termed "masks of conquest") urged upon architects of empire or those charged with counter-insurgency as to biologists.[8] Carson seems not to recognize the congruence of her map of DDT resistance with that of anticolonial resistance, but the analogy between resistant insects and restive natives is explicit in Briejer's 1958 report of watching flies "'disporting themselves in DDT as much at home as primitive sorcerers cavorting over red-hot coals'". After citing this analogy, Carson writes simply but ominously, "Similar reports come from other parts of the world" (1962, 273).

We have come full circle, back to the equation of insect pests with primi-tive superstition. In *Silent Spring*, however, the insects are immune to DDT and Carson offers the borrowed image unironically. Carson and Fanon write at a moment when spray guns had become a crucial Cold War weapon, but their shared antipathy to DDT is hardly solidarity in a single struggle. They see the man with spray gun as a proxy for broader destructive forces, but the vehicles of their spray-gun metaphors head in different directions. Fanon wants readers to recoil at treating people like pests and at colonizing projects where potentially beneficial technologies like DDT or Christianity become instruments of violence and coercion. He doesn't say anything about dead birds, silent springs or pervasive, persistent and biomagnifying toxic-ity. For that we need and read Carson. But rereading Carson, we also need Fanon to help us see that far from embracing or abetting communism, as her critics charged, Carson internalized (or strategically deployed) a Cold War discourse where waging war on insects was a way of containing communism, and the spread of insect resistance was a fearsome prospect not least because it mapped so neatly onto the dizzying spread and seeming success of anti-colonial resistance against Western European powers in the late 1950s and early 1960s. (Anticolonial resistance was, arguably, more easily contained than pesticide resistance.) Despite her brave critique of hubristic, reductive scientific certitude, Carson did not reject the militarism, Manicheism or eth-nocentrism of Cold War discourse. Rather, she deployed it to explain how to fight the war against pestilent insects better, with soft power, biological controls, "guiding natural processes in the desired direction".

My aim is not to discredit Carson but to show that neither her attack on DDT nor Fanon's is complete without the other – and to argue that an ade-quate understanding of environmentalism in its manifold genealogies must also be postcolonial, and vice versa. Fanon and Carson's shared antipathy to DDT only raises more questions about what we talk about when we talk about environmentalism at any given historical moment. Nixon is right that it is important to recognize why Fanon might not have described himself as an environmentalist, if environmentalism meant, as it evidently did for Carson, battling a dark tide of invaders disporting themselves like native sorcerers. But it is also important not to accept the hegemonic version of anything as the only game in town. Hegemonies are not born, they are made, and to recognize only Carson's concern about DDT as environmentalist is to miss the historical presence of alternative modes of environmental concern that postcolonial ecocriticism has (thanks to critics like Nixon) begun to recover.

In mainstream American ecocriticism, Cheryll Glotfelty has also worried about Carson's militarist images, the "many striking parallels between the rhetorics of the Cold War, *Silent Spring*, and modern environmentalism". For Glotfelty, these rhetorics assume a bipolar logic where "the possibility of a third, alternative position was denied. With only two choices, the question becomes simply, 'Which side are you on?'" (2000, 162). For Fanon and his wretched millions, the question was anything but simple (that word again), and sometimes even a matter of life and death on the Cold War's Third World battlefields. Neither naïve nor optimistic about the prospects of non-alignment, Fanon acknowledges the desire for a new, neither/nor answer to the Cold War version of the Manichean question, are you with us or against us? (1968, 82–83). This third choice remains invisible in Glotfelty's analysis. Third Worldism appears in *Silent Spring* only as an ominous shadow mode of resistance from which Carson constructs the image of dark enemy hordes.

But DDT was present at the birth of the Third World, its "slow and irresistible, humble and fierce thrust towards life" (Sauvy 1952, 14). This presence was not merely in the coincidence of reports of DDT resistance and the articulation of the Truman Doctrine, the Marshall Plan and containment discourse in 1947. One almost hears, in response to Glotfelty's voicing of the question, "Which side are you on?", French demographer Alfred Sauvy's observation in 1952 that it is all too easy to forget that there are actually three worlds, not two, and that the question for the third, "underdeveloped" world is not which of the former to follow but whether to try another way altogether. Like Sophocles adding a third character to the drama, Sauvy is credited for introducing a third term into the Cold War lexicon. His poignant conclusion invokes revolutionary France: "This ignored Third World, exploited, scorned like the Third Estate, also wants to be something". Sauvy saw one obstacle to this aspiration: burgeoning population in the Third World, resulting from the use of DDT. One could save lives with DDT for little money, but without substantial investments in social and economic development, its use only created a new "cycle of misery" and explosive instability. Sauvy doubted that the post-war crisis of world hunger (which he saw exacerbated by DDT's reduction of mortality rates) could compete with military defense as a First World budget priority. For Sauvy, the Third World, as it emerged on the geopolitical stage in the early 1950s, was literally the creation of DDT.

Gregg Garrard has suggested provocatively that population – the "P-word" – is what ecocriticism cannot say. Because many critics have convincingly argued that "anxiety about population is a cover for other, more sinister *political* objectives [...] ecocritics have had nothing to say about population beyond dark allusions to the perils of Malthusianism" (2012, 54–55). Sauvy ushered *Third World* into the Cold War lexicon at one such anxious moment. A perceived global food shortage sparked fierce debate about overpopulation at the1952 World Health Assembly in Geneva: optimists saw DDT as a solution whereby healthier workers could produce more food, while others (like the Food and Agriculture Organization) thought fewer malaria deaths would mean more people to feed (Litsios 1977, 263–265). What ecocriticism has not been able to say, postcolonial ecocriticism must confront head on. Its twinned genealogies trace directly back to such debates. The dialogue about DDT between Carson and Fanon that I have staged is incomplete without the perspective of someone like Sauvy. The Manichean thinking that Fanon diagnosed as endemic to colonialism (succeeded by Cold War binarisms) turns out to be complicated and overdetermined, rarely either/or or black and white. Fanon, Carson and Sauvy were all against DDT but they would have had difficulty recognizing each other as being on the same side.

In 1962, Rachel Carson charted a new planetary imaginary when she wrote, "[I]t is not possible to add pesticides to water anywhere without threatening the purity of water everywhere" (42). Carson described DDT as a global chemical, which persisted in soil and water, accumulated in fatty tissue and made its way up the food chain in organisms without passports, their movements unconstrained by Iron Curtains or ideological *cordons sanitaires*. Having raised concerns about Carson's ideological blind spots, I want to close by positing her "anywhere [...] everywhere" formulation as a topos for recognizing universal vulnerability and imagining global justice. Martin Luther King, Jr. wrote one year later in his "Letter from Birmingham Jail":

> I am cognizant of the interrelatedness of all communities and states. I cannot sit idly by in Atlanta and not be concerned about what happens in Birmingham. Injustice anywhere is a threat to justice everywhere. We are caught in an inescapable network of mutuality, tied in a single garment of destiny. Whatever affects one directly, affects all indirectly.

Read alongside Carson, King's vision of the concrete/universal aspect of justice seems distinctly ecological in the sense she popularized. "Interrelatedness" and enmeshment within an "inescapable network" are easily imagined as an ecosystem or biotic community. King's insistence upon the implication of all Americans within the civil rights movement (addressing the notion of "outside agitators", King rejects the premise of an "outside") has analogues in anticolonial thinkers from Nehru to Lumumba, who saw imperialism anywhere as a threat to decolonization everywhere. Fanon saw this synecdochic logic as a product of the Cold War: "This [superpower] competition gives an almost universal dimension to even the most localized demands" (1968, 75). These theorists demand attention to the local instance – pesticide in this stream, legalized racism in this town, colonialism in this country – combined with a capacity to imagine and actualize the relationship between local instance and planetary scale: the downstream consequences and mutual imbrications of this pesticide, this racism, this colonialism.

The task of postcolonial ecocriticism is to read such statements in counterpoint and to recognize the occult instabilities in their conjunctures. Malaria, too, is a global phenomenon (mosquitoes became world travelers in an era of mechanized transport), and its mid-twentieth-century foes understood that the success of eradication in any one site depended on the fate of eradication efforts elsewhere. Thus the WHO's global campaign: malaria anywhere was a threat to humans everywhere (Packard 1997, 280). But as Timothy Mitchell argues, transnational rivers and global insects are not generalizable instances of broader processes in the same way that human projects like "capitalism, the idea of the nation, or modern science" are for social theory (2002, 29). Toxic substances and racism have profound, interrelated effects, ranging from the cellular level to economic and political collectivities on a global scale, but they do not flow in the same way. Postcolonial theory articulates links between environmental injustice anywhere and its threat to every kind of justice everywhere by refusing easy distinctions between nature and society and insisting upon trans-corporeal, transnational connections among things like pesticide, racism and colonialism.[9] But there is nothing simple about it. Here, too, we should see postcolonial theory in dynamic, dialectical relationship to its anticolonial genealogy. Fanon's weak-anthropocentric accounting of colonialism's environmental aspects is necessary but insufficient to grasp the contradictory intersections of different kinds of actors and modes of agency in the making and unmaking of the colonial world. But reading Fanon amidst this multiplying *dramatis personae* helps keep in view the workings of power: who gains, who pays.

NOTES

1. See DeLoughrey and Handley (2001, 8–20) and Huggan and Tiffin (2010, 3).
2. Despite the general absence of environmental concerns in the field at large, Said's emphasis on geography and Spivak's engagement with Mahasweta Devi were important to the emergence of postcolonial ecocriticism.
3. Political ecology analyzes "convergences of culture, power, and political economy" that inform conflicts over "defining, controlling, and managing nature" and natural resources (Peluso and Watts 2001, 25).
4. PSNR was also codified in the International Covenant on Civil and Political Rights and the International Covenant on Economic, Social, and Cultural Rights (ICCPR and ICESCR). Both 1966, came into force 1976.
5. See Rangan 2004.

6. "This model of human-environmental relationship, one that avoids illusions of anthropological domination as well as those of illusory purification of nature, gives us the basis of precisely the kind of 'weak' anthropocentrism that green thinking is now beginning to use as a route out of the ... [ecocentrism/anthropocentrism] impasse" (Mukherjee 2010, 62).
7. Unlike earlier anti-malaria campaigns, WHO aimed to eradicate the *Plasmodium* parasite rather than the *Anopheles* mosquito. By interrupting transmission to humans for several years, WHO hoped to reduce parasite levels in the human host population sufficiently to render mosquitoes harmless, no longer a disease vector (Packard 1997, 279).
8. Note echoes of policies articulated by figures like Jan Smuts and Jawaharlal Nehru, where marginalized populations such as Africans in South Africa or indigenous peoples in India were to "develop along their own lines" or "along the lines of their own genius". Such "organic" approaches to development were sometimes carried out by force or coercion.
9. "Trans-corporeality" is Stacy Alaimo's term for flows of matter and power across human bodies and the body politic (2010).

REFERENCES

Alaimo, Stacy. 2010. *Bodily Natures: Science, Environment, and the Material Self.* Bloomington: Indiana University Press.

Anghie, Anthony. 2004. *Imperialism, Sovereignty and the Making of International Law.* Cambridge: Cambridge University Press.

Coronil, Fernando. 2000. "Towards a Critique of Globalcentrism: Speculations on Capitalism's Nature". *Public Culture* 12.2: 351–374.

Coronil, Fernando. 1997. *The Magical State: Nature, Money, and Modernity in Venezuela.* Chicago: University of Chicago Press.

DeLoughrey, Elizabeth and George Handley. 2011. *Postcolonial Ecologies: Literatures of the Environment.* Oxford: Oxford University Press.

Engels, Friedrich. 1954. *Dialectics of Nature.* Translated by Clements Dutt. Moscow: Foreign Languages Publishing House.

Evernden, Neil. 1996. "Beyond Ecology: Self, Place, and the Pathetic Fallacy". In *The Ecocriticism Reader*, edited by Cheryll Glotfelty and Harold Fromm, 92–104. Athens, GA: University of Georgia Press.

Fanon, Frantz. 1968. *The Wretched of the Earth.* Translated by Constance Farrington. New York: Grove.

Gearty, Conor. 2010. "Do Human Rights Help or Hinder Environmental Protection?" *Journal of Human Rights and the Environment* 1.1: 7–22.

Garrard, Gregg. 2012. "Worlds without Us: Some Types of Disanthropy". *SubStance* 41.1: 40–60.

Glotfelty, Cheryll. 2000. "Cold War, *Silent Spring*: The Trope of War in Modern Environmentalism". In *And No Birds Sing: Rhetorical Analyses of Rachel Carson's Silent Spring*, edited by Craig Waddell, 157–173. Carbondale: Southern Illinois University Press.

Haraway, Donna. 2008. *When Species Meet.* Minneapolis: University of Minnesota Press.

Huggan, Graham and Helen Tiffin. 2010. *Postcolonial Ecocriticism: Literature, Animals, Environment*. London: Routledge.

Kinkela, David. 2011. *DDT and the American Century*. Chapel Hill: University of North Carolina Press.

Leopold, Aldo. 1966. *A Sand County Almanac*. New York: Oxford University Press.

Litsios, Socrates. 1997. "Malaria Control, the Cold War, and the Postwar Reorganization of International Assistance". *Medical Anthropology: Cross-Cultural Studies in Health and Illness* 17.3: 255–278.

Mazel, David. 1996. "American Literary Environmentalism as Domestic Orientalism". In *The Ecocriticism Reader*, edited by Cheryll Glotfelty and Harold Fromm, 137–146. Athens, GA: University of Georgia Press.

McMillen, Wheeler. 1965. *Bugs or People?* New York: Appleton-Century.

Mitchell, Timothy. 2002. *Rule of Experts: Egypt, Techno-Politics, Modernity*. Berkeley: University of California Press.

Mukherjee, Upamanyu Pablo. 2010. *Postcolonial Environments: Nature, Culture, and the Contemporary Indian Novel in English*. Basingstoke, UK: Palgrave Macmillan.

Ngũgĩ wa Thiong'o. 2007. *The Wizard of the Crow*. New York: Anchor.

Nixon, Rob. 2005. "Environmentalism and Postcolonialism". In *Postcolonial Studies and Beyond*, edited by Ania Loomba *et al.*, 233–251. Durham, NC: Duke University Press.

Nixon, Rob. 2011. *Slow Violence and the Environmentalism of the Poor*. Cambridge: Harvard University Press.

O'Brien, Susie. 2001. "Articulating a World of Difference: Ecocriticism, Postcolonialism and Globalization". *Canadian Literature* 170/171: 140–158.

Packard, Randall M. 1997. "Malaria Dreams: Postwar Visions of Health and Development in the Third World". *Medical Anthropology: Cross-Cultural Studies in Health and Illness* 17.3: 279–296.

Peluso, Nancy and Michael Watts. 2001. *Violent Environments*. Ithaca: Cornell University Press.

Rangan, Haripriya. 2004. "From Chipko to Uttaranchal: The Environment of Protest and Development in the Indian Himalaya". In *Liberation Ecologies: Environment, Development, Social Movements*, 2nd edition, edited by Richard Peet and Michael Watts, 338–357. London: Routledge.

Sauvy, Alfred. 1952. "Tiers Monde, une planète". *L'Observateur* 118.14, August 14.

Scott, David. 2004. *Conscripts of Modernity: The Tragedy of Colonial Enlightenment*. Durham: Duke University Press.

12 Towards a Postcolonial Disaster Studies

Anthony Carrigan

Since its inception in the 1950s, disaster studies as an interdisciplinary field has been concerned with managing crisis situations, seeking to reduce vulnerability and assist post-disaster recovery. This has become increasingly important over the last few decades as the various risks that inhere in human–environmental relationships have been amplified not only by anthropogenic climate change but also by the capitalist exploitation of natural resources. Both of these processes have accelerated in the period of expansive globalization following World War II (see Fig. 12.1), resulting in natural hazards' frequent conversion into large-scale catastrophes. It is no surprise that these take a disproportionate toll on the world's poorest communities, many of which are still grappling with the legacies of Western colonialism and neocolonial practices. The World Bank is more than aware that "developing countries suffer the most from disasters" (World Bank 2014) and as Naomi Klein's work on "disaster capitalism" highlights (2007), these regions have been subjected to systematic dispossession through the spread of free market doctrine. In addition to increased environmental vulnerabilities, the social crises that have shadowed political decolonization – including war, genocide and systemic poverty – have been catastrophic for large numbers of people, radically transforming natural and built environments in ways that coincide with current forms of ecological imperialism. All this makes disaster response and management central to postcolonial concerns, with postcolonial studies emerging over the last three decades in the context of global problems such as accelerating economic disparities, resource scarcity, climate change and US-led wars. In particular, disaster analysis can shed light on how specific colonial practices produce differential forms of vulnerability, raising the question of what happens if we treat postcolonial studies as a form of disaster studies and vice versa, with an emphasis on the shaping influence of colonialisms on a global scale. The aim of this essay is to open up some perspectives on this relationship through consideration of what a postcolonial disaster studies might entail. Its core conviction is that postcolonial studies still has much to say, both in terms of recalibrating applied fields such as disaster studies and in imagining alternatives to the destructive processes that support the global proliferation of disasters.

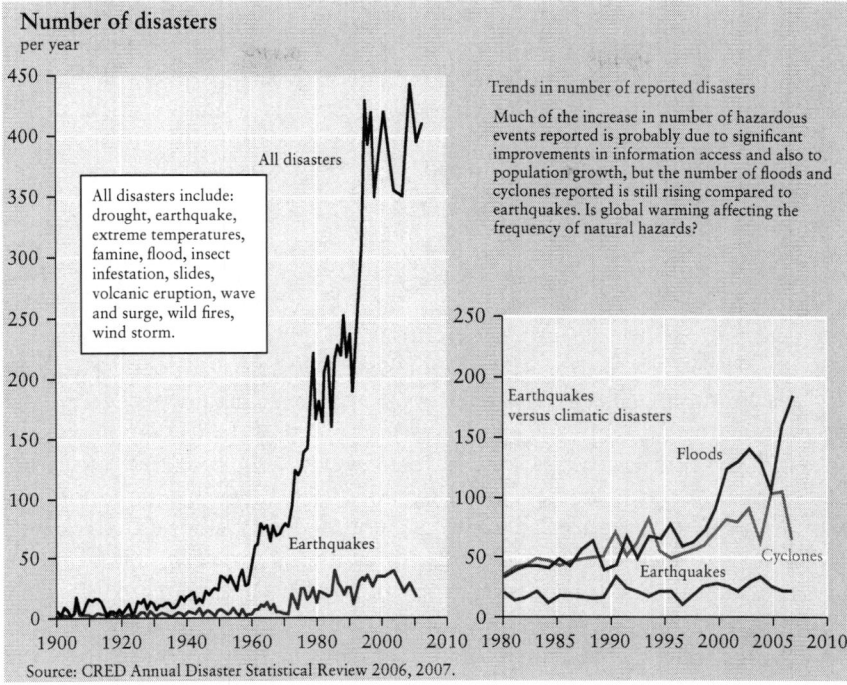

Number of disasters per year

All disasters

All disasters include: drought, earthquake, extreme temperatures, famine, flood, insect infestation, slides, volcanic eruption, wave and surge, wild fires, wind storm.

Trends in number of reported disasters

Much of the increase in number of hazardous events reported is probably due to significant improvements in information access and also to population growth, but the number of floods and cyclones reported is still rising compared to earthquakes. Is global warming affecting the frequency of natural hazards?

Earthquakes

Earthquakes versus climatic disasters

Floods

Cyclones

Earthquakes

Source: CRED Annual Disaster Statistical Review 2006, 2007.

Figure 12.1 Number of reported disasters p.a. since 1900. Credit: Riccardo Pravettoni, UNEP/GRID-Arendal (http://www.grida.no/graphicslib/detail/number-of-disasters-per-year_1408).

My contribution begins by tracing a genealogy of disaster studies and arguing for the need to bring it into productive exchange with postcolonial methodologies. The development of disaster studies is compelling for postcolonial researchers, partly because of how it embeds empirical findings in policy-oriented frameworks and partly for its role in situating disaster response as key to what Andrew Ross calls "planetary management" – a process in which "centralized rationalization" tends to obscure the social causes of global crises (1991, 207–208; see also Sachs 1993, 19–20). It is precisely this occlusion that a postcolonial approach to disaster must confront, and at the most fundamental level this involves reframing the question "What is a disaster?" in postcolonial contexts. At the same time, it is important to think through how postcolonial studies can benefit from confronting disaster head on, not least as the concept is enmeshed with many of the field's abiding concerns, from forced migration and displacement to trauma, memory and forgetting. To illustrate how this might operate conceptually, I turn in the second part of the article to the work of Barbadian poet and historian Kamau Brathwaite, and in particular his genre-defying epic *MR* (2002). I find Brathwaite's blend of creative and critical insights highly suggestive in establishing connections between cultural experiences of catastrophe and global concerns, and read it as a framework through which postcolonialism and disaster studies can be seen as mutually constitutive and causally linked. I conclude by speculating on how Brathwaite's work and the humanities-based observations I make here might be effectively integrated with disaster research.

DECOLONIZING DISASTER STUDIES

I would like to begin by tracing a genealogy of academic disaster studies following World War II as I see this as not only symptomatic of, but deeply entwined with, the historical processes that ushered in the "age of ecology" (Worster 1994, ix) and the "development era" (Sachs 1993, 4). There are obvious continuities between inter-empire disaster management practices in the nineteenth and early twentieth century and their post-1945 successors (see e.g. Davis 2001; Mukherjee 2013). However, I am primarily concerned here with how disaster studies was institutionalized in parallel to the post-war geopolitical shifts that are central to postcolonial studies, and to the global cultural–economic transitions that accompany the formation of the UN and the International Bank for Reconstruction and Development (to evoke the World Bank's original, disaster-responsive title). I am also interested in how the field has interpreted the exponential rise in catastrophes – both social and "natural" – since the mid-twentieth century, which has accompanied rapid economic globalization and continues to be magnified by accelerating gaps between rich and poor. There is a stark contradiction between the institutionalization of disaster risk reduction – signalled by the UN Office of that name – and the rising tide of global catastrophes, compounded by the sense that "never again" has become "wherever again", as Rwandan President Paul Kagame put it bluntly in 2000 (cited in Mirzoeff 2005, 36; see also e.g. Jennings 2013 for its continued reiteration). Considering disaster studies' post-1945 genealogy is therefore helpful for articulating how postcolonial research can critique and extend the field's commitment to vulnerability reduction through a reframing of the disaster concept.

Disaster studies began to emerge as a coherent field in the US in conjunction with the "Strategic Bombing Surveys" conducted during World War II, which were devised to assess civilian "morale" in the context of "sustained military attacks" (Bolin 2007, 119). Its growth as a sociological research area came in the context of Cold War militarization, with the US government sponsoring the formation of a Disaster Research Group under the aegis of the National Academy of Sciences in 1952 (Perry 2007, 5). In subsequent decades, the initial "reactive [...] command-and-control civil defense approach" has given way to more methodologically diverse perspectives, organized mainly "around the twin concepts of risk management and sustainable hazard mitigation" (Britton 2005, 66). This has been partly due to the rise of the risk paradigm in sociological research and partly due to critiques dating back to the 1970s from a number of materialist-inspired geographers, anthropologists and historians such as Kenneth Hewitt, Anthony Oliver-Smith and Ben Wisner. Their work helped reconfigure mainstream disaster studies approaches, emphasizing the need to address not just the agents of natural disasters (e.g. environmental phenomena such as hurricanes, earthquakes and droughts) but also the social, political and economic processes that put particular groups at risk and underpin the scale of disasters. Nevertheless, the durability of technocratic management strategies (focusing on the four stages of disaster management: mitigation, preparedness, response and recovery) coupled with a largely US-centric approach continue to perpetuate critical blindspots that limit the field's global applicability even as its findings are adopted by multinational actors like the UN and the World Bank.

Tellingly, it took until 1998 – the end of the UN-designated International Decade for Natural Disaster Reduction – for the landmark collection of essays *What is a Disaster?* to be published, with its stated intention being to bring sociological disaster studies into sustained dialogue with other disciplinary perspectives. The need for this is dramatized by the volume's title question, which seems to come a little late in the day for a field with five decades' development behind it, but which really serves to register an abiding tension between researchers who "assume physical happenings, independent from human actions, are necessary for disaster" and those who see disaster more as a "social construction", as the volume's editor puts it (Quarantelli 1998a, 3). Given that social and political debates over the causes of disasters go back at least as far as the nineteenth century, as Mike Davis (2001) and others have shown in relation to British imperial policy and famine, what the prolonged nature of this debate attests to is partly the tendency for disaster researchers to favor inductive approaches (i.e. responding empirically to experiential observations) over deductive methods (working from theoretically informed standpoints). Such prioritization has resulted in a number of prominent ellipses or, as Hewitt puts it more critically, "excluded perspectives" (1995), with scant attention paid to the relationship between history, identity politics and vulnerability – including categories like race, gender, class, religion, disability and a whole raft of non-human concerns – or to how economic processes like structural adjustment have increased hazard vulnerability and "magnified losses from disasters" (Bolin 2007, 118).

This leads to a number of observations that will no doubt perplex postcolonial researchers: the fact that in editing *What is a Disaster?*, Quarantelli admitted to failing to "find anyone [...] who used primarily a non-Western frame" (1998b, 271); the assertion by Bob Bolin, in the single chapter dedicated to "Race, Class, Ethnicity and Disaster Vulnerability" in the 2007 *Handbook of Disaster Research*, that disaster specialists tend to "rely on commonsensical treatments of racial and ethnic categories rather than using in-depth sociohistorical and ethnographic analyses" (2007, 117); and the predilection for separating out or "typologizing" disasters rather than considering the much messier ramifications of what the UN calls "*complex emergencies* (or sometimes *compound disasters*)", which can involve "mixtures of civil strife, famines, genocidal activities, epidemics, and large-scale displacement and movement of refugees" (Quarantelli 1998b, 263).

As several critics have observed, approaches to disaster that fail to engage with the social, economic and political dimensions of hazard production can work ultimately to sustain rather than mitigate catastrophes (see e.g. Hewitt 1995) – a point that is given a darker edge in Klein's work, which situates the manufacture of "sustainable disasters" as a deliberate neoliberal strategy. Indeed, if we accept the full force of Klein's argument (2007) – that free market hegemony has been attained on a global level through the exploitation of disasters – then the exponential rise in post-1945 disasters illustrated in Fig. 12.1 suggests such events are in fact products of neoliberal policies that both feed from and create entrenched vulnerability.

Certainly any approach that prioritizes returning post-disaster communities to a pre-disaster "norm" has serious flaws, given the differential forms of disenfranchisement that precede and are exploited by reconstruction processes (as the aftermath of Hurricane Katrina horrifically exposed). The inappropriateness of such models is even more pronounced in the many contexts where catastrophic events are consistently entwined with "ordinary", "chronic" or "slow onset" disasters – including poverty, debt, ecological degradation, underdevelopment and militarism – or where the state itself constitutes a "hazard". Yet the close affiliations disaster studies has shared with normative politics (especially, though not exclusively, in the US) has rendered it slow to reformulate itself in ways that might be responsive to these structural conditions. Put more polemically, the field has yet to disentangle itself fully from the epistemic violence associated with its institutional birth – forged during the Cold War and entwined with military–industrialism's global spread.

There has, encouragingly, been something of a transformation in disaster research over the last decade or so – catalyzed partly by considerations of 9/11 (Scanlon 2005, 13) – with increasing attention now being paid to the relationship between disasters, development and globalization (Bankoff *et al.* 2004; Collins 2009; Lewis 1999; O'Dempsey and Munslow 2006; Pelling 2003; Wisner *et al.* 2004); to indigenous knowledge and disaster risk reduction (Kelman *et al.* 2012; Shaw *et al.* 2009); and to the cultural dimensions of catastrophes (Bankoff 2003; Oliver-Smith and Hoffman 1998; Hoffman and Oliver-Smith 2002). The field has also been boosted through perspectives from political ecology and progressive humanitarian studies, with Anthony Oliver-Smith in particular emphasizing the need to address how disasters are manifestations of historical vulnerabilities that are produced at the intersection of environment and society, and cannot be disentangled from systemic power structures (1998, 189). Yet there remains virtually no sustained analysis of the relationship between colonialism and disaster. It is in this context, then, that I want to expand the sense of paradigm change captured in progressive disaster research by asserting the importance for the field to, first, find points of critical exchange with postcolonialism, with a particular focus on the connections between vulnerability production, imperialist practice and cultural response; and subsequently not to treat this as another "avenue" or "dimension" of interest to be appended in future handbooks but as necessarily constitutive of the field's future transformation and relevance.

In making this argument, I am aware of the usual barriers it presents for establishing meaningful synergies between postcolonialism and disciplines outside – and sometimes within – the humanities (as Simon Obendorf's chapter on International Relations in this volume aptly illustrates). I am more optimistic in this case, though, about the possibilities for sustained and substantive exchange precisely because the sheer scale of contemporary disasters is prompting serious methodological shifts in disaster research itself – so much so that the recent Routledge *Handbook of Hazards and Disaster Risk Reduction* opens with a plea for more "critical thinking, along with departure from disciplinary norms and expectations, and the euphemisms and politeness of diplomatic language used by United Nations organisations" (Wisner *et al.* 2012, 3). The unbridled effects of climate change coupled with the yawning wealth disparities that underpin global economic crises are two high-profile challenges to conventional vulnerability analysis, and disaster research must also respond to the many "resurgent" resistance movements across the Global South that highlight how "ecological and human disposability" have been catastrophically "conjoined" (Nixon 2011, 4). Turning to the cultural, historical and economic implications of postcolonial critique is in this sense crucial if the field is to achieve genuine and sustained disaster mitigation in global contexts. The corollary is that such a transformation requires not only significant input and exchange from postcolonialists but that postcolonial studies itself must engage in similarly transformative modes of *praxis* that takes it beyond its humanities-based comfort zone. Indeed, I would suggest that one thing postcolonial studies should avowedly stand for is progressive disaster mitigation, and this form of collaboration – uneasy and volatile as it may be – represents one way of achieving the real-world changes the field theoretically demands.

There is much to be learned, for instance, from how disaster researchers communicate beyond academic contexts, and postcolonial studies can look to build on disaster studies' success as an applied research formation that can speak to – and potentially challenge – political perspectives on crisis management and reconstruction. This does not mean foregoing postcolonialism's humanities-based strengths but rather channelling these towards a self-conscious reformulation of disaster studies methods. It is especially interesting in this light that, along with the lack of attention to identity categories, there has been scant consideration of disaster narratives and imaginative depictions more broadly in mainstream disaster research. This is something that literary and cultural critics can redress directly in conjunction with related disciplines like history by exploring how postcolonial texts challenge, reject or reconfigure key disaster studies concepts such as resilience, risk, adaption and vulnerability. At the same time, postcolonial researchers should ask how disaster research can frame and inform textual readings of specific disasters, and use this as a basis for establishing new methodologies that engage different audiences.

There is certainly a willingness in disaster studies to embrace literary and cultural findings, with a number of researchers emphasizing that disasters are less "accident[s]" than "representation[s] of reality" (Gilbert 1998, 9), and that "perception[s] of risk and vulnerability" are "clearly mediated through linguistic and cultural grids, accounting for great variability in assessments and understandings of disasters" (Oliver-Smith 2004, 17). Some, such as Hewitt, anticipate Rob Nixon's influential arguments in *Slow Violence and the Environmentalism of the Poor* (2011) by highlighting the need to listen to "the plight and *stories* of distinctly more vulnerable members of society" and create a discourse that speaks "of missing persons or unheard voices; of 'hidden damage' and 'shadow risks' and, more severely, of 'silent' or 'quiet violence'" (1995, 120; my emphasis). Postcolonial research can obviously foreground these concerns by exploring how writers, intellectuals and artists working in non-Western contexts theorize and represent specific experiences of disaster in relation to distributions of power. This involves attending to the resilience of what Ann Stoler calls "imperial formations" – a term she uses to "register the ongoing quality of processes of decimation, displacement, and reclamation" that remain active outside formal imperialism and create "*repositories of vulnerabilities* that [...] last longer than the political structures that produced them" (2008, 193, 203; my emphasis). It also requires a methodologically inclusive approach to how these narratives can help reconstruct the disaster field itself – attending to the "long emergencies of slow violence" (Nixon 2011, 3) and "dialectics of ordinary disaster" (Davis 1995) that are bound up with different forms of colonialism and that present fundamental challenges to the technocratic applicability of event-based disaster-modelling.

The rest of this essay puts these ideas into practice by using Kamau Brathwaite's recent literary–historical work as a platform from which to begin reframing the question of "What is a disaster?" in light of postcolonial concerns. Brathwaite's work represents a great example of what a postcolonial disaster studies might look like precisely because it rejects technocratic dictats in favor of comparative inquiry and seeks to act as a "witness/crossroad from world to word to self & from self to other selves w/what i can only call humility" (2002, 68). Moreover, given that the text under discussion (*MR*) is hard to get hold of and arguably inaccessible to the uninitiated, I want to use this as an opportunity to advertise its relevance as a meditation on colonialism and catastrophe, not least through how it sheds light on the conceptual adaptations needed for a postcolonial disaster studies to emerge.

MR, RADIANCE AND RECONSTRUCTION

Throughout his distinguished career, Kamau Brathwaite has been alive to the intersections of history, aesthetics and catastrophe in colonial and postcolonial contexts and the Caribbean in particular. He famously describes the need for Caribbean writers to re-forge English in ways that "approximate [...] the *natural* experience, the *environmental* experience", asserting that "[t]he hurricane does not roar in pentameters" (Brathwaite 1984, 10). This statement foregrounds the constitutive presence of natural hazards in the region, and elsewhere he observes how "[t]he beauty of the Caribbean is (re)born out of the catastrophic origins of the Yucatan-Atlantis cordillera and the volcanoes & earthQuake flues & flows that rim & ruim the Caribbean sea" (2006, 7; see also Carrigan 2011, 111). Since the 1990s, Brathwaite's interest in the double valence of disasters – both generative and destructive – has become increasingly manifest, and his recent work has led to a comparative and increasingly epic cosmology of catastrophe that situates it at the heart of postcolonial concerns.

One powerful example comes in a 2005 interview conducted by Joyelle McSweeney shortly after Hurricane Katrina hit New Orleans and the Gulf Coast. McSweeney opens by asking how Brathwaite interprets this and other recent disasters given his long-standing interest in the subject, to which he responds:

> My position on catastrophe [...] is, I'm so conscious of the enormity of slavery and the Middle Passage and I see that as an ongoing catastrophe. So whatever happens in the world after that, like tsunamis in the Far East and India and Indonesia, and 9/11, and now New Orleans, to me these are all aspects of that same original explosion, which I constantly try to understand. What is it that causes nature to lunge in this cataclysmic way, and what kind of message, as I suspect it is, what message is Nature [sic] trying to send to us? And how are they connected, these violent forces that hit the world so very often – manmade or nature-made or spirit-made – they hit us increasingly violently.
>
> (McSweeney 2005)

Brathwaite's eloquent response foregrounds a number of concerns that can be considered central to an emergent notion of postcolonial disaster. These include the ongoing effects of colonialism as catastrophe – or "worldquake", as Brathwaite calls it elsewhere (Brathwaite 2002, 127) – in relation to a series of seemingly disparate social and natural catastrophes; the intimate relationship between power, exploitation, violence and disaster; and a multivalent concept of "nature" as material and metaphysical entity (alluded to in the switch to capitalized form, "Nature"), which emphasizes its historical agency and corresponds with how Brathwaite uses "catastrophe" to evoke the cultural, psychological and metaphysical dimensions of "disaster" as a physical process. The significance of these points is partly that they speak to Stoler's historicized vision of imperial formations, which also involves "[m]aking connections where they are hard to trace" between psychological suffering and physical destruction of landscapes, homes and infrastructure (2008, 195). But whereas Stoler's interest resides in what she calls "imperial debris" – that is, material remnants of accretive disasters or various forms of "ruination" (193–194) – Brathwaite focuses more on the dialectic between destructive processes and disastrous events or, as disaster specialist Ilan Kelman puts it, the "fuzzy clusters" of experiences that elide "[c]atastrophic and chronic disasters" in global societies (2003, 118). Importantly, Brathwaite's comments indicate how the designation "postcolonial disaster" can help negotiate the dichotomy between event and process. This is because it always implies the kind of "complex emergencies" or "compound disasters" evoked in humanitarian and disaster relief discourse, which are conditioned by the "ruinous" (Stoler 2008, 195) consequences of specific imperial formations.

Where Brathwaite's work becomes even more compelling from the perspective of reconfiguring and extending the forms through which disasters are analyzed is in his insistence on the significance of conceptual transformation and imaginative response. Asserting that "Art must come out of catastrophe" (McSweeney 2005), Brathwaite sets out a provocative counterpoint to Adorno's famous assertion that writing poetry after Auschwitz is barbaric, reflecting elsewhere in his work on how "[t]here has been a vast river of postHiroshima [sic] catastrophe & suffering [...] yet creativity & hope" that calls for a "whole new *reconstruction* of history and possibility" (2005; 1990, 33; my emphasis). Such conceptual reconstruction crucially accompanies the more familiar forms of post-disaster reconstruction relating to flattened infrastructure and transfigured environments. It also underlines the importance of attuning post-disaster reconstruction policies to historical and imaginative insights, and identifying how artistic works and intellectual critique are implicated in recovery processes.

Brathwaite elaborates on this by commenting: "One thing about catastrophe, for me, is that it always seems to lead to *a kind of* magical realism. That moment of utter disaster, the very moment when it seems almost hopeless, too difficult to proceed, you begin to glimpse a kind of radiance on the other end of the maelstrom" (McSweeney 2005; my emphasis). The "glimpse [...] of radiance" Brathwaite evokes is enticing as it promises to shed light not only on literary representations of disaster (as the reference to magical realism seemingly implies) but on the way in which the concept is framed and understood in (largely Western) academic discourse. This is not because it somehow redeems the tarnished notion of a "radiant tomorrow" captured in mid-twentieth-century development discourse (Sachs 1999, 21); rather, the image conjures a sense of epiphanic transformation associated with epistemological change. This point forms the subject of Brathwaite's most extended engagement with catastrophe, conceptual reconstruction and aesthetic response: his epic, 700-page meditation on magical realism, *MR*.

Winner of the Casa de las Americas Prize for literary criticism in 1998 and published in full in 2002, *MR* is a formally dazzling inquiry into magical realism's emergence, concentrating on the Caribbean and Latin America in particular. While this single-genre focus might seem incompatible with a broader analysis of the many narrative and artistic forms used to represent disasters, Brathwaite's characterization of the term through multiple, often elusive definitions presents it more as an alternative epistemology or mode of understanding than a conventional literary genre as such, which emerges in contradistinction to the catastrophic epistemologies embedded in Western colonialism. Or as he puts it:

> this new work of the Caribbean Améric
> – as which collapses time & space
> & integrates them into new maps w/ a new
> vocab, opt ic & METAPHOR – another
> way therefore of hearing & VOICING
> the vision – seems to me a real

promethean
response to catastrophe (natural + social
like slavery & colon ialism & the ru le
of the cau dillo Plan tation)

an # orphean
response to NATURE (m kissi of landscape),
& the people – the FOLK CULTURE

– the # NATION
LANGUAGE CULTURE of that landscape

a # sycoraxian
nurturing of all this as a response
to downpression
[...]
& an

ogotemmellean
response to the need to restore
COSMOLOGY
(*problematic unmiracle of fragmentation*)
& when/wherever i find this
(these) breaking the scarface
of our culture i call out

MR

(2002, 382–384)

This visionary passage exemplifies how Brathwaite positions magical realism as "a form of post-catastrophe art istic cosmology [...] engaging prismatically [...] all [...] the elements of one's culture towards a moment of *transformation. healing*" (649–50). On one level, this involves a distinctly Caribbean response to compound disaster, which builds not least on Édouard Glissant's and Wilson Harris' sustained engagements in their oeuvres with crisis, catastrophe and regeneration (Harris is especially prominent in *MR*). The passage is representative of how *MR* itself disrupts conventional academic formats – along with any imagined boundary between the critical and the creative – in line with what Brathwaite elsewhere describes as a regional "geo-psyche" (1990, 26). This is shaped by experiences of fragmentation, which result partly from negotiating the transformations caused by recurring environmental hazards and partly from the abuses and transfigurations of "colon ialism & the ru le of the cau dillo Plan tation". The "mkissi" or spirits of local landscapes are necessarily responsive to the various ways in which the Caribbean has been "*inaugurated* in catastrophe" (Small Axe Project 2011, 134; see also Anderson 2011, 7), with the plantation system underpinning the region's location as a crucible of colonial modernity and globalization. This has been instrumental in creating a sense of alienation between nature and society (DeLoughrey *et al.* 2005, 1, 4) – along with the "cosmological" rupture Brathwaite describes – while at the same time shaping the many identifiable "cultures of disaster" across the region (to adapt Greg Bankoff's term for creative adaptation to environmental hazards in the Philippines; 2003).

On another level, it is precisely these features that underpin how "*MR*'s critical ideas/theory cross-reference other transcultural IIIW concerns" (2002, 347), making the artistic innovations Brathwaite describes relevant to the global forms of disaster evoked throughout his study and which are brought together in creative works such as his elegiac post-9/11 poem "Ark". This references a litany of postcolonial examples – Bhuj, Grenada, Jenin, Bhopal, Rwanda – before reaching the pregnant conclusion "Manhattan in Afghanistan" (2010, 82–86). The poem follows *MR*'s logic by foregrounding the conjuncture between imperialism, environmental exploitation and compound disaster in ways that unsettle assumptions that globalization's relationship with catastrophe is "inherently unpredictable" because the processes involved are supposedly "discontinuous in [...] space and time" (Oliver-Smith 1998, 193). By focusing on conditions that render certain disasters chillingly calculable, Brathwaite instead offers a globally oriented correlative to Derek Gregory's account of "the colonial present" in the Middle East, which likewise favors "recovering [...] spatial stories" and "connecting different places and combining different time-scales" (2004, 19–20). The parallel is accentuated by Gregory's interest in humanities-based (contra humanitarian) approaches to complex emergencies, drawing on postcolonial methodologies and quoting numerous literary and artistic intertexts, albeit without ever quite clarifying their implications for geopolitical exegesis.

While *MR* is more allusive than comprehensive in its examples, the text complements Gregory's work in resisting the tendency for disasters to be "treated as [...] archipelagos of extreme [...] random events" that are "cordoned off as areas of spatial disorganization or national security crisis" (Hewitt 1995, 117) or even "conceived of as existing beyond history and, therefore, politics" (Anderson 2011, 21). Resistance to this trend is key for disaster studies in order to refute the tendency for many economically disadvantaged states to be portrayed as crisis-ridden risk zones, situated less as sites of progressive reconstruction (or what Brathwaite calls "healing") than as security threats for Western states, ever-threatening to be "engulfed by disaster" (Sachs 1999, 21–22). Such rhetorics often determine approaches to disaster response and management, instituting exceptionality in place of comparative discussion of how vulnerability is produced (see also Franks 2013). Brathwaite's alternative cartography helps reframe understandings of disastrous history in this respect as it is not only temporally and geographically expansive but also asserts continuities between "natural + social" catastrophes that remain subdued in disaster studies but should be the subject of postcolonial critique (see e.g. Kelman 2012 and Hilhorst 2013 for work that is beginning to close this gap).

Brathwaite uses a literary method to approach this issue by looking at how creative works encode both what he calls "the literature of negative catastrophe" (associated, somewhat problematically, with social realism) and "the literature [...] of optimistic catastrophe" (aligned more with magical realism; 2002, 347). This is relevant for disaster studies more generally because the ambivalence it captures parallels the tensions associated with understanding the social and psychological conflicts that accompany catastrophes. Throughout *MR*, Brathwaite urges the need to strike a balance between how postcolonial representations of disaster on one hand hold "a broken mirror up to broeken [sic] nature" and on the other hand reconfigure these "broken parts [...] to go [...] beyond the crisis/disruption" and reveal "the [...] [**HINTERLAND**] of wholeness & restoration, re/vision, healing" (323). The tentative – even slightly distorted – wording here captures the sense of fragmentation that accompanies catastrophes (see Blanchot 1995), while at the same time responding to the violent dialectics of fracture and reconstruction that underpin the production of disaster in many postcolonial locations. This anticipates both a reading strategy for critics looking at postcolonial disaster texts and a platform for articulating how humanities-based work can advance comprehension of what disaster researchers readily admit is "the least understood aspect of emergency management": recovery (Smith and Wenger 2007, 234).

I have discussed elsewhere the need to alter mainstream recovery paradigms, including long-term toxicity and trauma, in relation to the many disabilities and disabling environments produced by disasters (Carrigan 2010). This seems crucial in developing what, according to hazard mitigation specialists Gavin Smith and Dennis Wenger, "does not exist:" a "comprehensive theory of sustainable community disaster recovery" (2007, 245). Brathwaite's approach in *MR* takes this thinking further by seeing one core element of *MR* epistemology as involving "the making/discovery/improvisationary recovery of new/ancient necessary survival/transcendent concept(s)/forms [...] thru habilitation/rememory/adaptation/improvization [...] into forms of maronage/possession/resistances into the emancipation/liberation of space/time" (2002, 370). The key terms in this passage chime provocatively with – even riff directly off – progressive disaster commentaries that see vulnerability reduction as dependent on replacing technocratic "attempts to control the environment" with "approaches that [...] stress flexibility, adaptability, resilience and capacity" (Hilhorst and Bankoff 2004, 4). Such resonances seem more than coincidental, given that Brathwaite was on the board of UNESCO and composed most of *MR* during the UN's International Decade for Natural Disaster Reduction in the 1990s (see also Brathwaite 2002, 58–62). Importantly, Brathwaite tempers uncritical celebration of qualities such as adaptation by emphasizing "emancipation/liberation" as part of long-term (and never linear) recovery processes, which can be politicized, augmented or set back in the aftermath of specific disasters. One of the benefits of comparing and historicizing postcolonial disaster representations in this light is that they provide culturally responsive insights into post-disaster adaptation and community solidarity while at the same time dramatizing the stresses and frictions that are exacerbated by differential experiences of colonialism (the reading strategy here again involves examining dialectics of negative and optimistic catastrophe). This is important, as we know that terms like "resilience" and "capacity" can also operate as Western discourses that are all too willingly appropriated in neoliberal discourse as a smokescreen for inaction (when there is no economic motivation for intervention) or continued exploitation (often under the banner of "aid").

The "glimpse of radiance" (McSweeney 2005) that Brathwaite associates with many creative responses to postcolonial catastrophes parallels academic convictions that disasters are always opportunities for change by situating anticolonialism at the heart of effective disaster response and mitigation. This in turn requires critical engagement with the challenges historical exploitation poses for conceptualizing sustainable community recovery. What does recovery mean, for instance, in a context such as Haiti, where the pre-disaster paradigm was characterized by enforced poverty, ecological exhaustion and political abuse (see also e.g. McRuer 2010)? How does recovery differ from its cognate, reconstruction, and do both work as thresholds between negative and optimistic catastrophe? Is recovery an appropriate term in contexts of collective trauma and long-term injustice? And how do postcolonial commentators activate the legal and pecuniary connotations of recovery (as in recovering losses) alongside the need to recover occluded narratives and voices? As *MR* demonstrates, the kind of epistemological reframings these questions demand rely on nuanced conversations between postcolonialists and disaster researchers working from various scientific, sociological and humanitarian backgrounds. However – and crucially for my argument here – such exchange can only be emancipatory in substance if the principles that emerge from *MR* are applied to the institutional treatment of disaster itself, and I would like to close with a few further reflections on the challenges of facilitating conceptual reconstruction in this light.

CONCLUSION: FROM CLOSURE TO COLLABORATION

Part of the brilliance of *MR* is that it functions as a performative example of what it claims magical realist or post-catastrophe art provides: a "promethean" response to compound disaster that offers "another way [...] of hearing & VOICING the vision" (2002, 382). Brathwaite's own comparative vision of catastrophic history emphasizes the importance of pushing back at the dominant strains of risk-based analysis, which tend to focus more on future apocalyptic scenarios, and to look instead at how postcolonial texts depict past and present experiences of real-world catastrophes along with their deep-lying causes. This is a change that needs to be effected still within literary and cultural studies, particularly as critics interested in issues of catastrophe, apocalypse and climate change have much more willing to turn to apocalyptic imaginings such as Cormac McCarthy's novel *The Road* (2006) or Roland Emmerich's film *The Day After Tomorrow* (2004) than to representations of lived disasters in global contexts (popular and sensationalist narratives also tend to make up the focus of the few chapters in disaster studies textbooks on disaster representation; see e.g. Webb 2007; Berger and Wisner 2013). Such transformation is vital both in terms of maximizing literary studies' contribution to humanizing disaster studies – placing identity politics and social stories at the core of understanding disaster – and in seeing vulnerability reduction as predicated on culturally and historically nuanced understandings of human–environmental relations. This includes how differential experiences of trauma, environmental devastation and post-disaster aid are inflected by histories of oppression that continue to evolve in the present, and attending to what Mark Anderson calls the "cultural politics of catastrophe" – a term he uses to elucidate how certain narratives compete to "hold sway over the collective imagination and [...] political establishment" in the wake of disasters (Anderson 2011, 2).

Instituting such an approach requires creative thinking if we are to negotiate the various and often catastrophic communication barriers that emerge between different stakeholders and constituencies. This is an issue that Brathwaite again identifies in *MR* by focusing on the distinction between what he calls "closed" and "open" systems of thought, with the former associated partly with the impetus for colonial conquest and the latter focusing on responses to fragmentation and reconstruction. As he puts it:

- CLOSE(D) ≈ 'critical', argumentative often nit-pickin (in defence of the invariant STATUS QUO even STATUS CROW), 'Aristotelian' rather than 'Platonic', MISSILIC ATTACK/COUNTERATTACK as crucial strategy in defence of their CADEUS/CITADEL/ESTABLISHMENT

- in "contrast" to the OPEN/CONSTITUATIVE (collecting/accumulation
of parts or fragments, trying to see/evoke/create a PATTERN - this pattern
is usually (but not necessarily) diff from the CLOSED/ESTAB in that for one
thing it will be DYNAMIC/IN MOTION/xhibiting
features of FISSION & KINESIS - xplosive or xploding in contrast to
CLOSE(D) Systems which tend towards implosion
on the way not to BLACK HOLES & MR
but to ENTROPY

(2002, 36)

While the contrast between open and closed systems sets up a seeming binary, along with the predictable political affiliations this entails, Brathwaite complicates this by suggesting that his work, and magical realism, and, I would argue, most forms of postcolonial critique emerge from the tensions and contradictions between these systems. In so doing, they all represent ways of negotiating the conflicts produced in what Brathwaite calls "western" society (with the pun troubling the distinction between geography, historical development and epistemology) and shed light on more open forms of practice. This contradiction needs to be positioned methodologically at the heart of a self-conscious decolonization of disaster studies, which does not simply involve labelling the various strands of the field as "open" or "closed" but considers how they might be brought together in a process of transformation towards a more open research formation as a whole.

Perhaps the most pertinent example here is the need to adapt the conceptual system that generated the "What is a disaster?" debate so as not only to accommodate alternative concepts of disaster (incorporating non-empirical perspectives and prioritizing culturally localized definitions) but also to be more deductive about the political links between vulnerability production, environmental exploitation and post-disaster reconstruction. The category of postcolonial disaster represents a further point of synthesis here because it clearly counters the segregated approach to historical and cultural processes that haunts mainstream disaster studies, hinting instead at a productive response to what Brathwaite calls "the lack of truly consistent collective interdiscipline" and the "'problematic' of conversation between academics & between academics & 'Other(s)'" (Brathwaite 2002, 89). It also implies a research formation in which the most obvious contribution to "policy and practice" involves a direct critique of closed-system disaster management that fails to contribute to the work of decolonization, and this is precisely where I see a form of postcolonial studies that situates itself as disaster studies making a productive intervention.

There is no doubt that "closed spaces abound" in the disaster management field, which tends to consolidate power rather than reduce risk (Mascarenhas and Wisner 2012, 56–57). It is also evident that a postcolonial disaster studies must confront the many exploitative, normalizing and deeply exclusionary practices that accompany managerial approaches to reconstruction. In fact, Brathwaite says as much when he complains in a 2006 interview that Caribbean aid gets "automatically contaminated [...] by donors *and* menagement-receivers" who represent organizations like "the IMF the WTO NAFTA the EPA" and are more "interested in imposing a solution – not soulution! – that has been already agreed-on somewhere on Madison Avenue or Wall Street or Paris or the G8 at Davos or Geneva or in the Br Museum" than in listening to the concerns of "*local people*" (Brathwaite and Sajé 2009, 247; original emphases). However, *MR* makes a case for negotiating these power structures in ways that are more strategically nuanced than belligerently oppositional. As the puns that characterize Brathwaite's work suggest, this involves emphasizing the power of language in revising key disaster studies tenets and risk reduction practices – an issue that postcolonial and humanities-based research is especially well placed to address.

Throughout this essay, I have highlighted how creative texts such as *MR* offer epistemological alternatives to the dominant rhetorics through which disasters are framed, providing new vocabularies for talking about the relationship between catastrophic events, histories and – perhaps most significantly – processes of recovery and reconstruction. The last quotation from Brathwaite builds on this directly through its use of language. The term "menagement-receivers" highlights patriarchy's inscription in managerial logics, while the distinction between "solutions" and "soulutions" intimates a vital recalibration of "menagement-speak". The technocratic language of "solutions" is rife in disaster studies, and is often complicit in exclusionary approaches to recovery and retrenchment of the very processes that exacerbate pre-disaster vulnerability through structural ignorance. This is because it is bound up in a logic of top-down, quick-fix intervention, disregarding the need for an ongoing and sustainable commitment to reconstruction that guards against the tendency for catastrophes to be exploited in ways that produce further disenfranchisement. Postcolonial disasters are not "problems" to be "solved"; rather, they are compound processes that demand attention to systemic factors, colonial histories and – no less importantly – forms of creative response. The significance of this is apparent from how Brathwaite refuses to reject entirely the discourse of solutions but instead reconstitutes it so as to place cultural and endogenous perspectives at its core, suggesting that meaningful reconstruction is not just participatory but must be attuned to the metaphysical and psychosocial needs of affected communities and environments. Transposing the term "solution" – with its dark historical resonances – to "soulution" is much more than a semantic sleight. It is an invitation to orient disaster studies away from its complicities with militarism, neocolonialism and capitalist exploitation, and towards the emancipatory vision of recovery and healing that Brathwaite avows. It is also a way of anticipating a shift towards more open systems of analysis and response that are consonant with postcolonial critique. Such transformation – at once linguistic and conceptual – is essential for strengthening the claims of postcolonialism and disaster studies to progressive mitigation, and is part of the work of decolonization on which the reduction of global vulnerability depends.

ACKNOWLEDGMENTS

The research for this chapter was supported by a Fellowship at the Rachel Carson Center for Environment and Society, Ludwig-Maximilians-Universität, and by the Arts and Humanities Research Council (UK). Thanks also to Routledge and my co-editors (Elizabeth DeLoughrey and Jill Didur) of *Global Ecologies and the Environmental Humanities: Postcolonial Approaches* (Routledge, 2015), which features a version of this chapter.

REFERENCES

Anderson, Mark. 2011. *Disaster Writing: The Cultural Politics of Catastrophe in Latin America*. Charlottesville: University of Virginia Press.

Bankoff, Greg. 2003. *Cultures of Disaster: Society and Natural Hazards in the Philippines*. London and New York: Routledge.

Berger, Gregory and Ben Wisner. 2013. "Hazards and Disasters Represented in Film". In *Handbook of Hazards and Disaster Risk Reduction*, edited by Ben Wisner, JC Gaillard and Ilan Kelman, 121–130. London and New York: Routledge, 2012.

Blanchot, Maurice. 1995 [1980]. *The Writing of the Disaster*. Translated by Ann Smock. Lincoln, NE: University of Nebraska Press.

Bolin, Bob. 2007. "Race, Class, Ethnicity and Disaster Vulnerability". In *Handbook of Disaster Research*, edited by Havidán Rodríguez, Enrico Quarantelli and Russell Dynes, 113–129. New York: Springer.

Brathwaite, Kamau. 1984. *History of the Voice: The Development of Nation Language in Anglophone Caribbean Poetry*. London: New Beacon.

Brathwaite, Kamau. 1990. "History, the Caribbean Writer, and *X/Self*". In *Crisis and Creativity in the New Literatures in English*, edited by Geoffrey Davis and Hena Maes-Jelinek, 23–45. Amsterdam: Rodopi.

Brathwaite, Kamau. 2002. *MR*. New York: Savacou North.

Brathwaite, Kamau. 2005. "CP No News is Not Good Newes". *Save CowPastor*. 4 September 2013. http://tomraworth.com/augupdate.html.

Brathwaite, Kamau. 2006. "Preface". In *Volcano: A Memoir* by Yvonne Weekes, 7. Leeds: Peepal Tree.

Brathwaite, Kamau. 2010. *Elegguas*. Middletown, CT: Wesleyan University Press.

Brathwaite, Kamau and Natasha Sajé. 2009. "KB in Utah". *Ariel* 40.2–3: 203–274.

Britton, Neil. 2005. "What's A Word? Opening Up The Debate". In *What is a Disaster? New Answers to Old Questions*, edited by Ronald Perry and Enrico Quarantelli, 113–121. Philadelphia: Xlibris.

Carrigan, Anthony. 2010. "Postcolonial Disaster, Pacific Nuclearization, and Disabling Environments". *Journal of Literary and Cultural Disability Studies* 4.3: 255–272.

Carrigan, Anthony. 2011. "(Eco)Catastrophe, Reconstruction, and Representation: Montserrat and the Limits of Sustainability". *New Literatures Review* 47–48: 111–128.

Collins, Andrew. 2009. *Disaster and Development*. London and New York: Routledge.

Davis, Mike. 1995. "Los Angeles After the Storm: The Dialectic of Ordinary Disaster". *Antipode* 27.3: 221–241.

Davis, Mike. 2001. *Late Victorian Holocausts: El Niño Famines and the Making of the Third World*. London: Verso.

DeLoughrey, Elizabeth, Renée Gosson and George Handley. 2005. "Introduction". In *Caribbean Literature and the Environment: Between Nature and Culture*, edited by Elizabeth DeLoughrey, Renée Gosson and George Handley, 1–30. Charlottesville: University of Virginia Press.

Emmerich, Roland. 2004. Dir. *The Day After Tomorrow*. 20th Century Fox.

Franks, Suzanne. 2013. *Reporting Disasters: Famine, Aid, Politics and the Media*. London: Hurst.

Gilbert, Claude. 1998. "Studying Disaster: Changes in the Main Conceptual Tools". In *What Is a Disaster?: Perspectives on the Question*, edited by Enrico Quarantelli, 11–18. London and New York: Routledge.

Gregory, Derek. 2004. *The Colonial Present*. Oxford: Blackwell.

Hewitt, Kenneth. 1995. "Sustainable Disasters? Perspectives and Powers in the Discourse of Calamity". In *Power of Development*, edited by Jonathan Crush, 115–128. London and New York: Routledge.

Hewitt, Kenneth. 1998. "Excluded Perspectives in the Social Construction of Disaster". In *What Is a Disaster? Perspectives on the Question*, edited by Enrico Quarantelli, 71–88. London and New York: Routledge, 1998.

Hilhorst, Dorothea, ed. 2013. *Disaster, Conflict and Society in Crises: Everyday Politics of Crisis Response*. London and New York: Routledge.

Hilhorst, Dorothea and Greg Bankoff. 2004. "Introduction: Mapping Vulnerability". In *Mapping Vulnerability: Disasters, Development and People*, edited by Greg Bankoff, Georg Frerks and Dorothea Hilhorst, 1–9. London: Earthscan.

Hoffman, Susanna and Anthony Oliver-Smith, eds. 2002. *Culture and Catastrophe: The Anthropology of Disaster*. Santa Fe: School of American Research Press.

Jennings, Christine. 2013. "From Bosnia to Syria: The Investigators Identifying Victims of Genocide". *The Guardian*. 13 November. http://www.theguardian.com/law/2013/nov/10/bosnia-syria-victims-of-genocide-dna.

Kelman, Ilan. 2003. "Beyond Disaster, Beyond Diplomacy". In *Natural Disaster and Development in a Globalizing World*, edited by Mark Pelling, 110–123. London and New York: Routledge.

Kelman, Ilan. 2012. *Disaster Diplomacy: How Disasters Affect Peace and Conflict*. London and New York: Routledge.

Kelman, Ilan, Jessica Mercer and JC Gaillard. 2012. "Indigenous Knowledge and Disaster Risk Reduction". *Geography* 97.1: 12–21.

Klein, Naomi. 2007. *The Shock Doctrine: The Rise of Disaster Capitalism*. London: Allen Lane.

Lewis, James. 1999. *Development in Disaster-prone Places: Studies of Vulnerability*. London: Intermediate Technology Publications.

Mascarenhas, Adolfo and Ben Wisner. 2012. "Politics: Power and Disasters". In *Handbook of Hazards and Disaster Risk Reduction*, edited by Ben Wisner, JC Gaillard and Ilan Kelman, 48–60. London and New York: Routledge.

McCarthy, Cormac. 2006. *The Road*. London: Picador.

McRuer, Robert. 2010. "Reflections on Disability in Haiti". *Journal of Literary and Cultural Disability Studies* 4.3: 327–332.

McSweeney, Joyelle. 2005. "Poetics, Revelations, and Catastrophes: An Interview with Kamau Brathwaite". *Rain Taxi Review of Books*. 4 September. http://www. raintaxi.com/online/2005fall/brathwaite.shtml.

Mirzoeff, Nicholas. 2005. "Invisible Again: Rwanda and Representation after Genocide". *African Arts* 38.3: 36–39; 86–95.

Mukherjee, Upamanyu Pablo. 2013. *Natural Disasters and Victorian Empire: Famines, Fevers and the Literary Cultures of South Asia*. Basingstoke, UK: Palgrave Macmillan.

Nixon, Rob. 2011. *Slow Violence and the Environmentalism of the Poor*. Harvard: Harvard University Press.

O'Dempsey, Tim and Barry Munslow. 2006. "Globalisation, Complex Humanitarian Emergencies and Health". *Annals of Tropical Medicine and Parasitology* 100.5–6: 501–515.

Oliver-Smith, Anthony. 1994. "Peru's Five Hundred Year Earthquake: Vulnerability in Historical Context". In *Disasters, Development and Environment*, edited by Ann Varley, 31–48. Chichester: Wiley.

Oliver-Smith, Anthony. 1998. "Global Changes and the Definition of Disaster". In *What Is a Disaster? Perspectives on the Question*, edited by Enrico Quarantelli, 177–194. London and New York: Routledge.

Oliver-Smith, Anthony. 2004. "Theorizing Vulnerability in a Globalized World: A Political Ecological Perspective". In *Mapping Vulnerability: Disasters, Development and People*, Edited by Greg Bankoff, Georg Frerks and Dorothea Hilhorst, 10–24. London: Earthscan.

Oliver-Smith, Anthony and Susanna Hoffman, eds. 1998. *The Angry Earth: Disasters in Anthropological Perspective*. London and New York: Routledge.

Quarantelli, Enrico. 1998a. "Introduction: The Basic Question, Its Importance, and How it is Addressed in this Volume". In *What Is a Disaster? Perspectives on the Question*, edited by Enrico Quarantelli, xii–xviii. London and New York: Routledge.

Quarantelli, Enrico. 1998b. "Epilogue: Where We Have Been and Where We Might Go". In *What Is a Disaster? Perspectives on the Question*, edited by Enrico Quarantelli, 234–273. London and New York: Routledge.

Pelling, Mark, ed. 2003. *Natural Disaster and Development in a Globalizing World*. London and New York: Routledge.

Perry, Ronald. 2007. "What is a Disaster?" In *Handbook of Disaster Research*, edited by Havidán Rodríguez, Enrico Quarantelli and Russell Dynes, 1–15. New York: Springer.

Ross, Andrew. 1991. *Strange Weather: Culture, Science and Technology in an Age of Limits*. London: Verso.

Sachs, Wolfgang. 1993. "Global Ecology and the Shadow of 'Development'". In *Global Ecology: A New Arena of Political Conflict*, ed. Wolfgang Sachs, 3–21. London: Zed.

Sachs, Wolfgang. 1999. *Planet Dialectics: Explorations in Environment and Development*. London: Zed.

Scanlon, T. Joseph. 2005. "Foreword". In *What is a Disaster? New Answers to Old Questions*, edited by Ronald Perry and Enrico Quarantelli, 13–18. Philadelphia: Xlibris.

Shaw, Rajib, Anshu Sharma and Yukio Takeuchi, eds. 2009. *Indigenous Knowledge and Disaster Risk Reduction: From Practice to Policy*. New York: Nova.

Small Axe Project. 2011. "The Visual Life of Catastrophic History: A Small Axe Project Statement". *Small Axe* 15.1: 133–136.

Smith, Gavin and Dennis Wenger. 2007. "Sustainable Disaster Recovery: Operationalizing an Existing Agenda". In *Handbook of Disaster Research*, edited by Havidán Rodríguez, Enrico Quarantelli and Russell Dynes, 234–247. New York: Springer.

Stallings, Robert. 2005. "Disaster, Crisis, Collective Stress, and Mass Deprivation". In *What is a Disaster? New Answers to Old Questions*, edited by Ronald Perry and Enrico Quarantelli, 237–274. Philadelphia: Xlibris.

Stoler, Ann. 2008. "Imperial Debris: Reflections on Ruins and Ruination". *Cultural Anthropology* 23.2: 191–219.

Webb, Gary R. 2007. "The Popular Culture of Disaster: Exploring a New Dimension of Disaster Research". In *Handbook of Disaster Research*, edited by Havidán Rodríguez, Enrico Quarantelli and Russell Dynes, 430–440. New York: Springer.

Wisner, Ben, Piers Blaikie, Terry Cannon and Ian Davis, eds. 2004. *At Risk: Natural Hazards, People's Vulnerability and Disasters*. 2nd ed. London and New York: Routledge.

Wisner, Ben, JC Gaillard and Ilan Kelman. 2012. "Challenging Risk". In *Handbook of Hazards and Disaster Risk Reduction*, edited by BenWisner, JC Gaillard and Ilan Kelman, 1–8. London and New York: Routledge.

World Bank. 2014. "Disaster Risk Management Overview". *The World Bank: IRBD IDA*. 25 March 2014. http://www.worldbank.org/en/topic/disasterriskmanagement/overview#1.

Worster, Donald. 1994 [1977]. *Nature's Economy: A History of Ecological Ideas*. 2nd ed. Cambridge: Cambridge University Press.

13 Postcolonial Nature? Or, "If Oil Could Speak, What Would it Say?"

Crystal Bartolovich

Among Ed Kashi's (2008) arresting photographs documenting the ravaging effects of oil extraction in the Niger Delta are several images of women laying out little white mounds of tapioca to bake near menacing tongues of smoky flame thrusting out of oil pipes. These gas flares are not an aberration but a standard industrial practice. When petroleum is tapped, natural gas is often dissolved in it or layered above it. For the oil corporations, it is often cheaper and more convenient to simply burn off this gas than to collect and sell it. Thus even the extraction of oil contributes massive amounts of CO_2 to the atmosphere well before refined fossil fuel residue spews out of vehicle exhaust pipes. Furthermore, this byproduct of oil drilling would be entirely wasted if it were not for the ad hoc transformation of the flares into communal kitchens by the poor.

Kashi's images testify to the remarkable capacity of people to turn adversity to advantage. At the same time, though, the admirable efforts of rural villagers and urban squatters to "make do" can exact terrible costs that romanticizing advocates of such practices (see McClellan 2012) typically fail to take into account. In the case of the oil-pipe ovens, for example, petro-toxins seep slowly, relentlessly into the food, as well as the soil, water and air, wreaking what Rob Nixon (2011) evocatively calls "slow violence" on the inhabitants whose life expectancy and quality of life are lowered dramatically. Nor can we distance ourselves from this violence when we turn the pages of Kashi's book to discover familiar oil company logos emblazoned on the uniforms of machete-wielding guards and the hard hats of engineers. Foreign as the scene of collective cookery at an oil well may be to readers in the global North, our encounter with the logos that we drive past every day shatters distance, linking us, disturbingly, to the scene.

Indeed, for those of us living in the parts of the world where politicians tell us that "foreign oil" means "dependency" on the Middle East and other oil-rich countries like Nigeria that threaten our "way of life", the images of depredation and survival Kashi captures demand a reversal of perspective. For the peoples who suffer the costs of oil extraction and refining while benefiting little or not at all from them, it's not the oil that is "foreign" but the corporations, not "dependency" on other countries' resources that poses a threat but economic and political dependencies imposed by global uneven development. Not just their way of life but their lives are under threat.

Thinking about these global relations is difficult. Their truths are often best seized in art, like Kashi's, that powerfully undermines our capacity to abjure complicity or prescribe easy answers. To tease out some of these truths, I will discuss here Patrick Chamoiseu's *Texaco* (1997; 1992), a novel in which the global conditions of oil use and abuse – as well as the aspiration to an alternative that I will call the "common" – has been captured evocatively, all the more so because oil is marginal to the book, despite its title. This is the case because the novel focuses on the lives of the poor, who do not drive cars and have no, or only sporadic and hacked, links to the power grid. For them, oil is primarily an odor, albeit an insistent one. "The gasoline smell made me open my eyes", observes the narrator, Marie-Sophie Laborieux, "a persistent smell going through your bones. That smell would never leave my life" (286). At this point in the narrative, Marie-Sophie has been taken to a healer's hut built on the fringes of an oil depot to recover from a severe depression. As she regains health and strength, she invades the "oil company's domain" and builds a hut there, eventually attracting other settlers to the place (297). Having established their camp, the squatters' struggle for "Texaco" ensues – a struggle permeated inextricably by the odor of oil, as the narrative reminds us every so often. Its constant presence raises the question of oil's role in the struggle, and why Chamoiseau figures it via "Texaco".

He does so, I will show, in order to underscore that the enclosure of resources for globally disproportionate use renders the inhabitants of rich countries complicit with the oppression of the world's poorest peoples, for whom the odor of oil – and the "slow violence" of which it is a sign – is far more familiar than the use of it in any form. Between these two groups lie the sleek fleets of tankers and the tasteful boardrooms of Total, Shell and Texaco (now Chevron). In Chamoiseau's novel, as in Kashi's photographs, the corporate name offers a starting place for confronting mediation – the capitalist relations of trade and consumption, politics and culture that link distant as well as nearby peoples and objects unevenly. As Timothy Mitchell (2011) reminds us, "[L]eading industrial countries [...] have developed ways of eating, travelling, housing themselves and consuming other goods and services that require very large amounts of energy from oil and other fossil fuels". However, this recognition does not prevent him from also asserting that "*humankind*" has "within a few generations" steadily depleted stocks of fossil fuel "that has accumulated in the earth over [...] 500 million years", unsettling delicate ecological balances as it does so (6, emphasis mine). This slippage from "leading industrial countries" to "humanity" is not an accident of phrase, I suggest, but is encouraged and enabled by Mitchell's network approach that, having junked mediation, loses the ability to disaggregate humanity in terms of planetary relations of oppression.

The vast majority of humankind has, of course, not depleted stocks of fossil fuel. The full benefits of oil's use and profits have been realized by only a tiny fraction of humanity – though the costs, of course, have been far more widely, albeit also unevenly, distributed, falling most heavily on those who derive none of the benefits, or comparatively few. Even now, 1.3 billion people – one-fifth of the global population – have no access to electricity at all, and two-fifths still rely on wood, charcoal or animal dung for cooking (IEA 2012, 7; Practical Action 2013). In large swathes of the underdeveloped world, nearly half the schools and clinics function without reliable access to electricity. In such communities, energy poverty remains one of the most dramatic signs of global uneven-ness. At the same time, the deleterious effects of global warming, extreme weather patterns and pollution of air, water and soil impact the poor far more than the wealthy. In this planetary uneven-ness the postcolonial and ecological meet, urgently raising the question of "Postcolonial Nature" in my title.

It would be wide of the mark to suggest that eco-criticism of oil belongs to the set of things about which postcolonial studies has had nothing to say, given the influential work of Ken Saro-Wiwa (1992), Fernando Coronil (1997), Ato Quayson (2003) and Imre Szeman (2007), as well as Mitchell (on postcolonial eco-criticism more generally see Huggan and Tiffin 2010). Bringing *Texaco* into this conversation, I show that a materialist position of a specific kind – Adorno's understanding of "Nature" and "Capitalism" as critical concepts – offers a formidable and necessary alternative to Bruno Latour's (2004) contention that "Nature" and "Capitalism" are neither descriptive of reality nor useful as concepts, a position that has influenced postcolonial critics such as Mitchell. A Marxist position, alternatively, insists that we understand "nature" – like "labor" – in the systemic terms of the mode of production in which it is deployed. Currently, oil is corporately enclosed, but if we did not take this planetary condition as a given, we could understand oil and other planetary resources to be properly common so that the injustice of fossil-fuel capitalism might be properly assessed – and transformed (Harvey 2003). While network approaches can enrich our understanding of local complexities and specificity, they necessarily fail at what mediation does best: foregrounding relations of exploitation not only locally but globally.

In the following section, I lay out some of the problems with current "oil talk", as Michael Watts (2013) has called it, especially its characterization of oil as "foreign". I then bring *Texaco* into the discussion to show how it intervenes in this oil talk by revealing corporations to be foreign rather than oil. My conclusion extends this observation by underscoring that corporations are foreign to the just, sustainable way of life that we – collectively, planetarily – might live, even for those of us who currently benefit, relatively, from uneven global development.

FOLLOW THE CARBON

Mitchell's *Carbon Democracy* (2011) enjoins us to "follow the carbon", although, for him (as for Latour), the thingly concreteness of coal or oil does not entail "replacing [...] idealist schemes with a materialist account" (7). Indeed, Mitchell specifically rejects "materialist account[s]" (physicalist or Marxist) in favor of network analysis that, he claims, does not "respect any divide between material and ideal, economic and political, natural and social, human and nonhuman, or violence and representation". Attempting to undermine binaries is hardly a novelty. Much depends, however, on whether we interrogate the "divide" Mitchell points to from a Latourian or a dialectical perspective. Like Michael Watts (2013; see also Huber 2013), I find Mitchell's book suggestive in many of its local arguments but emphatically not in its assertion that there is no "logic of capitalism" at work in global terms today (Mitchell 2011, 230).

To "follow the carbon", in my view, means we cannot evade a materialist account in the Marxist sense. This is so precisely because the global logic of capital – the profit imperative – enforces reifications, shores up corporate enclosures, hegemonizes resistances and operates through local and global unevenness, though not always in the same ways or with equal success in each particular. Indeed, with the same ferocity that it enforces reifications, it explodes them at the level of individual instances or absorbs tactical defeat in singular cases in order to extend its hegemony all the more thoroughly ("all that is solid melts into air"). Given the flexibility of capitalism, its global logic is not in any respect undermined by descriptions that declare the divide between the binaries it materially enforces to be null (Bartolovich 2002). Only changing the conditions would accomplish that. Nevertheless, attempting to listen to an object like oil through the din produced by a commodified world, while no easy matter, is a tactic that Adorno viewed as particularly fruitful in assessing structural conditions in order to change them.

Marx thought so too. Many readers will probably already have recognized my title as an allusion to the conclusion of the first chapter of *Capital* 1 in which Marx (1990) observes:

> If commodities could speak, they would say this: our use-value may interest men, but it does not belong to us as objects. What does belong to us as objects, however, is our value. Our own intercourse as commodities proves it. We relate to each other merely as exchange values. (176–177)

With derision, Marx then quotes passages from mainstream political economists who write as if, he says, "commodities [were] speak[ing] through their mouth[s]". One, for example, explains that "Riches (use-value[s]) are the attribute of man, value is the attribute of commodities. A man or a community is rich, a pearl or a diamond is valuable [...] as a pearl or diamond". Marx concludes that because they assume that "commodities" are "natural", bourgeois economists misrecognize the status of such objects in capitalist society, falsely attributing social aspects to them. "So far", Marx points out, "no chemist has ever discovered exchange value either in a pearl or a diamond. The economists who have discovered this chemical substance [...] nevertheless find that the use value of material objects belongs to them independently of their material properties, while their value, on the other hand, forms a part of them as objects". His point is that commodities do not speak but that bourgeois economists transform them into ventriloquists dummies of their own projections when they attribute human qualities to them.

Marx mocks the anthropomorphizing of commodities but having demystified the speaking commodity, he nonetheless leaves open the possibility that the "non-human" can be more or other than merely a tool of, or means for, the human, as John Bellamy Foster (2000) proposes. This latter project propels us to ask: Can an object – as opposed to the commodity – speak? That is to say, is there a role for the non-human in the struggles among "ideological forms" Marx famously described as the sites "in which men become conscious of [...] conflict and fight it out"? Arjun Appadurai's (1988) ruminations on the "Social Life of Things", Latour's (2005) vision of the "Parliament of things" and countless other attempts at "thing theory" (Brown 2004) have offered themselves as advocates for things. However, listening to things over the din of commodities is not so easy. Under conditions of capitalism, giving things a voice often ends up speaking for commodities in the very ways Marx warned us against, as Bruce Robbins (2005) suggests in his study of the recent proliferation of "commodity histories". Along these lines, it is telling that when Latour (1996) gives "Aramis", the proposed French transit system, a "voice" in his book of that title, "Aramis" (unsurprisingly) speaks as a Latourian for whom systemic forces have no role. The Latourian thing does not critique capitalism any more than a bourgeois economist would. Latour tells many stories in that book but none of them interrogates systemic problems such as the gender politics of techno-culture, the corruption of politics and science by capitalism, the conditions of labor in which the transit project would have been built or the ecological impact that building it might have had on the planet and its inhabitants, locally or globally (how many rare-earth metals would be required, etc.?). Network approaches promote themselves as attentive to details, lavishly appreciative of the translations that occur at each node in a network. What they are incapable of doing, by definition, though, is attend to the structural impingements on each node imposed by capital. If we are to hear dissident objects – unassimilated to the capitalist world as it is – speak, we must take a different approach: Adorno's insistence on the "preponderance of the object".

It is worth remembering the particular way that "preponderance of the object" emerges in *Negative Dialectics* in relation to the section of Marx's *Capital* I have cited above. Adorno (1994) emphasizes that the fetish character of commodities is not explained by Marx to be an effect of "errant consciousness" but is, instead, "objectively deduced from the [...] exchange process" (190). In this way, according to Adorno, Marx indicates that he knows what philosophical idealism and mainstream thought alike do not: reification cannot be undermined in thought alone – that is to say, a process of reflection, however mobile and reflexive, cannot, in itself, budge it. Adorno makes this very clear: "the trouble is with the *conditions* that condemn mankind to impotence and apathy and would yet be changeable by human action; it is not primarily with people and with the way that conditions appear to people". In this sense, then, which by no means exhausts Adorno's use of the concept, an object is preponderant under conditions of capitalism, so long as those conditions inhere, because it resists, because it is irreducibly foreign to not only our concepts but also our transformative desires, which are limited by the conditions in which they emerge. For Adorno, the non-human world is, in fact, formidably expressive in its intransigence. And, in effect, what it says, again and again, is "No!" – a negation that might be translated more extensively as "We object(ion)s are the evidence that neither wishing nor ignorance can save you from the limits we impose, or silence the alternatives we propose!" This non-human "no" also carries with it the promise of an other or beyond to capitalism, the yet unknown realm of free-dom, which cannot be produced in thought but only in active struggle with (rather than against) the material conditions that say "no" to capitalism. This is the critical function of Adorno's insistence on the "preponderance of the object" that I would have us bring to bear on oil.

Adorno did not junk concepts but deployed them critically – using "nature" to critique "history", "human", "culture" and so on, but also the reverse. To simply stop using a concept critically while it still maintains power in the social order doesn't work. Latour proposes that if a bunch of us just stop using the word "nature" then the "new constitution" will be ratified and the happy world will follow. But nature is not just a trump card that scientists use to win arguments unfairly, as Latour claims, but also a material limit to human hubris and fantasy, a set of preponderant objects that resist and refuse our theoretical, technological, social, political and economic pretensions.

This is why the prevalent accusation of oil's foreign-ness can be demysti-fied (its contradictions exposed) by interrogating it in planetary and sys-temic terms, which, of course, mainstream political and economic discourse tends not to do, or to do only very selectively. Since the 1970s oil shocks, US politicians have frequently resorted to the phrase, saturated with resentment and fear, that "we" must free ourselves of "dependence on foreign oil". This phrase received especially strenuous use in Bush energy policy post-9/11, though Barack Obama's campaign speeches and press conferences, as well as the White House blog, continue to worry about "our dependence on for-eign oil" too.[1] Indeed, the Obama administration has favored the increased domestic extraction of fossil fuels so vigorously that Citigroup (2013) was able to declare the immanent prospect of US energy "self-sufficiency" in its *Energy 2020: Independence Day—Global Ripple Effects of the North American Energy Revolution*. The report proposes that the "dynamic duo" of Canada and the US will achieve the "supply miracle" that propels North America from the "largest [...] importer to self-sufficiency" with profound implications for the "geopolitics of energy" in the near future (12, 9, 3). While in Citi's fantasy, the US "would see its role as a singular superpower enhanced and prolonged", this would not permit "isolationism". To the contrary, the report emphasizes that "the national security borders of the US are effectively totally global", and frankly observes that, even if its own dependence on "foreign oil" wanes, "it is not in the US interest to allow China or any other potential rival control over these resources" (58–59, 9–10). At the same time, the fantasy of US power with which it associates "energy independence" has permeated numerous discourses, where "foreign oil" is associated with threats to the American Way of Life.

Oil transnationals tend to see things very differently. Ostensibly wrenching us from a merely parochial to a "global" perspective, a recent high profile (*The New York Times*, *The Economist*, etc.) advertising campaign for Chevron declares: "There are 193 countries in the world", and then insists that "None of them are energy independent", before asking, pointedly, "So who's holding whom over a barrel?" These revisionist declarations appear next to a chart that indicates Saudi Arabia, Norway, UAE and Nigeria all import gasoline and Russia imports coal, natural gas and electricity. A nearby map of "Global Oil Flows" implies, with its tangle of interconnecting arrows, that oil binds the world together, rather than isolating its regions in competitive menace. Extended copy underscores this visual message by proposing that while a handful of "energy-producing nations" have "won the geological lottery blessing them with abundant hydrocarbons", we must recognize that "even regions with plenty of raw resources import some form of energy". No nation, it informs us, matter of factly, is "independent".

It is of course not surprising that Chevron would see the world this way since dependence on oil today means dependence on oil corporations. While based in California, Chevron explains on its webpage that in 2008, "about 75 percent" of its oil production "occurred outside the United States".[2] From Chevron's point of view, how could oil be foreign when it flows together into a single corporate reservoir from its "extensive oil and gas exploration and production operations around the world"? Thus, instead of dependence (which it has declared universal, in the sense of dependence on corporations) it identifies the energy problems confronting "us" all, globally, as "rising demand, supply disruptions, natural disasters, and unstable regimes", and it offers a neoliberal solution to these unhappy conditions: "When investment and expertise are allowed to flow freely across borders, the engine of innovation is ignited, prosperity is fueled and the energy available to everyone increases". Here oil is not merely a commodity, it is the fundamental commodity that not only "ignites" and "fuels" the market as a whole but, miraculously, "increases", like the Biblical loaves and fishes, if we let the market do its work. We are thus reassured that "succeeding in securing energy for everyone doesn't have to come at the expense of anyone". I shall return to this question of "expense", but we must first further interrogate the issue of "foreign oil" and the ways in which Chevron encourages the sanctioned ignorance of inhabitants of the global North regarding fossil fuels, even as it assures us that all people inhabit the oil crisis alike.

We do not, of course, all inhabit the oil crisis alike, because we do not all inhabit the world alike. The US discourse of "foreign oil" – despite its implication that some hazy, distant "they" are irrationally or cruelly keeping "our" oil from "us" – emerges after all under material conditions of grossly disproportionate use. Although less than five percent of the global population, the US consumes at least twenty percent of the global daily oil output, the bulk of which goes towards fuel for transportation (BP 2012, 9). If my students are any indication, this stunning disproportion in global usage is not widely known, but once the immediate shock wears off – a rather different sort of oil shock than the one the media draws our attention to most frequently – the global imbalance in resource use does not appear to strike its most intensive users as unjust. When the market is taken to be a "natural" means of allocating resources, and "we" pay for gasoline, the transactions can be rationalized as "fair".

An ability to listen over the din of politicians and public-relations specialists for oil's opinion on this subject would be helpful. Manifestly, and despite the industry and nationalist discourse to the contrary, oil is crying out, "No! This way of doing things cannot go on!" to us ever more insistently, simply by the increasing difficulty it imposes to extraction and the environmental and social costs of both drilling and use. The price of oil, however, by no means reflects these total global costs and thus, irreducibly, the behavior of the multitude of automobile drivers in the US puts us all in relations of complicity with the conditions of environmental degradation, war, economic corruption and ecosystem destruction on which oil-centered economies depend – that is, the very world that cannot continue in perpetuity.

However, if you surmised from Chevron's adoption of a variation on "we are the world" discourse to combat "foreign oil" fears in the global North that it advocates more equitable distribution of common global resources, or makes common cause with oil's own case for alternatives, you would, of course, be disappointed. It turns out that their assumptions about distribution and use, if not their preferred idiom for describing it, are not so different from mainstream political discourse in the US. The directions for a SimCity-type game, "Energyville", developed for Chevron's website by The Economist Group, for example, explains to players that "the implications of the energy decisions you make today for your city in 2020 are based on *current lifestyles* and the projected energy demands and costs *for developed countries throughout North America, Europe and Asia*" (emphasis mine) – a vision of the globe that obviously takes current disproportionate use as a given.[3] With one hand, then, Chevron naturalizes globally disproportionate energy consumption in the game while, with the other, it seeks in advertisements to soothe the concerns and resentments that ensue because the "countries" who reap most of the benefits of "cheap energy" and those who pay most of its costs do not correspond.

When we shift our gaze from the empyrean heights of the transnational corporations, who translate any local "dependence on foreign oil" to a general global dependence on their services, to the situation on the ground in those nations "blessed", as Chevron tells us, with "abundant hydrocarbons", a different definition of foreign oil emerges to contest corporate assertions. In sites such as the Niger Delta or the Caribbean, regions that have been in litigation (and other forms of resistance) with oil transnationals for years in a quest for redress for the devastation of their economies and ecologies, "foreign oil" refers not to the substance in the ground but to the corporations, such as Chevron, that come in from the outside to profit from it. These are the sites that bear the brunt of the environmental damage of oil drilling and the misery and social unrest of the economies it skews, while deriving none of the benefits of "cheap" energy, often becoming instead pawns in geopolitics. A dramatic case in point is the Ecuadorian rain forest, where Texaco was engaged in exploration and drilling operations with the state oil company Petroecuador in the 1970s and '80s. Chevron inherited a multi-billion-dollar reparations suit after it merged with Texaco at the turn of the millenium, and has been increasingly fierce in its denial of responsibility.[4] Meanwhile, the inhabitants of the Ecuadorian Amazon continue to struggle with toxic residue and blight. While elites fight out who will profit and who will pay, the poor and nature continue to suffer. A network approach, indifferent or suspicious of the global logic of capital, simply cannot adequately assess this situation. No matter how many nodes it traces, it loses sight of the capitalist conditions that impinge on them all. This is not the case with a novel like *Texaco*.

TEXACO

Patrick Chamoiseau's *Texaco* brilliantly evokes the threat of foreign intervention by transnationals while keeping the focus squarely on the experience of the poorest inhabitants of Martinique as they struggle valiantly to make lives for themselves under trying conditions at best. Written in a challenging mix of French and Creole, the novel subtly demonstrates a relation of global and local, colonizer and colonized, in the linguistic effect it produces. While this linguistic "créolité" has been much commented upon by critics, I am more interested in the studies that take a politico-economic rather than a postmodern approach (see, for example, Dawson 2004). Intriguingly, though the title puts the machinations of transnational capital at center stage, these forces remain as shadowy in the novel as they are, for the most part, in everyday life for most people in the global North or South. To be sure, their effects are experienced, but at a considerable distance from the decision-making processes that set them in motion, processes that thus remain largely invisible. Indeed, in its corporate form, Texaco is utterly marginalized in the novel, which traces the history and pre-history of a battle for an abandoned oil depot that is reinscribed by the indigenous poor as a settlement on the outskirts of "City", the "pedestal", as the novel's heroine, Marie-Sophie calls it, "of the rare things which bettered life", from which she and her comrades have been systematically excluded (316). She explains early on that as an active site of business, the corporation "Texaco [...] had left aeons ago". All that remains is the "smell of stale oil" and the bare minimum of infrastructure and staff to "keep one foot on the dear property". This absent presence is a figure in the novel of global forces that alienate and undermine local populations, against which the poor form "our very own Texaco, a company in the business of survival" (24). For Marie-Sophie and the other squatters, the land and life occupied by "Texaco", as well as by "City" more generally, have been rendered alien and forbidding by their corporate and bureaucratic enclosure.

Though a few critics have noted the eco-critical implications of these local and global relations, none has done so adequately, in my view. Richard Watts (2008) deals with *Texaco* briefly in his exploration of texts "that suggest a productive resolution of the tension" between ecocriticsm and postcolonial studies (253). For Watts, *Texaco* is preoccupied with "the persistent reshaping of Martinique's natural ecology by the centre" to which the squatter camp is a form of resistance that Watts takes to be (over-romantically in my view) "ecologically balanced" (257). Eric Prieto (2005) seems more correct when he observes that "it is far from clear that the cultural practices of Chamoiseau's Creoles are allied to ecological wisdom in any essential way", and that "Chamoiseau is ultimately more interested in understanding the adaptive strategies that have enabled Creole culture to survive than in extolling the virtues of the natural environment" (242–243). His treatment of the novel is very brief, however. Most recently, Michael K. Walonen (2012) discusses *Texaco* in an overview of a number of "texts from disparate cultural and linguistic traditions in terms of their responses to a common global and globalizing situation" of oil's extraction, refining and use – an intriguing and potentially excellent project (58). Unfortunately, like Watts, Walonen is somewhat given to romanticization in his reading of *Texaco* which he claims shows that "no matter how vast and powerful the corporate machinery of big oil might seem, [it is] in the end no more formidable than the will of the people", which is, alas, certainly not the case in the real world nor, I think, in the novel. In any case, Walonen, is certainly wrong that *Texaco* deals with a site in which the "oil extraction process" is relevant, since Martinique has no oil.

A word is in order here about the actual historical relation of "Texaco" to Martinique, since it is all too easy for the metropolitan reader – even one critical of unevenness – to assume that the South is everywhere alike. Martinique, however, has no oil at all, so it differs from the Niger Delta or the Ecuadorian Amazon in relation to oil corporations. The various oil depots that Marie-Sophie describes are not drilling operations but storage and refining facilities, mostly for the domestic market. They were located on the coasts because oil was imported to them, of course, but also because earlier generations of elite urban dwellers in Fort de France thought of the waterfronts as "unhealthy, repulsive swamps" and thus left them to ports, industry and squatters (Gidel 2011, 35). Further complicating the local politics of oil is the status of Martinique as a French Overseas Department since 1946. Even now, two-thirds of its trade is with mainland France. Oil is no exception. Though the politics of oil in general in the Caribbean have been strongly bound up with production for the United States, this was not the case for the French islands. There colonial elites viewed production for the local market as a strategic necessity in the Cold War period and, also, as vital to development policy for the island, which kept it solidly oriented towards Europe rather than the US.[5] Thus the bulk of the oil franchise in Martinique was, from the start, held by French companies.[6] This is still the case, though a series of other oil transnationals, including Texaco, have held relatively small stakes at different times. For readers virtually anywhere, though, "Texaco" would be immediately recognizable, despite its relatively marginal position in Martinique and its absorption by Chevron in 2000. This is all the more so because "Texaco" also refers to an actual slum on the periphery of Fort de France that exists to this day, one that had been brought to metropolitan attention in 1992 through a widely circulated book by Serge Letchimy.[7]

Texaco's resonant name, effected by the oil corporation's broad transnational reach, helps the novel suggest that the struggles of the squatters take place on several scales at once. As the squatters labor to make land common by resisting its corporate enclosure, they meet global resistance represented by watchmen, fences and other traces of corporate presence. The struggle with the traces of the foreign corporation links to a long history of resistance to colonialism, imperialism, slavery and other depredations narrated in previous chapters, a history that insists on a global dimension as well as the local for all of these struggles. On the one hand, the novel underscores the admirable capacity for survival of the squatters and their ancestors against so many formidable adversaries. On the other, it illustrates the imbrication of "City" – where the gasoline produced (from imported oil) by the coastal refineries is actually used – with global forces. "City" establishes its local privilege by inserting itself into relations with France, capitalism – and oil – in particular ways.

Significantly, the Texaco squatters only come to the attention of the "City" authorities when a road is built alongside it. This is, in fact, nearly the first thing we are told in the novel:

> … a road called Petetrante West had joined our Quarter to the center of City. That is why the ever-so-well-to-do *from the depths of their cars* had discovered our piled-up hutches which they said were insalubrious – and such a spectacle seemed to them contrary to the public order. (9–10, emphasis mine)

This marginality does not of course mean that the labor and capacities of the squatters were not already tapped, and would continue to be, by "City" but rather that the exchange was unequal. The politics of oil might be bound up with the French colonial past and a present dominated by transnational corporations but "City" is the site of exclusion and inequality in which the global battle is fought most immediately.

Hence, when Marie-Sophie eventually establishes her first claim on Texaco by erecting a tent there, she is confronted by a watchman, whose attempt to expel her she describes thus: "[I]t was through his voice that City was addressing me directly for the first time with its millennial *no*". The exasperated guard protests: "You black people really are no good, the beke puts his things here peacefully, asking nothing from no one, and here you come set your hutch right next to *his* things! As if there was no other space left in the world!" (298, emphasis mine). Marie-Sophie, however, refuses to budge and challenges him: "When the beke came to settle here did you go up to him to tell him what you're telling me here?" To (re)claim corporately enclosed "Texaco", Marie-Sophie makes clear, is to refuse to be excluded and to insist upon the earth and its resources as common – not only for people but in common with the planet. Thus, in reclaimed "Texaco", "each hutch, day after day, supported the other and so on. The same went for the lives which reached out to each other over the ghost fences writhing on the ground. In our mind, the soil under the houses remained strangely free, *definitively free [définitivement libre]*" (319; 409).

This common world in which the land – one might call it a preponderant object – remains "definitively free" becomes the struggled-for alternative to the corporately (or nationally) enclosed world. In subtle ways such as this, though the novel is not thematically or polemically ecological to any great extent, it opens a space to imagine a common world in which nature does not exist for humans alone: "We were part of the cliff in Upper Texaco", Marie-Sophie explains. However, because the "ghostly fences" are the traces of real social forces at work in the world, global and local, the encampment, with its "free" soil, maintains itself only by way of very hard struggle, which is not even fully accomplished by the novel's end. And one cannot romanticize it, first of all because it would have been better for the struggle not to be necessary and second, because by no means is "Texaco" depicted as a site to be preserved as a shining example of ecological balance. Marie-Sophie observes the triumphs but also the depredations – for example, the piles of garbage that accumulate because "everyone thought that, just like in the countryside, nature would digest the refuse" but it does not. She laments that she "would have liked to put together a few hands to take care of all that, but there were a thousand wars to wage merely to exist" (320). Existence is not futile, but it is not always pretty – or sustainable – under the conditions in which people find themselves. Indeed, when we turn to the last page of the novel, the give and take between "City" and an occupied "Texaco" has only just begun in an official sense, a process that cannot run smoothly because it provokes a transformation of "City" as much as "Texaco".

The anonymous urban planner to whom Marie-Sophie tells her story in a successful attempt to prevent the destruction of the squatter encampment describes the struggle this way: "The Western urban planner sees Texaco [the shanty town not the corporation] as a tumor on the urban order. [...] A dynamic contestation [...] denied any architectural or social value [...] a problem. But to raze it is to send the problem elsewhere or worse: not to consider it". So, he continues, tellingly: "No, we must dismiss the West [*l'Occident*] and re-learn to read: learn to re-invent the city" (269, 345). The work of the novel is to display to readers that the value of the reinscribed Texaco, the energy, hopes, dreams and talents of its inhabitants, must be brought to "City" to transform it, not simply to be absorbed or excluded. The urban planner's "No" – this time ventriloquizing the excluded instead of "City" – confronts (and inverts) the "No" with which "City", in the mouth of the hegemonized corporate watchman, earlier warned squatters away. "Texaco" being the site of such a struggle is of the utmost significance. The dominance of the foreign West and its corporate entities must be dismissed so that an alternative development can occur. Yet, for all the emphasis of the novel on the politics of language and the power of words, it also shows us – lest we mistakenly think, for example, that our reading of the novel is itself somehow a radical act – that "Texaco" can only be displaced through direct occupation and physical recoding of its putative space – the transformation, that is, of material conditions: the local and global relations that maintain uneven planetary divisions of costs and benefits.

PAYING THE PRICE

As *Texaco* eloquently protests, we cannot permanently set aside consideration of the issue of expense I suspended earlier. The price at the pump simply does not cover all the costs of oil. We have already seen the vast difference that point of view makes in the decoding of the phrase "foreign oil". The same circumstances that give rise to these vast differences in point of view also point to why the true price of oil is so difficult to calculate. Any commentator, on the right or left, North or South, will tell you oil dominates global energy markets at the moment because, even at over $80 or $100 a barrel, it is still the "cheapest" source. However, as with many prices, this one discounts the cost considerably, since what economists refer to as "negative externalities" are so conspicuously absent from it. What if the price of every barrel of oil included the costs of global warming and other environmental devastation? What if it included the costs of civil war, corrupt governments and undermined quality of life? What if it included the costs of a planet divided between haves and have-nots imposed by corporate enclosure of resources? To best approach questions like these, we need to deploy "foreign" as a critical concept.

Mitchell is right to question the divide Benjamin Barber (1995) sees between forces of corporate capital ("McWorld") and local "traditional" interests ("Jihad") and to propose that the situation in the Middle East is actually better described as "McJihad": alliances between oil corporations, intent on the production of scarcity (that is, controlling oil flow so that their rents from it are maintained at the highest possible rate), and a variety of local groups with disparate interests. It is odd, though, that he sees these alliances, however tenuous or conflicted, as evidence of the "absence of [...] a logic" to capitalism when the situation he describes is the familiar one of hegemony at work. Localities always make their own negotiated settlements with capital; that's what hegemony means. The "carbon copy" approach (assuming that all local situations can be settled the same way) that Mitchell argues against has not been a feature of sophisticated (Marxist, at least) analysis for decades, if ever. In any case, the apt term "McJihad" suggests in my view the opposite conclusion that Mitchell draws from it. Rather than the absence of a "logic", it indicates the flexible and dynamic attributes of capitalism that make it possible for corporations to further the interests of capital, despite the different balance of forces in each site or the fate of individual corporations in them.

Such lessons are instructive for inhabitants of privileged nations as well as the poor. Take, for example, the pundits at conservative US think tanks such as the Heritage Foundation, which, when it does its oil math, only counts the costs to Americans, who, it asserts "need answers [to the oil crisis] that will ensure the protection of *their* environment, the freedom and productivity of *their* economy, and the security of *their* lives and property".[8] They do not bother even to defend these assumptions; they take such possessive nationalism as a given. However, the oil corporation tactic of "production of scarcity" – well established by social scientists before Mitchell but used effectively by him – indicates the conflict between the nationalistic goals of even powerful countries and corporate interests. As economists explain, increased domestic production promoted by politicians in the US does not necessarily lead to cheaper prices at the pump.[9] Nor are the ecological costs of the fracking necessary to extract this domestic oil (water contamination, earthquakes and other environmental damage) accounted for by pundits intent on US security. From this point of view, the oil corporations are as foreign in relation to US domestic interests as they are in Nigeria or Afghanistan – though of course the corporations are forced to tread more lightly in the US, where environmental and other protections are greater, and local economic and political forces strong enough to exert some pressure on corporate power. While increased environmental and economic costs in the US should not distract us from global disparities, they still might contribute to a needful lesson concerning the foreign workings of corporate power in relation to relatively privileged populations as well as the most vulnerable ones.

The point is not to increase nationalist enclosure. If the goal is planetary social justice (Spivak 2003, 72), then oil must be seen as *common*, the critical concept we must bring to bear against both national and corporate enclosure. The savvy populist redistributions of oil wealth by the late Hugo Chavez should not blind us to this necessity.[10] Neoliberal claims to the contrary, the only fair and just way to distribute key resources is to make them common resources. Otherwise the haves will continue to benefit at the expense of the have nots, given the centrality of oil to capitalism as we know it. How to do this might be difficult to imagine, but is not impossible.

Like all concepts, however, "common" is not an answer (as it is sometimes problematically treated today) but a critical tool under conditions of capitalist enclosure. It is not a universal answer to injustice because it can, after all, be deployed by the privileged as well as the poor. Centuries ago, oceans were declared "common" by Hugo Grotius in his tortured arguments that sought to preserve private property while making a strategic case to open up the oceans (effectively enclosed by Portuguese and Spanish dominance) while European powers squabbled among themselves over shipping lanes and colonies. Today, as we have seen, Citigroup tells us that "the national security borders of the US are effectively totally global" – that is to say, the oceans are common in the limited sense that the stronger assert their rights to promote their interests in them freely. Like the ocean, oil is irreducibly necessary to the way of life of the rich nations. To move past the global inequality that underwrites that way of life, oil, as the oceans, must be managed globally, with an eye to costs as well as benefits for all concerned. However, true commonality is difficult to imagine in a capitalist world in which the corporate roar of commodities does its best to drown out the speaking of non-elite people and objects alike.

In such a world, "If oil could speak, what would it say?" As a "preponderant object", it has a certain mute Adornian eloquence and denies that the world can go on as it now does. What preponderant oil says, in brief, is "no", a "no" that keeps challenging commodification, corporate public-relations offices, US mainstream politics and even the "no" of "City" that attempts to undermine Chamoiseau's Marie-Sophie. The dissonance produced by the oily contradictions we inhabit globally and locally, though not all alike, emerge to full view when we "follow the carbon". In solidarity with Chamoiseau's urban planner, who would have the West "dismissed", it joins in the resistance to a world in which the only way to encounter oil is as a commodity, whose disproportionate and costly use seems just because the market says it is so. As long as geopolitics is structured in terms of possessive nationalism as well as corporate privatization, rather than a commoning of the planet in the interests of all peoples and the non-human world, oil will continue to say "no" to us by depletion and environmental degradation. Without heavy-handedly writing a novel about oil or even nature, Chamoiseau makes a space for this silent but eloquent "no", the cosmic shake of oil's preponderant head, to be recognized. This "no" points us towards a way of being that is not yet but could be: a common world that waits behind and beyond the corporate privatization and possessive nationalism that deform it – and us. To this other way of life, it is corporations, not nature or oil, that are foreign.

For opportunities to present earlier versions of this paper, I am grateful to Imre Szeman, Jennifer Wenzel and Anna Bernard.

NOTES

1. See for example: http://www.whitehouse.gov/the-press-office/updated-and-final-weekly-address-president-obama-calls-energy-bill-passage-critical; http://www.whitehouse.gov/blog/2012/03/01/our-dependence-foreign-oil-declining.
2. http://www.chevron.com/about/leadership/.
3. http://www.energyville.com/.
4. http://www.businessweek.com/articles/2013-05-03/plaintiffs-lawyers-jump-ship-in-pollution-fight-against-chevron#r=hpt-fs.
5. See the "historique" section of "La SARA", the French Caribbean oil conglomerate: http://www.sara.mq/RAF/sara.nsf/VS_OPM/A17CCDDA7EE5A62BC12573E200393D0D?OpenDocument; also see Mulchansingh (1971).
6. http://fr.wikipedia.org/wiki/Raffinerie_des_Antilles#Description_de_la_raffinerie.
7. Letchimy is a well-known politician in Martinique, having served in a number of key offices, including succeeding Aimé Césaire as mayor of Fort de France. Since 2010, he has been President of the Regional Council, the highest office in the French Department.
8. http://www.heritage.org/research/reports/2010/06/stopping-the-slick-saving-the-environment-a-framework-for-response-recovery-and-resiliency.
9. http://www.bloombergview.com/articles/2013-04-16/why-more-u-s-oil-may-not-mean-cheaper-u-s-gas.
10. See, for example, Fernando Coronil's ambivalent assessment of Chavez in *ReVista*: http://www.drclas.harvard.edu/publications/revistaonline/fall-2008/ch%C3%A1vez-venezuela.

REFERENCES

Adorno, Theodor. 1978. *Minima Moralia*. Translated by E. F. N. Jephcott. London: Verso.

Adorno, Theodor. 1994. *Negative Dialectics*. Translated by E.B. Ashton. New York: Continuum.

Appadurai, Arjun. 1988. *The Social Life of Things*. Cambridge: Cambridge University Press.

Barber, Benjamin. 1995. *Jihad vs. McWorld*. New York: Ballantine.

Bartolovich, Crystal. 2002. "Introduction". In *Marxism, Modernity and Postcolonial Studies*, edited by Crystal Bartolovich and Neil Lazarus, 1–17. Cambridge: Cambridge University Press.

Brown, Bill. 2004. *Things*. Chicago: University of Chicago Press.

BP. 2012. *Statistical Review of World Energy*.

Chamoiseau, Patrick. 1992. *Texaco*. Paris: Gallimard.

Chamoiseau, Patrick. 1997. *Texaco*. Translated by Rose-Myriam Rejouis and Val Vinokurov. New York: Vintage International.

Citi GPS. 2013. *Energy 2020: Independence Day – Global Ripple Effects of the North American Energy Revolution*.

Coronil, Fernando. 1997. *The Magical State*. Chicago: University of Chicago Press.

Dawson, Ashley. 2004. "Squatters, Space and Belonging in the Underdeveloped City". *Social Text* 22.4: 17–34.

Foster, John Bellamy. 2000. *Marx's Ecology*. New York: Monthly Review Press.

Gidel, Melanie. 2011. "Fragmentation on the Waterfront: Coastal Squatting Settlements and Urban Renewal Projects in the Caribbean". In *Transforming Urban Waterfronts: Fixity and Flow*, edited by Gene Desfor *et al.*, 35–53. New York: Routledge.

Harvey, David. 2003. *The New Imperialism*. Oxford: Oxford University Press.

Huber, Matt. 2013. *Lifeblood*. Minneapolis: University of Minnesota Press.

Huggan, Graham and Helen Tiffin. 2010. *Postcolonial Ecocriticism: Literature, Animals, Environment*. New York and London: Routledge.

IEA. 2012. *World Energy Outlook 2012: Executive Summary*.

Kashi, Ed and Michael Watts. 2008. *Curse of the Black Gold: 50 Years of Oil in the Niger Delta*. Brooklyn: Powerhouse Books.

Latour, Bruno. 1996. *Aramis*. Translated by Catherine Porter. Cambridge: Harvard University Press.

Latour, Bruno. 2004. *Politics of Nature*. Cambridge: Harvard University Press.

Letchimy, Serge. 1992. *De l'habitat précaire à la ville: l'exemple martiniquais*. Paris: L'Harmattan.

McClellan, Philip. 2012. "Is Jugaad Going Global?" *New York Times*. http://india.blogs.nytimes.com/2012/10/11/is-jugaad-going-global/.

Marx, Karl. 1990 [1867]. *Capital*, Volume 1. Translated by Ben Fowkes. London: Penguin Books.

Mitchell, Timothy. 2011. *Carbon Democracy: Political Power in the Age of Oil*. London and New York: Verso.

Mulchansingh, Vernon. 1971. "The Location of Oil Refining in Latin America and the Caribbean". *Revista Geografica* 75: 85–126.

Nixon, Rob. 2011. *Slow Violence and the Environmentalism of the Poor*. Cambridge: Harvard University Press.

Practical Action. 2013. *Poor People's Energy Outlook 2013*. Rugby, UK: Practical Action Publishing.

Prieto, Eric. 2005. "The Uses of Landscape". In *Caribbean Literature and the Environment: Between Nature and Culture*, edited by Elizabeth M. DeLoughrey *et al.*, 236–246. Charlottesville, VA and London: University of Virginia Press.

Quayson, Ato. 2003. *Calibrations: Reading for the Social*. Minneapolis: University of Minnesota Press.

Robbins, Bruce. 2005. "Commodity Histories". *PMLA* 120.2: 454–463.

Spivak, Gayatri. 2003. *Death of a Discipline*. New York: Columbia University Press.

Saro-wiwa, Ken. 1992. *Genocide in Nigeria*. London: Soros International Publishers.

Szeman, Imre. 2007. "System Failure: Oil, Futurity, and the Anticipation of Disaster". *South Atlantic Quarterly* 106.4: 805–823.

Walonen, Michael K. 2012. "'The Black and Cruel Demon' and its Transformation of Space: Toward a Comparative Study of World Literature". *Interdisciplinary Literary Studies* 14.1: 56–78.

Watts, Michael. 2013. "Oil Talk". *Development and Change* 44.4: 1013–1026.

Watts, Richard. 2008. "Towards an Ecocritical Postcolonialism: Val Plumwood's Environmental Culture in Dialogue with Chamoiseau". *Journal of Postcolonial Writing* 44.3: 251–261.

14 Inherit the World

World-Literature, Rising Asia and the World-Ecology

Sharae Deckard

Postcolonial studies arose alongside the first wave of what has been idealistically labeled globalization but might more properly be called neoliberalization, a global redistribution of wealth enforced through the brutal imposition of structural adjustment policies across the decolonized world (Harvey 2005). If, as Neil Lazarus argues, the trajectory of the discipline's subsequent concentration on the problem of imperialism rather than capitalism itself can be read in correlation to "the epochal reversal" of the insurgent revolutionary ideologies of the Third World (Lazarus 2011, 9), then we should ask how the blindspots of the contemporary discipline might be symptomatic of our current conjuncture of intensified liberalization, asset-stripping, accelerated US imperialist aggression – combined with a paradoxical impotence implicit in its inability to defeat insurgencies in Iraq and Afghanistan, despite bringing to bear all the might of the US military-industrial complex – and incipient cold war with China. Postcolonial studies provides valuable tools for the analysis of colonial formations of race, class, ethnicity and gender that continue to haunt independent nations. However, it seems less able to account for the proliferation of new forms of militarization and securitization under the aegis of the American imperium and the neoliberal state, the transition into capitalism of China and the countries of the former Soviet Empire or the vertiginous wealth accumulation amongst the elites of Brazil, India and South Africa.

Rather than perpetually looking back to Western European high imperialism, postcolonial studies ought to theorize new imperial formations and geographies, such as the ecological imperialism implicit in the scramble for resources as China and India compete with Western cores to secure raw materials in Africa and South America for their ongoing industrializations. It should be able to address the changing world order implied by the incipient terminal crisis of American hegemony, the US pivot to Asia and the so-called rise of the BRICS, re-establishing capitalism as the primary horizon of its analysis. This requires moving beyond disciplinary strategies that overdetermine the problem of Eurocentrism or fetishize the category of the West in binary terms in order to find new analytics that can account for the complex polygonal logics that govern the inter-relations of cores, semi-peripheries and peripheries throughout the contemporary capitalist world-system. As Daniel Vukovich remarks, world-systems theorists such as Roy Bin Wong (1997) and Giovanni Arrighi (2007) have been wrestling with the question of Chinese capitalism and the shifting centers of the global economy for decades, but "China is obviously something that postcolonial criticism and theory have yet to come to terms with" (Vukovich 2013, 591).

A world-systemic approach offers analytical tools through which to comprehend the present restructuring of the uneven geographies of the capitalist world order within a world-historical context, as well as the ways in which emergent literary forms mediate the effects, dispositions and social relations produced by these transformations. I have argued elsewhere that "'world-literature' with a hyphen might refer specifically to those works in which the world-system is not a distant horizon only unconsciously registered in immanent form, but rather consciously or critically mapped" – that is, to literature that takes the global, rather than the nation or the imperium, as its operative totality[1] – while the term "world-literary criticism" might correspondingly denote a world-systemic mode of literary studies (Graham *et al.* 2012, 468). In this essay, using the discourse of rising Asia and the literary fictions that emerge in connection to it as a point of entry, I want to explore what world-literary criticism might be able to say or identify about its literary form and content that postcolonial studies doesn't or can't.

I will begin with an illustrative example. At a recent Postcolonial Studies Association conference in Britain, a panel devoted to Aravind Adiga's *White Tiger* tried desperately to read the novel as writing back to the West, challenging Eurocentric ideas of development and provincializing imperialist hegemony through the jubilant ventriloquization of successful Indian capitalist entrepreneurship. The novel's primary aim was torturously described as "Othering the Other" and its aesthetic strategies characterized as linguistic hybridization and subversive minority. By straining to align their readings with the axis of postcolonial theoretical frameworks of hybridity, subalternity and provincializing Europe offered by Homi Bhabha, Gayatri Spivak and Dipesh Chakrabarty, the papers perversely failed to recognize that the novel is not primarily oriented towards critique of post-imperial metropolitan Britain but rather towards the internal impacts of neoliberalization and uneven development within contemporary India, and the rise of imperial ambitions and economic alliances outside the Western Anglophone cores of the US and Britain. *White Tiger*'s narrative structure is fundamentally organized around India's relation with emergent centers of economic hegemony such as China and around the internal relation between India's own cores and peripheries (urban centers and rural hinterlands), not the relation between post-colony and the former empire. As such, it is incongruous with binary, identitarian analytics and more productively read via world-literary criticism.

The novel is written in the first person from the perspective of Balram, the eponymous White Tiger, a self-made man who has dragged himself out of rural poverty by migrating to a city to serve as a chauffeur, and then killing his employer and stealing his capital in order to start his own taxi business ferrying prostitutes to foreign IT executives in Bangalore. In the novel's epistolary form, Balram writes nightly to the Chinese premier, Wen Jiabao, who is then visiting the country, in order to provide insights into the Indian entrepreneurial mindset on which India's economic boom is allegedly predicated. Adiga describes the novel as satirizing the self-help discourse of Indian corporate literature and its myth of meritocracy:

> India is being flooded with "how to be an Internet businessman" kind of books, and they're all dreadfully earnest and promise to turn you into Iacocca in a week. This is the kind of book that my narrator mentions, mockingly – he knows that life is a bit harder than these books promise. There are lots of self-made millionaires in India now, certainly, and lots of successful entrepreneurs. But remember that over a billion people live here, and for the majority of them, who are denied decent health care, education, or employment, getting to the top would take doing something like what Balram has done.
>
> (Adiga 2008a)

Rather than recuperating subaltern alterity and or refuting orientalized Western perceptions of Indians, the novel produces its own derogatory representations of class, caste, tribal and gender Others within the neocolonial state. Village life in the rural periphery is characterized as insectoid and subhuman: women sleep together "like one creature, a millipede"; teashop workers are "human spiders" (Adiga 2008b, 21, 51). Class conflict and poverty are reduced to the grotesque neo-Darwinist parable of the "Rooster Coop", imagining human laborers as hundreds of chickens, "pecking each other and shitting on each other, jostling just for breathing space; the whole cage giving off a horrible stench" (Adiga 2008b, 147). The peripheral province of Bihar from which the protagonist migrates goes unnamed, described only via a Conradian soubriquet, "The Darkness". The novel's aesthetics verge on the cartoonish, lacking the sociological detail, narrative complexity and range of class subjectivities mediated in other contemporary novels about the neoliberalization of India, such as Tarun Tejpal's *Story of My Assassins*.

Due to these shortcomings, the novel's critical reception acted as a lightning rod for the politics of representation of New India. Amitava Kumar criticized Adiga's "cynical anthropology" of a venal ruling class for reducing the complex caste system and circumstances of rural poverty to a portrayal of a "desperate and brazenly cannibalistic" victim class (Kumar 2008, 8). Kumar perceptively characterized the misanthropy of *White Tiger*'s narrator as playing off "middle-class Indian fear of domestic servants", corroborating bourgeois stereotypes of the underclass without offering any contradicting glimmer of peasant subjectivity or agency (2008, 1). From the opposite side, nationalist champions of "shining India" excoriated Adiga for blackening the international image of India and reducing the neoliberal fairy tale of entrepreneurial success to a story of violence and corruption, which exploited the Western literary market's hunger for slum tourism and poverty porn. Replying to the controversy, Adiga blamed the novel's classist and racist content on the unreliable narrator, the offensively self-described "half-baked Indian" whose escape from abject poverty is dependent on his internalization of class violence and cronyism. He pleaded that his aim was not to oppose neoliberal policies, merely to criticize their excesses:

> People have a right to question how fast liberalisation is going and whether it's damaging some sections of society. In the short term India might lag [behind] China if we're more introspective about our growth – but in the long term, we will surely outrun them. Those who interpret my novels as opposing liberalisation are misreading them. They're marked by ambivalence, not opposition, to the changes. [...] I'm not opposed to the great economic boom going on now. My role as a novelist is only to dramatize certain conflicts taking place because of the generation of so much new wealth.
>
> (Das 2011, 2)

In his cherished belief that India and China will "inherit the world from the west" (Jeffries 2008, 2), Adiga expresses the same myth of rising Asia that *White Tiger*'s protagonist trumpets. Balram's letter to Chinese premier Wen Jiabao champions "Sino-Indian relations" and exclaims, "In twenty years' time, it will be just us yellow men and brown men at the tip of the pyramid and we'll rule the whole world" (Adiga 2008b, 305). The novel may be written for the Euro-American Anglophone market, capitalizing on American fears of the decline of the West and the rise of Asia with its narrative of the collapse of white global hegemony, but the address of its epistolary form is pointedly to China, not Britain or even the US, and the subject of its flattery is clearly a sense of Indian nationalism situated in economic development.[2] As such, the geographic logic of the novel is not binary but triangular, triangulating between the current core-hegemon, the US imperium, with its signs of terminal crisis; China, the semi-periphery on the cusp of hegemony; and India, another semi-periphery rising in global influence.

Irrespective of the novel's aesthetic limitations, it is precisely the contradiction between its attempt to critique neocolonial class relations within the state while at the same time championing India's economic rise and prospect of capitalist alliance with China that makes the novel a useful object-example, less suited to the epistemological strategies of postcolonial studies than those of a world-systemic approach. The text's ideological ambivalence captures that of a nation in which the legacies of European colonialism live on in economic and political structures, class and geographical divisions, but that also nurses imperial ambitions of its own. India is the semi-periphery to which US telephony and information technology labor are outsourced, not to mention more exploitative industries such as garment manufacture and pharmaceutical production. But India is also a regional core, consumed by its own imperialistic development and resource-extraction projects throughout Africa and the global South. Culturalist and identitarian postcolonial frameworks are insufficient to the task of critiquing the class formations of neoliberal India, of reading the particular way in which this novel encodes, however problematically, lives that are characterized by the violent precarity, ecological crisis and brute inequalities of uneven development between rural peripheries and hypermodern urban centers in the contemporary nation. Nor are they able to examine the larger operative totality at the text's heart: its concern to "inherit the world".

Discussing his *Capital Gains* project on the rise of Indian oligarchy, Rana Dasgupta observes a paradoxical dynamic in the myth of the rise of India. While many of the class distinctions and racial prejudices inherited from colonialism and rightly critiqued by postcolonial studies persist in India, within nationalist rhetoric discourses of postcolonial victimization are manipulated to legitimate the nation's attempts to dominate the twenty-first century:

> India has moved very fast from being a country that was exploited to a country that is looking to exploit. It's true that the wounds of exploitation have not healed. [...] If a white person comes into a restaurant in Delhi, the waiters will drop everything they're doing to serve that person, though the Indian person that they're serving might be much more politically and economically significant than that white guy. [...] And the English language [...] is now the language of commerce and politics and intellectual life: Many people who didn't grow up with that language feel this great sense of exclusion and insecurity. These are all post-colonial problems which continue to afflict the place. *But* the country also has to wake up to the fact that *it* is now stealing resources from other countries. [...] It says, "But we're not – We don't have those kinds of responsibilities, because we are a post-colonial country and we don't have to take on these kinds of responsibilities. We are still struggling. We are still poor. So we have every right to take opportunities where we can get them". [...] It's becoming increasingly disingenuous of India to on the one hand *take* a lot of stuff [...] and *rejoice* over the acquisition of British companies or the successes of Indian corporations abroad, and continue to play this small, wounded character that doesn't have any responsibilities.
>
> (Colbert 2011, 12)

For Dasgupta, the best contemporary Indian novelists "are not particularly concerned anymore by their country's colonised past: they are preoccupied instead by its expanding, imperial future" (Dasgupta 2010). He argues that the contemporary writer should generate new forms through which to narrate the present world-historical order and to overcome the reification of earlier forms and critical methods, rather than recycling old "images of the world" (Colbert 2012, 11). In particular, he calls for Indian aesthetics that move beyond "sari-and-mango" novels and "brooding trans-generational dramas delivered in monsoon-drenched prose" in order to criticize the "brutal excesses of the new economy" (Dasgupta 2010).

This point can be made more broadly. The orientation of many novels from so-called postcolonies is increasingly towards a critique of global neoliberal capitalism rather than the former imperial metropolis, seeking to generate new art forms capable of capturing the polygonal relations of the global market and the new sensibilities it generates. Within these novels, the residual legacies of nineteenth-century European imperialism within the postcolonial nation-state are only one subtext amongst many, rather than the overarching narrative. While these novels have been frequently interpreted within the rubrics of transnationalism, cosmopolitanism, diaspora or postnationalism, their ultimate horizon is better understood as that of the capitalist world-system, of which "transnational relations and imperial power are but partial expressions" (Medovoi 2011, 62). In Leerom Medovoi's path-breaking essay on the global remapping of American literature, he reads Mohsin Hamid's *The Reluctant Fundamentalist* as exemplifying not postcolonial aesthetics but rather "'world-system literature' about America and its global position", and calls for a literary analysis that would "rigorously consider how literature from different locations in the global order registers unequal exchanges and politico-military applications of power" (Medovoi 2011, 645, 653).

Given that socio-ecological violence is inextricable from the current phase of neoliberal capitalism, in which accumulation is dependent on new frontiers and enclosures of the commons, world-literary criticism ought to draw not only on world-systems theory but also on Jason W. Moore's understanding of capitalism as "world-ecology", constituted by ecological regimes, those "relatively durable patterns of class structure, technological innovation and the development of productive forces" that have sustained and propelled successive phases of world accumulation (Moore 2010, 405). To imagine a world-literature whose operative totality is the world-system is necessarily to imagine a literature that mediates the crises of capitalism-in-nature. This essay employs a critical practice that unites a theory of combined and uneven development across the striated cores and peripheries of the world-system with a conceptualization of capitalism as a world-ecology constituted by ecological regimes. Before returning to literary examples, I will examine the BRICS thesis, which helps fuel the myth of rising Asia and explore the world-ecological relations particular to the neoliberal accumulation regimes in the BRICS.

THE MYTH OF THE BRICS AND RISING ASIA

The idea of the rise of the BRICS first appeared in a 2003 Goldman Sachs economics paper, "Dreaming with BRICs: The Path to 2050", in which

Dominic Wilson and Roopa Purushothaman argued that Brazil, Russia, India and China were the largest-growing forces in the world economy, projecting that their combined GDP would overtake the industrialized G7 by 2027.[3] As their economies grew, so too might their political clout increase. The "miracle" of the BRICS – large but poor countries outpacing small but rich countries, drawing on their huge demographic reserves of human resources – seemed to confirm the triumph of neoliberal economic policies, particularly in the rosy twilight of the boom. In India, the "demography is destiny" theme was enthusiastically adopted by propertied elites and nationalist boosters as proof of their emergence into the bright light of free market capitalism from the dark night of underdevelopment (Desai 2007, 787). Amongst US and Western European investors, the prospect of new investment opportunities was embraced with euphoria, though it also provoked anxiety about reverse imperialism, particularly in post-Fordist cores such as Britain, where the large majority of industrial jobs are now controlled by the oligarchal Indian megacorporation Tata (Willsdon 2008).

However, the demographically biased BRICS thesis rests disproportionately on the Indian and Chinese cases, while its projections depend on the ideological assumption that so long as the BRICS maintain "sound" neoliberal policies, financial crises or trade imbalances will not inhibit their growth – a glaring failure to predict the effects of the 2008 crisis (Desai 2007, 787–788). As the product of employees of a private bank that played a central role in instigating the credit crunch, the model was chiefly aimed at providing benchmarks for Goldman Sachs investors seeking to make a killing in emergent markets. For Radhika Desai, the BRICS thesis was embraced with such alacrity because it "was more than a narrative about the sources of new growth in the world economy", acting rather as "a directive to first world political and corporate leaders about where opportunities lay and another to third world political and corporate leaders about the conditions – mainly consistency of neoliberal policy – they must secure if the fruits foreseen were to be theirs" (Desai 2007, 785). She heralds the BRICS thesis as the latest in a series of hegemonic discourses – modernization, development theory, globalization and now neoliberalism – which articulate the prospects of peripheral economic development in terms of core interests.

Although the BRICS model was widely held up as validation of trickle-down economics and proof that the structural adjustment policies had produced the "correct" results of unleashing entrepreneurship and defeating socialist-induced stagnation, the authors of the paper never claimed that the people of BRICS countries would be any better off. In their projections, the world's largest economies might no longer be the richest, and the large poor countries might gain economic power, but "despite much faster growth, individuals are still likely to be poorer on average than individuals in the G6" (Wilson and Purushottaman 2003, 5). Indeed, in the case of India, the wealth-creation under the neoliberal reforms led by Finance Minister Manmohan Singh emerged from a deeply polarized accumulation regime that benefited only a tiny handful of financial and political elites. The "New Industrial Policy" privatized public goods and state services – water, telecommunications, health, electricity, education – and handed over nationalized manufacturing sectors in iron, steel, shipbuilding, mining and banking to private ownership and investment. The turn of the century witnessed the vertiginous rise of Indian oligarchs up the Forbes list of the world's richest, prompting one editorial to shriek in alarm, "Beware India's manifest destiny" (Willson 2008).

Mass enclosure of the commons has been central to the neoliberal ecological regime, not only in its Indian manifestation but across the BRICS. According to Jason W. Moore, the ecological regimes that constitute capital accumulation always rely on a dialectic of plunder and productivity, in which nature's allegedly free gifts outside the commodity system are plundered through new forms of frontier enclosure and commodity extraction in order to maximize labor productivity and intensify profits. The hegemony of finance capital over the accumulation process since the 1970s has prioritized short-term profits over productive investment, favoring asset-stripping, plunder and speculation in volatile commodity markets over forms of infrastructural fixed capital. Lacking a sufficient revolution in labor productivity, the neoliberal regime sustained itself through intensified rounds of appropriation of whatever "free gifts" remained after nineteenth-century industrialization and imperialism: "[T]he oil frontiers of the North Sea, Alaska, West Africa, and the Gulf of Mexico; the crest of Green Revolution agriculture in South Asia, appropriating and exhausting fertile soil and cheap water; the integration of the old Soviet Bloc into the world market, allowing cheap metals and oils to reduce production costs after 1989; the appropriation of the Chinese peasantry as a vast labor surplus; the privatization of state and quasi-state firms and public services" (Moore 2012, 245). This "great frontier" is now closed, however, and its free gifts will not recur.

Moore reads the 2008 recession as telegraphing the collapse of the neoliberal ecological regime, which had been dependent on driving down the costs of strategic inputs – the "four cheaps" of labor, energy, food and resources. The acceleration of yield suppression for major cereal crops, looming peak oil, water scarcity, reductions in global cropland due to climate change, and faltering productivity due to soil exhaustion and pesticide resistance all signal the exhaustion of the biophysical natures that fueled the cheap food regime. Indian agriculture – a cornerstone of "cheap food" – is in the throes of a "'post-green revolution' crisis" (Desai 2007, 800). Cereal production and consumption per capita have declined due to the diversion of land to the cultivation of non-grain and non-food cash export products. The application of free-market orthodoxy – lifting subsidies, tightening credit – has exacerbated malnutrition and increased the vulnerability of small peasant farmers, catalyzing a spate of farmer suicides. At the same time, the short-term profit-maximizing strategies of financialization have created property bubbles in urban centers such as Delhi, fuelling intense corruption and driving speculation via "parasitic" foreign capital inflows used to finance surplus imports, rather than investing in infrastructure or industry (Shrivastava and Kothari 2012).

If anything, the pattern has been one of disinvestment from the national economy, shunting domestic investment into outflows to more vulnerable economies. Indian financial elites increasingly invest in Africa and South America, seeking "backwards integration" for their corporations by monopolizing global resources and securing commodity supply lines (Shiva 2011, 105). The majority of Indian investments in agricultural land are in the sub-Saharan countries of Sudan, Ethiopia, Ghana, Nigeria and Mozambique, where huge plantations, often worked by imported Indian labor, grow food crops such as rice, millet and vegetable oils that can no longer be produced at home due to diversion of land to cash-exports, as well as other commodities such as flowers. From national land grabs, Indian financial elites have progressed to global land grabs, especially as they are faced with the costs of increasing indigenous resistance, resource conflicts and labor unrest at home. In this form of new colonialism, formerly colonized nations reconfigure European imperialist practices, such as eighteenth-century sugar plantation in the Caribbean, and the nineteenth-century appropriation of large tracts of African farmland for coffee and cacao production (Rowden 2013, 8).

Far from showing anxiety at the ecological degradation unleashed by their mode of accumulation, India's financial elites seem elated at the opportunity to fashion themselves as disaster capitalists, as captured in Dasgupta's interview with an Indian executive overseeing mass sugar plantations in Guinea:

> "We're approaching a global food crisis, the climate is changing, a lot of established food markets are having problems [...] there is so much scarcity". He says it with exultation, and I'm reminded that this is an elite bred for the era of catastrophe, delighted by food shortages, climatic disturbance and turbulence of all sorts. Unlike American elites that might have come to maturity in belief in era that might be less assailed by catastrophe, this elite comes to age in an era where catastrophe is just beginning.
>
> (Dasgupta 2012)

The image of India may have been transformed in national and transnational media narratives from a land of darkness and destitution to that of Shining India, one of globalization's winners, but the wealth of the emerging economy is concentrated amongst a few influential families with political clout, and is fundamentally based on the tactics of "resource grab" (Shiva 2011, 82). The neoliberal model has not so much unleashed entrepreneurial potential and enabled class mobility into India's middle classes as opened avenues for the "economic rise of India's billionaires, misleadingly presented as the 'rise of India'" (Shiva 2011, 81). What the BRICS model presents as wealth creation is really a process of wealth accumulation via socio-ecological dispossession, a massive transfer of wealth from billions of poor to about fifty billionaire oligarchs, which has further polarized the India-Bharat divide between the privileged consuming classes in urban centers and the millions of impoverished peasants and evicted tribals in rural peripheries, whose land has been seized for mass agro-business, mining operations, hydroelectric projects and resource extraction carried out by the corporate recipients of the state's water and land "give-outs".

Comparative examination of other BRICS, particularly China, reveals similar characteristics of wealth accumulation by mass dispossession and enclosure; socio-ecological contradictions produced by the myth of linear development and catch-up; and a move towards ecological imperialism and resource-grabbing in the peripheries. That is not to deny the particularities of each nation. Brazil's early twenty-first-century alignment with the left-leaning extractive democracies of the South American axis means that its relation to external pressures to liberalize has been quite different from that of India or Russia, while China offers its own peculiar mixture of authoritarian state party communism, socialist mode of production and neoliberal marketization, and faces so many internal ecological limits and domestic political contradictions that its capacity to emerge as the unipolar global empire that the US fears is by no means certain. Indeed, Li Minqi has argued that China's rise is unsustainable in the context of climate change and will provoke an epochal crisis of the whole capitalist world-system (Li 2009). The differences between the BRICS are so many that certain critics argue the BRICS label is a generalization without substance.

Others, however, argue that the geopolitical dimension of the BRICS summits is more significant than the economic thesis, and point to plans for development banks and reserve pooling arrangements as evidence that the BRICS are dedicated to building a new multipolar world order that challenges American supremacy (Tisdall 2012; Desai 2013). We might recall here how *White Tiger*'s narrator fantasizes Sino-Indian economic hegemony cemented through racialized political solidarity between rising core nations. However, India's role in such a project is ambivalent, given its participation in the Trans-Pacific Partnership (a US-led trade organization that excludes China) and the extent to which the recent US pivot to Asia and corresponding Indian pro-US tilt has made India central to the US's anti-China strategy, both military and economic. Inter-state co-operation on civilian nuclear technology and promises to "make India a great power" characterize US attempts to enlist India in anti-Chinese militarization, what Arundhati Roy calls the "new cold war" (Roy 2012). The shifting contours of geopolitical power are encapsulated in President Obama's recent declaration that the US's primary military strategy will abandon counterterrorism for the fortification of military presence in the Asia-Pacific region, the new "center of gravity" of world economic activity (Klare 2012, 2).

Yet it seems increasingly unlikely that the economically weakened American imperium will be able to maintain its staggering empire of bases – over one thousand spanning the globe – and prevail in multiple regions simultaneously whilst also containing its largest creditor, China. From a world-historical perspective, the unraveling hegemony of US unipolar power in relation to the signal crisis of neoliberalism seems only delayed, not arrested (Arrighi 2005). Nonetheless, the politico-military system of Western cores is undergoing an aggressive expansion in the attempt to preserve hegemony, incorporating Eastern Europe up to the Baltic states and buttressing its security architecture in the Asia-Pacific region through alliances with Japan, Taiwan, South Korea, Australia and New Zealand. Within the North American and European cores, the drive for energy sufficiency aims to stave off decline through new extreme, intensified methods of oil and gas extraction: fracking, tar sands, deep-water drilling (Engelhardt 2013, 3). Externally, the US Navy strives to dominate the sea lanes of the South China Sea, through which the majority of China's oil arrives by tanker, while in response, China frantically builds pipelines across the entire Asian continent to the Caspian Sea (Klare 2012, 4). In all, it is a recipe for aggravated socio-ecological violence on a world-historical scale.

SOME DIRECTIONS FOR WORLD-LITERARY CRITICISM

Whether the ongoing reconfiguration of the world order will result in a bi-polar or multi-lateral system, much less a new accumulation regime, remains to be seen, but it certainly ought to be an object of world-literary analysis, given that it is increasingly the subject of literary representation. India and China loom large in the imagination of contemporary world-literature, refracting the double connotations of the discourse of rising Asia as the expression of nationalist triumph for former peripheries and a source of ambivalent hysteria for a Western imperium obsessed with decline. "Asia" is a deeply vexed term that should not be incorporated unambiguously into postcolonial studies. It is an inaccurate cartographic designation and a misleading civilizational concept that makes little sense of the different cultures it attempts to elide. It also fails as an identitarian construct, since few people within Asia actually identify as Asians (Vukovich 2013, 588). Daniel Vukovich argues that the contemporary designation of Asia as defined by the Chinese sphere of economic and political influence marks a shift in the concept from the "traditional, philological, overtly 'othering'" way of thinking about Asia towards a more "empirical, social-based" construct associated in the context of the "neo-imperial, globalized scene" (Vukovich 2013, 588). India's own relation to Asia is contradictory. It is currently identified as part of Asia now that its economy is shining, but was excluded before, a tendency directly reflective of changing world-systemic relations and the neoliberal construction of the rise and fall of Asian tigers. For these reasons, it is not possible to simply add Asia to postcolonial studies, since the globalist discourse of rising Asia can only be understood in terms of the capitalist world-system and does not fit neatly into analyses of high European imperialism. Yet as ideology, the concept clearly has force. One has only to look to the work of the imperial cheerleader Niall Ferguson, oscillating wildly between hopes of "Chimerica", a "Sino-American symbiosis", and dire proclamations of the end of "500 years of western ascendancy" with the dawning of the "Chinese century" (Mishra 2011, 10–12).

Mohsin Hamid's latest novel, *How to Get Filthy Rich in Rising Asia* (2013), tackles the bi-valent myth of Asia head on with its ironic title and its chapter titles satirizing self-help books: "Work for Yourself", "Be Prepared to Use Violence", "Befriend a Bureaucrat", "Patronize the Artists of War", "Dance with Debt". With greater aesthetic skill than Adiga's *White Tiger*, Hamid's novel charts the rise of a rural migrant to an unnamed city from junior delivery boy to small-business entrepreneur, who makes his money through a scam of bottling tap water and selling it as mineral water, and who then becomes a water mogul with a monopoly on the city's underground aquifers, depleting the water table in order to divert resources to gated communities for the nation's financial elites. The protagonist dispenses advice on wealth-creation that unblinkingly accepts the violence immanent to neoliberal accumulation:

> Distasteful though it may be, it was inevitable in a self-help book such as this, that we would eventually find ourselves broaching the topic of violence. Becoming filthy rich requires a degree of unsqueamishness, whether in rising Asia or anywhere else. For wealth comes from capital, and capital comes from labor, and labor comes from [...] the leanness of biological machines that must be bent to your will with some force if you are to loosen your own financial belt, and sighingly, expand.
>
> (Hamid 2013, 121)

Water privatization and hydrological exhaustion are at the center of the tale. The nameless protagonist, referred to in the unusual second-person narration only as "you", is an exemplar of the same mode of wealth-accumulation demonstrated by India's oligarchs, achieved not through the meritocratic magic of the market but through his connections to corrupt officials, his deployment of mafia violence to secure his monopoly and his appropriation of the city's water resources, intensifying urban hydrological crisis.

All of Hamid's work has been oriented to charting the changing economy and culture of South Asia in relation to US hegemony. If Hamid's first novel, *Moth Smoke*, mapped the decadent affects and subjectivities of the tiny fraction of Lahore's ascendant financial elites, and *The Reluctant Fundamentalist* cognitively mapped a world in which Pakistan orbits the US in the larger global system of wealth, *Filthy Rich* is his most explicit mapping of a changing geopolitical order. The novel is set in an unnamed city, reminiscent of Lahore, and the nation's culture and geography seem to be that of Pakistan but are left unspecified. This indeterminate setting might be read as a deliberate attempt to circumvent postcolonial readings of the novel in order to enable more world-systemic comparisons of the dynamics of liberalization, corruption, financialization, urbanization and authoritarian state power in "emergent" economies throughout the Global South. The novel foregrounds the entrepreneur's "relationship with the state" but the influence of the nation-state quickly gives way to inter-state pressures and the conjoined flows of finance and military power, culminating in the US's "imperial economic grip": "We exist in a financial universe that is subject to massive gravitational pulls from states. States tug at us. States bend us. And, tirelessly, states seek to determine our orbits" (Hamid 2013, 139).

Another novel to make the reconfigurations of the world economy its main theme is Tash Aw's *Five Star Billionaire* (2013), set in the Guangdong economic corridor of China, moving between mass industrial cities staffed by cheap migrant labor and the gleaming skyscrapers and glassy financial districts of the Shanghai property bubble. The novel represents the pace of capitalist transformation and commodification of relations in China as vertiginous but also strangely monotonous, so pervasive in national propaganda that it seems simultaneously spectral and banal. Yanyan, a former factory worker explains:

> "You open a newspaper or turn on the TV and all you see is CHANGE. Every village, every city, everything is changing. I get so bored with it. It's as if we're possessed by a spirit – like in a horror film. Sometimes I think we're all on drugs. I used to speak to foreigners on the phone at work; all they would say was 'I hear things are changing really fast over there'".
>
> (Aw 2013, 324)

The novel cognitively maps the territory of China's frenzied accumulation and dispossession through a form uncannily similar to Hamid's novel. It too adopts the conceit of anonymous narration by a self-made billionaire, providing advice on how to become "superabundantly, incalculably wealthy" (Aw 2013, 1) and deploys chapter titles satirizing Chinese corporate jargon such as "Move to the City", "Bravely Set the World on Fire", "How to Be Inventive – Property Management Case Study". The geographic logic triangulates between the territories of the ASEAN +3, charting financial and labor flows between the Chinese core and its semi-peripheries, particularly Malaysia, while demonstrating the waning influence of Britain and other Western European economic states.

Adiga, Hamid, Aw: three examples of thematic content organized around rising Asia and of a novel form reconfiguring the tropes and structures of self-help literature.[4] Self-help fiction is emerging as a distinct subgenre in

Anglophone world-literature from industrializing economies, an object for world-literary criticism alongside the emergence of other literary forms specifically engaged in charting the effects of globalization and the affects corresponding to neoliberal accumulation and crisis. The BRICS thesis and rising Asia may be myths, but the socio-ecological effects of accumulation by dispossession, oligarchical concentration of wealth and new forms of ecological enclosure are all too real. In India, as Tarun Tejpal observes, "the dominant mood is frenzied accumulation [...] the corporations and the state are in bed with each other, eating and drinking the country out of everything it has" (Dasgupta 2009, 5). Rana Dasgupta writes, "It is difficult to live here and not be stupefied by the speed and brutality with which every resource is being fenced in, mined and commodified" (Dasgupta 2009, 5). The affects, cultural formations and dispositions corresponding to these effects are already being mediated in the new forms of literature emerging from these economies. The changing parameters of the world-system can be most clearly glimpsed in literature emerging from semi-peripheries where, as Dasgupta observes, "the surface of the earth has broken open, and one can see the precise churn of the 21st century in a very real way, in a way that one can wander around in the west for quite a long time without really encountering" (Colbert 2012, 14).

World-literary criticism should specifically seek out the world-ecological content of this literature, both as the expression of internal national dynamics – the "churning of the earth" requisite to the creation of hyper-rich national elites (Shrivastava and Kothari, 2012) – and as the expression of ecological imperialism abroad, not just European oil extraction in Nigeria or the Arctic but Indian flower plantations in Ethiopia, Chinese coltan extraction in the Congo or Russian petro-imperialism in the Ukraine. This would not be to approach world-literature as a mere list of food commodity prices or drone missiles – though both of these appear in the fictions I have discussed – but rather to seek to discover the aesthetics and forms that subjectivize the reconfiguration of socio-ecological relations within this literature: the turn away from fragrant lyricism towards genre elements including those of self-help, the epistolary, crime fiction, the thriller and the science-fictional; the plotted emphasis on mobility, versatility, celerity; the geographic and temporal narrative logics of unlikely convergence and time-space compression; and the adoption of registers oscillating between euphoria and dread in their registration of the world and what it might be.

NOTES

1. For the term "operative totality", I am indebted to Hvroje Tutek's paper "Narrating the World-System: Capitalist Universality and the Novel", delivered at ACLA, NYU, 21 March 2014.
2. One mark of the conservatism of the novel's analysis of neoliberal capitalism and its appeal to a Western Anglophone readership might be that it was the favorite of Booker Prize judge Michael Portillo, a former Tory cabinet minister.

3. In this essay, I use the amended acronym BRICS, which reflects the recent addition of South Africa to the BRICS summits.
4. The appearance of the "self-help" novel in connection with the industrialization of the BRICS economies raises interesting questions about the periodicity of forms in relation to the moving geographies of capitalist accumulation, if we recall that self-help philosophy first consolidated as a distinct genre tied to the rise of the middle class and to the nineteenth-century industrial revolution in Britain, and achieved a second apotheosis in relation to American industrial capitalism in books such as Andrew Carnegie's *How to Win Friends and Influence People*. The rise of the literary self-help parody also reflects on the enormous popularity of self-help books in non-Western literary markets and the contradictions of second-hand ideology implicit in their importation, and to the fact that reading publics in these markets often conversely approach novels not as fictions to be read purely for pleasure but as manuals for self-improvement and bourgeois subject-formation.

REFERENCES

Adiga, Aravind. 2008a. "An Interview with Aravind Adiga". *Bookbrowse*. http://www.bookbrowse.com/author_interviews/full/index.cfm?author_number=1552.
Adiga, Aravind. 2008b. *The White Tiger*. London: Atlantic Books.
Ahmad, Aijaz. 1992. *Against Theory: Classes, Nations, Literatures*. London: Verso.
Arrighi, Giovanni. 2005. "Hegemony Unravelling – Part I". *New Left Review* 32. http://newleftreview.org/II/32/giovanni-arrighi-hegemony-unravelling-1.
Arrighi, Giovanni. 2007. *Adam Smith in Beijing: Lineages of the Twenty-First Century*. New York: Verso.
Aw, Tash. 2013. *Five Star Billionaire*. London: Fourth Estate.
Colbert, Jade. 2012. "Future is – Rana Dasgupta, Solo (Interview): On tragic optimism and ethical creativity". *The Varsity* CXXXVIII: 21. http://thevarsity.ca/2012/03/26/future-is-rana-dasgupta-solo-interview/.
Colbert, Jade. 2012b. "Psychoanalyzing the City". *The Varsity* CXXXVIII: 21. http://thevarsity.ca/2012/03/18/psychoanalyzing-the-city/.
Das, Srijana Mitra. 2011. "They Mocked Me Because I Didn't Know Who Lionel Richie Was". *The Times of India*, 26 June. http://timesofindia.indiatimes.com/home/stoi/They-mocked-me-because-I-didnt-know-who-Lionel-Richie-was/articleshow/8995173.cms.
Dasgupta, Rana. 2009. "Capital Gains" *Granta*, 28 July. http://www.ranadasgupta.com/texts.asp.
Dasgupta, Rana. 2010. "A New Bend in the River: The Future of the Indian Novel in English". *The National*. http://www.thenational.ae/arts-culture/a-new-bend-in-the-river# ixzz2QuVx2NQ9.
Dasgupta, Rana. 2012. "Intimations of Futurity: Delhi, New Elites and the World". Talk at Brown University, 12 October. http://mediacapture.brown.edu:8080/ess/echo/presentation/97b41914-2470-4272-bb89-025d63df8746.
Desai, Radhika. 2007. "Dreaming in Technicolour? India as a BRIC Economy". *International Journal* 62.4: 781–804.
Desai, Radhika. 2013. "The Brics Are Building a Challenge to Western Economic Supremacy". *The Guardian,* 2 April. http://www.guardian.co.uk/commentisfree/2013/apr/02/brics-challenge-western-supremacy.

Engelhardt, Tom. 2013. "And Then There Was One: Imperial Giganticism and the Decline of Planet Earth". *TomDispatch*, 7 May. http://www.tomdispatch.com/blog/175696/.

Graham, James, Michael Niblett and Sharae Deckard. 2012. "Postcolonial Studies and World-Literature". *Journal of Postcolonial Writing* 48.5: 465–471.

Hamid, Mohsin. 2000. *Moth Smoke*. London: Penguin.

Hamid, Mohsin. 2007. *The Reluctant Fundamentalist*. London: Penguin.

Hamid, Mohsin. 2013. *How to Get Filthy Rich in Rising Asia*. London: Penguin.

Harvey, David. 2005. *A Brief History of Neoliberalism*. Oxford: Oxford University Press.

Jeffries, Stuart. 2008. "Roars of Anger". *The Guardian,* 16 October. http://www.guardian.co.uk/books/2008/oct/16/booker-prize.

Klare, Michael. 2011. "A New Cold War in Asia?" *TomDispatch,* 6 December. http://www.tomdispatch.com/post/175476/tomgram%3A_michael_klare,_a_new_cold_war_in_asia/.

Kumar, Amitava. 2008. "Bad News: Authenticity and the South Asian Political Novel". *Boston Review* 33.6, November/December. http://bostonreview.net/BR33.6/kumar.php.

Lazarus, Neil. 2011. *The Postcolonial Unconscious*. Cambridge: Cambridge University Press.

Li, Minqi. 2009. *The Rise of China and the Demise of the Capitalist World Economy*. New York: Monthly Review.

Medovoi, Leerom. 2011. "'Terminal Crisis?' From the Worlding of American Literature to World-System Literature". *American Literary History* 23.3: 643–659.

Mishra, Pankaj. 2011. "Watch This Man". *London Review of Books* 33.21: 10–12.

Moore, Jason W. 2010. "The End of the Road? Agricultural Revolutions in the Capitalist World-Ecology, 1450–2010". *Journal of Agrarian Change* 10.3: 389–413.

Moore, Jason W. 2012. "Cheap Food and Bad Money: Food, Frontiers, and Financialization in the Rise and Demise of Neoliberalism". *Review: A Journal of the Fernand Braudel Center* 33(2–3): 1–29.

Roy, Arundhati. 2012. "Capitalism: A Ghost Story". *Outlook India Magazine*, 26 March. http://www.outlookindia.com/article.aspx?280234.

Rowden, Rick. 2013. *India's New Role in the Global Farmland Grab*. New Delhi: Indian Social Action Forum (INSAF).

Shiva, Vandana. 2011. "The Indian Oligarchs". In *Outing the Oligarchy: Billionaires who Benefit from Today's Climate Crisis*, edited by Victor Menotti *et al.* San Francisco, CA: A Special Report of the International Forum on Globalization. http://www.ifg.org/pdf/IFG_OTO_report.pdf.

Shrivastava, Aseem and Ashish Kothari. 2012. *Churning the Earth: The Making of Global India*. New Delhi: Penguin India. Kindle.

Tejpal, Tarun. 2009. *The Story of My Assassins*. New Delhi: HarperCollins India.

Tisdall, Simon. 2012. "Can the Brics Create a New World Order?" *The Guardian,* 29 March. http://www.guardian.co.uk/commentisfree/2012/mar/29/brics-new-world-order.

Vukovich, Daniel. 2013. "Postcolonialism, Globalization and the 'Asia Question'" *Oxford Handbook of Postcolonial Studies*, edited by Graham Huggan. Oxford: Oxford University Press.

Willson, Benjamin. 2008. "A Case of Reverse Imperialism". *Forbes*, 6 June. http://www.forbes.com/2008/06/06/tata-uk-imperialism-oped-cx_bw_0606india.html.

Wilson, Dominic and Roopa Purushothaman. 2003. "Dreaming with BRICs: The Path to 2050". *Goldman Sachs CEO Confidential* 12: 1–4. http://www.goldmansachs.com/ceoconfidential/CEO-2003-12.pdf.

Wong, Roy Bin. 1997. *China Transformed: Historical Change and the Limits of European Experience*. Ithaca: Cornell University Press.

Contributors

Pasi Ahonen is Lecturer in Management at Essex Business School, University of Essex. With a background in cultural history and professional and scholarly experience in management, his research draws on a multi-disciplinary background in history, the social sciences and organizational studies. He is currently interested in three overlapping areas: the dynamics of history, memory and change in organizations; the formation of subjectivity and identity in organizations; and the ethics and politics of management knowledge. His work has been published in collected editions and journals including *Competition and Change, Organization* and *Human Relations*.

Crystal Bartolovich is an Associate Professor of English at Syracuse University. She has published widely in postcolonial and Marxist topics in venues such as *New Formations, Angelaki, Cultural Critique* and *Interventions*. With Neil Lazarus, she edited the collection *Marxism, Modernity and Postcolonial Studies* (Cambridge University Press, 2002). Her current book project is entitled "A Natural History of the Common".

Eva Bischoff teaches International History at the University of Trier. Her research interests include colonial and imperial history, postcolonial theory and gender/queer studies. She published *Kannibale-Werden: Eine postkoloniale Geschichte deutscher Männlichkeit um 1900* (Bielefeld: transcript Verlag, 2011) and is co-editor of *Provincializing the United States: Colonialism, Decolonization, and (Post)Colonial Governance in Transnational Perspective* (American Studies – A Monograph Series Vol. 248, Heidelberg: Winter Verlag, 2014). She is currently conducting a book project investigating the history of a group of Quaker families and their roles in the process of settler imperialism in early nineteenth-century Australia.

Anthony Carrigan is Lecturer in Postcolonial Literatures and Cultures at the University of Leeds. He is the author of *Postcolonial Tourism: Literature, Culture, and Environment* (Routledge, 2011), and editor of (with Elizabeth DeLoughrey and Jill Didur) *Global Ecologies and the Environmental Humanities: Postcolonial Approaches* (Routledge, 2015), and a special issue of *Moving Worlds* on Catastrophe and Environment

(2014). He is a Fellow of the Rachel Carson Center for Environment and Society, Ludwig-Maximilians-Universität, and an AHRC Early Career Fellow, and is currently writing a book on postcolonial literature and disaster.

Sharae Deckard is a Lecturer in World Literature at University College Dublin. Her research interests include world-ecological approaches to world literature, postcolonial ecocriticism and global ecogothic. She recently edited a special issue of *Green Letters* on "Global and Postcolonial Ecologies" and co-edited a special issue of *The Journal of Postcolonial Writing* on "Postcolonial Studies and World Literature". Her monograph, *Paradise Discourse, Imperialism and Globalization*, was published by Routledge in 2010. Recent articles have appeared in *Interventions*, *MLQ*, *JPW* and *Moving Worlds*, as well as multiple book chapters in collections on global ecologies, postcolonial ecocriticism and environmental humanities.

Alison Fraunhar, PhD is Associate Professor of Art History at Saint Xavier University in Chicago. Her research interests include the representation and performance of race and gender in Cuban culture, with a particular interest in the instability of these categories. She has published widely on Cuban visual culture, cinema and the built environment, and at present she is preparing a book manuscript on the *mulata* in Cuban cultural production. Future projects include a series of essays on vernacular built environments in the Americas, and a history of the intersection of art and punk rock in Los Angeles in the 1980s.

Mrinalini Greedharry is Assistant Professor in the Department of English at Laurentian University, Canada. A graduate of the University of London, she has taught in universities in Finland, the UK and Canada. Her three main areas of research are the history of English literary studies as colonial governmentality; the interdisciplinary encounter between postcolonial theory and organization studies; and critique of psychoanalytic theory. All of these projects continue her interest in how postcolonial critique might produce new ways of thinking about subjectivity and subject formation. She is the author of *Postcolonial Theory and Psychoanalysis* (Palgrave Macmillan 2008).

Ashleigh Harris is Senior Lecturer at the Department of English, Uppsala University, Sweden. She is currently working on a monograph on sub-Saharan African fiction of the 2000s, paying particular attention to the ways that contemporary economic, environmental and health challenges are shaping the forms and styles of African fiction today.

John C. Hawley is Professor of English at Santa Clara University, CA, and former chair of the department. Among his books are *Encyclopedia of Postcolonial Studies*; *India in Africa, Africa in India*; *The Postcolonial and the Global*; *Postcolonial, Queer*; *Cross-Addressing*; *Historicizing Christian Encounters with the Other*; *Amitav Ghosh: An Introduction*;

The Postcolonial Crescent and others. He has published in *Research in African Literatures*, the *Journal of Postcolonial Writing*, *Ariel*, and elsewhere. He has served on three executive committees of the Modern Language Association and chaired the US chapter of the Association for Commonwealth Literature and Language Studies.

Rob Nixon holds the Barron Family Professorship in Humanities and the Environment at Princeton University. He is the author of four books, most recently *Slow Violence and the Environmentalism of the Poor* (Harvard University Press 2011), which has been awarded an American Book Award and three other prizes. Nixon contributes frequently to *The New York Times*. His writing has also appeared in *The New Yorker, Atlantic Monthly, London Review of Books, Times Literary Supplement, Village Voice, Slate, The Nation, The Guardian, Public Culture, PMLA* and *Critical Inquiry*. He has been a recipient of a Guggenheim, an NEH and a MacArthur Foundation Peace and Security Award.

Simon Obendorf is Senior Lecturer in International Relations at the University of Lincoln, UK. He was educated at the University of Melbourne, where he read for degrees in political science and law before completing a PhD in international relations theory. His research spans the fields of international theory, postcolonial studies, and gender and sexuality. He is a member of the Institute of Postcolonial Studies.

Cristina Şandru currently works as managing editor for *The Literary Encyclopedia* (www.litencyc.com) and teaches at Cardiff Metropolitan University. She previously taught at the universities of Northampton and Wales, at UCL, Goldsmiths and Lucian Blaga University of Sibiu, Romania. She co-edited the special issue of the *Journal of Postcolonial Writing* on Postcommunism/Postcolonialism (May 2012) and the collection *Rerouting the Postcolonial: New Directions for the New Millennium* (Routledge 2009). She has published articles and reviews in *Critique, Euresis, The Journal of Postcolonial Studies* and *English*. Her monograph, *Worlds Apart? A Postcolonial Reading of Post-1945 East-Central European Culture*, was published in 2012 by Cambridge Scholars.

Jennifer Wenzel is an Associate Professor in the Department of English and Comparative Literature and the Department of Middle Eastern, South Asian and African Studies at Columbia University. Her book *Bulletproof: Afterlives of Anticolonial Prophecy in South Africa and Beyond* (Chicago and KwaZulu-Natal, 2009) was awarded Honorable Mention for the Perkins Prize by the International Society for the Study of Narrative. Her current book projects are "Reading for the Planet: World Literature and Environmental Crisis" and "Contrapuntal Environmentalisms: Nature, North and South". She is also co-editing *Fueling Culture: Energy, History, Politics* (Fordham 2016) with Imre Szeman and Patricia Yaeger.

Claire Westall is a Lecturer in the Department of English and Related Literature at the University of York, UK. She is co-editor of *Cross-Gendered Literary Voices: Appropriating, Resisting, Embracing* (Palgrave Macmillan, 2012) and *Literature of an Independent England* (Palgrave Macmillan, 2013). She is co-writing a book entitled *The Public on the Public* (Palgrave Macmillan, 2014). Much of her published work has examined cricket's place in the Caribbean literary imagination, including "Reading Brian Lara and the Traditions of Caribbean Cricket Poetry" in Jeff Hill and Anthony Bateman (eds.), *The Cambridge Companion to Cricket* (Cambridge University Press, 2011).

Patrick Williams is Professor of Literary and Cultural Studies at Nottingham Trent University, where he teaches courses on postcolonial theory and culture, film, diaspora, and race and nation in twentieth-century Britain. His publications include *Colonial Discourse and Post-Colonial Theory*, Columbia University Press, 1993; *Introduction to Post-Colonial Theory*, Routledge, 1996; *Ngũgĩ wa Thiong'o*, Manchester University Press, 1999; *Edward Said*, Sage, 2000; *Postcolonial African Cinema*, Manchester University Press, 2007. Forthcoming books include a collection on Orientalism in Routledge's Major Works series. He is on the editorial boards of *Theory, Culture and Society*, and *Journal of Postcolonial Writing*.

Index

An environmentally friendly book printed and bound in England by www.printondemand-worldwide.com

PEFC Certified

This product is
from sustainably
managed forests
and controlled
sources

www.pefc.org

This book is made entirely of sustainable materials; FSC paper for the cover and PEFC paper for the text pages.

#0038 - 061015 - C0 - 229/152/15 [17] - CB - 9780415857970